1, 7, 9, 12, 33, 3
37 (2), 50-51, 6
119, 123, 139, 147, 155, 162-3, 176

PHILIPPIANS

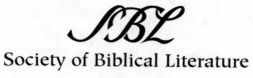

Society of Biblical Literature

Early Christianity and Its Literature

Number 3

PHILIPPIANS
Let Us Rejoice in Being Conformed to Christ

PHILIPPIANS

Let Us Rejoice in Being Conformed to Christ

John Paul Heil

Society of Biblical Literature
Atlanta

PHILIPPIANS
Let Us Rejoice in Being Conformed to Christ

Copyright © 2010 by the Society of Biblical Literature

Library of Congress Cataloging-in-Publication Data

Heil, John Paul.
    Philippians : let us rejoice in being conformed to Christ / by John Paul Heil.
        p.   cm. — (Society of Biblical Literature early Christianity and its literature ; 3)
Includes bibliographical references and index.
ISBN 978-1-58983-482-8 (paper binding : alk. paper) — ISBN 978-1-58983-483-5 (electronic library copy)
    1. Bible. N.T. Philippians—Criticism, interpretation, etc. I. Title.
BS2705.52.H44 2010b
227'.6066—dc22
                                         2010007843

17 16 15 14 13 12 11 10   5 4 3 2 1

Printed in the United States of America on acid-free, recycled paper conforming to ANSI/NISO Z39.48-1992 (R1997) and ISO 9706:1994 standards for paper permanence.

CONTENTS

Abbreviations

AcT	*Acta theologica*
AnBib	Analecta biblica
AUSS	*Andrews University Seminary Studies*
BBR	*Bulletin for Biblical Research*
BDAG	Bauer, W., F. W. Danker, W. F. Arndt, and F. W. Gingrich. *Greek–English Lexicon of the New Testament and Other Early Christian Literature*. 3d ed. Chicago, 1999
BECNT	Baker Exegetical Commentary on the New Testament
Bib	*Biblica*
BibInt	*Biblical Interpretation*
BIS	Biblical Interpretation Series
BJRL	*Bulletin of the John Rylands University Library of Manchester*
BNTC	Black's New Testament Commentaries
BSac	*Bibliotheca sacra*
BT	*The Bible Translator*
BTZ	*Berliner Theologische Zeitschrift*
BZNW	Beihefte zur Zeitschrift für die neutestamentliche Wissenschaft
CBET	Contributions to Biblical Exegesis and Theology
CBQ	*Catholic Biblical Quarterly*
CBQMS	Catholic Biblical Quarterly Monograph Series
ConBNT	Coniectanea biblica: New Testament Series
DPL	*Dictionary of Paul and His Letters*. Edited by G. F. Hawthorne and R. P. Martin. Downers Grove, 1993
EDNT	*Exegetical Dictionary of the New Testament*. Edited by H. Balz, G. Schneider. ET. Grand Rapids, 1990–1993
ExpTim	*Expository Times*
FRLANT	Forschungen zur Religion und Literatur des Alten und Neuen Testaments
Greg	*Gregorianum*
HBT	*Horizons in Biblical Theology*

HTR	*Harvard Theological Review*
Int	*Interpretation*
JBL	*Journal of Biblical Literature*
JETS	*Journal of the Evangelical Theological Society*
JSNT	*Journal for the Study of the New Testament*
JSNTSup	Journal for the Study of the New Testament: Supplement Series
JTS	*Journal of Theological Studies*
LNTS	Library of New Tesament Studies
LS	*Louvain Studies*
MSJ	*The Master's Seminary Journal*
Neot	*Neotestamentica*
NICNT	New International Commentary on the New Testament
NIGTC	New International Greek Testament Commentary
NovT	*Novum Testamentum*
NovTSup	Supplements to Novum Testamentum
NTM	New Testament Monographs
NTS	*New Testament Studies*
PRSt	*Perspectives in Religious Studies*
PTMS	Pittsburgh Theological Monograph Series
RdT	*Rassenga di teologia*
RevExp	*Review and Expositor*
RevScRel	*Revue des sciences religieuses*
RHPR	*Revue d'histoire et philosophie religieuses*
RivB	*Rivista biblica italiana*
SBLAbib	Society of Biblical Literature Academia Biblica
SBLDS	Society of Biblical Literature Dissertation Series
SBLMS	Society of Biblical Literature Monograph Series
ScrB	*Scripture Bulletin*
ScrC	*Scripture in Church*
ScrTh	*Scripta theologica*
SNTSMS	Society for New Testament Studies Monograph Series
SP	Sacra pagina
SVTQ	*St. Vladimir's Theological Quarterly*
Them	*Themelios*
TJ	*Trinity Journal*
TLNT	*Theological Lexicon of the New Testament*. C. Spicq. Translated and edited by J. D. Ernest. 3 vols. Peabody, Mass., 1994
TynBul	*Tyndale Bulletin*
TZ	*Theologische Zeitschrift*
WTJ	*Westminster Theological Journal*

| WUNT | Wissenschaftliche Untersuchungen zum Neuen Testament |
| ZNW | *Zeitschrift für die neutestamentliche Wissenschaft und die Kunde der älteren Kirche* |

1

INTRODUCTION

A. PHILIPPIANS: LET US REJOICE IN BEING CONFORMED TO CHRIST

The words in the title of this book, "Philippians: Let Us Rejoice in Being Conformed to Christ," have been chosen very carefully to express what I consider to be the main theme running through the entirety of Paul's letter to the Philippians. This book will deal in a comprehensive way with the whole of this NT document. In it I present a proposal for an entirely new chiastic structure embracing the ten units that comprise and organize this letter. In addition, I show that within this overall macrochiastic structure each and every one of the letter's ten units likewise exhibits its own individual chiastic structure. These macro- and microchiastic patterns will serve as a key to understanding what and how Paul, the implied author of the letter to the Philippians, is communicating to his implied audience.[1]

The words "let us rejoice" capture the overall tone of Philippians as a letter exhorting its audience to rejoice along with Paul. Although "let us rejoice," the first-person plural hortatory subjunctive or cohortative form of the Greek verb χαίρω, does not occur as such in Philippians, this verbal form was chosen for the title because it combines and summarizes the various forms of the verb "rejoice" and its cognates in the letter, which, taken together, express Paul's exhortation for his audience to rejoice with him. The verb "rejoice" (χαίρω) occurs nine times throughout the letter, at least once in each chapter (1:18[2x]; 2:17, 18, 28; 3:1; 4:4[2x], 10). In addition, the verb "rejoice with" (συγχαίρω) occurs twice (2:17, 18). These verbs expressing joy are complemented by the noun "joy" (χαρά), which occurs five times throughout the letter (1:4, 25; 2:2, 29; 4:1).

The noun "joy" is employed in the letter to refer to the joy of both Paul (1:4; 2:2; 4:1) and of his Philippian audience (1:25; 2:29). With regard to the verb "rejoice," in 1:18 Paul employs it twice to express his own joy—"I rejoice (χαίρω)

---

1. For similar presentations of the comprehensive chiastic structures in Philemon, Ephesians, and Colossians, see John Paul Heil, "The Chiastic Structure and Meaning of Paul's Letter to Philemon," *Bib* 82 (2001): 178–206; idem, *Ephesians: Empowerment to Walk in Love for the Unity of All in Christ* (Studies in Biblical Literature 13; Atlanta: Society of Biblical Literature, 2007); idem, *Colossians: Encouragement to Walk in All Wisdom as Holy Ones in Christ* (forthcoming).

and I will be joyful (χαρήσομαι)." In 2:17 Paul expresses his own joy—"I rejoice (χαίρω)"—and the joy he shares with his audience—"I rejoice with (συγχαίρω) all of you." In 2:18 Paul exhorts his audience to "rejoice (χαίρετε)" and to share their joy with him—"rejoice with (συγχαίρετε) me." In 2:28 Paul states that his audience "may rejoice (χαρῆτε)." In 3:1 and 4:4 Paul thrice exhorts his audience to "rejoice (χαίρετε)." And finally, in 4:10 Paul climactically expresses his own joy—"I am joyful (ἐχάρην) in the Lord greatly." Hence, "let us rejoice" aptly sums up Paul's concerted exhortations throughout the letter for his audience to rejoice together with him and with one another.

But the theme of joy and rejoicing that pervades Philippians is not limited to the noun χαρά and the various verbal forms of χαίρω. It is included in the closely related concept of "grace" with its connotation of joy in both the noun form χάρις and the verb form χαρίζομαι. Thus, it may be said that a connotation of joy envelops the letter, which begins with the greeting of "grace (χάρις) to you" (1:2a) and concludes with the greeting of "the grace (χάρις) of the Lord Jesus Christ be with your spirit" (4:23). Joy is connoted when Paul says, "I give thanks (εὐχαριστῶ) to my God at every remembrance of you" (1:3), since "give thanks," like "joy" and "grace," also comes from the χαρ- root. Joy is also connoted when Paul states that the Philippians are all partners with him in "grace" (χάριτος, 1:7b). With regard to the verbal forms, joy is connoted in the assertions that "to you has been granted (ἐχαρίσθη) for the sake of Christ, not only to believe in him but also for the sake of him to suffer" (1:29), and that God "granted (ἐχαρίσατο) him [Christ] the name that is above every name" (2:9). Hence, God's grace is implicitly one of the reasons for Paul and his audience to rejoice.[2]

Included within the "joy" word field are other connotations and/or synonyms and antonyms of joy in the letter. After Paul expresses his hope of sending Timothy to the Philippians, he looks forward to the joy that will result—"so that I also may be glad (εὐψυχῶ), knowing the things concerning you" (2:19). After stating that God had mercy on both Epaphroditus in his illness and on Paul himself, Paul expresses his joy in terms of the elimination of some of its opposites, namely, sorrow and anxiety—"so that I may not have sorrow (λύπην) upon sorrow (λύπην)" (2:27) and "so that seeing him you may rejoice again and I may be less sorrowful (ἀλυπότερος)" (2:28). With sadness Paul informs his audience that "many are walking, about whom many times I told you, and now even weeping (κλαίων) I tell you, that they are enemies of the cross of Christ" (3:18). Paul also exhorts his audience to "have anxiety (μεριμνᾶτε) for nothing" (4:6).

A note of joy can also be readily detected in the various exuberant doxologies and expressions of praise to God throughout the letter—"for the glory (δόξαν) and

---

2. William G. Morrice, "Joy," *DPL*, 512: "It is significant that the most common cognates for joy (χαρά, 'inner joy,' and χαίρειν, 'to rejoice') are derived from the same root χαρ–as is the Greek word for 'grace,' χάρις. There is a very close connection between the two concepts." BDAG, 1079: "It seems that χάρις is not always clearly differentiated in meaning from χαρά."

praise (ἔπαινον) of God" (1:11), "to the glory (δόξαν) of God the Father" (2:11), and "to our God and Father, glory (δόξα) for the ages of the ages, amen" (4:20).[3]

The choice of the phrase "in being conformed to Christ" as the cause of the rejoicing is intended to summarize the letter's emphasis on its audience being united with Paul, Timothy, Epaphroditus, and one another in their conformity to the suffering, death, and resurrection-exaltation of Christ. Both the noun and verb expressing "conformity" make noteworthy appearances in Philippians. Paul voices his desire "to know him [Christ] and the power of his resurrection and the fellowship of his sufferings, being conformed (συμμορφιζόμενος) to his death, if somehow I may arrive at the resurrection from the dead" (3:10–11). After exhorting his audience to "become imitators of me" (3:17a), Paul promises that the Lord Jesus Christ "will transform the body of our humility (to be) conformed (σύμμορφον) to the body of his glory according to the force that empowers him to subject all things to himself" (3:21). Paul and his audience are thus to be "conformed" to the Christ who, though he was in the "form" (μορφῇ) of God (2:6), nevertheless emptied himself as he took the "form" (μορφήν) of a slave (2:7), and humbly became obedient to the point of dying on a cross (2:8) before being exalted to glory (2:9–11).

But there are several other word fields, expressions, and terms for unity, union, fellowship, being of the same mind, and so on, that, as I would propose, can be considered to be embraced in one way or another by the phrase, "in being conformed to Christ." Paul prays with joy for his audience (1:4), based upon their "fellowship" (κοινωνίᾳ) for the gospel (1:5), which is about Christ. Paul tells his audience that they are all "fellow sharers" (συγκοινωνούς) with him in grace (1:7). Paul speaks of his audience's "fellowship" (κοινωνία) of the Spirit (2:1) before he exhorts them to fill up his joy (2:2). And Paul deeply desires to know the "fellowship" (κοινωνίαν) of the sufferings of Christ (3:10).

Paul hopes to hear that his audience are standing firm "in one Spirit" (ἐν ἑνὶ πνεύματι), "with one mind" (μιᾷ ψυχῇ), "struggling together" (συναθλοῦντες) with regard to the faith of the gospel (1:27), which is about Christ. For it has been granted to them for the sake of Christ, not only to believe in him but for the sake of him to suffer, having the "same struggle" (αὐτοῦ ἀγῶνα), as they saw in Paul and now hear in him (1:29–30). Paul then exhorts his audience to complete his joy so that "you think the same thing" (τὸ αὐτὸ φρονῆτε), having "the same" (τὴν αὐτήν) love, being "united in mind" (σύμψυχοι), "thinking one thing" (τὸ ἓν φρονοῦντες) (2:2). Indeed, Paul's Philippian audience are to "think among you" (φρονεῖτε ἐν ὑμῖν) this which is also in Christ Jesus (2:5).

Continuing his exhortation, Paul urges, "Whoever, then, are mature, let us think this (τοῦτο φρονῶμεν), and if you think otherwise (ἑτέρως φρονεῖτε), this

---

3. Ceslas Spicq, "δόξα," *TLNT* 1.372–73. On the theme of joy in Philippians, particularly on the relationship between joy and suffering and death, see L. Gregory Bloomquist, "Subverted by Joy: Suffering and Joy in Paul's Letter to the Philippians," *Int* 61 (2007): 270–82.

too God will reveal to you" (3:15). He then tells them to follow "the same thing" (τῷ αὐτῷ) (3:16) and to become "fellow imitators" (συμμιμηταί) of him (3:17), rather than enemies of the cross of Christ (3:18). Paul even exhorts two members of the audience, Euodia and Syntyche, "to think the same thing (τὸ αὐτὸ φρονεῖν) in the Lord" (4:2), as they have "struggled together" (συνήθλησάν) with Paul in the gospel (4:3). In sum, then, there seems to be a concerted exhortation throughout the letter that allows for a preliminary claim that my chosen title, "Let us rejoice in being conformed to Christ," when "conformity to Christ" is understood in as broad a way as possible, aptly expresses the main theme and purpose of Paul's letter to the Philippians.

B. AUTHORSHIP AND PROVENANCE

The letter to the Philippians initially presents itself as authored and sent by both Paul and Timothy (1:1), but with the occurrence of first-person singular forms after the opening greeting Paul quickly establishes himself as the primary authorial voice—"I thank my God . . . in my every prayer" (1:3-4), and so on. Timothy never really speaks for himself as a co-author of the letter. Paul does eventually speak about Timothy, however, when he voices his hope of sending him to the Philippians (2:19-23).[4]

Several times it is indicated that the letter was composed and sent while Paul was in "my chains" or "my bonds" (δεσμοῖς μου in 1:7, 14, 17; δεσμούς μου in 1:13) of imprisonment. But the precise location of his imprisonment is never explicitly stated in the letter. Several possibilities have been proposed: Caesarea, Corinth, Ephesus, Rome. There is no direct literary evidence that Paul was ever imprisoned in Corinth or Ephesus. According to Acts, Paul was imprisoned for a considerable length of time in both Caesarea (23:23-27:1) and Rome (28:16-31). Since in Philippians Paul has reconciled himself to the distinct possibility of being executed (1:21-23), and since Rome is the most likely place for Paul as a Roman citizen (Acts 16:37-38; 22:25-29; 23:27) to be executed, Rome, during Paul's imprisonment there as narrated in Acts 28:16-31 probably in 60-62 A.D., is the most likely location of his imprisonment for the composition and sending of the letter to the Philippians.[5]

---

4. Timothy, a key co-worker and frequent delegate of Paul (Acts 16:1; 17:14-15; 18:5; 19:22; 20:4; 1 Thess 3:2, 6; Rom 16:21; 1 Cor 4:17; 16:10) was a co-author of several other Pauline letters (1 Thess 1:1; 2 Thess 1:1; 2 Cor 1:1; Phlm 1:1; Col 1:1) as well as the recipient of an additional two Pauline letters (1 Tim 1:2; 2 Tim 1:2).

5. For fuller discussions of the view that Philippians was composed while Paul was imprisoned in Rome, see Peter Thomas O'Brien, *The Epistle to the Philippians: A Commentary on the Greek Text* (NIGTC; Grand Rapids: Eerdmans, 1991), 19-26; Ben Witherington, *Friendship and Finances in Philippi: The Letter of Paul to the Philippians* (Valley Forge: Trinity Press International, 1994), 24-26; Gordon D. Fee, *Paul's Letter to the Philippians* (NICNT; Grand Rapids: Eerdmans, 1995), 34-37; Markus N. A. Bockmuehl, *The Epistle to the Philippians* (BNTC 11; London: Hendrickson, 1998), 25-32; Richard J. Cassidy, *Paul in Chains: Roman Imprisonment and the Letters of St. Paul* (New York:

C. AUDIENCE

Paul, the primary author with Timothy as his co-author, is sending the letter "to all the holy ones in Christ Jesus who are in Philippi with the overseers and ministers" (1:1). The intended audience of the letter are thus all the "holy ones," that is, all those who are separated from the rest of society and consecrated to God as those who believe in and are united to Christ Jesus together with those who have a leadership role among them, described as their "overseers and ministers." According to Acts, Paul and Timothy, together with Silas (and Luke?), spent some time in Philippi, described as a "first city of the region of Macedonia, a [Roman] colony" (16:12).[6] While in Philippi, Paul converted Lydia and her household (16:13–15), was briefly imprisoned together with Silas for exorcizing a slave girl (16:16–23), converted his Roman jailer along with his household (16:24–34), and was released when it was learned that both Paul and Silas were Roman citizens (16:35–40). As we will see, the close relationship between Rome as the letter's provenance and Philippi as its destination comes into play within the letter's rhetorical dynamics in view of Philippi's special status as a Roman colony.[7]

What does the letter itself tell us about the situation of its Philippian audience and their relationship with the co-authors of the letter, Paul and Timothy? First, Paul is grateful to God (1:3–4) that his Philippian audience have been in "fellowship" (κοινωνία) with him for the gospel (1:5). Indeed, the Philippians are "partners" or "fellow sharers" (συγκοινωνούς) with Paul both in the bonds of his imprisonment and in the defense and confirmation of the gospel (1:7). Like Paul (1:15–17), the audience have opponents (1:28; cf. 3:2). And it has been granted to the audience not only to believe in Christ but to suffer on behalf of him (1:29).

Crossroad, 2001), 124–209; Stephen E. Fowl, *Philippians* (Grand Rapids: Eerdmans, 2005), 9–10; Moisés Silva, *Philippians* (BECNT; Grand Rapids: Baker, 2005), 5–7; David E. Garland, "Philippians," in *The Expositor's Bible Commentary: Revised Edition* (Vol. 12; ed. Tremper Longman and David E. Garland; Grand Rapids: Zondervan, 2006), 178–80; Craig L. Blomberg, *From Pentecost to Patmos: An Introduction to Acts Through Revelation* (Nashville: Broadman & Holman, 2006), 325–27. For information on prisons in the ancient Roman world and its significance for the letter to the Philippians, see Craig S. Wansink, *Chained in Christ: The Experience and Rhetoric of Paul's Imprisonments* (JSNTSup 130; Sheffield: Sheffield Academic Press, 1996); J. L. Bailey, "Perspectives from Prison: Reading Philippians," *Trinity Seminary Review* 27 (2006): 83–97; Stephen Finlan, *The Apostle Paul and the Pauline Tradition* (Collegeville: Liturgical Press, 2008), 136–37.

6. On the difficulty of the translation here, see BDAG, 632.

7. For more on Philippi at the time of the letter, see Lukas Bormann, *Philippi: Stadt und Christengemeinde zur Zeit des Paulus* (NovTSup 78; Leiden: Brill, 1995); Peter Pilhofer, *Philippi: Die erste christliche Gemeinde Europas* (WUNT 87; Tübingen: Mohr–Siebeck, 1995); Peter Oakes, *Philippians: From People to Letter* (SNTSMS 110; Cambridge: Cambridge University Press, 2001), 1–54; Richard J. Cassidy, *Four Times Peter: Portrayals of Peter in the Four Gospels and at Philippi* (Collegeville: Liturgical Press, 2007), 109–12. On the social context of the Philippian Christian community, see Richard S. Ascough, *Paul's Macedonian Associations: The Social Context of Philippians and 1 Thessalonians* (WUNT 161; Tübingen: Mohr Siebeck, 2003), 110–61.

Indeed, they have the same struggle that they saw in Paul and now hear in him
(1:30).

According to Paul, the audience know the worth of Timothy, who has great
concern for them and whom Paul hopes to send to them in the near future. As a
"child" of a "father" he served with Paul for the gospel (2:19–23). Paul also finds it
necessary to return Epaphroditus, who has recovered from a serious illness, to the
Philippians. He had been sent by them to assist the imprisoned Paul in his need,
coming close to death to fill up what was lacking in the Philippians' own assistance
of Paul (2:25–30).

Apparently the audience are in danger of being influenced by those who claim
that believers must be circumcised in the flesh and thus become Jewish (3:1–2).
Paul, however, assures his Philippian audience that, as believers in Christ, they
already are spiritually "the circumcision," so that, like Paul, they should not place
any confidence in being circumcised in the flesh (3:3–21).

Among the audience there are two named individuals—Euodia and Syntyche—who had been co-workers of Paul but who now need assistance in resolving
a misunderstanding between the two of them (4:2–3). When Paul was in Thessalonica, the Philippians were the only church to send him something in his need
(4:15–16). And now Paul is grateful to them for sending more assistance to him
in his current imprisonment through Epaphroditus (4:18–20). In short, then, the
audience of the letter to the Philippians seem to have a rather close relationship
with Christ, Paul, Timothy, Epaphroditus, and among themselves, which serves as
a basis for the dynamics of Paul's exhortation for them to rejoice together with him
and with all who are in conformity to Christ.

D. LITERARY-RHETORICAL, AUDIENCE-ORIENTED METHOD

In the past the letter to the Philippians has been plagued by various theories that it
is a composite of parts of different letters, so that it lacks literary unity and integrity. Recent research, however, seems to have largely discredited such theories, so
that one could speak of a current consensus against the idea. At any rate, in accord
with these recent studies, I will treat Philippians as a single, unified letter. In addition, the chiastic structures that I will propose for Philippians may be considered
as yet another indication of such literary integrity and unity.[8]

---

8. Those who have argued for the literary integrity and unity of Philippians include: William J.
Dalton, "The Integrity of Philippians," *Bib* 60 (1979): 97–102; David E. Garland, "The Composition and
Unity of Philippians: Some Neglected Literary Factors," *NovT* 27 (1985): 141–73; Duane F. Watson, "A
Rhetorical Analysis of Philippians and Its Implications for the Unity Question," *NovT* 30 (1988): 57–88;
Philippe Rolland, "La structure littéraire et l'unité de l'Épître aux Philippiens," *RevScRel* 64 (1990):
213–16; O'Brien, *Philippians*, 10–18; L. Gregory Bloomquist, *The Function of Suffering in Philippians*
(JSNTSup 78; Sheffield: JSOT, 1993), 97–103; Fee, *Philippians*, 21–23; George H. Guthrie, "Cohe-
sion Shifts and Stitches in Philippians," in *Discourse Analysis and Other Topics in Biblical Greek* (ed.
Stanley E. Porter and D. A. Carson; JSNTSup 113; Sheffield: Sheffield Academic Press, 1995), 36–59;

I consider Philippians, then, to be a single, unified letter written to be read and heard in a public, communal setting, most likely in a liturgical assembly, as an oral performance substituting for the personal presence of the imprisoned Paul.[9] I employ a literary-rhetorical method that treats Philippians as a hortatory letter with a rhetorical strategy of persuading its implied audience to the viewpoint of Paul, the primary implied author. I use the term *rhetorical* in its broadest and most general sense. Rather than applying the categories and terminology of either ancient Greco-Roman rhetoric or the modern "new rhetoric" to Philippians, the rhetorical method I follow is entirely and rigorously text-centered. I determine Paul's rhetorical or persuasive strategy by carefully and closely listening to the chiastic structures of the text as they unfold within the letter to the Philippians.[10]

My method is audience-oriented in that it is concerned to determine how the implied audience are meant to respond to Paul's rhetorical strategy as it develops

---

Veronica Koperski, *The Knowledge of Christ Jesus My Lord: The High Christology of Philippians 3:7–11* (CBET 16; Kampen: Pharos, 1996), 69–72; Jeffrey T. Reed, *A Discourse Analysis of Philippians: Method and Rhetoric in the Debate Over Literary Integrity* (JSNTSup 136; Sheffield: Sheffield Academic Press, 1997); Bockmuehl, *Philippians*, 20–25; Paul Andrew Holloway, *Consolation in Philippians: Philosophical Sources and Rhetorical Strategy* (SNTSMS 112; Cambridge: Cambridge University Press, 2001), 7–33; Demetrius K. Williams, *Enemies of the Cross of Christ: The Terminology of the Cross and Conflict in Philippians* (JSNTSup 223; London: Sheffield, 2002), 42–54; Bonnie B. Thurston and Judith M. Ryan, *Philippians and Philemon* (SP 10; Collegeville: Liturgical Press, 2005), 30–34; Fowl, *Philippians*, 8–9; Silva, *Philippians*, 12–14.

9. For treatments of the oral performance of NT documents, see: Whitney Taylor Shiner, *Proclaiming the Gospel: First Century Performance of Mark* (Harrisburg: Trinity, 2003); Holly E. Hearon, "The Implications of Orality for Studies of the Biblical Text," in *Performing the Gospel: Orality, Memory, and Mark: Essays Dedicated to Werner Kelber* (Richard A. Horsley, et al.; Minneapolis: Fortress, 2006), 3–20; Bridget Gilfillan Upton, *Hearing Mark's Endings: Listening to Ancient Popular Texts Through Speech Act Theory* (BIS 79; Leiden: Brill, 2006); William David Shiell, *Reading Acts: The Lector and the Early Christian Audience* (BIS 70; Boston: Brill, 2004), 209 : "Paul's letters also give examples of the kinds of documents that need to be discussed in light of delivery. How were they performed, and what vocal inflection would have been used?" On the public performance of Paul's letters, see also Pieter J. J. Botha, "The Verbal Art of the Pauline Letters: Rhetoric, Performance and Presence," in *Rhetoric and the New Testament: Essays from the 1992 Heidelberg Conference* (ed. Stanley E. Porter and Thomas H. Olbricht; JSNTSup 90; Sheffield: JSOT, 1993), 409–28; Luther M. Stirewalt, *Paul: The Letter Writer* (Grand Rapids: Eerdmans, 2003), 13–18; E. Randolph Richards, *Paul and First-Century Letter Writing: Secretaries, Composition and Collection* (Downers Grove, IL: InterVarsity, 2004), 202; Kenneth J. Thomas and Margaret Orr Thomas, *Structure and Orality in 1 Peter: A Guide for Translators* (UBS Monograph 10; New York: United Bible Societies, 2006). On oral patterns in Philippians, see John D. Harvey, *Listening to the Text: Oral Patterning in Paul's Letters* (Grand Rapids: Baker, 1998), 231–58; Casey Wayne Davis, *Oral Biblical Criticism: The Influence of the Principles of Orality on the Literary Structure of Paul's Epistle to the Philippians* (JSNTSup 172; Sheffield: Sheffield Academic Press, 1999); idem, "Oral Biblical Criticism: Raw Data in Philippians," in *Linguistics and the New Testament: Critical Junctures* (ed. Stanley E. Porter and D. A. Carson; JSNTSup 168; Sheffield: Sheffield Academic Press, 1999), 96–124.

10. For a text-centered approach to the rhetoric of another Pauline letter, see D. Francois Tolmie, *Persuading the Galatians: A Text-Centered Rhetorical Analysis of a Pauline Letter* (WUNT 190; Tübingen: Mohr Siebeck, 2005). For a recent treatment of the background and rhetorical force of the various metaphors employed in Philippians, see Raymond F. Collins, *The Power of Images in Paul* (Collegeville: Liturgical Press, 2008), 40–67.

in the progression of the chiastically arranged textual units of the letter to the Philippians.[11] With regard to the literary genre of Philippians, several have proposed that it is a "friendship letter."[12] Others have rightly pointed out problems with this designation, among them being that the words *friend* or *friendship* never occur in the letter and Paul does not really present himself as the "friend" of the Philippians.[13] I treat Philippians rather as a hortatory letter whose overall theme can be summarized as "Let us rejoice in being conformed to Christ."[14]

---

11. For more on the audience-oriented method to be employed in this investigation, see Warren Carter and John Paul Heil, *Matthew's Parables: Audience-Oriented Perspectives* (CBQMS 30; Washington: Catholic Biblical Association, 1998), 8–17; John Paul Heil, *The Meal Scenes in Luke–Acts: An Audience-Oriented Approach* (SBLMS 52; Atlanta: Society of Biblical Literature, 1999), 2–4; idem, *The Transfiguration of Jesus: Narrative Meaning and Function of Mark 9:2–8, Matt 17:1–8 and Luke 9:28–36* (AnBib 144; Rome: Editrice Pontificio Istituto Biblico, 2000), 22–24; idem, *The Rhetorical Role of Scripture in 1 Corinthians* (Studies in Biblical Literature 15; Atlanta: Society of Biblical Literature, 2005), 5–10.

12. L. Michael White, "Morality Between Two Worlds: A Paradigm of Friendship in Philippians," in *Greeks, Romans, and Christians* (ed. David L. Balch, et al.; Minneapolis: Fortress, 1990), 201–15; Fee, *Philippians*, 2–7, 12–14; Stanley K. Stowers, "Friends and Enemies in the Politics of Heaven: Reading Theology in Philippians," in *Pauline Theology* (Vol. I; ed. Jouette M. Bassler; Minneapolis: Fortress, 1991), 105–21; John T. Fitzgerald, "Philippians in the Light of Some Ancient Discussions of Friendship," in *Friendship, Flattery, and Frankness of Speech: Studies on Friendship in the New Testament World* (ed. John T. Fitzgerald; NovTSup 82; Leiden: Brill, 1996), 141–60.

13. John Reumann, "Philippians, Especially Chapter 4, as a 'Letter of Friendship': Observations on a Checkered History of Scholarship," in *Friendship, Flattery, and Frankness of Speech: Studies on Friendship in the New Testament World* (ed. John T. Fitzgerald; NovTSup 82; Leiden: Brill, 1996), 83–106. According to Garland, "Philippians," 184: "That the letter reflects the coincidence of friendship language does not make it in form a 'letter of friendship,' a literary category. Philippians is friendly in tone, but it is not simply a friendship letter. Paul never uses the terms 'friendship' or 'friend'. He is not simply the Philippians' friend, having equal status and obligated to reciprocate in gift giving, and the church is not simply an association of friends. Paul is their founder, apostle, and teacher. Friends do not have congregations. . . . Philippians is best categorized as a hortatory letter that is reinforced with appeals to examples." Marc J. Debanné, *Enthymemes in the Letters of Paul* (LNTS 303; New York: Clark, 2006), 96: "Philippians is not a pure ritual of friendship, but one in which the apostle and founder of the Philippian Church has blended into the gesture of affection a pastoral aim that can be described both as paraenesis (παραίνεσις) and as deliberative rhetoric." See also Joseph A. Marchal, "With Friends Like These... : A Feminist Rhetorical Reconsideration of Scholarship and the Letter to the Philippians," *JSNT* 29 (2006): 77–106.

14. For other proposals for the main theme of Philippians, see James P. Ware, *The Mission of the Church in Paul's Letter to the Philippians in the Context of Ancient Judaism* (NovTSup 120; Leiden: Brill, 2005), 168 n. 19. Ware's own proposal that the main theme is the Philippians' cooperation with Paul for the advancement of the gospel, while an important theme, does not extend throughout the entire letter as does the theme of rejoicing in being conformed to Christ, which includes but is not limited to their role in advancing the gospel. In other words, the theme of rejoicing in being conformed to Christ includes the audience's own profound relationship with Christ, which is the basic and fundamental presupposition for their work of advancing the gospel of Christ.

E. SUMMARY

1. In this book I propose and demonstrate new chiastic structures for the entire letter to the Philippians as a key to understanding it as an exhortation to rejoice in being conformed to Christ.

2. Although Paul and Timothy are initially presented as the co-authors of the letter to the Philippians, Paul alone quickly emerges as the primary author.

3. Although there is no absolute certainty on where Paul was imprisoned when he composed and sent the letter, in all probability he was in Rome during the imprisonment narrated at the end of the Acts of the Apostles. An imprisonment in Rome is important for the interpretation of the letter, as the relationship between Rome and Philippi, with its special status as a Roman colony, comes into play within the rhetorical dynamics of the letter.

4. The audience of the letter to the Philippians seem to have a rather close relationship with Christ, Paul, Timothy, Epaphroditus, and among themselves, which serves as a basis for Paul's exhortation for them to rejoice together with him and all who are in conformity to Christ.

5. In this investigation I employ a text-centered, literary-rhetorical and audience-oriented method concerned with demonstrating how the implied audience are persuaded and exhorted by the dynamic progression of the letter's chiastic structures to rejoice along with Paul and other believers in being conformed, with all of the broad implications of such conformity, to Christ.

2

THE CHIASTIC STRUCTURES OF PHILIPPIANS

A. THE TEN MICROCHIASTIC UNITS OF THE LETTER

To be absolutely convincing the determination of an extended chiastic structure should be based upon a methodology with very rigorous criteria. It must be clear that the chiasm has not been subjectively imposed upon the text but actually subsists and operates objectively within the text. My investigation will be guided by the following list of nine criteria for detecting an extended chiasm:

(1) There must be a problem in perceiving the structure of the text in question, which more conventional outlines fail to resolve.

(2) There must be clear examples of parallelism between the two "halves" of the hypothesized chiasm, to which commentators call attention even when they propose quite different outlines for the text overall.

(3) Linguistic (or grammatical) parallelism as well as conceptual (or structural) parallelism should characterize most if not all of the corresponding pairs of subdivisions.

(4) The linguistic parallelism should involve central or dominant imagery or terminology important to the rhetorical strategy of the text.

(5) Both linguistic and conceptual parallelism should involve words and ideas not regularly found elsewhere within the proposed chiasm.

(6) Multiple sets of correspondences between passages opposite each other in the chiasm as well as multiple members of the chiasm itself are desirable.

(7) The outline should divide the text at natural breaks which would be agreed upon even by those proposing very different structures to account for the whole.

(8) The central or pivotal as well as the final or climactic elements normally play key roles in the rhetorical strategy of the chiasm.

(9) Ruptures in the outline should be avoided if at all possible.[1]

---

1. For a slightly different and more detailed version of this list, as well as an example of an extended biblical chiasm, see Craig L. Blomberg, "The Structure of 2 Corinthians 1–7," *CTR* 4 (1989): 4–8. And for more discussion of criteria and more biblical examples of extended chiasms, see Wayne Brouwer, *The Literary Development of John 13–17: A Chiastic Reading* (SBLDS 182; Atlanta: Society

An important and distinctive feature of this investigation is that all of the proposed chiasms are based on precise linguistic parallels found objectively in the text, rather than on thematic or conceptual parallels, which can often be subjective. Indeed, the main criterion for the establishment of chiasms in this investigation is the demonstration of these linguistic parallels. I will seek to determine how the subsequent occurrence(s) of a paralleled word or phrase develops the first occurrence after a central unparalleled element or central parallel elements serve as a pivot from the first to the second half of the chiasm.

Since they are based strictly on linguistic parallels, some of the proposed chiasms may or may not exhibit a balance in the length of the various parallel elements or units—one parallel element or unit may be much longer or much shorter than its corresponding parallel. This may seem odd to a modern audience, but an ancient audience would presumably be attuned to the key linguistic parallels that are heard rather than the balance of length between the elements or units of a given chiasm. The main presupposition of this investigation is that if there are demonstrable linguistic parallels with a pivotal section between them, then a chiasm is operative regardless of a certain lack of balance between various elements or units.

Furthermore, some of the linguistic parallels involve what might be considered by a modern audience as rather ordinary or trivial words, unlikely to be key words in chiastic parallels. But it should be kept in mind that what may seem to be insignificant words or phrases on the surface to a modern audience may have been very significant indeed to the particular rhetorical strategy of the author and the particular situation of the original audience as they listened to the entire oral performance of the letter to the Philippians. In some cases the parallels are between cognates or between synonyms, antonyms, and/or alliterative terms. And in some cases an identical grammatical form of a word determines the chiastic parallel.

Not all of the proposed chiasms have the same number of elements or units. Some chiasms may exhibit a single unparalleled central element, e.g. A–B–C–B′–A′, while others may exhibit dual, parallel central or pivotal elements, e.g. A–B–C–C′–B′–A′. Nevertheless, both of these types operate as chiasms in the ears of the implied audience, since they both involve a pivot from the first to the second half of the chiasm. In one type a central unparalleled element serves as the pivot, whereas in the other type two parallel elements together serve as the pivot to the second half of parallel elements. In addition, it may often be more accurate to

of Biblical Literature, 2000). See also Joachim Jeremias, "Chiasmus in den Paulusbriefen," *ZNW* 49 (1958): 145–56; John W. Welch, "Chiasmus in the New Testament," in *Chiasmus in Antiquity: Structures, Analyses, Exegesis* (ed. John W. Welch; Hildesheim: Gerstenberg, 1981), 211–49; idem, "Criteria for Identifying and Evaluating the Presence of Chiasmus," in *Chiasmus Bibliography* (ed. John W. Welch and Daniel B. McKinlay; Provo, Utah: Research, 1999), 157–74; Ian H. Thomson, *Chiasmus in the Pauline Letters* (JSNTSup 111; Sheffield: Sheffield Academic Press, 1995), 13–45; Mark Wilson, *The Victor Sayings in the Book of Revelation* (Eugene, OR: Wipf and Stock, 2007), 3–8; David A. DeSilva, "X Marks the Spot? A Critique of the Use of Chiasmus in Macro-Structural Analyses of Revelation," *JSNT* 30 (2008): 343–71.

speak of the central element or elements as the pivotal point of the chiasm and the final A´ element as the climax. This is important to keep in mind, lest one think that chiastic patterns are a type of circular or merely repetitive argument, rather than exhibiting an ongoing, dynamic development.

Chiastic patterns serve to organize the content to be heard and not only aid the memory of the one delivering or performing a document, but also make it easier for the implied audience to follow and remember the content. A chiasm works by leading its audience through introductory elements to a central, pivotal point or points, and then reaching its conclusion by recalling and developing, via the chiastic parallels, aspects of the initial elements that led to the central, pivotal point or points. Since chiasms were apparently very common in ancient oral–auricular and rhetorical cultures,[2] the original ancient audience may and need not necessarily have been consciously identifying or reflecting upon any of these chiastic structures in themselves as they heard them. They unconsciously experienced the chiastic phenomenon as an organizing dynamic, which had a subtle but purposeful effect on how they perceived the content.[3] But I would suggest that a discovery, delineation, and bringing to consciousness of the underlying chiastic structures of ancient documents can greatly aid the modern audience to a more proper and precise interpretation of them.

In what follows, then, I will first demonstrate how the text of Paul's letter to the Philippians naturally divides itself into ten distinct literary units based upon their microchiastic structures as determined by very precise linguistic parallels found objectively in the text. Where applicable I will point out how other lexical and grammatical features often confirm the integrity of these units. Secondly, I will demonstrate how these ten units form a macrochiastic pattern based upon very precise linguistic parallels found objectively in the text between the chiastically paired units.[4] Thirdly, I will point out the various transitional words that

---

2. For some of the evidence of this see Brouwer, *Literary Development*, 23–27. On Paul's use of chiasm, see John L. White, "Apostolic Mission and Apostolic Message: Congruence in Paul's Epistolary Rhetoric, Structure and Imagery," in *Origins and Method: Towards a New Understanding of Judaism and Christianity: Essays in Honour of John C. Hurd* (ed. Bradley H. McLean; JSNTSup 86; Sheffield: Sheffield Academic Press, 1993), 157.

3. On chiasms as an aid to both listener and performer, see Joanna Dewey, "Mark as Aural Narrative: Structures as Clues to Understanding," *Sewanee Theological Review* 36 (1992): 50–52.

4. On the interpretive significance of chiastic structures, see Ronald E. Man, "The Value of Chiasm for New Testament Interpretation," *BSac* 141 (1984): 146–57; Augustine Stock, "Chiastic Awareness and Education in Antiquity," *BTB* 14 (1984): 23–27; John Breck, "Biblical Chiasmus: Exploring Structure for Meaning," *BTB* 17 (1987): 70–74. For a discussion of chiasm in relation to chain-link interlock, see Bruce W. Longenecker, *Rhetoric at the Boundaries: The Art and Theology of the New Testament Chain-Link Transitions* (Waco, Texas: Baylor University Press, 2005), 16–17, 22–23. A chiastic structure for Philippians has been proposed by A. Boyd Luter and Michelle V. Lee, "Philippians as Chiasmus: Key to the Structure, Unity and Theme Questions," *NTS* 41 (1995): 89–101. But it has not proved to be entirely successful as indicated by Stanley E. Porter and Jeffrey T. Reed, "Philippians as a Macro-Chiasm and Its Exegetical Significance," *NTS* 44 (1998): 213–31. On the structure of Philippians, see also Ronald Russell, "Pauline Letter Structure in Philippians," *JETS* 25 (1982): 295–306; Robert C.

connect a unit to the unit that immediately precedes it. These various transitional words, which occur at the conclusion of one unit and at the beginning of the following unit, indicate that the chiastic units are heard as a cohesive sequence. These various transitional words are capitalized in the translations of the units below.

1. Grace from the Lord Jesus Christ to the Holy Ones (1:1–2)
Paul and Timothy to Those in Philippi[5]

A: [1:1a] Paul and Timothy, slaves of Christ Jesus (Χριστοῦ Ἰησοῦ),
   B: [1b] to all those (τοῖς) holy ones in (ἐν) Christ Jesus,
   B′: [1c] those (τοῖς) who are in (ἐν) Philippi with overseers and ministers,
A′: [2] grace to you and peace from GOD our Father and the Lord Jesus Christ (Ἰησοῦ Χριστοῦ).[6]

Directed to "all the holy ones in Christ Jesus who are in Philippi with the overseers and ministers," the opening address and greeting from both Paul and Timothy of "grace to you and peace *from* God *our* Father" in Phil 1:1–2 is grammatically set off from the thanksgiving that begins in 1:3, which is voiced by Paul alone and directed *to* "*my* God." The integrity of this first unit is further secured by its A–B–B′–A′ chiastic structure. The only occurrences in this unit of the genitive singular of "Jesus Christ"—"slaves of Christ Jesus (Χριστοῦ Ἰησοῦ)" in 1:1a and "Lord Jesus Christ (Ἰησοῦ Χριστοῦ)" in 1:2—determine the parallelism of the A (1:1a) and A′ (1:2) elements of this chiasm.[7] The only occurrences in this unit of the dative masculine plural of the definite article "the" or "those" and of the preposition "in"—"those (τοῖς) holy ones in (ἐν) Christ Jesus" in 1:1b and "those (τοῖς) who are in (ἐν) Philippi" in 1:1c—establish the parallelism of the B (1:1b) and B′ (1:1c) elements.

Swift, "The Theme and Structure of Philippians," *BSac* 141 (1984): 234–54; Loveday C. A. Alexander, "Hellenistic Letter-Forms and the Structure of Philippians," *JSNT* 37 (1989): 87–101; Peter Wick, *Der Philipperbrief: Der formale Aufbau des Briefs als Schlüssel zum Verständnis seines Inhalts* (BWANT 135; Stuttgart: Kohlhammer, 1994); David Alan Black, "The Discourse Structure of Philippians: A Study in Textlinguistics," *NovT* 37 (1995): 16–49; Ralph Brucker, *"Christushymnen" oder "epideiketische Passagen"? Studien zum Stilwechsel im Neuen Testament und seiner Umwelt* (FRLANT 176; Göttingen: Vandenhoeck & Ruprecht, 1997), 280–300; Stefano Bittasi, *Gli esempi necessari per discernere: Il significato argomentativo della struttura della lettera di Paolo ai Filippesi* (AnBib 153; Rome: Editrice Pontificio Istituto Biblico, 2003); David E. Aune, *The Westminster Dictionary of New Testament and Early Christian Literature and Rhetoric* (Louisville: Westminster John Knox, 2003), 356–59. I shall attempt to propose more satisfying chiastic structures with an objective basis in the text of Philippians.

5. The main heading of each unit is intended to summarize the unit as it relates to its parallel unit within the overall macrochiastic structure of the letter, while the subheading of each unit is intended to summarize or characterize the microchiastic dimension of each unit.

6. The translation of this and all subsequent units of the letter is my own, striving to be as literal as possible to the Greek text for the purpose of clarifying the exegesis.

7. "Christ Jesus" occurs also in 1:1b, but in the dative rather than genitive case. Note that the two occurrences of the name in the A and A′ elements form a mini-chiasm: (a) Christ (b) Jesus in 1:1a and (b′) Jesus (a′) Christ in 1:2.

*2. My Prayer That You Abound
and Be Filled to Glory and Praise of God (1:3–11)
Paul Makes His Petitions with Joy*

A: ³ I thank my GOD (θεῷ) at every remembrance of you,

B: ⁴ always in my every petition on behalf of all of you, making the petition with joy ⁵ at your fellowship for the gospel from the first day (ἡμέρας) until now, ⁶ having confidence of this very thing, that he who began in you a good work will perfect it until the day (ἡμέρας) of Christ (Χριστοῦ) Jesus.

C: ⁷ Just as it is right for me to think this on behalf of all of you because I have you in my heart, as both in my bonds and in the defense and confirmation of the gospel, all of you (πάντας ὑμᾶς) are my fellow sharers of the grace.

D: ⁸ᵃ For my witness is God,

C′: ⁸ᵇ how I long for all of you (πάντας ὑμᾶς) with the affection of Christ Jesus.

B′: ⁹ And this I pray, that your love even more and more may abound in knowledge and every perception ¹⁰ in order that you determine the things that matter, so that you may be sincere and faultless for the day of Christ (ἡμέραν Χριστοῦ),

A′: ¹¹ having been filled up with the fruit of righteousness that is through Jesus CHRIST for the glory and praise of God (θεοῦ).⁸

The word "God" (θεῷ) in the expression "I thank my God" that introduces this unit in 1:3 recalls "God" (θεοῦ) at the beginning of the greeting "grace to you and peace from God our Father" in 1:2 that concludes the preceding unit. These occurrences of "God" thus serve as the transitional words linking the first unit (1:1–2) to the second unit (1:3–11).

An A–B–C–D–C′–B′–A′ chiastic pattern secures the integrity and distinctness of this second unit (1:3–11). The only two instances in this unit in which God is the recipient of a prayerful action—"I thank my God (θεῷ)" in 1:3 and "to the glory and praise of God (θεοῦ)" in 1:11—constitute the parallelism of the A (1:3) and A′ (1:11) elements of this chiasm.⁹ The only occurrences in this unit of the terms "day" and "day of Christ"—from the first day (ἡμέρας) in 1:5, "until the day of Christ (ἡμέρας Χριστοῦ) Jesus" in 1:6, and "for the day of Christ (ἡμέραν Χριστοῦ)" in 1:10—determine the parallelism of the B (1:4–6) and B′ (1:9–10) elements. The only two occurrences in this unit of "all of you" in the accusative plural—"all of you (πάντας ὑμᾶς) who are my fellow sharers" in 1:7b and "how I long for all of you (πάντας ὑμᾶς)" in 1:8b—form the parallels for the C (1:7) and

---

8. For a discussion of the variant readings in 1:11, see Fee, *Philippians*, 96 n. 3; Bockmuehl, *Philippians*, 70–71; Silva, *Philippians*, 58.

9. The term "God" (θεός) occurs also in this unit in 1:8a, but in the nominative case as the subject of a sentence, and thus not as the recipient of a prayerful action as in 1:3 and 1:11.

C′ (1:8b) elements.[10] The unparalleled, central, and pivotal D (1:8a) element contains the only occurrence of the word "witness" (μάρτυς) in the letter.

3. I Rejoice and I Will Be Joyful (1:12–18)
Christ Is Proclaimed Even While Paul Is in the Bonds of Imprisonment

A: [12] I want you to know, brothers, that the things regarding me have come rather to an advancement of the gospel, [13] so that my bonds (δεσμούς μου) have become in CHRIST manifest in the whole praetorium and to all (πάσιν) the rest, [14] and most of the brothers, in the Lord having confidence by my bonds (δεσμοῖς μου), more abundantly dare fearlessly to speak the word.[11]

    B [15] Some even on account of envy and rivalry, but others even on account of good pleasure, preach the Christ (τὸν Χριστόν).

        C: [16] The latter out of love, knowing that for the defense of the gospel I am set,

    B′: [17a] the former out of self-seeking, proclaim the Christ (τὸν Χριστόν),

A′: [17b] not sincerely, supposing to raise affliction in my bonds (δεσμοῖς μου).
[18] What then? Only that in all (παντί) manner, whether in pretense or in truth, CHRIST is proclaimed, and in this I rejoice. And indeed I will be joyful,

The word "Christ" (Χριστῷ) in the statement "that my bonds have become in Christ manifest" in 1:13 at the beginning of this unit recalls "Christ" (Χριστοῦ) in the phrase "through Jesus Christ" in 1:11 at the conclusion of the preceding unit. These occurrences of "Christ" thus serve as the transitional words linking the second unit (1:3–11) to the third unit (1:12–18).

An A–B–C–B′–A′ chiastic pattern secures the integrity and distinctness of this third unit (1:12–18). The only occurrences in this unit of "my bonds"—"my bonds (δεσμούς μου) have become manifest in Christ" in 1:13, "confident by my bonds (δεσμοῖς μου)" in 1:14, and "supposing to raise affliction in my bonds (δεσμοῖς μου)" in 1:17, as well as the only occurrences in this unit of "all"—"to all (πάσιν) the rest" in 1:13 and "in all (παντί) manner" in 1:18, constitute the parallels between the A (1:12–14) and A′ (1:17b–18) elements of the chiasm.[12] The only occurrences in this unit of the term "Christ" with the article and in the accusative case—"preach the Christ (τὸν Χριστόν)" in 1:15 and "proclaim the Christ (τὸν Χριστόν)" in 1:17a—determine the parallelism between the B (1:15) and B′ (1:17a) elements. The unparalleled and pivotal C (1:16) element contains the only occurrences of the terms "love" (ἀγάπης) and "defense" (ἀπολογίαν) in this unit, as well as the only occurrence of the verb "I am set" (κεῖμαι) in the letter.

---

10. "All of you" occurs in both 1:4 and 1:7a, but in the genitive rather than in the accusative case.

11. For the preference of the shorter reading "to speak the word" (τὸν λόγον λαλεῖν) over the longer variant "to speak the word of God" (τὸν λόγον τοῦ θεοῦ λαλεῖν), see Bruce Manning Metzger, *A Textual Commentary on the Greek New Testament: Second Edition* (Stuttgart: Deutsche Bibelgesellschaft, 1994), 544–45. See also Bockmuehl, *Philippians*, 76; Cf. Ware, *Mission*, 180 n. 60.

12. The phrase "my bonds" (δεσμοῖς μου) occurred previously in 1:7.

4. Death in My Body Is Gain
But Remaining in the Flesh Is for Your Faith (1:19–30)
Not Only to Believe in Christ but to Suffer on Behalf of Him

A: [19] for I know that this for me will lead to salvation (σωτηρίαν) through the petition of you and supply of the Spirit of Jesus CHRIST [20] according to my eager expectation and hope, that in nothing (ἐν οὐδενί) I will be put to shame but in all boldness as always and now Christ will be magnified in my body, whether through life or through death. [21] For to me to live is Christ and to die is gain. [22] If it is to live in the flesh, this for me is fruitful work, and which I will choose I do not know. [23] I am constrained between the two, having (ἔχων) the desire for release and to be with Christ, for that is much better by far.[13] [24] But to remain in the flesh is more necessary on account of you.

    B: [25] And having confidence of this, I know that I will remain, indeed I will remain beside all of you for your advancement and joy in the faith (τῆς πίστεως), [26] so that your boast may abound in Christ Jesus in me through my presence again with you. [27a] Only, live as citizens worthy of the gospel (τοῦ εὐαγγελίου) of the Christ,

        C: [27b] so that, whether coming (εἴτε ἐλθών) and seeing you,

        C′: [27c] or being absent (εἴτε ἀπών), I hear the things concerning you,

    B′: [27d] that you are standing firm in one Spirit, with one mind struggling together for the faith of the gospel (τῇ πίστει τοῦ εὐαγγελίου),

A′: [28] and not being intimidated in anything (ἐν μηδενί) by the opponents, which is for them a demonstration of destruction, but of your salvation (σωτηρίας), and this is from God, [29] for to you has been granted that which is on behalf of Christ, not only in him to believe but also on behalf of him to suffer, [30] having (ἔχοντες) the same struggle, such as you saw in me and now hear in me.

The word "Christ" (Χριστοῦ) in the phrase "of the Spirit of Jesus Christ" in 1:19 at the beginning of this unit recalls "Christ" (Χριστός) in the statement "Christ is proclaimed" in 1:18 at the conclusion of the preceding unit. These occurrences of "Christ" thus serve as the transitional words linking the third unit (1:12–18) to the fourth unit (1:19–30).

    An A–B–C–C′–B′–A′ chiastic pattern secures the integrity and distinct-

---

13. We translate ἀναλῦσαι with its most basic meaning of "loose," "untie," or "release." The implicit object would be release from Paul's "bonds" (cf. 1:7, 13, 14, 17; and BDAG, 67, for the variant reading in Acts 16:26) and thus from his body by being put to death. Craig A. Smith, *Timothy's Task, Paul's Prospect: A New Reading of 2 Timothy* (NTM 12; Sheffield: Sheffield Phoenix, 2006), 126: "I propose that Paul uses ἀναλύω in Phil. 1.23 because he is drawing from his understanding of death in terms of being released from the body in order to enter the intermediate state. The idea of the intermediate state as being the place to which the disembodied soul goes is one of many interpretations of 2 Cor. 5.1–4. . . . Paul is simply reflecting his eschatological understanding of death as the release of the spirit from the body in order to be with Christ."

ness of this fourth unit (1:19–30). The only occurrences in this unit of the term "salvation"—"will lead to salvation (σωτηρίαν)" in 1:19 and "of your salvation (σωτηρίας)" in 1:28, the only occurrences in this unit of the prepositional phrase "in nothing/anything"—"in nothing (ἐν οὐδενί) I will be put to shame" in 1:20 and "not being intimidated in anything (ἐν μηδενί)" in 1:28, and the only occurrences in this unit of the verb "to have"—"having (ἔχων) the desire" in 1:23 and "having (ἔχοντες) the same struggle" in 1:30, constitute the parallels in the A (1:19–24) and A′ (1:28–30) elements of this chiasm.

The only occurrences in this unit of the terms "the faith" and "the gospel"—"joy in the faith (τῆς πίστεως)" in 1:25, "the gospel (τοῦ εὐαγγελίου) of the Christ" in 1:27a, and "for the faith of the gospel (τῇ πίστει τοῦ εὐαγγελίου)" in 1:27d—determine the parallels in the B (1:25–27a) and B′ (1:27d) elements. The only occurrences in this unit of the coordinating conjunctions "whether/or" with participles—"whether coming (εἴτε ἐλθών)" in 1:27b and "or being absent (εἴτε ἀπών)" in 1:27c—establish the parallels in the central and pivotal C (1:27b) and C′ (1:27c) elements.[14]

5. Joy in Humility for the Day of Christ
Who Humbled Himself to Death (2:1–16)
Be Conformed to Christ Who Was Obedient Even to Death on a Cross

A: [2:1] If then there is any encouragement in CHRIST, if there is any consolation of love (ἀγάπης), if there is any fellowship of Spirit, if there is any affection and compassion, [2] fill up my joy and think the same thing, having the same love (ἀγάπην), united in mind, thinking the one thing, [3] nothing according to self-seeking nor according to vainglory (κενοδοξίαν), but in humility considering one another more important than yourselves (ἑαυτῶν), [4] each of you looking out not for the things of yourselves (ἑαυτῶν), but everyone also for the things of others. [5] This go on thinking in you, which is also in Christ Jesus,

   B: [6] who, existing (ὑπάρχων) in the form of God (θεοῦ), not something to be exploited did he consider (ἡγήσατο) being equal to God, [7] but emptied himself, taking the form of a slave, becoming in the likeness (ὁμοιώματι) of human beings, and in outward appearance found to be as a human being,

      C: [8a] he humbled himself, becoming obedient to the point of death (θανάτου),

      C′: [8b] even of death (θανάτου) on a cross.

   B′: [9] therefore indeed God exalted (ὑπερύψωσεν) him and granted (ἐχαρίσατο) him the name that is above every name, [10] so that at the name (ὀνόματι) of Jesus every knee should bend, of those in heaven and of

---

14. The same coordinating conjunctions occur in 1:20 of this unit, but with prepositional phrases rather than with participles. Note also the use of these same conjunctions in 1:18 with nouns.

those on earth and of those under the earth, [11] and every tongue confess that Jesus Christ is Lord to the glory of God (θεοῦ) the Father.

A´: [12] So that, my beloved (ἀγαπητοί), just as you have always obeyed, not as in my presence only, but now much more in my absence, with reverence and awe continue to work out your own (ἑαυτῶν) salvation. [13] For God is the one working in you both to desire and to work for the sake of his good pleasure. [14] Do everything without grumbling or questioning, [15] so that you may become blameless and innocent, children of God without blemish in the midst of a crooked and perverse generation, among whom you shine as lights in the world, [16] holding forth the word of life, so that MY boast for the day of Christ— that I did not run in vain (κενόν) or labor in vain (κενόν).[15]

The word "Christ" (Χριστῷ) in the phrase "in Christ" in 2:1 at the beginning of this unit recalls "Christ" (Χριστοῦ) in the phrase "on behalf of Christ" in 1:29 at the conclusion of the preceding unit. These occurrences of "Christ" thus serve as the transitional words linking the fourth unit (1:19–30) to the fifth unit (2:1–16).

An A-B-C-C´-B´-A´ chiastic pattern secures the integrity and distinctness of this fifth unit (2:1–16). The only occurrences in this unit of terms for "love"—"if there is any consolation of love (ἀγάπης)" in 2:1, "having the same love (ἀγάπην)" in 2:2, and "my beloved (ἀγαπητοί)" in 2:12, the only occurrences in the letter of terms for "vainglory" and "vain"—"according to vainglory (κενοδοξίαν)" in 2:3 and "I did not run in vain (κενόν) or labor in vain (κενόν)" in 2:16, and the only occurrences in this unit of the masculine plural genitive of the reflexive pronoun—"more important than yourselves (ἑαυτῶν)" in 2:3, "the things of yourselves (ἑαυτῶν)" in 2:4, and "your own (ἑαυτῶν) salvation" in 2:12, constitute the parallels in the A (2:1–5) and A´ (2:12–16) elements of this chiasm.

Terms related by alliteration determine the parallels in the B (2:6–7) and B´ (2:9–11) elements—"of God (θεοῦ)" in 2:6 and "of God (θεοῦ)" in 2:11, "existing (ὑπάρχων)" in 2:6 and "exalted (ὑπερύψωσεν)" in 2:9, "regard (ἡγήσατο)" in 2:6 and "granted (ἐχαρίσατο)" in 2:9, "likeness (ὁμοιώματι)" in 2:7 and "name (ὀνόματι)" in 2:10. And the only occurrences in this unit of the term "death" in the genitive singular—"to the point of death (θανάτου)" in 2:8a and "even of death (θανάτου) on a cross" in 2:8b—establish the parallels in the central and pivotal C (2:8a) and C´ (2:8b) elements of this chiasm.

6. Rejoice with Those Who Neared Death for the Work of Christ (2:17–30)
Rejoice with Paul over Timothy and Epaphroditus

A: [17] But if indeed I am being poured out like a drink offering upon the sacrifice and service (λειτουργίᾳ) of your faith, I am rejoicing (χαίρω), indeed I

---

15. The basis for translating λόγον ζωῆς ἐπέχοντες as "holding forth the word of life" is provided by Ware, *Mission*, 256–70.

am rejoicing with (συγχαίρω) all of you. [18] And in the same way you are to be rejoicing (χαίρετε), indeed you are to be rejoicing with (συγχαίρετέ) ME.

B: [19a] I hope (ἐλπίζω) in the Lord (δὲ ἐν κυρίῳ) Jesus soon (ταχέως) to send (πέμψαι) Timothy to you,

C: [19b] so that I also may be heartened, coming to know (γνούς) the things concerning you. [20] For I have no one like minded, who genuinely will be anxious for the things concerning you.

D: [21a] For they all seek the things (τά) of themselves,

D′: [21b] not the things (τά) of Jesus Christ.

C′: [22] For you know (γινώσκετε) his worth, that as a child to a father he served with me for the gospel.

B′: [23] This one then I hope (ἐλπίζω) to send (πέμψαι) as soon as I perceive the things concerning me. [24] But I have confidence in the Lord (δὲ ἐν κυρίῳ) that I myself will also come soon (ταχέως). [25] I have considered it necessary Epaphroditus, my brother and co-worker and fellow soldier, and your apostle and servant in my need, to send (πέμψαι) to you,

A′: [26] since he was longing for all of you and was distressed, because you heard that he was sick. [27] For indeed he was sick, close to death, but God had mercy on him, not on him only but also on me, so that I might not have sorrow upon sorrow. [28] More eagerly then I send him, so that seeing him you may REJOICE (χαρῆτε) again and I may be less sorrowful. [29] Welcome him then in the Lord with all JOY (χαρᾶς) and have such people in esteem, [30] for on account of the work of Christ he came near to the point of death, risking his life, so that he might fill up your lack of service (λειτουργίας) toward me.

The pronoun "me" (μοι) in the statement "you are to be rejoicing with me" in 1:18 at the beginning of this unit recalls the pronoun "my" (ἐμοί) in the phrase "my boast" in 1:16 at the conclusion of the preceding unit. These occurrences of the first-person singular pronoun referring to Paul thus serve as the transitional words linking the fifth unit (2:1–16) to the sixth unit (2:17–30).

An A–B–C–D–D′–C′–B′–A′ chiastic pattern secures the integrity and distinctness of this sixth unit (2:17–30). The only two occurrences in the letter of the term for "service"—"upon the sacrificial service (λειτουργίᾳ) of your faith" in 2:17 and "your lack of service (λειτουργίας) toward me" in 2:30, the only occurrences in this unit of the verbs "rejoice" and "rejoice with" as well as the noun "joy"—"I am rejoicing (χαίρω), indeed I am rejoicing with (συγχαίρω) all of you" in 2:17, "you are to be rejoicing (χαίρετε), indeed you are to be rejoicing with (συγχαίρετέ) me" in 2:18, "you may rejoice (χαρῆτε)" in 2:28, and "with all joy (χαρᾶς)" in 2:29, constitute the parallels in the A (2:17–18) and A′ (2:26–30) elements of this chiasm.

The only two occurrences in the letter of the verb "to hope"—"I hope (ἐλπίζω)" in 2:19a and in 2:23, the only two occurrences in this unit of the prepositional phrase "in the Lord" preceded by the coordinating conjunction δέ—"in the Lord (δὲ ἐν κυρίῳ)" in 2:19a and in 2:24,[16] the only two occurrences in the letter of the adverb "soon"—"soon (ταχέως) to send" in 2:19a and "I myself will also come soon (ταχέως)" in 2:24, and the only occurrences in the letter of the aorist active infinitive "to send"—"to send (πέμψαι) Timothy to you" in 2:19a, "this one then I hope to send (πέμψαι)" in 2:23, and "to send (πέμψαι) to you" in 2:25,[17] determine the parallels in the B (2:19a) and B′ (2:23–25) elements.

The only occurrences in this unit of the verb "know"—"coming to know (γνούς) the things concerning you" in 2:19a and "you know (γινώσκετε) his worth" in 2:22—establish the parallels in the C (2:19b–20) and C′ (2:22) elements. And the only occurrences in this unit of the accusative neuter plural of the definite article "the things" not followed by the preposition "concerning" (περί; see 2:19–20, 23)—"the things (τά) of themselves" in 2:21a and "the things (τά) of Jesus Christ" in 2:21b establish the parallels in the pivotal D (2:21a) and D′ (2:21b) elements at the center of this chiasm.

7. Gain in Faith in the Death of Christ and the Body of His Glory (3:1–21) Become My Fellow Imitators as We Await the Lord Jesus Christ

> A: [3:1a] Furthermore, my brothers, REJOICE in the Lord (κυρίῳ).
>
> B: [1b] To write the same things to you (ὑμῖν), to me is not burdensome, but to you (ὑμῖν) is assuring.
>
>> C: [2] Beware of the dogs, beware of the evil workers, beware of the mutilation. [3] For we are the circumcision, the ones who by the Spirit of God are worshiping and boasting in Christ Jesus (ἐν Χριστῷ Ἰησοῦ), and not having put confidence in the flesh, [4] although I myself (ἐγώ) have (ἔχων) confidence even in the flesh. If someone else supposes to be confident in the flesh, I (ἐγώ) even more, [5] with circumcision on the eighth day, from the race of Israel, tribe of Benjamin, a Hebrew from Hebrews, according to the Law (νόμον) a Pharisee, [6] according to zeal persecuting (διώκων) the church, according to righteousness (δικαιοσύνην) that is in the Law (νόμῳ) I became blameless.
>>
>> D: [7] But whatever things were for me gains (κέρδη), these things I have considered (ἥγημαι) on account of the Christ a loss (ζημίαν). [8a] But indeed I even consider (ἡγοῦμαι) all things (πάντα) to be a loss (ζημίαν)
>>
>>> E: [8b] on account of the surpassing greatness of the knowledge of Christ Jesus my Lord,
>>
>> D′: [8c] on account of whom I have suffered the loss (ἐζημιώθην) of all things (πάντα), indeed I consider (ἡγοῦμαι) them rubbish, that Christ I may gain (κερδήσω)

---

16. The identical phrase does occur later in the letter in 4:10.

17. The verb "to send" does occur in the first-person singular aorist indicative active (ἔπεμψα) in 2:28 of this chiastic unit.

C´: [9] and I may be found in him, not having (ἔχων) my own righteousness (δικαιοσύνην) that is from the Law (νόμου) but that is through faith in Christ, the—from God—righteousness (δικαιοσύνην) based on the faith, [10] to know him and the power of the rising of him and the fellowship of the sufferings of him, being conformed to the death of him, [11] if somehow I may arrive to the resurrection from the dead. [12] Not that I have already taken it or already been perfected, but I am pursuing (διώκω) it, if indeed I may apprehend it, for which indeed I have been apprehended by Christ Jesus.[18] [13] Brothers, I (ἐγώ) do not consider that I myself have apprehended. But just one thing—forgetting the things behind but stretching out for the things ahead, [14] according to the goal, I am pursuing (διώκω) to the prize of the upward calling of God in Christ Jesus (ἐν Χριστῷ Ἰησοῦ).

B´: [15] As many as then (would be) perfect,[19] this let us think. And if something otherwise you are thinking, this also God will reveal to you (ὑμῖν). [16] Nevertheless, to what we have attained, to the same hold fast. [17] Become my fellow imitators, brothers, and look at those who are thus walking, just as you have us as a model. [18] For many are walking, about whom many times I told you (ὑμῖν), and now even weeping I tell you, that they are the enemies of the cross of Christ. [19] Their end is destruction, their God is their stomach and their glory is in their shame, those who are thinking the things of the earth.

A´: [20] For our citizenship is existing in heaven, from which indeed a savior we are awaiting, the LORD (κύριον) Jesus Christ, [21] who will transform the body of our humbleness (to be) conformed to the body of his glory according to the working that empowers him even to subject to himself all things.

The verb "rejoice" (χαίρετε) in the injunction "rejoice in the Lord" in 3:1 at the beginning of this unit recalls both the noun "joy" (χαρᾶς) and the verb "rejoice" (χαρῆτε) in the statement "that seeing him you may rejoice again and I may be less sorrowful. Welcome him then in the Lord with all joy" in 2:28–29 at the conclusion of the preceding unit. These expressions of joy thus serve as the transitional words linking the sixth unit (2:17–30) to the seventh unit (3:1–21).

An A–B–C–D–E–D´–C´–B´–A´ chiastic pattern secures the integrity and distinctness of this seventh unit (3:1–21). The only two anarthrous occurrences in this unit of the word "Lord"—"rejoice in (the) Lord (κυρίῳ)" in 3:1a and "Lord

---

18. For the translation of the phrase ἐφ ᾧ here (see also 4:10) as "for which" with a final sense, see Maximilian Zerwick, *Biblical Greek* (Rome: Biblical Institute, 1963), 43; Joseph A. Fitzmyer, "The Consecutive Meaning of ἐφ ᾧ in Romans 5.12," *NTS* 39 (1993): 330; Fee, *Philippians*, 346 n. 31.

19. This translation follows from the context in which Paul has stated in 3:12 that he has not yet been "perfected."

(κύριον) Jesus Christ" in 3:20,[20] constitute the parallels in the A (3:1a) and A′ (3:20–21) elements of this chiasm.

The only occurrences in this unit of the second-person dative plural pronoun—"to write the same things to you (ὑμῖν), to me is not burdensome, but to you (ὑμῖν) is assuring" in 3:1b as well as "this also God will reveal to you (ὑμῖν)" in 3:15 and "about whom many times I told you (ὑμῖν)" in 3:17—establish the parallels in the B (3:1b) and the B′ (3:15–19) elements.[21]

The only occurrences in this unit of the phrase "in Christ Jesus"—"boast in Christ Jesus (ἐν Χριστῷ Ἰησοῦ)" in 3:3 and "the upward calling of God in Christ Jesus (ἐν Χριστῷ Ἰησοῦ)" in 3:14, the only occurrences in this unit of "I"—"although I myself (ἐγώ)" and "I (ἐγώ) even more" in 3:4 and "I (ἐγώ) do not reckon" in 3:13,[22] the only occurrences in this unit of the participle "have"—"although I myself have (ἔχων) confidence" in 3:4 and "not having (ἔχων) my own righteousness" in 3:9,[23] the only occurrences in the letter of the word "Law"—"according to the Law (νόμον) a Pharisee" in 3:5, "in the Law (νόμῳ) I became blameless" in 3:6, and "from the Law (νόμου)" in 3:9, the only occurrences in the letter of the verb "pursue/persecute"—"persecuting (διώκων) the church" in 3:6, "but I am pursuing (διώκω) it" in 3:12, and "I am pursuing (διώκω) to the prize" in 3:14, and the only occurrences in the letter of the word "righteousness" in the accusative singular—"according to righteousness (δικαιοσύνην) that is in the Law" in 3:6, "my own righteousness (δικαιοσύνην) that is from the Law" in 3:9a, and "the—from God—righteousness (δικαιοσύνην) based on the faith" in 3:9b,[24] determine the parallels in the C (3:2–6) and C′ (3:9–14) elements.

The only occurrences in this unit of words for "gain"—"whatever things were for me gains (κέρδη)" in 3:7 and "that Christ I may gain (κερδήσω)" in 3:8c, the only occurrences in this unit of the verb "consider"—"these things I have considered (ἥγημαι)" in 3:7, "indeed I even consider (ἡγοῦμαι)" in 3:8a, and "indeed I consider (ἡγοῦμαι) them rubbish" in 3:8c, the only occurrences in the letter of the terms for "loss"—"on account of the Christ a loss (ζημίαν)" in 3:7, "to be a loss (ζημίαν)" in 3:8a, and "I have suffered the loss (ἐζημιώθην)" in 3:8c, establish the parallels in the D (3:7–8a) and D′ (3:8c) elements. And the only occurrence in the letter of the word "knowledge" (γνώσεως) distinguishes the unparalleled, central, and pivotal E (3:8b) element of the chiasm.

---

20. In 3:8b of this unit the word "Lord" occurs, but with the article—"Christ Jesus my Lord (τοῦ κυρίου μου)."

21. These are the last four of the twelve occurrences in the letter of the second-person dative plural pronoun.

22. The only other occurrence in the letter of the first-person singular personal pronoun "I" (ἐγώ) is in 4:11.

23. The only other place in the letter that this particular form of the verb "to have" occurs is in 1:23.

24. "Righteousness" (δικαιοσύνης) occurs in the genitive singular in 1:11.

8. Brothers in the Lord and in the Gospel, Rejoice in the Lord (4:1–5)
Rejoice in the Lord Who Is Near

A: ⁴ˈ So that, my brothers beloved and longed for, my joy (χαρά) and crown, thus stand firm in the LORD (ἐν κυρίῳ), beloved. ²Euodia I exhort and Syntyche I exhort to think the same thing in the Lord (ἐν κυρίῳ).

   B: ³ᵃYes, I ask also you, genuine yokemate (σύζυγε),

      C: ³ᵇbring them together (συλλαμβάνου),

      C′: ³ᶜthose who in the gospel have struggled together (συνήθλησάν) with me,

   B′: ³ᵈwith also Clement and the rest of my co-workers (συνεργῶν), whose names are in the book of life.

A′: ⁴Rejoice (χαίρετε) in the Lord (ἐν κυρίῳ) always. Again I will say, rejoice (χαίρετε). ⁵Let your forbearance be KNOWN to all human beings. The Lord (κύριος) is near.

The word "Lord" (κυρίῳ) in the injunction "stand firm in the Lord" in 4:1 at the beginning of this unit recalls "Lord" (κύριον) in the phrase "Lord Jesus Christ" in 3:20 at the conclusion of the preceding unit. These occurrences of "Lord" thus serve as the transitional words linking the seventh unit (3:1–21) to the eighth unit (4:1–5).

An A–B–C–C′–B′–A′ chiastic pattern secures the integrity and distinctness of this eighth unit (4:1–5). The only occurrences in this unit of words for joy/rejoice—"my joy (χαρά) and crown" in 4:1 and "rejoice (χαίρετε)" twice in 4:4, and the only occurrences in this unit of the word "Lord"—"in the Lord (ἐν κυρίῳ)" in 4:1, 2, 4 and "the Lord (κύριος) is near" in 4:5, constitute the parallels in the A (4:1–2) and A′ (4:4–5) elements of this chiasm. The only occurrences in this unit of the terms "yokemate/co-workers"—"genuine yokemate (σύζυγε)" in 4:3a and "the rest of my co-workers (συνεργῶν)" in 4:3d—determine the parallels in the B (4:3a) and B′ (4:3d) elements. And the only occurrences in this unit of the verbs "bring together" and "struggle together"—"bring them together (συλλαμβάνου)" in 4:3b and "they have struggled together (συνήθλησάν) with me" in 4:3c—establish the parallels in the central and pivotal C (4:3b) and C′ (4:3c) elements of this chiasm.

9. Glory to God Who Will Fulfill You as I Am Filled and Abound (4:6–20)
My God Will Fulfill Your Every Need in Christ Jesus

A: ⁶Be anxious about nothing, but in everything, by prayer and petition, with thanksgiving, let your requests be made KNOWN before God (θεόν). ⁷And the peace of God (θεοῦ) that surpasses all understanding will guard your hearts and your minds in Christ Jesus (ἐν Χριστῷ Ἰησοῦ). ⁸Furthermore, brothers, whatever is true, whatever is honorable, whatever is right, whatever is pure, whatever is pleasing, whatever is commendable, if there is any excellence, and if there is any praise, these things consider. [9] And the things you have learned and received and heard and saw in me, these things practice. And the God (θεός) of peace will be with you.

B: [10] I am joyful in the Lord greatly that now at last you have begun again to think on behalf of me, for which indeed you were thinking, but had no opportunity. [11] Not that I say this on account of want, for I have learned in whatever things I am involved to be content. [12] I know indeed to be humble, I know indeed to abound (περισσεύειν). In every situation and in all things I have learned the secret, both to be satisfied and to hunger, both to abound (περισσεύειν) and to be in want. [13] I am strong for everything (πάντα) in the one who empowers me!

C: [14] Nevertheless, you did well, sharing with me in my affliction. [15] And you indeed know, Philippians, that in the beginning of the gospel, when I went out from Macedonia, not a single church shared with me in an account (εἰς λόγον) of giving (δόσεως) and receiving except you alone,

D: [16] for even in Thessalonica not only once but twice you sent to me in my need.

C′: [17] Not that I am seeking the gift (δόμα), but I am seeking the fruit that increases in your account (εἰς λόγον).

B′: [18a] For I have received in full everything (πάντα) and I am abounding (περισσεύω). I have been filled up, having received from Epaphroditus the things from you, an aroma of fragrance, an acceptable sacrifice,

A′: [18b] well pleasing to God (θεῷ). [19] My God (θεός) will fill up your every need according to his wealth in glory IN CHRIST JESUS (ἐν Χριστῷ Ἰησοῦ). [20] To our God (θεῷ) and Father, glory to the ages of the ages, Amen.

The verb "be made known" (γνωριζέσθω) in the appeal to "let your requests be made known to God" in 4:6 at the beginning of this unit recalls the similar verb form "be known" (γνωσθήτω) in the appeal to "let your kindness be known to all human beings" in 4:5 at the conclusion of the preceding unit. These very similar verbal expressions of making known serve as the transitional words linking the eighth unit (4:1–5) to the ninth unit (4:6–20).

An A–B–C–D–C′–B′–A′ chiastic pattern secures the integrity and distinctness of this ninth unit (4:6–20). The only occurrences in this unit of words for "God"—"before God (θεόν)" in 4:6, "the peace of God (θεοῦ)" in 4:7, "the God (θεός) of peace" in 4:9, "well-pleasing to God (θεῷ)" in 4:18a, "My God (θεός) will fulfill" in 4:19, and "to our God (θεῷ) and Father" in 4:20, and the only occurrences in this unit of the phrase "in Christ Jesus"—"your hearts and your minds in Christ Jesus (ἐν Χριστῷ Ἰησοῦ)" in 4:7 and "according to his wealth in glory in Christ Jesus (ἐν Χριστῷ Ἰησοῦ)" in 4:19, constitute the parallels in the A (4:6–9) and A′ (4:18b–20) elements of this chiasm.

The only occurrences in this unit of the verb "abound"—"I know indeed to abound (περισσεύειν)" in 4:12a, "both to abound (περισσεύειν) and to be in want" in 4:12b, and "I am abounding (περισσεύω)" in 4:18a, and the only occurrences in this unit of the neuter plural accusative adjective functioning as the object of a first-person singular verb and meaning "everything"—"I am strong for everything (πάντα)" in 4:13 and "I have received in full everything (πάντα)" in 4:18a,[25] determine the parallels in the B (4:10–13) and B′ (4:18a) elements.

The only occurrences in the letter of the prepositional phrase "in an account"— "in an account (εἰς λόγον) of giving" in 4:15 and "in your account (εἰς λόγον)" in 4:17, and the only occurrences in the letter of the terms "giving/gift"—"in an account of giving (δόσεως)" in 4:15 and "not that I am seeking the gift (δόμα)" in 4:17, establish the parallels in the C (4:14–15) and C′ (4:17) elements. And the unparalleled, central, and pivotal D (4:16) element of this chiasm is distinguished by the only occurrences in the letter of the terms "Thessalonica" (Θεσσαλονίκη), "once" (ἅπαξ), and "twice" (δίς).

10. Greeting from Holy Ones and Grace from the Lord Jesus Christ (4:21–23)
The brothers and all the holy ones greet you

A: [21a] Greet every holy one IN CHRIST JESUS (Χριστῷ Ἰησοῦ).
B: [21b] The brothers who are with me greet you (ἀσπάζονται ὑμᾶς).
B′: [22] All the holy ones greet you (ἀσπάζονται ὑμᾶς), especially those from the household of Caesar.
A′: [23] The grace of the Lord Jesus Christ (Ἰησοῦ Χριστοῦ) be with your spirit.

The phrase "in Christ Jesus" (ἐν Χριστῷ Ἰησοῦ) in the injunction to "greet every holy one in Christ Jesus" in 4:21 at the beginning of this unit recalls the same phrase "in Christ Jesus" (ἐν Χριστῷ Ἰησοῦ) in Paul's promise that "My God will fill up your every need according to his wealth in glory in Christ Jesus" in 4:19 at the conclusion of the preceding unit. The repetition of these phrases thus serve as the transitional words linking the ninth unit (4:6–20) with the tenth unit (4:21–23).

An A–B–B′–A′ chiastic pattern secures the integrity and distinctness of this final tenth unit (4:21–23). The only occurrences in this unit of the names "Jesus" and "Christ"—"in Christ Jesus (Χριστῷ Ἰησοῦ)" in 4:21a and "Lord Jesus Christ (Ἰησοῦ Χριστοῦ)" in 4:23—constitute the parallels in the A (4:21a) and A′ (4:23) elements of this final chiasm. And the only occurrences in the letter of the third person plural indicative present middle verb "greet" followed by the second person accusative plural pronoun "you"—"the brothers who are with me greet you (ἀσπάζονται ὑμᾶς)" in 4:21b and "all the holy ones greet you (ἀσπάζονται ὑμᾶς)" in 4:22—determine the parallels in the pivotal B (4:21b) and B′ (4:22) elements.[26]

---

25. The same adjective occurs, but as a neuter singular accusative modifying a noun rather than functioning as a noun, in 4:7 of this unit—"the peace of God that surpasses all (πάντα) understanding."

26. The same verb "to greet" occurs in 4:21a of this unit, but as second person plural imperative—"Greet (ἀσπάσασθε) every holy one."

B. THE MACROCHIASTIC STRUCTURE OF THE LETTER

Having illustrated the various microchiastic structures operative in the ten distinct units of the letter to the Philippians, I will now demonstrate how these ten main units form an A–B–C–D–E–E′–D′–C′–B′–A′ macrochiastic structure organizing the entire letter.

A: Grace from the Lord Jesus Christ to the Holy Ones (1:1–2)
A′: Greeting from Holy Ones and Grace from the Lord Jesus Christ (4:21–23)

Repetitions of significant words indicate the parallelism between the opening A unit (1:1–2) and the closing A′ unit (4:21–23) within the macrochiastic structure of the letter to the Philippians. The occurrences of "every holy one" (πάντα ἅγιον) in 4:21a and "all the holy ones" (πάντες οἱ ἅγιοι) in 4:22 of the A′ unit at the end of the letter recall and parallel the occurrence of "to all the holy ones" (πᾶσιν τοῖς ἁγίοις) at the beginning of the letter in 1:1b of the A unit. That these are the only occurrences in the letter of the term "holy one" enhances the distinctiveness of this parallelism. The words "grace" (χάρις) and "Lord Jesus Christ" (κυρίου Ἰησοῦ Χριστου) in the final greeting at the end of the letter in 4:23 recall and parallel the identical words "grace" (χάρις) and "Lord Jesus Christ" (κυρίου Ἰησοῦ Χριστου) in the initial greeting at the beginning of the letter in 1:2.[27]

B: My Prayer That You Abound and Be Filled to Glory and Praise of God (1:3–11)
B′: Glory to God Who Will Fulfill You as I Am Filled and Abound (4:6–20)

Paul's directive about the praying of the audience—"be anxious about nothing, but in everything, by prayer and petition (δεήσει), with thanksgiving (εὐχαριστίας), let your requests be made known before God"—in 4:6 of the B′ unit recalls and parallels what he says about his own praying—"I thank (εὐχαριστῶ) my God at every remembrance of you, always in my every petition (δεήσει) on behalf of all of you, making the petition (δέησιν) with joy"—in 1:3–4 of the B unit. That these are the only occurrences in the letter of cognate words for "thanksgiving" and of the word "petition" in the dative singular (δεήσει) enhances the distinctiveness of these parallels.[28]
Paul's promise that "the peace of God that surpasses all understanding will guard your hearts (καρδίας)" in 4:7 of the B′ unit recalls and parallels his assurance that "I have you in my heart (καρδίᾳ)" in 1:7 of the B unit. That these are the

---

27. The word "grace" occurs elsewhere in the letter in 1:7, but in the genitive singular rather than in the nominative singular as in 1:2 and 4:23.

28. The same word for "petition" occurs only once elsewhere in the letter in 1:19.

only two occurrences in the letter of the word "heart" enhances the distinctiveness of this parallel. "Whatever is right (δίκαια)" in 4:8 of the B´ unit recalls and parallels "it is right (δίκαιον)" in 1:7 of the B unit. That these are the only two occurrences of the word "right" in the letter enhances the distinctiveness of this parallel. "If there is any praise (ἔπαινος)" in 4:8 of the B´ unit recalls and parallels "to the glory and praise (ἔπαινον) of God" in 1:11 of the B unit. That these are the only two occurrences of the word "praise" in the letter enhances the distinctiveness of this parallel.

The occurrence of the present active infinitive of the verb "to think" together with the preposition "on behalf of"—"that now at last you have begun again to think on behalf of me(ὑπὲρ ἐμοῦ φρονεῖν)"—in 4:10 of the B´ unit recalls and parallels the previous occurrence of this combination—"it is right for me to think this on behalf of all of you (φρονεῖν ὑπὲρ πάντων ὑμῶν)" in 1:7 of the B unit. That these are the only occurrences of this combination in the letter enhances the distinctiveness of this parallel.[29] "I know indeed to abound (περισσεύειν) . . . both to abound (περισσεύειν) and to be in want" in 4:12 and "I am abounding (περισσεύω)" in 4:18 of the B´ unit recall and parallel "that your love even more and more may abound (περισσεύῃ)" in 1:9 of the B unit.[30]

The occurrence of the word "fruit" in the accusative singular—"But I am seeking the fruit (καρπόν) that increases in your account"—in 4:17 of the B´ unit recalls and parallels "filled up with the fruit (καρπόν) of righteousness" in 1:11 of the B unit. That these are only occurrences in the letter of the noun "fruit" in the accusative singular enhances the distinctiveness of this parallel.[31] "I have been filled up (πεπλήρωμαι)" in 4:18 and "my God will fill up (πληρώσει)" in 4:19 of the B´ unit recall and parallel "having been filled up (πεπληρωμένοι) with the fruit of righteousness" in 1:11 of the B unit.[32] And "in glory (δόξῃ) in Christ Jesus" in 4:19 and "glory (δόξα) to the ages of the ages" in 4:20 of the B´ unit recall and parallel "to the glory (δόξαν) and praise of God" in 1:11 of the B unit.[33]

C: I Rejoice and I Will Be Joyful (1:12–18)
C´: Rejoice in the Lord, Rejoice (4:1–5)

The occurrence of the adjective for "rest of" in the plural form—"the rest (λοιπῶν) of my co-workers"—in 4:3 of the C´ unit recalls and parallels "to all the rest (λοιποῖς)" in 1:13 of the C unit. That these are the only two occurrences in the

---

29. The only other occurrence of the present active infinitive of the verb "to think" in the letter is in 4:2, but without the preposition "on behalf of." Other forms of the verb "to think" occur elsewhere in the letter in 2:2(2x), 5; 3:15(2x), 19; 4:2, 10.

30. The only other occurrence of the verb "to abound" in the letter is in 1:26.

31. The only other occurrence of the noun "fruit" in the letter is in 1:22, but in the nominative rather than accusative case.

32. The only other occurrence of the verb "to fill up" in the letter is in 2:2.

33. Other occurrences of the word "glory" in the letter are in 2:11; 3:19, 21.

letter of the adjectival use of the term for "rest of" enhances the distinctiveness of this parallel.[34] The emphatic double occurrence of the verb "rejoice"—"rejoice (χαίρετε) in the Lord always. Again I will say, rejoice (χαίρετε)"—in 4:4 of the C′ unit recalls, parallels, and complements a similar emphatic double occurrence of this verb—"in this I rejoice (χαίρω). And indeed I will be joyful (χαρήσομαι)" in 1:18 of the C unit.[35]

D: Death in My Body Is Gain But Remaining Is for Your Faith (1:19–30)
D′: Gain in Faith in the Death of Christ and the Body of His Glory (3:1–21)

The three occurrences of the prepositional phrase "in the flesh"—"do not put confidence in the flesh (ἐν σαρκί), although I myself have confidence even in the flesh (ἐν σαρκί). If someone else supposes to be confident in the flesh (ἐν σαρκί), I even more"—in 3:3–4 of the D′ unit recall and parallel the same phrase in 1:22— "if it is to live in the flesh (ἐν σαρκί)," and in 1:24—"to remain in the flesh ([ἐν] τῇ σαρκί)," of the D unit. That these are the only occurrences of the phrase "in the flesh" in the letter enhances the distinctiveness of these parallels.

"But whatever things were for me a gain (κέρδη)" in 3:7 and "that Christ I may gain (κερδήσω)" in 3:8 of the D′ unit recall and parallel "to die is gain (κέρδος)" in 1:21 of the D unit. That these are the only occurrences of the word "gain" in the letter enhances the distinctiveness of these parallels. The occurrence of the noun "faith" in the dative singular with the article—"the righteousness from God based on the faith (τῇ πίστει)" in 3:9 of the D′ unit recalls and parallels "struggling together for the faith (τῇ πίστει) of the gospel" in 1:27 of the D unit. That these are the only two occurrences of this form of the noun "faith" in the letter enhances the distinctiveness of this parallel.

"Their end is destruction (ἀπώλεια)" in 3:19 of the D′ unit recalls and parallels "a demonstration of destruction (ἀπωλείας)" in 1:28 of the D unit. That these are the only two occurrences in the letter of the word "destruction" enhances the distinctiveness of this parallel. "Who will transform the body (σῶμα) of our humility (to be) conformed to the body (σώματι) of his glory" in 3:21 of the D′ unit recalls and parallels "Christ will be magnified in my body (σώματί)" in 1:20 of the D unit. That these are the only occurrences in the letter of the word "body" enhances the distinctiveness of this parallelism.

E: Joy in Humility for the Day of Christ Who Humbled Himself to Death (2:1–16)
E′: Rejoice with Those Who Neared Death for the Work of Christ (2:17–30)

---

34. The term λοιπός is used adverbially in 3:1 and 4:8.
35. A similar pattern of double occurrences of the verbs for "rejoice" occurs in 2:17–18, but in that case the second verb in each double occurrence is the compound verb "rejoice with."

The occurrence of the noun for "joy"—"welcome him then in the Lord with all joy (χαρᾶς)"—in 2:29 of the E´ unit recalls and parallels its previous occurrence—"fill up my joy (χαράν)" in 2:2 of the E unit.[36] The occurrence of "Lord"—"I hope in the Lord (κυρίῳ) Jesus"—in 2:19 of the E´ unit recalls and parallels its previous occurrence—"Jesus Christ is Lord (κύριος)" in 2:11 of the E unit.[37] The occurrence of the verb "to have"—"I have (ἔχω) no one like–minded"—in 2:20 of the E´ unit recalls and parallels its previous occurrence —"having (ἔχοντες) the same love" in 2:2 of the E unit.[38] The occurrence of the genitive masculine plural reflexive pronoun referring to one's own self—"they all seek their own (ἑαυτῶν) things"—in 2:21 of the E´ unit recalls and parallels its previous occurrences—"to work out your own (ἑαυτῶν) salvation" in 2:12 and "considering one another more important than yourselves (ἑαυτῶν), each of you looking out not for your own (ἑαυτῶν) things" in 2:3–4 of the E unit. That these are the only occurrences in the letter of the plural form of this pronoun enhances the distinctiveness of these parallels.[39]

The occurrence of the title "Christ" in the genitive singular—"not those of Jesus Christ (Χριστου)"—in 2:21 of the E´ unit recalls and parallels its previous occurrence—"the day of Christ (Χριστου)" in 2:16 of the E unit.[40] The occurrence of the word "father"—"as a child to a father (πατρί)"—in 2:22 of the E´ unit recalls and parallels its previous occurrence—"to the glory of God the Father (πατρός)" in 2:11 of the E unit.[41] The occurrence of the word "child"—"as a child (τέκνον) to a father" in 2:22 of the E´ unit recalls and parallels its previous occurrence—"children (τέκνα) of God" in 2:15 of the E unit. That these are the only occurrences of the word for "child" in the letter enhances the distinctiveness of this parallel.

The occurrence of the verb "to consider"—"I have considered (ἡγησάμην) it necessary"—in 2:25 of the E´ unit recalls and parallels its previous occurrences—"did not consider (ἡγήσατο) being equal to God something to be grasped" in 2:6 and "in humility considering (ἡγούμενοι) one another more important than yourselves" in 2:3 of the E unit.[42] The occurrence of the prepositional phrase "to the point of death"—"he came near to the point of death (μέχρι θανάτου)"—in 2:30 of the E´ unit recalls and parallels "becoming obedient to the point of death (μέχρι θανάτου)" in 2:8 of the E unit. That these are the only occurrences in the letter of this phrase enhances the distinctiveness of this parallel.[43]

---

36. The noun "joy" occurs elsewhere in the letter in 1:4, 25; 4:1. In addition, forms of the verb for "rejoice" occur in 2:17–18 and 2:28 in the E´ unit.

37. "Lord" occurs again in 2:24 and 2:29 of the E´ unit.

38. The verb "to have" also occurs in 2:27 and 2:29 of the E´ unit.

39. Singular forms of the reflexive pronoun occurs elsewhere in the letter in 2:7–8.

40. The genitive singular of "Christ" occurs also in 2:30 of the E´ unit, as well as several other times throughout the letter.

41. The only other occurrences in the letter of the word "father" are in 1:2 and 4:20.

42. The only other occurrences in the letter of the verb "to consider" are in 3:7–8.

43. The same word for "death" occurs again in 2:8 of the E unit, in 2:27 of the E´ unit, and elsewhere in the letter in 1:20 and 3:10.

C. Overview of the Parallels of the Macrochiasm in Philippians

A 1:1–2: to all the holy ones (πᾶσιν τοῖς ἁγίοις, v. 1b)—grace (χάρις, v. 2)—Lord Jesus Christ (κυρίου Ἰησοῦ Χριστοῦ, v. 2)
A′ 4:21–23: every holy one (πάντα ἅγιον, v. 21a)—all the holy ones (πάντες οἱ ἅγιοι, v. 22)—grace (χάρις, v. 23)—Lord Jesus Christ (κυρίου Ἰησοῦ Χριστοῦ, v. 23)

B 1:3–11: I thank (εὐχαριστῶ, v. 3) my God—in my every petition (δεήσει, v. 4)—making the petition (δέησιν, v. 4)—it is right (δίκαιον v. 7)—to think this on behalf of all of you (φρονεῖν ὑπὲρ πάντων ὑμῶν, v. 7)—I have you in my heart (καρδίᾳ, v. 7)—that your love even more and more may abound (περισσεύῃ, v. 9)—having been filled up (πεπληρωμένοι, v. 11)—the fruit (καρπόν, v. 11) of righteousness—to the glory (δόξαν, v. 11)—praise (ἔπαινον, v. 11) of God
B′ 4:6–20: by prayer and petition (δεήσει, v. 6), with thanksgiving (εὐχαριστίας, v. 6)—will guard your hearts (καρδίας, v. 7)—whatever is right (δίκαια v. 8)—if there is any praise (ἔπαινος, v. 8)—to think on behalf of me (ὑπὲρ ἐμοῦ φρονεῖν, v. 10)—I know indeed to abound (περισσεύειν, v. 12)—both to abound (περισσεύειν, v. 12) and to be in want—I am abounding (περισσεύω, v. 18a)—I have been filled up (πεπλήρωμαι, v. 18b)—my God will fill up (πληρώσει, v. 19)—in glory (δόξῃ, v. 19) in Christ Jesus—glory (δόξᾳ v. 20) to the ages of the ages

C 1:12–18: to all the rest (λοιποῖς, v. 13)—in this I rejoice (χαίρω, v. 18)—I will be joyful (χαρήσομαι, v. 18)
C′ 4:1–5: the rest (λοιπῶν, v. 3) of my co-workers—rejoice (χαίρετε, v. 4a) in the Lord always—again I will say, rejoice (χαίρετε, v. 4b)

D 1:19–30: Christ will be magnified in my body (σώματί, v. 20)—to die is gain (κέρδος, v. 21)—to live in the flesh (ἐν σαρκί, v. 22)—to remain in the flesh ([ἐν] τῇ σαρκί, v. 24)—struggling together for the faith (τῇ πίστει, v. 27)—a demonstration of destruction (ἀπωλείας, v. 28)
D′ 3:1–21: confidence in the flesh (ἐν σαρκί, v. 3)—confidence even in the flesh (ἐν σαρκί, v. 4a)—confident in the flesh (ἐν σαρκί. v. 4b)—for me a gain (κέρδη, v. 7)—Christ I may gain (κερδήσω, v. 8)—the righteousness from God based on the faith (τῇ πίστει, v. 9)—their end is destruction (ἀπώλειαν. 19)—transform the body (σῶμα, v. 21a)—conformed to the body (σώματι, v. 21b)

E 2:1–16: fill up my joy (χαράν, v. 2)—having (ἔχοντες, v. 2) the same love—considering (ἡγούμενοι, v. 3) one another—more important than yourselves (ἑαυτῶν, v. 3)—not for your own things (τὰ ἑαυτῶν, v. 4)—did not consider (ἡγήσατο, v. 6)—to the point of death (μέχρι θανάτου, v. 8)—Jesus Christ is

Lord (κύριος, v. 11)—God the Father (πατρός, v. 11)—your own (ἑαυτῶν, v. 12) salvation—children (τέκνα, v. 15) of God—day of Christ (Χριστοῦ, v. 16)

E´ 2:17–30: in the Lord (κυρίῳ, v. 19)—I have (ἐχω, v. 20) no one like-minded—they all seek their own (ἑαυτῶν, v. 21) things—as a child (τέκνον, v. 22) to a father (πατρί, v. 22)—I have considered (ἡγησάμην, v. 25) it neces-sary—with all joy (χαρᾶς, v. 29)—the work of Christ (Χριστοῦ, v. 30)—to the point of death (μέχρι θανάτου, v. 30)

D. Outline of the Macrochiastic Structure of Philippians

A: 1:1–2: Grace from the Lord Jesus Christ to the Holy Ones
    B: 1:3–11: My Prayer That You Abound and Be Filled to Glory and Praise of God
        C: 1:12–18: I Rejoice and I Will Be Joyful
            D: 1:19–30: Death in My Body Is Gain But Remaining Is for Your Faith
            E: 2:1–16: Joy in Humility for the Day of Christ Who Humbled Himself to Death
            E´: 2:17–30: Rejoice with Those Who Neared Death for the Work of Christ
            D´: 3:1–21: Gain in Faith in the Death of Christ and the Body of His Glory
        C´: 4:1–5: Rejoice in the Lord, Rejoice
    B´: 4:6–20: Glory to God Who Will Fulfill You as I Am Filled and Abound
A´: 4:21–23: Greeting from Holy Ones and Grace from the Lord Jesus Christ

E. Summary

1. There are ten distinct units in the letter to the Philippians with each exhibit-ing its own microchiastic structure.

2. The ten units comprising Philippians operate as a macrochiastic struc-ture with five pairs of parallel units and with the pivot of the entire macrochiastic structure occurring in the progression from the E unit in 2:1–16 to the E´ unit in 2:17–30.

3

PHILIPPIANS 1:1–2: GRACE FROM THE LORD JESUS CHRIST TO THE HOLY ONES (A)

Paul and Timothy to Those in Philippi

A: [1:1a] Paul and Timothy, slaves of *Christ Jesus,*
  B: [1b] to all *those* holy ones *in* Christ Jesus,
  B′: [1c] *those* who are *in* Philippi with overseers and ministers,
A′: [2] grace to you and peace from God our Father and the Lord *Jesus Christ.*[1]

A. AUDIENCE RESPONSE TO PHILIPPIANS 1:1–2

1. *Phil 1:1a (A): Paul and Timothy, Slaves of Christ Jesus*

The letter presents itself as sent by both Paul, who founded the community of believers at Philippi (Acts 16:11–40), and Timothy, who accompanied him (Acts 16:1; 17:14–15; 18:5) and later revisited Macedonia, undoubtedly including Philippi located in that region (Acts 19:22; 20:4). That Paul is mentioned first indicates that he is the primary sender and author of the letter. The mention of Timothy as a co-sender, however, lends additional pertinence to the letter for the Philippians. He was a prominent co-worker of Paul well known to the Philippians, who can thus vouch for what Paul will say in the letter. Although Timothy is mentioned as a co-sender, this does not necessarily mean he had a major role to play in the actual composition of the letter. At any rate, Paul himself will immediately emerge in 1:3 as the sole authorial voice for the remainder of the letter.[2]

The letter is being sent to its Philippian audience by both Paul and Timothy, described as "slaves of Christ Jesus" (1:1a).[3] This designation evokes a double response from the audience. First, they are to be duly impressed by, with perhaps the

---

1. For the establishment of Phil 1:1–2 as a chiasm, see ch. 2.

2. There is not much evidence to indicate that co-senders actively composed together with Paul the letters in which they are mentioned, according to Samuel Byrskog, "Co-Senders, Co-Authors and Paul's Use of the First Person Plural," *ZNW* 87 (1996): 230–50.

3. For more on the metaphor of slavery in Paul, see Dale B. Martin, *Slavery as Salvation: The Metaphor of Slavery in Pauline Christianity* (New Haven: Yale University Press, 1990). On slavery at the time of the NT, see Jennifer A. Glancy, *Slavery in Early Christianity* (Minneapolis: Fortress, 2006);

hint of imitating, the submissive humility of Paul and Timothy as fellow "slaves" of Christ Jesus, who is thus portrayed as their "owner" or "master."[4] Secondly, they are to be attuned to hearing what these "slaves," especially Paul as the primary author, have to say to them as authoritative agents of their "master," Christ Jesus. In other words, it is in fulfillment of their role as "slaves" that Paul and Timothy are bringing the Philippians an authoritative communication from their "master," Christ Jesus himself, who by implication is also the "master" of those who believe in him at Philippi. What the audience will hear in the letter, then, ultimately comes to them from the "master" Christ Jesus through his designated "slaves," Paul and Timothy.[5]

2. Phil 1:1b (B): To All Those Holy Ones in Christ Jesus

The recipients of the letter are designated as "all those holy ones in Christ Jesus" (1:1b). That the letter is addressed to "all" (πᾶσιν) those holy ones makes the audience aware that they are being addressed as a unified totality, with no member of the community left out.[6] That the audience are described as all those "holy ones" refers to the totality of those who are "holy" (ἁγίοις), that is, those who have been separated from the rest of society and consecrated by God for service to God. They have been separated and consecrated "in Christ Jesus," that is, within the dynamic sphere or realm of existence established by the life, death, and resurrection of Christ Jesus. Addressing the audience as "holy ones" who are "in Christ Jesus," then, makes them reflect not only on their close union with Christ Jesus, but that there is a sense in which they are living separate from the profane and political domain of society and within the sacred and spiritual domain dominated by Christ Jesus.[7]

J. Albert Harrill, *Slaves in the New Testament: Literary, Social, and Moral Dimensions* (Minneapolis: Fortress, 2006).

4. Garland, "Philippians," 188: "Identifying himself and Timothy as slaves drives home the point that they are not ministry volunteers but are in bondage to Christ, who owns the title deed to their lives." See also M. Sydney Park, *Submission Within the Godhead and the Church in the Epistle to the Philippians: An Exegetical and Theological Examination of the Concept of Submission in Philippians 2 and 3* (LNTS 361; London: Clark, 2007), 126–28.

5. Garland, "Philippians," 189: "Slaves frequently served as agents or managers for their masters, and the title can convey Paul's authority as Christ's manager. Paul understands all Christians to be Christ's slaves since they all were bought at a price (1Co 6:20). He has no interest in emphasizing his status and makes no pretensions to some special dignity. Introducing himself and Timothy as Christ's slaves at the outset must be intended to highlight lowly service and humility, an emphasis that echoes throughout the letter."

6. Davorin Peterlin, *Paul's Letter to the Philippians in the Light of Disunity in the Church* (NovTSup 79; Leiden: Brill, 1995), 24: "So already in the very opening of the letter Paul may be hinting at divisions in the church . . . By addressing the letter to *all* Philippian Christians Paul makes it clear that he has a message to *all* irrespective of the side they find themselves on."

7. O'Brien, *Philippians*, 46: "ἐν Χριστῷ Ἰησοῦ frequently points to Christ Jesus as the sphere in which the Christian lives and moves." Fee, *Philippians*, 65: "The Philippian believers are 'in Christ Jesus' precisely because they are first of all 'by Christ Jesus.' That is, Christ Jesus is both responsible for their

3. Phil 1:1c (B´): Those Who Are in Philippi with Overseers and Ministers

The recipients of the letter are further specified as "those who are in Philippi with overseers and ministers" (1:1c). At this point the audience hear a pivot in the chiastic parallels from "all those (τοῖς) holy ones in (ἐν) Christ Jesus" (1:1b) in the B element to "those (τοῖς) who are in (ἐν) Philippi" in the B´ element. The audience are thus reminded that as "those" who are "holy ones" they live in two realms at the same time—the sacred and spiritual realm of being united with and located "in" Christ Jesus and the profane and physical realm as "those" who presently are geographically, socially, and politically located "in" the Roman colony of Philippi. The explicit use of the present participle in the clause "those who are," literally "those being presently (οὖσιν)," emphasizes that whereas the audience are always "in Christ Jesus" (1:1b), they are only at the present time "in Philippi" (1:1c).

The additional notice, "with overseers and ministers" (1:1c), makes the audience of "all those holy ones" realize that there are those individuals among them who exercise certain leadership roles within their community.[8] The members of the audience thus include "overseers" (ἐπισκόποις), those who in some way supervise the other members of the audience, and "ministers" (διακόνοις), those who perform some kind of assistance in the community. That these members of the audience are singled out affirms their leadership roles for acknowledgment from the rest of the audience.[9]

---

becoming the people of God, and as the crucified and risen One, he constitutes the present sphere of their new existence. They are those who belong to Christ Jesus, as those whose lives are forever identified with Christ." Fowl, *Philippians*, 18: "Being in Christ locates one within that community founded by Christ, and thereby, within the realm governed by Christ. What is not always recognized, however, is that when Paul speaks this way he is speaking in political terms. He is speaking of a community whose character and common life are defined by the lordship of Christ."

8. Fee, *Philippians*, 67: "The language used for this addition, 'together with/along with,' is the sure giveaway as to the role of leadership in the Pauline churches. The community as a whole is addressed, and in most cases therefore the 'overseers and deacons' are simply reckoned as being within the community. When they are singled out, as here, the leaders are not 'over' the church, but are addressed 'alongside of' the church, as a *distinguishable* part of the whole, but as *part of the whole*, not above or outside it."

9. Bockmuehl, *Philippians*, 55: "Paul's address here, then, appears at the very least to recognize and respect a group of people who in his own absence exercise a ministry of supervision and care for the Christian polity at Philippi." Garland, "Philippians," 190: "The most that can be said with complete confidence is that they had roles of supervision and service that were distinctive in the community." See also John Reumann, "Church Office in Paul, Especially in Philippians," in *Origins and Method: Towards a New Understanding of Judaism and Christianity: Essays in Honour of John C. Hurd* (ed. Bradley H. McLean; JSNTSup 86; Sheffield: Sheffield Academic Press, 1993), 82–91; Peterlin, *Paul's Letter*, 20–22. For a possible but ultimately indecisive text-critical point that the words "with overseers and ministers" might not be original, see T. C. Skeat, "Did Paul Write to 'Bishops and Deacons' at Philippi? A Note on Philippians 1:1," *NovT* 37 (1995): 12–15. See also Wolfgang Schenk, *Die Philipperbriefe des Paulus: Kommentar* (Stuttgart: Kohlhammer, 1984), 78–82.

4. Phil 1:2 (A´): Grace to You and Peace from God Our Father and Lord Jesus Christ

The opening address by the senders of the letter to its recipients is followed by the letter's introductory greeting: "Grace to you and peace from God our Father and the Lord Jesus Christ" (1:2).[10] Paul and Timothy's greeting of God's "grace" expresses their prayer-wish that God, who has already graced the audience in making them holy ones in Christ Jesus (1:1b), will grant them yet further "grace" (χάρις)—God's gracious, generous, and freely given favor.[11] This concept of the "grace" or "favor" of God is thus not only a gift from God but carries with it a connotation of divine empowerment or enablement.[12] God's grace has empowered the audience to become holy ones in Christ Jesus and will empower them to live as holy ones who are also in Philippi (1:1bc).

After hearing themselves addressed in the third person, as "all *those* holy ones in Christ Jesus, *those* who are in Philippi" (1:1bc), the audience now hear themselves addressed more directly and personally with the second-person plural pronoun—"grace *to you* (ὑμῖν)" (1:2). The prayer-wish, then, is for grace "to you," that is, to all of you who are holy ones in Christ Jesus and who are in Philippi, including overseers and ministers (1:b–2).

Coupled with God's grace that Paul and Timothy pray to be given to their audience is "peace" (εἰρήνη)—a state of overall well-being or harmony.[13] Paul and Timothy pray that with the grace of God their audience may live in peace with God, with one another as holy ones who are in Christ Jesus (1:1b), and, as holy ones who are in Christ and in Philippi, with non–believers who are not in Christ Jesus but in Philippi, and with the overseers and ministers among them (1:1c).[14]

---

10. Fee, *Philippians*, 70: "It is worth noting that this is the invariable order of Paul's words, not 'grace and peace to you' as in most translations. Very likely there is significance to this order: the grace of God and Christ is what is given to God's people; peace is what results from such a gift. Hence, 'grace to you—and peace.'" Garland, "Philippians," 190: "'Grace' is the source of Christian life, and 'peace' is its consummation."

11. A. Boyd Luter, "Grace," *DPL*, 374: "[T]he Pauline letters all begin and end by sounding a note of grace. It is not unlikely that the apostle intended all of his writings to be viewed within the all–encompassing framework of divine grace, from beginning to end."

12. James R. Harrison, *Paul's Language of Grace in Its Graeco-Roman Context* (WUNT 172; Tübingen: Mohr Siebeck, 2003), 243: "It is worth remembering that Paul links χάρις with the language of glory, wealth, mystery, and power." See also John Nolland, "Grace as Power," *NovT* 28 (1986): 26–31.

13. Ceslas Spicq, "εἰρενεύω," *TLNT* 1.424–38. O'Brien, *Philippians*, 51: "In the LXX εἰρήνη ('peace') had the general sense of well-being, the source and giver of which is Yahweh alone. It included everything given by God in all areas of life, and had a social dimension."

14. Judith M. Lieu, "'Grace to You and Peace': The Apostolic Greeting," *BJRL* 68 (1985): 161–78. See also Klaus Berger, "Apostelbrief und apostolische Rede: Zum Formular frühchristlicher Briefe," *ZNW* 65 (1974): 190–231. Fee, *Philippians*, 71 n. 62: "In Paul 'peace' can refer in turn to (1) peace with God (= cessation of hostilities), (2) peace within the believing community, (3) inner peace in place of turmoil, and (4) rest or order within a context of worship." Garland, "Philippians," 190: "The peace offered through Jesus Christ rivals that of the peace established and propagated by the emperor, who

With the use of the first-person plural pronoun "our," that the grace and peace are to come from "God our (ἡμῶν) Father" (1:2) plays a double rhetorical role. First, it bonds the audience more closely to the senders of the letter, Paul and Timothy (1:1a), as together sharing in the common Fatherhood of God. And secondly, more broadly and generally, it reminds the audience that, as holy ones in Christ Jesus, there is a sense in which they are united with all the other holy ones in Christ Jesus, who do not reside in Philippi but share in this common Fatherhood of God as *our* Father.[15]

That the grace and peace are to come not only from God our Father but from "the Lord Jesus Christ" (1:2) functions for the audience as the parallel between the A (1:1a) and A´ (1:2) elements of this first chiastic unit. The order of the parallel is itself a mini–chiasm: Paul and Timothy are slaves of (a) Christ (b) Jesus in the A element, while the grace and peace come from the Lord (b) Jesus (a) Christ in the A´ element. But "the Lord Jesus Christ" also functions as the climax of a rhetorical triplet heard by the audience. First of all, not only are Paul and Timothy "slaves of Christ Jesus" (1:1a), but, secondly, all the holy ones are united with them as those who are "in Christ Jesus" (1:1b), and, thirdly, the audience of holy ones, including overseers and ministers (1:1c), are further united with the "slaves" Paul and Timothy, as they share with them and with all other believers in the "lordship" of Jesus Christ.[16] The progression that moves from "of Christ Jesus" (1:1a) to "in Christ Jesus" (1:1b) and climaxes with "the Lord Jesus Christ" (1:2) thus serves as the dominant theme ringing in the ears of audience, now poised to hear the body of the letter.[17]

B. SUMMARY ON PHILIPPIANS 1:1–2

1. In the opening of the chiastic unit in 1:1–2 the senders of the letter, Paul and Timothy, present themselves as "slaves" owned and authorized by Christ Jesus to address the audience to whom they are sending the letter (1:1a).

---

is portrayed in Roman imperial propaganda as the world's great savior and benefactor. The emperor's peace is built on the backs of conquered peoples who must submit to political oppression, religious crackdowns, and impoverishing taxation. Christ's peace comes through his own death for others, which was driven by God's fatherly love. It brings true peace—reconciliation to God and to one another."

15. Bockmuehl, *Philippians*, 56: "It is not that God is *like* an idealized human father, but rather that God *is* the one from whom human parenthood receives its very definition."

16. Thurston, *Philippians*, 46–47: "As Philippi was governed by Roman law and closely connected to Rome, to call anyone other than the Caesar 'Lord' was bold and probably dangerous." Garland, "Philippians," 191: "Caesar and his loyalists would regard this confession as high treason because it means that Caesar is not lord."

17. Davis, *Oral Biblical Criticism*, 105: "The beginning and end of the unit are marked by an inclusio with a chiasm on the name Χριστοῦ Ἰησοῦ (Christ Jesus). While the senders and recipients are named, the three–fold repetition of the name, Ἰησοῦ Χριστός (Jesus Christ), which echoes in the ears of the audience, gives it the position of primary importance in the unit."

2. That the letter is sent to "all the holy ones in Christ Jesus" (1:1b) unites the audience to the senders through their common relationship to Christ Jesus.

3. The audience are not only "in" Christ Jesus but also "in" the Roman colony of Philippi and includes members designated as "overseers and ministers" (1:1c).

4. The senders greet the audience directly and personally as "you," with a prayer-wish that they be granted "grace" and its resulting "peace" from the God who is "our" Father—the Father of Paul and Timothy, of all the holy ones in Philippi, and of all other holy ones—and from "the Lord Jesus Christ," thus uniting the audience under the lordship of Jesus Christ to the senders of the letter as "slaves" of that same Lord Jesus Christ (1:2). This is the third and climactic time that the audience have heard a reference to Jesus Christ, the dominant theme echoing throughout this first chiastic unit of the letter (1:1–2).

4

PHILIPPIANS 1:3–11: MY PRAYER THAT YOU ABOUND AND BE FILLED TO GLORY AND PRAISE OF GOD (B)

Paul Makes His Petitions with Joy

A: [3] I thank my *God* at every remembrance of you,

B: [4] always in my every petition on behalf of all of you, making the petition with joy [5] at your fellowship for the gospel from the first *day* until now, [6] having confidence of this very thing, that he who began in you a good work will perfect it until the *day of Christ* Jesus.

C: [7] Just as it is right for me to think this on behalf of all of you because I have you in my heart, as both in my bonds and in the defense and confirmation of the gospel, *all of you* are my fellow sharers of the grace.

D: [8a] For my witness is God,

C′: [8b] how I long for *all of you* with the affection of Christ Jesus.

B′: [9] And this I pray, that your love even more and more may abound in knowledge and every perception [10] in order that you determine the things that matter, so that you may be sincere and faultless for the *day of Christ,*

A′: [11] having been filled up with the fruit of righteousness that is through Jesus Christ for the glory and praise of *God.*[1]

A. AUDIENCE RESPONSE TO PHILIPPIANS 1:3–11

1. *Phil 1:3 (A): I Thank My God at Every Remembrance of You*

The opening address and greeting (1:1–2) is followed by a thanksgiving section beginning with the pronouncement that "I thank my God at every remembrance

---

1. For the establishment of Phil 1:3–11 as a chiasm, see ch. 2.

of you" (1:3).[2] With the first-person singular verb "I thank" (εὐχαριστῶ), the audience hear a progression from being addressed by Paul and Timothy (1:1) to being addressed by Paul alone, confirming that he is the primary sender and author of the letter. When the audience hear of Paul's thanking my "God" (θεῷ), they hear the transitional word that links this chiastic unit (1:3–11) with the previous one (1:1–2), which concluded with Paul's greeting of grace and peace from our "God" (θεοῦ) and the Lord Jesus Christ (1:2). The audience also hear a development from the prayer-wish of "grace to you and peace from God *our* (ἡμῶν) Father" (1:2) to Paul's thanking "*my* (μου) God," further emphasizing the focus on Paul alone with this expression of his personal gratitude to God.[3] The audience are assured that every time Paul thinks of them, with the implication that he thinks of them quite often, it is an occasion for Paul to render thanks to God. The audience are thus being made aware of and further drawn into Paul's close relationship with them.[4]

2. Phil 1:4–6 (B): God Will Perfect Your Good Work until the Day of Christ Jesus

Paul continues the introduction to the thanksgiving section of the letter with the words "always in my every petition on behalf of all of you" (1:4a). The audience hear an alliterative intensification of the accent on "all" or "every" in Paul's thanking God at "*every* (πάσῃ) remembrance of you" (1:3), as he adds "*always* (πάντοτε) in my *every* (πάσῃ) petition on behalf of *all* (πάντων) of you."[5] The audience are further assured not only that Paul thanks God at his frequent remembrances of them, but that each and every time that he does so it is in a special petition to God

---

2. Davis, *Oral Biblical Criticism*, 105: "The beginning of the unit, and its form, are clearly marked by the introductory thanksgiving clause. Upon hearing the thanksgiving formula the audience would know that the greeting has ended. The thanksgiving was a common epistolary form which Paul adapted to his use and usually placed at the beginning of the letter, immediately after the greeting." Paul Schubert, *Form and Function of the Pauline Thanksgiving* (BZNW 20; Berlin: Töpelmann, 1939); Alexander, "Hellenistic Letter-Forms," 87–101.

3. O'Brien, *Philippians*, 57: "It is to the one true God that he offers his thanksgiving, and stressing the consciousness of a personal relation to him he adds the pronoun μου." Garland, "Philippians," 192: "Thanking '*my* God' reflects Paul's personal relationship to God, whom he has identified as 'our Father' (1:2); it does not mean that he is thanking *his* God as opposed to other so-called gods."

4. For the suggestion that an alternative rendering of 1:3a, "because of your remembrance of me," be considered the preferred translation, see Kuo-Wei Peng, "Do We Need an Alternative Rendering for Philippians 1.3?" *BT* 54 (2003): 415–19. But this seems questionable and not at all convincing; see also Fee, *Philippians*, 78–80; Bockmuehl, *Philippians*, 58. Phil 1:3 should be translated something like "I give thanks to my God *for* every remembrance of you," according to Paul Andrew Holloway, "Thanks for the Memories: On the Translation of Phil 1.3," *NTS* 52 (2006): 419–32. But this seems to be a strained and unusual way to construe the preposition ἐπί with the dative, which usually means "at" or "on the basis of." For the questionable view that Paul is here thanking God for a monetary gift from the Philippians, see Gerald W. Peterman, *Paul's Gift from Philippi: Conventions of Gift-Exchange and Christian Giving* (SNTSMS 92; Cambridge: Cambridge University Press, 1997), 93–99.

5. According to Peterlin (*Paul's Letter*, 25), this fourfold alliteration in 1:3–4 "conveys to the Philippians that Paul thinks of them as the whole, and does not want anyone to feel excluded."

on behalf of "*all* of you" as a completely united community, "*all* (πᾶσιν) the holy ones in Christ Jesus who are in Philippi (1:1).[6]

Paul makes every special petition to God on behalf of his Philippian audience not only in a context of gratitude to God but with an emphasis on his joy in doing so: "making the petition with joy" (1:4b).[7] With this participial clause the audience hear a mini–chiasm based on alliterative, linguistic, and grammatical parallels: (a) always (πάντοτε) (b) in my every petition (δεήσει) (c) on behalf of all of you (ὑπὲρ πάντων ὑμῶν) (c´) with joy (μετὰ χαρᾶς) (b´) the petition (δέησιν) (a´) making (ποιούμενος).

The adverb "always" (πάντοτε) in the "a" sub-element forms an allitera-tive parallel with the participle "making" (ποιούμενος) in the "a´" sub-element, which serves as a literary inclusion tightly framing the mini-chiasm between the introductory adverb and the concluding verbal form it modifies.[8] "In my every pe-tition (δεήσει)" in the "b" sub-element is linguistically paralleled by "the petition (δέησιν)" in the "b´" sub-element. The audience hear the pivot of the mini-chiasm in a parallel progression of prepositional phrases from "on behalf of all of you (ὑπὲρ πάντων ὑμῶν)" in the "c" sub-element to "with joy (μετὰ χαρᾶς)" in the "c´" sub-element. The close alignment of the emphatically positioned prepositional

---

6. Fowl, *Philippians*, 23 n. 6: "This is the second time in the first four verses of the epistle where Paul has used some version of 'all' to emphasize the whole church in Philippi." On the meaning of "petition" (δέησις), Ulrich Schoenborn ("δέησις," *EDNT* 1.287) states: "Δέησις as 'special' request is to be distinguished from προσευχή as the 'general' request. . . . The absolute use of the word implies God as object."

7. In the Greek text the prepositional phrase "with joy" (μετὰ χαρᾶς) stands in an emphatic position at the beginning of the participial clause in 1:4b. O'Brien, *Philippians*, 58: "Then, somewhat unusually, a phrase of manner μετὰ χαρᾶς, is added. Paul makes his petition 'with joy'; and the jubilant note struck here at the beginning rings throughout the whole letter (cf. 1:18, 25; 2:2, 17, 18 [twice], 28, 29; 3:1; 4:1, 4 [twice], 10)." Fee, *Philippians*, 81: "The word order ('with joy the prayer making') gives this phrase special emphasis; indeed this is the first of 16 occurrences of this word group ('joy') in the letter." Thurston, *Philippians*, 49: "The prepositional phrase describes the quality of Paul's prayer and is the first use of the root word χαρά, which characterizes the Philippian letter, Paul's epistle of joy and rejoicing. It is the only use of the word in Pauline thanksgivings and sets the emotional tone of this whole epistle."

8. According to O'Brien (*Philippians*, 57), the adverb "always" (πάντοτε) "modifies the principal verb εὐχαριστέω and indicates the frequency with which the apostle gave thanks." But this construal would make the adverb redundant after the statement that "I thank my God at *every* (πάσῃ) remem-brance of you" (1:3). Rather, the adverb modifies the participle "making" (ποιούμενος) that follows it, thus emphasizing that Paul *always makes* every petition on behalf of his audience *with joy* (1:4). Hollo-way, "Thanks," 428: "Following Westcott and Hort, the 27th edition of *Novum Testamentum Graece* sets 1.4b (μετὰ χαρᾶς τὴν δέησιν ποιούμενος) in commas, on the assumption that the ἐπί-clause in v. 5 is the object of εὐχαριστῶ in v. 3 and that, accordingly, v. 4b is parenthetical. But we have argued that the object of εὐχαριστῶ is the ἐπί-clause in v. 3, not the ἐπί-clause in v. 5. These commas should therefore be removed, and instead a comma should be placed at the end of v. 3. All of vv. 4–5 should then be read as epexegetical of v. 3, with the ἐπί-clause in v. 5 understood to be the object of χαρά in v. 4b: μετὰ χαρᾶς . . . ἐπὶ τῇ κοινωνίᾳ ὑμῶν εἰς τὸ εὐαγγέλιον ('with joy over your partnership in the gospel')." See also Fee, *Philippians*, 75–76.

phrase "with joy" to the prepositional phrase "on behalf of all of you" begins to give the audience the impression that there is a very close relationship between themselves and the emphatic joy with which Paul makes these special petitions on behalf of his Philippian audience with gratitude to God.[9]

The strong implication that the audience are at the basis of Paul's joy is confirmed for them as he continues, "at your fellowship for the gospel from the first day until now" (1:5). At this point the audience hear a progression from an ἐπί prepositional phrase with the dative for a temporal meaning—"I thank my God at (ἐπί) every remembrance of you" (1:3), that is, Paul thanks God every time he remembers the audience, to the use of the same preposition with the dative for a more causal meaning—making the petition with joy "at" or "on the basis of" or "because of" (ἐπί) "your fellowship for the gospel." The audience have now heard a primary reason for Paul's close relationship with them. He thanks God at every remembrance "of you" (ὑμῶν, 1:3), and makes his petitions to God with a distinct joy on behalf of all "of you" (ὑμῶν, 1:4), because of "your" (ὑμῶν) mutual "fellowship" or "partnership" (κοινωνία), both with Paul and with one another as a united community, for the gospel (1:5).[10] That this fellowship began from the first day the Philippian audience heard the gospel mediated to them by Paul and has persisted until the present time affirms them in their comprehensive commitment to the fellowship for the gospel.

Paul then expresses his strong conviction about what the God to whom he petitions will do for the audience: "having confidence of this very thing, that he who began in you a good work will perfect it until the day of Christ Jesus" (1:6). The audience now hear an alliterative progression involving the "p" sound in participles modifying Paul—from ποιούμενος ("making," 1:4) to πεποιθώς ("having confidence," 1:6). This alliterative progression has a causal implication. Because

---

9. Holloway, "Thanks," 428 n. 35: "[W]e should note that v. 4b has clear verbal ties to v. 4a and makes good sense when read together with it: ἐν πάσῃ δεήσει . . . τὴν δέησιν ποιούμενος." It should also be noted that although the audience hear 1:4 as a mini-chiasm, this verse is not an independent, self-enclosed grammatical unit. Rather, 1:4a continues the grammatical flow from 1:3, and 1:4b is closely connected to its grammatical completion in 1:5–6. Indeed, the mini-chiasm in 1:4 is framed by a literary inclusion beginning with "at (ἐπί) every remembrance of you (ὑμῶν)" in 1:3b and concluding with "at (ἐπί) your (ὑμῶν) fellowship" in 1:5a. Cf. Harvey, *Listening*, 233.

10. Josef Hainz, "κοινωνία," *EDNT* 2.304: "Paul uses κοινωνία also for various common relationships of Christians with each other. Thus he thanks the Philippians for their '*partnership* in the gospel' (Phil 1:5). This partnership is based on the mediation of the gospel by the apostle and in the common participation in the gospel and is expressed in common service for the gospel (or for Paul as its mediator)." According to O'Brien (*Philippians*, 62), it is best "to understand κοινωνία in an active sense, so that the phrase ἐπὶ τῇ κοινωνίᾳ ὑμῶν εἰς τὸ εὐαγγέλιον means 'your cooperation [in promoting] the gospel.'" Fee, *Philippians*, 82: "By 'the gospel,' especially in Philippians, Paul refers primarily neither to a body of teaching nor to proclamation. Above all, the gospel has to do with Christ, both his person and his work. . . . Thus Paul's joy in prayer is prompted by their 'partnership *for (the furtherance of) the gospel* (Fee's emphasis).'" Fowl, *Philippians*, 22: "Paul incorporates all aspects of his relations with the Philippians under the rubric of κοινωνία which is often translated as 'fellowship,' 'partnership,' 'sharing,' or 'communion.'"

Paul is "making" (ποιούμενος) his every petition for the audience to his God (1:4), the God he thanks at every remembrance of the audience (1:3), he has been and is still "confident" (πεποιθώς, perfect tense) by his strong faith in God "of this very thing," namely,[11] the assured hope that the God who began "in you" (ἐν ὑμῖν)—in each of them as individuals and in all of them together as a unified community— this "good work" of believing in and committing themselves to the gospel within the fellowship they share with Paul and one another will "complete" or "perfect" (ἐπιτελέσει) it until the day of Christ Jesus.[12]

That God is the one who began this "good work" in the audience from the first "day" (ἡμέρας) until the present time (1:5) assures the audience of the hope that God will also continue to perfect it all the way until the "day" (ἡμέρας) of Christ Jesus (1:6), the "day" of his triumphant return in glory at the end of time.[13] This not only assures the audience of the hope for God's continual, complete, and final activity on their behalf but also indirectly encourages them to continue to play their own role in the "good work" of their fellowship with Paul and one another for the advancement of the gospel of Christ.

In sum, then, Paul has confidently assured the audience that God will continue to perfect, right up until the final day of Christ Jesus, the good work that God began in them in bringing them to faith in and fellowship for the gospel, the fellowship with one another and with Paul that has motivated Paul to thank and

---

11. Fee, *Philippians*, 85 n. 62: "αὐτὸ τοῦτο (lit., 'this same thing'), an emphatic combination stressing 'this very thing' that has been or is about to be mentioned. In this case, the ὅτι that follows makes it clear that it points forward."

12. O'Brien, *Philippians*, 64: "The ἔργον ἀγαθόν ('good work') that God commenced is that work of grace in the readers' lives that began with their reception of the gospel (cf. 2:13, which states that God is at work in them both to will and to do his good pleasure). The expression refers to the new creation that he had begun in them, while their eager participation in Paul's gospel ministry was not the good work itself, but clear evidence of this work of salvation." Fee, *Philippians*, 87: "[T]he term [good work] points to their 'salvation in Christ,' and in this case is yet another way of speaking about their 'participating in the gospel.'" Bockmuehl, *Philippians*, 62: "Paul's confidence is not in the Christianity of the Christians but in the God–ness of God, who is supremely trustworthy, able, and committed to finish the work he has begun. The 'good work', at the end of the day, is not Paul's, nor that of the Philippians, but God's; as such, participation in it frees one from both self–assurance and despondency." On further implications of 1:6, see J. G. Janzen, "Creation and New Creation in Phlippians 1:6," *HBT* 18 (1996): 27–54.

13. Wolfgang Trilling, "ἡμέρα," *EDNT* 2.121: "The center of gravity in NT use of ἡμέρα is in references to the eschatological *day* of the end, the day of judgment and redemption. This usage is derived from the OT and Jewish tradition of 'the day of Yahweh.' . . . Only Paul, in all the NT, speaks of the parousia *of Christ* as '*the day* of the Lord' (1 Cor 1:8; 5:5; 2 Cor 1:14; 1 Thess 5:2; in the Pauline tradition: 2 Thess 2:2); cf. 'the *day* of (Jesus) Christ' (in the NT only in Phil 1:6, 10; 2:16). Paul knows also the absolute ἡμέρα (1 Cor 3:13; 1 Thess 5:4; cf. Rom 2:16; Heb 10:25; 2 Pet 1:19)." Gordon D. Fee, *Pauline Christology: An Exegetical-Theological Study* (Peabody: Hendrickson, 2007), 407: "Paul refers to this future hope simply as 'the Day of Christ Jesus.' But it still carries the obvious identification of Christ with the κύριος = Yahweh of the prophetic phrase." On the eschatology in 1:6, as well as in the remainder of the Letter, see Heinz Giesen, "Eschatology in Philippians," in *Paul and His Theology* (ed. Stanley E. Porter; Pauline Studies 3; Leiden: Brill, 2007), 217–82.

petition God on behalf of his audience with a distinctive note of joy. With such assurance of divine assistance the audience are encouraged to continue their own personal and communal efforts regarding their fellowship with Paul and with one another for the gospel (1:3–6).

3. Phil 1:7 (C): All of You Are My Fellow Sharers of the Grace

Paul continues to express his close relationship with his Philippian audience: "Just as it is right for me to think this on behalf of all of you because I have you in my heart, as both in my bonds and in the defense and confirmation of the gospel, all of you are my fellow sharers of the grace" (1:7). Paul's profound persuasion of "this" (τοῦτο) very thing—the hope that the God who began a good work in the Philippians will continue to perfect it until the day of Christ Jesus (1:6)—receives further justification in his subsequent statement that it is right for him to think "this" (τοῦτο) on behalf of his audience.[14] The audience continue to hear of Paul's deep personal concern for the welfare of all of them as a unified community. Paul not only makes with joy every petition to God "on behalf of all of you" (ὑπὲρ πάντων ὑμῶν, 1:4), but acknowledges that it is right for him to think as he does "on behalf of all of you" (ὑπὲρ πάντων ὑμῶν) with regard to God's concern for them because he himself personally has "you" (ὑμᾶς) in his heart (1:7a).

With emphasis on no one of them being left out, Paul further describes his audience at Philippi as "all of you" (πάντας ὑμᾶς) who are his fellow sharers of the "grace" (χάριτος) (1:7b), the "grace" (χάρις) which is the freely given gift that both Paul and they have received from God our Father and the Lord Jesus Christ (1:2).[15] The audience hear their "fellowship" (κοινωνία) for the "gospel" (εὐαγγέλιον) (1:5) further specified in terms of all of them being "fellow sharers" (συγκοινωνούς) of the grace both in the bonds or chains of Paul's imprisonment and in the defense and confirmation of the "gospel" (εὐαγγελίου) (1:7b).[16] The audience, then, are to realize that they are fellow sharers closely aligned with Paul, who is deeply con-

---

14. On "to think" (φρονεῖν) here Fee (*Philippians*, 89) points out: "It refers neither to 'thinking' in general, nor 'reasoning' as such, nor is it used for a specific act of thought; rather, it has to do with having or developing a certain 'mind-set,' including attitudes and dispositions."

15. O'Brien, *Philippians*, 70: "The article (τῆς) before 'grace' (χάριτος) shows it is the grace of God that is in view. . . . That grace was manifested both in his bonds and in the defence and confirmation of the gospel."

16. According to BDAG, 219, "bonds" or "chains" (δεσμοῖς) often simply refer "to the locale where bonds or fetters are worn," thus to imprisonment. Cassidy, *Paul in Chains*, 168: "Paul proceeds in 1:7 to the subject of his chains and to the subject of 'the defense and confirmation of the gospel.' Seemingly, he uses these expressions in their root juridical meanings, thereby indicating his continued sharing with the Philippians whether as a prisoner in chains or as a defendant upholding the gospel before an imperial tribunal." Garland, "Philippians," 194: " 'Defense' and 'confirmation' are jurisprudential terms in this context. He is going to be on trial, but more importantly the gospel is on trial."

cerned for their welfare, in the defense and confirmation of the gospel even though Paul is in prison (probably in Rome) while they remain in Philippi.[17]

4. Phil 1:8a (D): For My Witness Is God

To further assure his Philippian audience of his close bond with them, Paul calls upon God himself: "For my witness is God" (1:8a). To bolster his assertion that it is right for "me" (ἐμοί), Paul, to think as he does on behalf of all in his audience because "I" (με) have you in my heart, as both in "my" (μου) bonds and in the defense and confirmation of the gospel all of you are "my" (μου) fellow sharers of the grace (1:7), Paul declares that "my" (μου) witness is God himself. Paul thus invokes the witness of God as the ultimate verification of his close relation with his audience even while he is in prison.[18] Paul's witness is thus "God" himself, the "God" who is the source of the grace and peace that Paul wishes for his audience (1:2), the "God" whom Paul thanks at every remembrance of his audience (1:3).

5. Phil 1:8b (C'): How I Long for All of You with the Affection of Christ Jesus

Paul then continues to express his personal and inner feelings toward his audience for which God himself is his witness: "how I long for all of you with the affection of Christ Jesus" (1:8b).[19] After the unparalleled, central, and pivotal D element of this chiastic unit—"For my witness is God" (1:8a)—the audience hear a progression, via the chiastic parallelism, from Paul's declaration that "all of you" (πάντας ὑμᾶς) are my fellow sharers of the grace (1:7) in the C element to his dis-

---

17. Fee, *Philippians*, 93: "Just as he is imprisoned for the defense of the gospel—and thus for its vindcation as well—so, too, they will be urged both to live in a way that is worthy of the gospel and to contend for it side by side in the face of similar (Roman) opposition in Philippi. In this way they exhibit their real participation with him in the cause of the gospel." Bockmuehl, *Philippians*, 64: "The Philippian Christians continue their partnership in support of Paul's ministry, even where his detention prevents him from exercising it freely; they have thus accepted a co-responsibility for his mission." See also J. Schlosser, "La communauté en charge de L'Évangile: A propos de Ph 1,7," *RHPR* 75 (1995): 67–76.

18. Johannes Beutler, "μάρτυς," *EDNT* 2.394: "Paul frequently calls on God as *witness* to his thoughts, intentions, and prayers (Rom 1:9; Phil 1:8; 2 Cor 1:23; 1 Thess 2:5)." O'Brien, *Philippians*, 71: "God is spoken of as a witness (μάρτυς) not in a judicial sense of witness to facts, but in a more general sense of his witnessing to the processes and motives in Paul's inner life or the reasons for his behaviour under particular circumstances, since no other factual witnesses could be produced to prove the truthfulness and authenticity of what he affirmed." Debanné, *Enthymemes*, 110: "As such the expression in Phil. 1.8 is not backing up an affirmation with the evidence of an actual testimony; it offers the desperate oath of a prisoner with no one to vouch for him but God himself."

19. Fee, *Philippians*, 94 n. 104: "ἐν σπλάγχνοις (= the entrails), referring to the 'inner parts' of one's being—probably because of the physical, deeply visceral, internal 'feelings' that one sometimes experiences in the emotion of deep affection for another." Nikolaus Walter, "σπλάγχνον," *EDNT* 3.266: "In Phil 1:8 Paul speaks of his own yearning for the Philippians 'with the σπλάγχνα of Christ Jesus'; it is, as it were, the *heart* of the Kyrios himself that 'speaks' in Paul's heart and yearns for fellowship with his brethern; that is how Paul describes the depth of his yearning." Silva, *Philippians*, 48: "Paul uses the most expressive term available to indicate the source of human emotion, σπλάγχνα used here by metonymy of the affection itself; moreover, the use of that term with the qualifying genitive, 'of Christ Jesus,' is unique to this passage and adds pathos to an already powerful statement."

closure of how he longs for "all of you" (πάντας ὑμᾶς) with the affection of Christ
Jesus in the C′ element. The audience thus continue to hear of Paul's intensely
warm feelings, his "longing," for each and every one of them, "all of you" (1:4,
7, 8), as a unified community in fellowship with him for the advancement of the
gospel.[20]

The audience at Philippi are to be duly touched by how Paul has the same affection for them as does Christ Jesus himself, to whom Paul belongs as a "slave"
(1:1a), in whom they are holy ones (1:1b), from whom they may continue to receive grace and peace (1:2), and for whose final "day" God will perfect the good
work he has begun in them (1:6).[21] How Paul longs for each and every member of
his audience with the affection of Christ Jesus (1:8b) is verified and complemented
by the only One who can attest to Paul's inner thoughts and feelings—"my witness
is God himself" (1:8a).

6. Phil 1:9–10 (B′): That You May Be Sincere and Faultless for the Day of Christ

Paul then begins to express a specific prayer on behalf of his audience: "And
this I pray, that your love even more and more may abound in knowledge and
every perception in order that you determine the things that matter, so that you
may be sincere and faultless for the day of Christ" (1:9–10). The audience now hear
a progression, via the chiastic parallelism, from the affirmation of their fellowship for the gospel from the first "day" (ἡμέρας) until the "day of Christ" (ἡμέρας
Χριστοῦ) Jesus (1:5–6) in the B element to the prayer that they may be sincere and
faultless for the "day of Christ" (ἡμέραν Χριστοῦ) (1:10) in the B′ element.

The audience continue to be made aware of Paul's very favorable disposition
toward them as they hear a third emphatic use of the demonstrative pronoun
"this." The audience have already heard how Paul is confident of "this" (τοῦτο)
very thing, namely, "that he who began in you a good work will perfect it until
the day of Christ Jesus" (1:6). It is appropriate for Paul to think "this" (τοῦτο) on
behalf of all in his audience (1:7). And now, with the demonstrative pronoun in an
emphatic position before the verb, Paul introduces the content of his prayer for his
audience, "and this (τοῦτο) I pray" (1:9a).

With a second use of the second-person plural pronoun as a subjective genitive (rather than as an objective genitive, as in 1:3, 4, 7), Paul's affirmation of "your"

---

20. Fee, *Philippians*, 94: "Thus, his 'longing' for them in the present instance is probably not simply to be with them again, true as that may be, but suggests an especially deep yearning *for* (= concern
about) his friends themselves, that they remain true to the gospel to which they have been so faithfully
committed over these many years." Peterlin, *Paul's Letter*, 26: "On the whole it must be concluded that
the repetition of 'you all' in 1:4–8 is significant. It hints at the reality of tension and disunity in the
church among the Christians, but also at subdued dissatisfaction with Paul and uncertainty about his
response on the part of some."

21. Bockmuehl, *Philippians*, 65: "His assertion of the affection of Christ is not so much a claim
to embody the exalted Lord and his emotions, but rather that he loves them with and through (ἐν) the
same love which Christ has for them."

(ὑμῶν) fellowship for the gospel (1:5) progresses to his prayer that "your" (ὑμῶν) love even more and more may abound in knowledge and every perception (1:9b). Paul thus prays that "your love," already evident in the fellowship they share with Paul and one another, may continue to abound even more and more.[22] As Paul thanks God at "every" (πάσῃ) remembrance of his audience (1:3) in his "every" (πάσῃ) petition on behalf of them (1:4), so he aptly prays that their love may abound within the domain of knowledge and "every" (πάσῃ) perception (1:9b).[23]

With a second use of the second-person plural pronoun as a subjective accusative (rather than as an objective accusative, as in 1:7a, 8b), Paul's affirmation that all of "you" (ὑμᾶς) who are his fellow sharers in the grace (1:7b) progresses to his prayer that your love even more and more may abound in knowledge and every perception in order that "you" (ὑμᾶς) determine or discern the things that matter (1:10a).[24] As a fitting complement to his conviction that the God who began in you a good work will perfect it until the "day of Christ" (ἡμέρας Χριστοῦ) Jesus (1:6), Paul prays to God that you may be morally sincere and faultless for the "day of Christ" (ἡμέραν Χριστοῦ) (1:10b).[25]

In sum, then, Paul's prayer "that your love even more and more may abound in knowledge and every perception in order that you determine the things that matter, so that you may be sincere and faultless for the day of Christ" (1:9–10) functions not only as a prayer for God to fulfill for the audience, but also as an

---

22. O'Brien, *Philippians*, 75: "His earnest desire was that there be no limit to the growth or increase of the Philippians' love, and in order to stress the idea of continuous growth he used the progressive present tense, περισσεύῃ." Bockmuehl, *Philippians*, 66: "The collective phrase 'your love' also highlights the corporate dimension of Christian love, which is not merely a matter of relationships between individuals but also finds expession in communal life and common ventures."

23. On the meaning of the prepositional phrase to express the domain within which the love is to abound, O'Brien (*Philippians*, 75 n. 11) notes that "when the verb is used intransitively of things and is followed by ἐν with the dative, it is best to regard this as the sphere in which the thing operates." Garland, "Philippians," 195: "Paul prays for them to abound in love that is instructed and morally discerning."

24. According to Gerd Schunack ("δοκιμάζω," *EDNT* 1.342), the verb to "determine" or "discern" (δοκιμάζειν) consists in "critical discernment (examination) and in practical testing of the experience of knowing or of being known in relation to oneself and to others." And on "the things that matter" (τὰ διαφέροντα) he remarks: "In its concrete but undetermined content τὰ διαφέροντα (a common Hellenistic colloquial phrase) in Phil 1:10 indicates, with respect to content, what is involved in the Church's critical testing and examining: an overflowing of the love which determines thought as well as action." See also Stefano Bittasi, "'. . . per scegliere ciò che conta di più' (*Fil* 1,10): Il criterio cristologico dello scegliere nella lettera di san Paolo ai Filippesi," *RdT* 47 (2006): 831–49.

25. Fee, *Philippians*, 99, 103: "[T]he prayer, after all, emphasizes 'love' not as 'affection' but as behavior, behavior that is both 'pure' (stemming from right motives) and 'blameless' (lacking offense). . . . Paul prays that they may stand blameless on the day of Christ, not having offended others through equivocal behavior." O'Brien, *Philippians*, 79: "The preposition εἰς ἡμέραν Χριστοῦ does not simply denote a time limit meaning 'until'. It is better to translate it 'in preparation for' or 'against' the day of Christ, since the ideas of preparation for the scrutiny of that great day as well as the ability to stand its test are suggested by the word in this context."

indirect exhortation for the audience to play their part, with the help of God, to bring about the prayer's fulfillment.[26]

7. Phil 1:11 (A'): Through Jesus Christ to the Glory and Praise of God

Paul concludes his prayer with a further description of the situation of his audience: "having been filled up with the fruit of righteousness that is through Jesus Christ for the glory and praise of God" (1:11). At the end of this prayer the audience hear a progression, via the chiastic parallels, in expressions with God as an object of the action—from "I thank my God (θεῷ)" in the A element (1:3) to "the glory and praise of God (θεοῦ)" in the A' element (1:11).[27]

With an alliterative resonance to Paul's "having been and still being confident" (πεποιθώς, perfect tense) that the God who began a good work in the Philippian audience will continue to perfect it until the day of Christ Jesus (1:6), the audience hear themselves described as those "having been and still being filled up" (πεπληρωμένοι, perfect tense)[28] with the fruit of righteousness that is through Jesus Christ (1:11a).[29] The audience are thus reminded of how they have been and continue to be beneficiaries of the "righteousness" (δικαιοσύνης), that is, their being placed in a right covenantal relationship with God, through the death and resurrection of Jesus Christ, the Christ Jesus in the domain of whom and in union with whom they are the holy ones in Philippi (1:1bc), the Lord Jesus Christ from whom—it is Paul's prayer-wish—they may continue to receive "grace" and "peace" (1:2), as the "fruit of righteousness."[30]

The audience are to realize that Paul's prayer that they, with divine assistance, may be sincere and faultless "for" (εἰς) the day of Christ (1:10b) has its ultimate goal in their being prepared "for" (εἰς) the glory and praise of God (1:11b). Paul employs his own personal appreciation for God to bring his audience to an appreciation not only for how they, by God, "have already been filled and are still

---

26. Silva, *Philippians*, 53: "Paul's prayer is in effect a commandment that the Philippians give evidence of their sanctification now. All the same, the apostle is focusing, as he did when writing to the Thessalonians, on the perfection of the sanctifying process, on his desire that God will sanctify them."

27. The term "God" is the grammatical subject rather than object in 1:8a.

28. Fee, *Philippians*, 103 n. 30: "This is an excellent example of the nuance of the Greek perfect, which is not easily carried over into English. It reflects the present state of something that happened in the past."

29. O'Brien, *Philippians*, 80: "'Filled with the fruit of righteousness' is not a further definition of 'pure and blameless' but a quality or characteristic that the apostle wishes to see in the Philippians together with purity and blamelessness.... Paul desires not only that they be acquitted; he also prays that through a right relationship with God they may be filled with the fruit of godly deeds.... We ... interpret δικαιοσύνης as a genitive of origin. καρπόν then refers to ... the result, outcome, or product of righteousness." The translation, "having been fully paid the dividends of righteousness" for πεπληρωμένοι καρπὸν δικαιοσύνης in 1:11 has been proposed by C. Rico and Gregory T. Tatum, "Une métaphore financière de l'Épître aux Philippiens: πεπληρωμένοι καρπῶν δικαιοσύνης (Ph 1,11)," *RB* 114 (2007): 447–53.

30. Karl Kertelge, "δικαιοσύνη," *EDNT* 1.326: "For Paul δικαιοσύνη stands in close relationship to the central salvific event, which has its historical place in the death and resurrection of Jesus."

being filled up" (πεπληρωμένοι, as divine passive in the perfect tense) with the fruit of righteousness through Jesus Christ (1:11a), but also for the hope of how God will continue to perfect the good work he has begun in them until the day of Christ Jesus (1:6). The audience, then, have been and will continue to be prepared by God for the glory and praise of God (θεοῦ, 1:11b), the One whom Paul personally thanks as "my God (θεῷ)" at every remembrance of his audience (1:3), and the God (θεός) who is Paul's personal ("my") witness for the close fellowship Paul shares with his Philippian audience (1:5, 7–8).

In sum, Paul wants his Philippian audience, through this thanksgiving section of the letter (1:3–11), to realize that what God has done, continues to do, and will do for them through and for Jesus Christ (1:6, 11a) is ultimately to lead them to the glory and praise of God himself (1:11b).[31]

B. Summary on Philippians 1:3–11

1. The audience are assured that every time Paul thinks of them, with the implication that he thinks of them quite often, it is an occasion for Paul to render thanks to God. The audience are thus being made aware of Paul's close relationship with them (1:3).

2. Paul has confidently assured the audience that God will continue to perfect, right up until the final day of Christ Jesus, the good work that God began in them in bringing them to faith in and fellowship for the gospel, the fellowship with one another and with Paul that has motivated Paul to thank and petition God on behalf of his audience with a distinctive note of joy. With such assurance of divine assistance the audience are encouraged to continue their own personal and communal efforts regarding their fellowship with Paul and with one another for the gospel (1:3–6).

3. The audience are to realize that they are fellow sharers closely aligned with Paul, who is deeply concerned for their welfare, in the defense and confirmation of the gospel even though Paul is in prison (probably in Rome) while they remain in Philippi (1:7).

4. How Paul longs for each and every member of his audience with the affec-

---

31. O'Brien, *Philippians*, 82: "The apostle concludes his prayer report on a note of praise. His thanksgiving thus returns to the divine basis on which it had begun. God's saving work among the Philippians eventually redounds to the divine glory." Fee, *Philippians*, 105: "In v. 6 Paul reminded the Philippians that 'the good work' begun in them was God's doing, as also will be its completion. Now he prays for them—that the fruit of righteousness that comes through Christ Jesus might increase among them more and more, precisely so that God will receive glory through the work that he is doing in their lives. Everything is to that end." Garland, "Philippians," 196: "What is often neglected is Paul's final phrase that expresses the purpose of it all. God's ultimate goal in saving humanity is to bring himself glory and praise as the unrivaled and rightful Sovereign of creation." See also J. Schlosser, "La Figure de Dieu selon l'Épître aux Philippiens," *NTS* 41 (1995): 378–99. On 1:1–11 as already an integral part of Paul's argumentation in the letter, see Andreas H. Snyman, "A Rhetorical Analysis of Philippians 1:1–11," *AcT* 24 (2004): 81–104.

tion of Christ Jesus (1:8b) is verified and complemented by the only One who can attest to Paul's inner thoughts and feelings—"my witness is God himself" (1:8a).

5. Paul's prayer "that your love even more and more may abound in knowledge and every perception in order that you determine the things that matter, so that you may be sincere and faultless for the day of Christ" (1:9–10) functions not only as a prayer for God to fulfill for the audience, but also as an indirect exhortation for the audience to play their part, with the help of God, to bring about the prayer's fulfillment.

6. Paul wants his Philippian audience, through this thanksgiving section of the letter (1:3–11), to realize that what God has done, continues to do, and will do for them through and for Jesus Christ (1:6, 11a) is ultimately to lead them to the glory and praise of God himself (1:11b).

5

PHILIPPIANS 1:12–18: I REJOICE AND I WILL BE JOYFUL (C)

Christ Is Proclaimed Even While Paul Is in the Bonds of Imprisonment

A: [12] I want you to know, brothers, that the things regarding me have come rather to an advancement of the gospel, [13] so that *my bonds* have become in Christ manifest in the whole praetorium and to *all* the rest, [14] and most of the brothers, in the Lord having confidence by *my bonds*, more abundantly dare fearlessly to speak the word.

    B [15] Some even on account of envy and rivalry, but others even on account of good pleasure, preach *the Christ*.

        C: [16] The latter out of love, knowing that for the defense of the gospel I am set,

    B′: [17a] the former out of self-seeking, proclaim *the Christ*,

A′: [17b] not sincerely, supposing to raise affliction in *my bonds*. [18] What then? Only that in *all* manner, whether in pretense or in truth, Christ is proclaimed, and in this I rejoice. And indeed I will be joyful,[1]

A. AUDIENCE RESPONSE TO PHILIPPIANS 1:12–18

1. Phil 1:12–14 (A): Paul's Bonds of Imprisonment Advance the Gospel

After the introductory salutation (1:1–2) and thanksgiving sections (1:3–11) Paul begins the main body of the letter: "I want you to know, brothers, that the things regarding me have come rather to an advancement of the gospel, so that my bonds have become in Christ manifest in the whole praetorium and to all the rest, and most of the brothers, in the Lord having confidence by my bonds, more abundantly dare fearlessly to speak the word" (1:12–14). The audience have heard Paul pray that "your love even more and more may abound in knowledge (ἐπιγνώσει) and every perception in order that you (ὑμᾶς) determine the things (τά) that matter" (1:9–10a). And now they hear Paul begin to fulfill his own prayer by providing knowledge by which they, whom he addresses as "brothers" (ἀδελφοί), that is, his

---

1. For the establishment of Phil 1:12–18 as a chiasm, see ch. 2.

fellow Christians (both men and women),[2] may discern what is really important, as he declares, "I want you (ὑμᾶς) to know (γινώσκειν)" about "the things (τά) regarding me" (1:12a).[3] Thus, the audience hear "the things that matter," previously left undetermined in 1:10a, begin to be specified in 1:12a as "the things regarding me," that is, the things regarding Paul in his situation of imprisonment (1:7).

The audience hear what Paul wants them to know in the form of a mini–chiasm (1:12b–14b), based on alliterative, conceptual, and linguistic parallels: (a) the things regarding me have come rather to an advancement of *the gospel* (12b), (b) so that *my bonds* (13a) (c) have become *in Christ* manifest (13b) (d) in the *whole* praetorium (13c) (e) and (13d) (d´) to *all* the rest (13e), (c´) and most of the brothers, *in the Lord* having confidence (14a) (b´) by *my bonds* (14b), (a´) more abundantly dare fearlessly to speak *the word* (14c).

That the things regarding Paul, literally, "to an advancement of the gospel have come (εὐαγγελίου ἐλήλυθεν)" at the end of the "a" sub-element (1:12b) forms an alliterative (through the "g," "l," and "n" sounds) and conceptual parallel with "to speak the word" (τὸν λόγον λαλεῖν) at the end of the "a´" sub-element (1:14c), as "the word" here is more or less synonymous with "the gospel" (cf. 2:16).[4] "My bonds" (δεσμούς μου) in the "b" sub-element (1:13a) is linguistically paralleled by "my bonds" (δεσμοῖς μου) in the "b´" sub-element (1:14b); and "in Christ" (ἐν Χριστῷ) in the "c" sub-element (1:13b) is conceptually paralleled by the synonymous "in the Lord" (ἐν κυρίῳ; cf. 1:2) in the "c´" sub-element (1:14a). "Whole" in the phrase, "in the whole praetorium," in the "d" sub-element (1:13c) is conceptually parallel to "all" in the phrase, "to all the rest," in the "d´" sub-element (1:13e). The conjunction "and" constitutes the central, unparalleled, and pivotal "e" sub-element (1:13d).[5]

---

2. According to BDAG, 18, the plural "brothers" (ἀδελφοί) can also mean "brothers and sisters." On the meaning of "brothers" for Paul, Johannes Beutler ("ἀδελφός," *EDNT* 1.28) states: "The prevailing sense in Paul is that of *fellow Christians*, the foundational statement being Rom 8:29: the redeemed are conformed to Christ the 'first-born among many brethren.'" See also Alanna Nobbs, "'Beloved Brothers' in the New Testament and Early Christian World," in *The New Testament in Its First Century Setting: Essays on Context and Background in Honour of B. W. Winter on His 65th Birthday* (ed. P. J. Williams et al.; Grand Rapids: Eerdmans, 2004), 143–50; Andrew D. Clarke, "Equality or Mutuality? Paul's Use of 'Brother' Language," in *The New Testament in Its First Century Setting: Essays on Context and Background in Honour of B. W. Winter on His 65th Birthday* (ed. P. J. Williams et al.; Grand Rapids: Eerdmans, 2004), 151–64.

3. Holloway, *Consolation*, 102: "Paul's choice of γινώσκειν here recalls the ἐπίγνωσις of 1:9. The implication is that he will now impart the 'knowledge and perception' that, on his view, the Philippians need in order to distinguish the things that matter from the things that do not."

4. Hubert Ritt, "λόγος," *EDNT* 2.358: "For Paul the creative 'word of God' (ὁ λόγος τοῦ θεοῦ), which was originally directed to Israel, 'has not failed' (Rom 9:6); this would not be at all possible, for God himself is the source of this *word* (1 Cor 14:36; 2 Cor 4:2), the gospel, which is clearly distinguishable from any 'human *word*' (λόγος ἀνθρώπων, 1 Thess 2:13; 1:5; 2:5)."

5. Fee, *Philippians*, 112 n. 25: "This is conventional hyberbole, where 'the whole' stresses the considerable breadth to which this has become known. On the other hand, even as hyberbole, this phrase tends to cut the ground from under the hypotheses of either an Ephesian or Caesarean provenance for

The audience, who are in fellowship with Paul for the "gospel" (εὐαγγέλιον, 1:5) and fellow sharers with Paul of the grace in the defense and confirmation of the "gospel" (εὐαγγελίου, 1:7), are to be surprised yet pleased that Paul's situation of imprisonment rather "has come and continues" (ἐλήλυθεν, perfect tense) to promote an advancement of the "gospel" (εὐαγγελίου, 1:12).[6] With this knowledge, the audience, then, are to discern or determine that "the things that matter" (1:10) are not "the things regarding me," that is, the things involved in Paul's being imprisoned, but rather the advancement of the gospel (1:12).[7]

Paul then begins to explicate how it is that his imprisonment has actually served to advance the gospel as a thing that really matters to his Philippian audience. First of all, "my bonds" (δεσμούς μου) of imprisonment, recalling that the audience are fellow sharers with Paul of the grace even while Paul is in "my bonds" (δεσμοῖς μου, 1:7), "have become in Christ manifest" (1:13a).[8] When the audience hear that Paul's bonds have become in "Christ" (Χριστῷ) manifest, they hear the transitional word that links this chiastic unit (1:12–18) to the previous one (1:3–11), which concluded with the phrase "through Jesus Christ (Χριστοῦ) for the glory and praise of God" (1:11).

That it has become manifest that the bonds of Paul's imprisonment are in the

---

this letter, since (1) the guard cannot be demonstrated ever to have existed in Ephesus and (2) Herod's *praetorium* in Caesarea was scarcely of a size to call for this emphasis." Ware, *Mission*, 176: "Almost all modern commentators who accept a Roman provenance for the letter follow Lightfoot in identifying the πραιτώριον (a Latin loan-word, from *praetorium*) of which Paul speaks with the soldiers of the praetorian guard. This sense of the word is well-attested, and is on balance the most probable interpretation of the term. However, ancient interpreters are unanimous in referring the word to the imperial palace. This latter sense seems well suited to the context, especially in view of the reference to the imperial staff in 4:22, and is difficult to exclude entirely." See also Ware, *Mission*, 177.

6. Ware, *Mission*, 174: "The verbal phrase ἔρχεσθαι εἰς expresses result, and the perfect form ἐλήλυθεν emphasizes its abiding character. Paul has already spoken in the thanksgiving period of his imprisonment as a participation in divine grace (1:7), and implicit in the impersonal construction εἰς προκοπὴν τοῦ εὐαγγελίου ἐλήλυθεν is doubtless a reference to God's activity and providential ordering of events. As in 1:5, τὸ εὐαγγέλιον is a *nomen actionis* referring to the preaching of the gospel. Through the grace of God Paul's imprisonment has resulted, contrary to expectation, in the greater progress of the gospel preaching."

7. Holloway, *Consolation*, 103.

8. Holloway, *Consolation*, 102 n. 7: "φανεροὺς ἐν Χριστῷ γενέσθαι is awkward. I would supply an εἶναι after φανεροὺς: 'so that my chains have been manifest [to be] in Christ.'" But the placing of ἐν Χριστῷ before the verb ("became") and immediately after the adjective ("manifest") without an εἶναι serves as added emphasis upon the manifestation of Paul's bonds as being "in Christ." According to Fee (*Philippians*, 113), Paul here "probably means something like, 'it has become clear that I am in chains because I am a man *in Christ* (Fee's emphasis), and that my chains are in part a manifestation of my discipleship as one who is thereby participating in the sufferings of Christ himself.' As Paul says in this letter and everywhere else, his life finds its meaning 'in Christ' (1:21), even as he himself is 'in Christ' and thus lives 'for Christ' in the sense of making him known to others." According to Bockmuehl (*Philippians*, 75), "Paul is indeed 'in Christ,' not just as his slave (1.1) but—plain to see—also as his prisoner." Thurston, *Philippians*, 57: "The idea is that Paul's bonds, his imprisonment, is for or because of Christ (but also 'in Christ,' within Christ's sphere of influence)."

realm or sphere of his being in union with Christ—"in Christ" (ἐν Χριστῷ)—further binds him to his audience as "all the holy ones" who are spiritually "in Christ Jesus" (ἐν Χριστῷ Ἰησοῦ), at the same time as they are physically "in" Philippi (1:1). Similarly, Paul's physical imprisonment "in bonds" is also, and ultimately, a spiritual imprisonment "in Christ"—he is in bonds because of, in union with, and on behalf of Christ (1:13a).[9] And this is what has become publicly and widely manifest not only in the "whole" Roman praetorium where Paul is in bonds but also to "all" the rest (1:13b),[10] as a further advancement of the gospel of Christ.[11]

Secondly, most of the "brothers," that is, fellow Christians in the location of Paul's imprisonment,[12] are described as having confidence "in the Lord" (ἐν κυρίῳ, 1:14a),[13] the synonymous complement both to Paul's being "in Christ" (ἐν Χριστῷ, 1:13a) and to the Philippian audience's being "in Christ Jesus" (ἐν Χριστῷ Ἰησοῦ, 1:1), a reminder to the audience that they, Paul, and all Christians are united

---

9. Fowl, *Philippians*, 39: "[B]eing in chains is not inconsistent with being 'in Christ.' That is, Paul's current circumstances are not only consistent with his convictions about Christ, but are the sorts of circumstances one who shared those convictions might also expect to share." Ware (*Mission*, 175–76) misses this richer sense of the phrase "in Christ" here, as he limits the meaning to merely the means of the manifestation: "it is through the agency of Christ that Paul's chains have become manifest." But Paul could have employed διά Χριστοῦ, if agency is all he wished to convey. Instead, he employed the more comprehensive phrase ἐν Χριστῷ as the dynamic sphere or realm in which Paul's bonds became manifest. See also Friedrich Büchsel, " 'In Christus' bei Paulus," *ZNW* 42 (1949): 141–58; Fritz Neugebauer, "Das Paulinische 'In Christo,'" *NTS* 4 (1957–58): 124–38; John A. Allan, "The 'In Christ' Formula in Ephesians," *NTS* 5 (1958–59): 54–62; Michel Bouttier, *En Christ: Étude d'exégèse et de théologie pauliniennes* (Paris: Presses Universitaires, 1962); Alexander J. M. Wedderburn, "Some Observations on Paul's Use of the Phrases 'in Christ' and 'with Christ,'" *JSNT* 25 (1985): 83–97; Celia E. T. Kourie, "In Christ and Related Expressions in Paul," *Theologia Evangelica* 20 (1987): 33–43; James D. G. Dunn, *The Theology of Paul the Apostle* (Grand Rapids: Eerdmans, 1998), 396–401; Mehrdad Fatehi, *The Spirit's Relation to the Risen Lord in Paul: An Examination of Its Christological Implications* (WUNT 128; Tübingen: Mohr Siebeck, 2000), 269–74; Mark A. Seifrid, "In Christ," *DPL*, 433–36.

10. Fee, *Philippians*, 114: "This refers to another group of people outside the Praetorian Guard, most likely to others who had dealings with imperial affairs. Thus anyone in Rome who had occasion to know about Paul's confinement had also come to learn that it had to do with his being the propagator of the nascent Christian religion."

11. Bockmuehl, *Philippians*, 75: "This statement . . . clearly aims to encourage his readers in the Roman colony of Philippi: even at a time of hardship for him and persecution for them (1.29–30), the gospel's progress continues into the very seat of imperial power." Thurston, *Philippians*, 57: "Paul's point is that instead of hindering the progress of the Gospel, his imprisonment has advanced it because all of those guarding him, all of those in the administrative center, have been introduced to the Gospel." Ware, *Mission*, 174–75: "The thought in 1:12–13 is that, as a result of Paul's preaching brought about by his bonds (1:12), the knowledge of his imprisonment on behalf of Christ has spread throughout the pagan populace at Rome (1:13). In Paul's thinking his sufferings and his proclamation of the message worked together for a missionary purpose."

12. Ware, *Mission*, 181: "ἀδελφοί, like οἱ ἅγιοι, is a general desgination referring to all Christians, or (as here) to all Christians in a given locality."

13. O'Brien, *Philippians*, 95: "ἐν κυρίῳ is best taken with πεποιθότας, and although one would normally expect the phrase to follow the participle, here it seems to have been placed first for emphasis." And see the discussion in Silva, *Philippians*, 66.

within the realm of being in Christ who is also *the* Lord (cf. 1:2).[14] Most of these brothers "have been and continue to be confident" (πεποιθότας, perfect tense) by "my bonds" (δεσμοῖς μου, 1:14a), that is, "my bonds" (δεσμούς μου) in which it has become manifest that Paul is imprisoned "in Christ" (1:13a).[15] The manifestation that the "bonds" of Paul's imprisonment are "in Christ" has "in the Lord" made confident these fellow Christians of Paul more abundantly to dare fearlessly to speak "the word" (1:14b), the gospel of the Lord Jesus Christ (cf. 2:16).[16]

In sum, the audience are to be pleased not only that it has become manifest in the whole Roman praetorium and to all the rest that Paul's imprisonment is "in Christ" (1:13), but that most of the "brothers," their fellow Christians, having been confident "in the Lord" by Paul's bonds, despite the danger of being imprisoned like Paul, more increasingly and without fear dare to speak "the word" (1:14), thus playing their part, and encouraging the audience at Philippi to likewise play their part, in advancing the gospel, the word about Christ (1:12).[17]

2. Phil 1:15 (B): Preaching the Christ

Paul then discloses the differing motivations of those who more abundantly and fearlessly speak the word of the gospel while he is in prison (1:14): "Some even on account of envy and rivalry, but others even on account of good pleasure,

---

14. Fee, *Philippians*, 114: "To the world—and especially to the citizens of a Roman colony—Caesar may be 'lord': but to Paul and to the believers in Philippi, only Jesus is Lord."

15. Fee, *Philippians*, 116: "The phrase 'in the Lord,' therefore, refers to the *ground* of their confidence, while the following phrase, 'by my chains,' is *instrumental* (= the means God has used). Thus his 'chains' have served to make them all the more 'confident *in the Lord*' so as to proclaim Christ more boldly."

16. Fee, *Philippians*, 116: "This absolute use of 'the word' occurs frequently in Paul to describe the gospel, the message about Christ." O'Brien, *Philippians*, 95: "[T]he point is not that the majority had been unduly timid before this, but that their courage had risen to new heights, when they might have been intimidated." Ware, *Mission*, 180: "Through the accumulation of terms denoting courage (πεποιθότας, τολμᾶν, ἀφόβως), Paul strongly emphasizes the boldness and fearlessness of the Roman believers. The comparative adverb περισσοτέρως highlights both the *increase* in courage shown by the believers, and its *amplitude*. Paul's language clearly presupposes the presence of some form of danger or personal risk for the believers at Rome, and the particular threat envisaged appears to be connected, not with their adherence to Christianity alone, but with the open proclamation of the Christian message to outsiders. . . . The adverb ἀφόβως modifies λαλεῖν, and its strongly emphatic position stresses the hazardous nature of this speech, and its fearless character." Fowl, *Philippians*, 40: "Paul claims in v. 14 that God has used his circumstances to make others more confident to speak the word."

17. Ware, *Mission*, 185: "[T]he function of 1:12–14 is not apologetic, but rather paradigmatic and paraenetic: the Roman Christians, in speaking the word of God even more courageously as a result of Paul's bold proclamation of the word in his imprisonment, function as a model for the Philippians of partnership with Paul for the extension of the gospel. Like the Romans, the Christians at Philippi are, despite opposition, fearlessly to spread the gospel. The paraenetic context of 1:12–14 is extremely significant, for it implies that in Paul's mind the active spread of the message is an essential element of Christian identity."

preach the Christ" (1:15).[18] That these two groups "preach the Christ" specifies, confirms, and emphasizes that the more abundant and fearless "speaking of the word" by most of the "brothers" (1:14b) indeed refers to the word of the gospel about "the Christ" (τὸν Χριστόν)—the Christ "in whom" (ἐν Χριστῷ) are Paul's bonds of imprisonment manifest (1:13). Here the audience learn that even among the "brothers" who speak the word of the gospel there are some who are opponents of Paul, taking advantage of his imprisonment, to preach the Christ even on account of their envy of and rivalry with Paul.[19] But the audience also learn that, on the other hand, there are "brothers" more favorable to the imprisoned Paul, who even on account of the "good pleasure" (εὐδοκίαν) of God,[20] further his mission by preaching the Christ.[21]

3. Phil 1:16 (C): Some Preach out of Love as Paul Is Set for the Defense of the Gospel

Paul then further describes those who on account of the good pleasure of God preach the Christ (1:15b): "The latter out of love, knowing that for the defense of the gospel I am set" (1:16). That some of the Christians at Rome are preaching the Christ out of "love" (ἀγάπης) not only contrasts with the "envy and rivalry" of the others (1:15a),[22] but provides a suggestive model for the audience, for whom Paul prays "that your love (ἀγάπη) even more and more may abound in knowledge and

---

18. On the twofold occurrence of καί in 1:15, translated as "even," Ware (*Mission*, 187–88) notes: "The majority of interpreters either ignore or misinterpret the twofold καί which follow μὲν and δὲ respectively. The two conjunctions are in fact correlative and contrastive, and serve to heighten the antithesis between the different motivations for preaching. They might seem superfluous beside μέν and δέ, but are in fact not so: as μέν / δέ function to set the two groups (τινὲς μὲν . . . τινὲς δὲ) in antithesis, the twofold καί functions to set in contrast their motives (καὶ διὰ φθόνον καὶ ἔριν . . . καὶ δι' εὐδοκίαν)."

19. This "envy and rivalry" did not involve differences in the content of the preaching, but was motivated by the concern of local church leaders in Rome to protect their own status and influence according to Christfried Böttrich, "Verkündigung aus 'Neid und Rivalität'? Beobachtungen zu Phil 1, 12–18," *ZNW* 95 (2004): 84–101.

20. Ware, *Mission*, 189–91: "The word εὐδοκία . . . in the great majority of its occurrences in the LXX and in the New Testament, is used with reference to the divine good pleasure. . . . both the immediate context of the passage, as well as the wider usage of the term [cf. 2:13], suggest that εὐδοκία in Philippians 1:15, while referring primarily to the 'eagerness' or 'glad purpose' of Christians at Rome to spread the message, also carries overtones of God's good pleasure at work in this activity. . . . While the motivation of those who preach the gospel out of envy is merely human and fleshly (φθόνος καὶ ἔρις), the impulse of those who engage in mission out of noble motives is from God (εὐδοκία)." Bockmuehl, *Philippians*, 79: "[T]he sincere evangelists are primarily motivated by the will of God."

21. Fee, *Philippians*, 120: "They see that Paul can no longer be involved in preaching Christ publicly, so they have stepped in to pick up the slack."

22. Ware, *Mission*, 191: "This love, in not being linked to any specific object, connotes not only love for Paul but also the general Christian grace of love. As such this motive of love, like εὐδοκία of 1:15b, and unlike φθόνος καὶ ἔρις in 1:15a, is divine in its origin."

every perception in order that you determine the things that matter" (1:9–10a).[23]
The love of the audience may thus more and more abound by their own advancement of the gospel of Christ.

That these Christians are preaching the gospel about the Christ, knowing that for the "defense" (ἀπολογίαν) of the "gospel" (εὐαγγελίου) Paul "is set" by God (divine passive),[24] reinforces the model they are providing for the Philippian audience, who are in fellowship with Paul for the "gospel" (εὐαγγέλιον, 1:5a), and are fellow sharers with Paul of the grace, in Paul's bonds and in the "defense" (ἀπολογίᾳ) and confirmation of the "gospel" (εὐαγγελίου) (1:7b).[25] Those preaching the Christ out of love while Paul is in prison for the defense of the gospel (1:16) thus provide the audience with a model persuading them out of love to play their role in the advancement of the "gospel" (εὐαγγελίου) (1:12).

4. Phil 1:17a (B´): Some out of Self-Seeking Proclaim the Christ

Then Paul further describes those who on account of envy and rivalry preach the Christ (1:15a): "the former out of self-seeking, proclaim the Christ" (1:17a). After the central and unparalleled C element (1:16) of this chiastic unit (1:12–18) the audience hear a pivot of antithetical parallels—from those who on account of the good pleasure of God preach "the Christ" (τὸν Χριστόν) in the B element (1:15) to those who out of self-seeking proclaim "the Christ" (τὸν Χριστόν) in the B´ element (1:17a).[26] The "envy and rivalry" out of which some preach the Christ (1:15a) thus progresses to the notice of their "self-seeking," and those who proclaim the Christ "out of self-seeking" (ἐξ ἐριθείας, 1:17a) thus stand in stark contrast to those who, in fellowship with Paul like the Philippians (cf. 1:5, 7), proclaim the Christ selflessly "out of love" (ἐξ ἀγάπης, 1:16a).[27]

---

23. Bockmuehl, *Philippians*, 79–80: "It is intriguing that in Paul's prayer for the Philippians love is also explained in terms of an ability to perceive 'what really matters' (1.9–10). The same perceptive love here applies also to Paul's captivity: he is put there, divinely appointed and destined for the defence not of himself but of the gospel." Fowl, *Philippians*, 40: "Hence, the emboldened preaching of these Christians stems from having perceived that Paul's circumstances are both the result and the manifestation of his defense of the gospel."

24. Hans Hübner, "κεῖμαι," *EDNT* 2.280: "Of theological relevance is the meaning *be destined for* (by God), which is seen in . . . Phil 1:16 (Paul was '*put in place* for the defense of the gospel')." O'Brien, *Philippians*, 101: "κεῖμαι, originally a military term, here indicates that Paul is under orders, issued by God. There is therefore no sense of divine disfavour in his captivity. Quite the reverse. Because he has been divinely appointed for the defence of the gospel, his captivity is entirely understandable. They are not embarrassed or put off by his bonds. Instead, they identify with him in proclaiming Christ, doing so out of true Christian love."

25. Ware, *Mission*, 192: "[T]he expressed object of Paul's defense is not the charges brought against him, but the gospel."

26. That they "proclaim" (καταγγέλλουσιν) the Christ alliteratively echoes both the synonymous verb—they "preach" (κηρύσσουσιν) the Christ (1:15b)—and the nearly cognate noun—"gospel" (εὐαγγελίου, 1:16).

27. Ware, *Mission*, 193–94: "Recognizing this commission of the apostle, the believers of whom Paul speaks in 1:15b–16 work in partnership with him for the advancement of the gospel. Others (οἱ δέ,

5. Phil 1:17b–18 (A ´): Supposing to Raise Affliction in My Bonds

Paul concludes his description of those Christians who, out of self-seeking, proclaim the Christ (1:17a), as he elaborates on their negative motivation: "not sincerely, supposing to raise affliction in my bonds" (1:17b).²⁸ At this point the audience hear, via the chiastic parallels, a contrast in motivations arising from the bonds of Paul's imprisonment, from a positive motivation—"my bonds (δεσμούς μου) have become in Christ manifest in the whole praetorium and to all the rest, and most of the brothers, in the Lord having confidence by my bonds (δεσμοῖς μου), more abundantly dare fearlessly to speak the word" (1:13–14)—in the A element, to a negative motivation—"supposing to raise affliction in my bonds (δεσμοῖς μου)" (1:17b)—in the A´ element.

The audience have now heard a conceptual mini–chiasm in 1:15–17, contrasting the differing motivations of those Christians in Rome who are preaching the gospel of Christ while Paul is in the bonds of his imprisonment: (a) Some even on account of envy and rivalry (1:15a), (b) but others even on account of good pleasure, preach the Christ (1:15b). (b´) The latter out of love, knowing that for the defense of the gospel I am set (1:16), (a´) the former out of self-seeking, proclaim the Christ, not sincerely, supposing to raise affliction in my bonds (1:17).²⁹

With their description of those negatively motivated, the "a" and "a´" sub-elements serve as a literary inclusion framing the "b" and "b´" sub-elements, with their description of those positively motivated in preaching/proclaiming the Christ. In addition, the audience hear an alliterative progression contrasting a positive motivation—"out of love" (ἐξ ἀγάπης)—in the "b´" sub-element with a negative motivation—"not sincerely" (οὐχ ἁγνῶς)—in the "a´" sub-element, and a contrasting progression of participles from a perceptive "knowing" (εἰδότες) in the "b´" sub-element to a mere "supposing" (οἰόμενοι) in the "a´" sub-element. The mini-chiasm thus moves the audience through a description of those proclaiming the Christ not only on account of envy and rivalry (1:15a) and out of self-seeking (1:17a), but also with a destructive aim toward Paul—"not sincerely, supposing to raise affliction in my bonds" (1:17b).³⁰ The overall rhetorical effect of

1:17), however, proclaim Christ, not in partnership with Paul, but out of selfish interests. Paul portrays the preaching of these persons as motivated by self-seeking (ἐξ ἐριθείας, 1:17)," 194 n. 109: "Found prior to the New Testament only in Aristotle, ἐριθεία is distinct from ἔρις (1:15), both etymologically and in usage, and denotes self-seeking as opposed to seeking the common good."

28. Silva (Philippians, 64, 67) suggests a translation that seeks to preserve the play on words: "supposing that they will add pressure to my chains."

29. See also Fee, Philippians, 118–19.

30. O'Brien, Philippians, 101–2: "While the first 'know' that Paul has been appointed by God for the defence of the gospel and interpret correctly the meaning of his captivity, the second group 'suppose' that through their preaching they will stir up trouble for Paul as a prisoner. They stumble at Paul's captivity and weakness, not recognizing that Christ's saving activity is manifested in his imprisonment, and so through it the gospel advances. οἴομαι, meaning to 'think, suppose, expect', is distnguished from εἰδότες in v. 16, for Paul hints by this purposely chosen word, which he uses nowhere else, that what they 'imagine' fails to happen. . . . The meaning is not that they deliberately set themselves to aggravate

this mini-chiasm, then, presents the audience with a climactic emphasis in which the negative motivations seem to overshadow the positive.

But in the climactic conclusion to the A´ element (1:17b–18) in the broader chiastic unit (1:12–18) Paul overturns this negative emphasis with a surprising explanation that imparts to his audience an overwhelmingly positive perspective: "What then? Only that in all manner, whether in pretense or in truth, Christ is proclaimed, and in this I rejoice. And indeed I will be joyful" (1:18). At this point the audience hear a progression, via the chiastic parallels, in the scope of the advancement of the preaching of the gospel from the manifestation "to all (πᾶσιν) the rest" that Paul's bonds are in Christ (1:13) in the A element to Christ being proclaimed "in all (παντί) manner" (1:18) in the A´ element.

The phrase "whether in pretense or in truth" (1:18a) sums up for the audience the negative and positive motivations respectively of those proclaiming the Christ (1:15–17). The audience then hear the climactic conclusion of the alliterative and conceptual progression that moves through every element of this chiastic unit (1:12–18): from "the advancement of the gospel (εὐαγγελίου)" (1:12) to "speak the word" (τὸν λόγον λαλεῖν, 1:14) to "preach the Christ" (τὸν Χριστὸν κηρύσσουσιν, 1:15) to "defense of the gospel (εὐαγγελίου, 1:16)" to "proclaim the Christ" (τὸν Χριστὸν καταγγέλλουσιν, 1:17a) and finally to "in all manner, whether in pretense of in truth, Christ is proclaimed (Χριστὸς καταγγέλλεται)" (1:18a). Paul caps off this dynamic description of the advancement of the gospel as a thing that really matters (1:10) in his imprisonment with an emphatic and exuberant outburst that reverberates in the ears of his Philippian audience: "and in this I rejoice. And indeed I will be joyful!" (1:18b).[31]

That Paul is presently "rejoicing" (χαίρω) because of the advancement of the gospel as in all manner Christ is being proclaimed (1:18a) and that he looks forward to the extension of his joy in the future—"and indeed I will be joyful (χαρήσομαι)" (1:18b) reminds the audience that every petition that Paul makes on behalf of them is made with "joy" (χαρᾶς, 1:4) based on their fellowship with

---

Paul's sufferings or to cause him physical harm and injury, but rather to stir up some inward annoyance, and restraints of his condition (which they misunderstood) as contrasted with their own unfettered freedom." Ware, *Mission*, 195: "Paul in 1:17b thus describes, not the confessed aim of these leaders, but rather the effect of their factious behavior upon the apostle. In seeking to undermine his missionary work in order to promote their own selfish interests, they are in effect seeking to bring emotional duress upon Paul."

31. I take the clause at the end of 1:18 "and indeed I will be joyful" (ἀλλὰ καὶ χαρήσομαι) as the conclusion of the chiastic unit in 1:12–18, because it emphatically reinforces and extends to the future the expression of rejoicing in the previous clause, "and in this I rejoice" (καὶ ἐν τούτῳ χαίρω). This is not to deny the grammatical connection of the clause "and indeed I will be joyful" with 1:19, which, through a clause introduced by γάρ, gives expression to a further basis for Paul's future rejoicing, a basis which confirms and specifies the audience's role in that future rejoicing. Fowl, *Philippians*, 43–44: "Clearly, the future tense verb in v. 18b is connected to the rejoicing in v. 18a." Cf. Ware, *Mission*, 201; Holloway, *Consolation*, 108; O'Brien, *Philippians*, 108; Silva, *Philippians*, 69.

him for the gospel (1:5) even while he is in the bonds of his imprisonment (1:7).[32] After Paul's concerted description of the surprising advancement of the gospel by those proclaiming the Christ while Paul is in prison in Rome (1:12–18a), an advancement that has resulted in Paul presently "rejoicing," the implication for the audience is that they can play their role in contributing to the future joy of their partner in the gospel, Paul—"and indeed I will be joyful" (1:18b)—by similarly advancing the gospel of Christ.[33]

In sum, in this A′ element, despite the insincere motivation of some who proclaim the Christ while Paul is in bonds (1:17b), Paul is presently "rejoicing" in the fact that in all manner, whether in pretense or in truth, Christ is being proclaimed. And that Paul indeed "will be joyful" invites the audience, as partners of Paul, to play their role in furthering the "joy" of Paul by advancing the gospel of Christ (1:18).

B. Summary on Philippians 1:12–18

1. The audience are to be pleased not only that it has become manifest in the whole Roman praetorium and to all the rest that Paul's imprisonment is "in Christ" (1:13), but that most of the "brothers," their fellow Christians, having confidence "in the Lord" by Paul's bonds, despite the danger of being imprisoned like Paul, more increasingly and without fear dare to speak "the word" (1:14), thus playing their part, and encouraging the audience at Philippi to likewise play their part, in advancing the gospel, the word about Christ (1:12).

2. The audience learn that even among the "brothers" who speak the word of the gospel there are some who are opponents of Paul, taking advantage of his imprisonment, to preach the Christ even on account of their envy of and rivalry with Paul (1:15a). But the audience also learn that, on the other hand, there are "brothers" more favorable to the imprisoned Paul, who even on account of the "good pleasure" of God, further his mission by preaching the Christ (1:15b).

3. Those preaching the Christ out of love while Paul is in prison for the defense of the gospel (1:16) provide the audience with a model persuading them out of love to play their role in the advancement of the gospel of Christ.

4. Those who proclaim the Christ "out of self-seeking" (1:17a) stand in stark contrast to those who, in fellowship with Paul like the Philippians (cf. 1:5, 7), proclaim the Christ selflessly "out of love" (1:16a).

5. Despite the insincere motivation of some who proclaim the Christ while

---

32. Ware, *Mission*, 195: "Given the desperate character of Paul's circumstances, the mood of joy which pervades the letter is striking indeed. In 1:18a the ground of Paul's joy is explicitly the spread of the gospel message."

33. Ware, *Mission*, 198: "Through his paradigmatic portrayal of the Christians at Rome who boldly proclaim the gospel in unity with the apostle, alongside the negative example of those who engage in mission through impure motives, Paul exhorts the Philippians to work for the extension of the gospel in unity with him and with one another."

Paul is in bonds (1:17b), Paul is presently "rejoicing" in the fact that in all manner, whether in pretense or in truth, Christ is being proclaimed. And that Paul indeed "will be joyful" invites the audience, as partners of Paul, to play their role in furthering the "joy" of Paul by advancing the gospel of Christ (1:18).

6

PHILIPPIANS 1:19–30: DEATH IN MY BODY IS GAIN BUT REMAINING IN THE FLESH IS FOR YOUR FAITH (D)

Not Only in Christ to Believe but on Behalf of Him to Suffer

A: [19] for I know that this for me will lead to *salvation* through the petition of you and supply of the Spirit of Jesus Christ [20] according to my eager expectation and hope, that *in nothing* I will be put to shame but in all boldness as always and now Christ will be magnified in my body, whether through life or through death. [21] For to me to live is Christ and to die is gain. [22] If it is to live in the flesh, this for me is fruitful work, and which I will choose I do not know. [23] I am constrained between the two, *having* the desire for release and to be with Christ, for that is much better by far. [24] But to remain in the flesh is more necessary on account of you.

    B: [25] And having confidence of this, I know that I will remain, indeed I will remain beside all of you for your advancement and joy in *the faith*, [26] so that your boast may abound in Christ Jesus in me through my presence again with you. [27a] Only, live as citizens worthy of *the gospel* of the Christ,

        C: [27b] so that, *whether coming* and seeing you,

        C': [27c] *or being absent*, I hear the things concerning you,

    B': [27d] that you are standing firm in one Spirit, with one mind struggling together for *the faith of the gospel*,

A': [28] and not being intimidated *in anything* by the opponents, which is for them a demonstration of destruction, but of your *salvation*, and this is from God, [29] for to you has been granted that which is on behalf of Christ, not only in him to believe but also on behalf of him to suffer, [30] *having* the same struggle, such as you saw in me and now hear in me.[1]

A. AUDIENCE RESPONSE TO PHILIPPIANS 1:19–30

1. Phil 1:19–24 (A): This for Me Will Lead to Salvation

Having heard that Paul is rejoicing in the fact that in all manner Christ is proclaimed and that "indeed I will be joyful" (1:18), the audience now hear further

---

1. For the establishment of Phil 1:19–30 as a chiasm, see ch. 2.

elaboration of that hope for future joy in the form of a mini-chiasm in 1:19–24:
(a) for I know that this for me (τοῦτό μοι) will lead to salvation through (διά) the
petition of you (ὑμῶν) and supply of the Spirit of Jesus Christ (1:19) (b) according to my eager expectation and hope, that in nothing I will be put to shame but
in all boldness as always and now Christ (Χριστός) will be magnified in my body,
whether through life (ζωῆς) or through death (θανάτου) (1:20).[2] (b´) For to me to
live (ζῆν) is Christ (Χριστός) and to die (ἀποθανεῖν) is gain (1:21). (a´) If it is to
live in the flesh, this for me (τοῦτό μοι) is fruitful work, and which I will choose I
do not know. I am constrained between the two, having the desire for release and
to be with Christ, for that is much better by far. But to remain in the flesh is more
necessary on account of you (δι᾽ ὑμᾶς) (1:22–24).[3]

The audience hear the central pivot of the mini–chiasm as a progression of
parallels from the nominative form of "Christ" (Χριστός), the noun "life" (ζωῆς),
and the noun "death" (θανάτου) in the "b" sub-element (1:20) to the verb "to
live" (ζῆν), the nominative form of "Christ" (Χριστός), and the verb "to die"
(ἀποθανεῖν)in the "b´" sub-element (1:21).[4] The audience then hear, via the chiastic parallels, a progression from "this for me (τοῦτό μοι) will lead to salvation" and
"through (διά) the petition of you (ὑμῶν)" in the "a" sub-element (1:19) to "this for
me (τοῦτό μοι) is fruitful work" (1:22) and "on account of you (δι᾽ ὑμᾶς)" in (1:24) in
the "a´" sub-element (1:22–24).

After having heard that in "this" (τούτῳ), that is, in the fact that Christ is
being proclaimed, Paul is presently rejoicing, the audience begin to hear the basis
for Paul's future joy—"And indeed I will be joyful" (1:18). Paul knows that "this"
(τοῦτό), that is, the fact that Christ is being proclaimed even while Paul is in
the bonds of imprisonment, "for me will lead to salvation" (1:19a).[5] These words
are a verbatim echo of LXX Job 13:16. Paul's implicit comparison of his hope for

---

2. The integral unity of this "b" sub-element is secured by the only two occurrences in this mini-
chiasm of the genitive of the first-person singular personal pronoun—"my (μου) eager expectaion and
hope" and "in my (μου) body."

3. The integral unity of this "a´" sub-element is secured through a literary inclusion formed by
the only two occurrences in this mini-chiasm of the prepositional phrase "in the flesh"—"to live in the
flesh (ἐν σαρκί)" and "to remain in the flesh ([ἐν] τῇ σαρκί)." Note that "to live" (ζῆν) in 1:22a, although
identical with "to live" (ζῆν) in 1:21, functions here not as a chiastic parallel but as a transitional hook
word to introduce the "a´" sub-element.

4. The term "Christ" occurs in 1:19 and 1:23, but not in the nominative form.

5. "This" (τοῦτό) in 1:19 thus functions as a transitional hook word, recalling "in this (τούτῳ)"
from 1:18, referring to Christ being proclaimed. Some relate the "this" in 1:19 to τὰ κατ᾽ ἐμέ in 1:12,
Paul's present circumstances of imprisonment. See, for example, O'Brien, *Philippians*, 109; Fee, *Philippians*, 131. But this is very unlikely, as it conflicts with the whole tenor of Paul's rhetorical strategy
here, which is to deflect attention from his imprisonment to the all-important proclamation of Christ.
In other words, it is not so much Paul's imprisonment but rather the proclaiming of the Christ during
and as a result of that imprisonment that will lead to his salvation. *Contra* Fee, *Philippians*, 131 n. 22.
Ware, *Mission*, 208: "[I]n Philippians 1:19a the direct antecedent of τοῦτο, as of τούτῳ in the previous
verse, is not only the preaching of Paul himself, but also the proclamation of Christ by other Christians
described in 1:18a." See also Bittasi, *Gli esempi*, 47–48.

salvation with that of Job's, the paradigmatic righteous sufferer, reinforces his encouragement for the audience.[6] Paul's hope for "salvation" (σωτηρίαν)—not only for "deliverance" in his present situation but especially and primarily for his ultimate vindication in the heavenly court, part of his eschatological "salvation"—as a result of his role in Christ being proclaimed in all manner, is to encourage the audience, with the same hope, to continue to play their own role in the proclamation of Christ.[7]

In the thanksgiving section of the letter the audience heard Paul declare: "I thank my God at every remembrance of you, always in my every petition (δεήσει) on behalf of all of you, making the petition (δέησιν) with joy at your fellowship for the gospel from the first day until now" (1:3–5). Just as Paul makes petitions to God on behalf of his Philippian audience, so they are to return the favor and make petitions to God on behalf of Paul—"through the petition (δεήσεως) of you"

---

6. Ware, *Mission*, 202–3: "Paul's allusion to Job is skillful, and functions on two levels. First, Paul, imprisoned and facing death for his preaching of the gospel, identifies himself with Job, the paradigmatic righteous sufferer. But second, . . . in LXX Job 13:14b–16 the ground (τοῦτό) of Job's assurance of salvation (μοι ἀποβήσεται εἰς σωτηρίαν) is his *fearless speech and reproof before the ruler who seeks to put him to death*. The similarity of the situation envisaged in LXX Job 13:14b–16 to Paul's own circumstances is remarkable, and suggests that this wider Septuagintal context, in which Job's confidence in deliverance is grounded in his bold speech before the ruler who threatens his life, is tacitly intimated in Paul's citation of Septuagint Job 13:16a. Paul, whose purposes in this section, as we have seen, are hortatory and didactic, thus draws in Job's example alongside his own to encourage the Philippians. . . . The echo of Job 13:16 thus greatly enriches Paul's paradigmatic self–description in 1:18b–19," and 203 n. 3: "While a few interpreters have doubted whether Paul intended a reference to Job here, the fact that Paul's words correspond exactly to the wording and sequence of LXX Job 13:16 and that the word ἀποβαίνω occurs nowhere else in Paul, strongly suggests that Paul's words reflect a deliberate echo of the passage." See also Lukas Bormann, "Triple Intertextuality in Philippians," in *The Intertextuality of the Epistles: Explorations of Theory and Practice* (ed. Thomas L. Brodie et al.; NTM 16; Sheffield: Sheffield Phoenix, 2006), 92–93. Bockmuehl, *Philippians*, 82: "Paul weaves into his discourse the words of a biblical man of faith which, although self–explanatory, nevertheless would evoke in a biblically literate readership both the tense drama and the reassurance of a familiar text." For doubt that the audience would recognize an allusion to Job here, see John Reumann, "The (Greek) Old Testament in Philippians 1:19 as Parade Example—Allusion, Echo, Proverb?" in *History and Exegesis: New Testament Essays in Honor of Dr. E. Earle Ellis for His 80th Birthday* (ed. Sang–Won Son; London: Clark, 2006), 189–200.

7. Karl Hermann Schelkle, "σωτηρία," *EDNT* 3.328: "In Philippians Paul speaks of the present peril of imprisonment though he knows (1:19) that it 'will turn out for *deliverance*' (cf. Job 13:16 LXX). 'Salvation' refers to deliverance from pressing circumstances, but also to the ultimate, eschatological experience." Garland, "Philippians," 202: "[H]e [Paul] does not allude here to his acquittal before an earthly court but instead is confident, like Job, that he will be acquitted in the heavenly court that will annul all human pronouncements." Fee, *Philippians*, 131 n. 20: "In Paul's sentence, therefore, the word σωτηρία carries in part its ordinary sense of 'salvation before God,' but in this case, as in the LXX, in the special sense of the final vindication of the passion of Paul's life, the gospel of Christ and therefore of Christ himself." Ware, *Mission*, 209: "Paul is thus assured that his bold defense of the gospel will bring about not only eternal salvation at the advent of Christ, but also his deliverance here and now from death and prison as well." See also Moisés Silva, "Philippians," in *Commentary on the New Testament Use of the Old Testament* (ed. Gregory K. Beale and Donald A. Carson; Grand Rapids: Baker, 2007), 836.

(1:19b). This continues to underline the mutuality between Paul and his audience as partners in fellowship for the gospel. It also confirms and develops the role the audience have to play in Paul's hope that "indeed I will be joyful" (1:18b). As partners of Paul, the audience can contribute to Paul's hope for future joy not only by themselves proclaiming the Christ out of love but also by making petitions to God that Christ being proclaimed in all manner will lead to Paul's "salvation" (1:19).[8]

It is Paul's hope that Christ being proclaimed will lead to his salvation not only through the petitions to God on Paul's behalf by his Philippian audience, but also through the "supply of the Spirit of Jesus Christ" (1:19b). It is thus "through" (διά) the petition of the Philippians, who have been filled up with the fruit of righteousness that is "through" (διά) Jesus Christ (1:11), and "through" the supply of the Spirit of Jesus Christ that Christ being proclaimed will lead to Paul's salvation (1:19a). The implication is that it is through the petition of the Philippians to God on behalf of Paul that Paul will receive the supply of the Spirit of Jesus Christ, that is, that Paul will be fully supplied with the Spirit that comes from Jesus Christ.[9] When the audience hear the word "Christ" (Χριστοῦ) in the phrase "the Spirit of

---

8. O'Brien, *Philippians*, 110–11: "δέησις, which originally denoted a 'lack' or 'need' and then an 'entreaty', is used exclusively in the NT of a 'prayer' addressed to God, especially a 'petition' or 'supplication'. . . . Here at Phil 1:19 Paul's entreaty corresponds to his earlier petition for the Philippians. . . . δέησις appears in the singular and directs attention to the single, specific nature of the request, while ὑμῶν, placed first for emphasis, is plural and points to the united offering of prayer by the Philippians for this particular object, namely his furthering of the gospel by life or by death so that he will finally be vindicated on the occasion of the great Assize." Fee, *Philippians*, 132 n. 26: "Even though δεήσεως is singular, this . . . is almost certainly a 'distributive singular'. . . . The word order τῆς ὑμῶν δεήσεως is striking. The ὑμῶν has probably been brought forward for clarity and emphasis." Bockmuehl, *Philippians*, 83–84: "[T]heir [the Philippians'] prayers play an integral and instrumental part in how God accomplishes that salvation. Clearly this is another vivid example of the Philippians' stake-holding 'partnership' in the gospel (1.5)!" Garland, "Philippians," 202: "He [Paul] does not believe he has the power to survive on his own without the prayer partnership of a supporting faith community. In listing the intercessory prayers of the Philippians as a contributing factor, he shows that he implicitly expects them to be unified in their prayers for him and to become like those who proclaim Christ in love, recognizing that he is put here for the defense and confirmation of the gospel."

9. O'Brien, *Philippians*, 110: "The apostle's vindication will come through (διά) the intercessory prayers of the Philippian Christians and the supply of the Spirit of Jesus Christ, thus enabling him to acquit himself well during his trials, whatever the outcome. The two terms mentioned in this long phrase, that is, δεήσεως ('petition') and ἐπιχορηγίας ('supply'), are closely related: they are governed by one preposition (διά) and connected by a single article (τῆς). The supply of the Spirit is the answer to his friends' prayer, the final result of which is Paul's vindication." Gordon D. Fee, *God's Empowering Presence: The Holy Spirit in the Letters of Paul* (Peabody, Mass.: Hendrickson, 1994), 743: "Thus this phrase is not incidental. Here is the key to Christ's being glorified in every way: by Paul's being 'supplied' the Spirit of Jesus Christ, who will live powerfully through Paul as he stands trial. . . . the Philippians—and others—are inextricably bound together with him through the Spirit. Therefore, he assumes that their praying, and God's gracious supply of the Spirit of his Son, will be the means God uses yet once more to bring glory to himself through Paul and Paul's defense of the gospel." Bockmuehl, *Philippians*, 84: "The Spirit is identified as being of Jesus Christ, a phrase which in this form occurs nowhere else in the New Testament. It must mean that the Spirit is *sent* by Jesus Christ, but beyond that it is also clear from other passages that Paul believed the Spirit to be in a distinctive sense the spirit *of* Christ, the power-

Jesus Christ" (1:19b), they hear the transitional word that links this chiastic unit (1:19–30) to the previous one (1:12–18), whose conclusion contains the assertation that "Christ (Χριστός) is proclaimed" (1:18).

Paul continues the elaboration of his hope for future joy (1:18b): "according to my eager expectation and hope, that in nothing I will be put to shame but in all boldness as always and now Christ will be magnified in my body, whether through life or through death" (1:20). It is in accord with Paul's confidently "eager expectation and hope,"[10] that in nothing "I will be put to shame" (αἰσχυνθήσομαι) by God (divine passive), either before opponents in his present situation in the bonds of imprisonment in Christ (1:13) or before God in the future heavenly court (1:19).[11]

Rather, in contrast to "*in* nothing" (ἐν οὐδενί) by way of a strikingly alliterative and assonant expression—"*in* all boldness as always and now" (ἐν πάσῃ παρρησίᾳ ὡς πάντοτε καὶ νῦν)—emphasizing the persistence of his public "openness" or "boldness," Paul expresses a confident hope that Christ "will be magnified" (μεγαλυνθήσεται) by God (divine passive) in Paul's body,[12] whether through his ongoing life or through his being put to death.[13] The audience have now heard a progression in the basis for Paul's future joy, from "Christ" (Χριστός) presently being proclaimed (1:18), which "will lead" to Paul's salvation (1:19), in which there is no way that "I will be put to shame" (1:20a), but rather "Christ" (Χριστός) "will

---

ful presence of the risen and exalted Messiah. In a profound sense the Spirit *is* the Lord (2 Cor. 3.17)" (Bockmuehl's emphases).

10. Ware, *Mission*, 204 n. 6: "ἀποκαραδοκία and ἐλπις united by one article express a single attitude under two different aspects; ἀποκαραδοκία signifies here not anxious and uncertain longing, but rather intense expectation." See also D. R. Denton, "Ἀποκαραδοκία," *ZNW* 73 (1982): 138–40; H.-K. Chang, "(ἀπο)καραδοκία bei Paulus und Aquila," *ZNW* 93 (2002): 268–78.

11. O'Brien, *Philippians*, 114: "[I]n a situation where Paul is awaiting trial, he knows that whatever happens he will not be put to shame—a shame that has nothing to do with public opinion but relates to his standing before God. His confidence lies not in his relation to his environment (since the extreme alternatives of life and death could not bring such an assurance) but in God's faithfulness." Bockmuehl, *Philippians*, 85: "Being put to shame has to do with the outcome not just of Paul's trial before Caesar, but even more of his eschatological standing before God: in that sense, Paul's statement may well be deliberately ambiguous."

12. Fee, *Philippians*, 137–38: "[H]e [Paul] is writing about what will happen to him 'physically,' that is, whether his trial will result in (physical) life or (bodily) death."

13. O'Brien, *Philippians*, 115: "Paul is simply the instrument by which the greatness of Christ shines out: behind the passive voice the activity of God is implied, with Paul being the instrument in the divine hands.... The expression ἐν πάσῃ παρρησίᾳ ... μεγαλυνθήσεται contrasts ἐν οὐδενὶ αἰσχυνθήσομαι, with the words ἐν πάσῃ[παρρησίᾳ] being antithetical to ἐν οὐδενί. παρρησία, which has a wide range of meanings, could here connote 'openness', to draw attention to the free and unrestricted way in which the glorifying of Christ will be manifested; or it might mean 'boldness', to show that Christ will be magnified in Paul's body in a bold and uncompromising manner as the apostle bears faithful witness to his Lord. That open and plain, or bold, glorification of Christ will occur in the present and the immediate future." Fee, *Philippians*, 137: "[T]hus, in a very open and public way Christ will be magnified through Paul's bold defense of the gospel, however the trial turns out."

be magnified" (1:20b).[14] The audience are thus, through Paul's confident hope, to be encouraged about the certainty of their own future salvation, if they likewise publicly and openly proclaim Christ, so that Christ will be magnified in them.[15]

The audience then experience a pivot of parallels in the mini-chiasm (1:19–24) from "Christ (Χριστός) will be magnified in my body, whether through *life* (ζωῆς) or through *death* (θανάτου)" in the "b" sub-element (1:20) to "for to me *to live* (ζῆν) is *Christ* (Χριστός) and *to die* (ἀποθανεῖν) is gain" in the "b'" sub-element (1:21).[16] The audience thus hear a progression from Paul's hope that Christ will be magnified in his body through his life to the basis for that hope—for Paul to live actually *is* Christ, that is, his life is totally identified with and completely dedicated to promoting Christ.[17] They likewise hear a progression from Paul's hope that Christ will be magnified in his body through his death to the basis for that hope—for Paul to die is gain. Through the striking alliteration and assonance between "Christ" (Χριστός) and "gain" (κέρδος),[18] the implication is that for Paul to die is not in any way a loss, but rather an opportunity for Christ to be magnified in Paul's body, and thus a "gain" or "profit."[19]

---

14. O'Brien, *Philippians*, 114: "In the Psalter the man of God often prays that he will not be covered with shame before his enemies; instead he desires that he may be vindicated and the Lord exalted (μεγαλυνθήτω ὁ κύριος, Ps. 34:26–27; 39:15–17). See also Fee, *Philippians*, 136; idem, *Pauline Christology*, 407–8. Silva, *Philippians*, 72: "[E]ven if σωτηρία in verse 19 alludes in some way to deliverance from prison (could we have a deliberate ambiguity in Paul's use of the term?), the primary reference is to Paul's perseverance in faith: the magnification of Christ—not his own freedom or even his life—is Paul's salvation."

15. Fee, *Philippians*, 138: "Paul's singular passion—and this is what he surely wants his beloved Philippians to hear—is that even though he expects a favorable outcome, he wants Christ to be glorified as he stands trial, and beyond, even if it were to result in death. That would only hasten Paul's eschatological 'salvation/vindication' before the heavenly tribunal. But for now, his singular 'hope' is that Christ—and thus the gospel—will be 'vindicated' through his life or death. . . . The sililoquy, therefore, has another reason for existence: to encourage the Philippians regarding the certainty of their own future, as long as for them, too, 'to live is Christ.'"

16. Thurston, *Philippians*, 63: "The sentence begins with an emphatic pronoun in Greek [ἐμοί, 'to me'], and the 'for' [γάρ] indicates that what follows explains what preceded."

17. O'Brien, *Philippians*, 120: "Paul asserts that living (τὸ ζῆν) has no meaning apart from Christ; he is the object, motive, inspiration, and goal of all that the apostle does."

18. Fee, *Philippians*, 140 n. 8: "The assonance between κέρδος and Χριστός could hardly have been missed. Four consonants correspond (ch/k, r, t/d, s), with only one vowel/consonant transposition (ri/er) and an additional sigma in the first syllable." In addition, for a possible wordplay here between Χριστός (Christ) and χρέστος (good), see Arthur J. Droge and James D. Tabor, *A Noble Death: Suicide and Martyrdom Among Jews and Christians in Antiquity* (San Francisco: Harper Collins, 1992), 121.

19. O'Brien, *Philippians*, 123: "[H]is death will give him the ultimate possibility of witnessing to Christ." See also D. W. Palmer, "'To Die Is Gain' (Philippians 1:21)," *NovT* 17 (1975): 203–18; David E. Garland, "Philippians 1:1–26: The Defense and Confirmation of the Gospel," *RevExp* 77 (1980): 327–36. These authors hold that "to die is gain" expresses how Paul would be free of the burdens of his life. But against this, O'Brien (*Philippians*, 123) notes: "[A]lthough being in deeper fellowship with his Lord beyond death would obviously mean that his present earthly troubles would cease, it is not the latter that Paul emphasizes." See also N. Clayton Croy, "'To Die Is Gain' (Philippians 1:19–26): Does Paul Contemplate Suicide?" *JBL* 122 (2003): 517–31. Fee, *Philippians*, 142: "[T]he *sense* lies in Paul's

Paul then explicates how for him to go on living is Christ while dying is gain (1:21): "If it is to live in the flesh, this for me is fruitful work, and which I will choose I do not know. I am constrained between the two, having the desire for release and to be with Christ, for that is much better by far.[20] But to remain in the flesh is more necessary on account of you" (1:22–24). For Paul "to live (τὸ ζῆν) is Christ" (1:21a) receives clarification as a reference to the continuance of Paul's physical, earthly life: "If it is to live (τὸ ζῆν) in the flesh" (1:22a).[21] The audience then hear a development, via the chiastic parallels, from "this for me (τοῦτό μοι) will lead to salvation" (1:19a) in the "a" sub-element of the mini-chiasm (1:19–24) to "this for me (τοῦτό μοι) is fruitful work (literally, 'fruit of work')" (1:22b) in the "a´" sub-element.

The audience are to realize, then, that whereas "this" in the statement that "this for me will lead to salvation" refers to Christ being proclaimed by Paul and others (1:18), "this" in the statement that "this for me is fruitful work" refers to the possibility of Paul continuing to live in the flesh, so that his "fruitful work" or "fruit of work" refers to his proclaiming Christ.[22] The audience can more clearly grasp that for Paul "to live is Christ" (1:21a) connotes that his life is for the purpose of Christ being proclaimed. And the alliteration between "gain" (κέρδος) and "fruit" (καρπός), as well as the conceptual similarity of these two terms, enhances the audience's realization that although Paul's death is "gain" of Christ (1:21b), his living in the flesh is also a "gain" for Christ, namely, the "fruit" of work (1:22a), that is, proclaiming Christ.[23]

The audience then experience the expression of Paul's intense personal dilemma: "Which," that is, the "gain" (of and for Christ) that is dying (1:21b) or the "fruitful work" of proclaiming Christ that is living in the flesh (1:22ab), "I will

---

understanding death to be the ultimate 'gaining' of his lifelong passion. This expresses neither a death wish nor dissatisfaction with life nor desire to be 'done with troubles and trials'; it is the forthright assessment of one whose future in terms of 'life in the flesh' is somewhat uncertain, but whose ultimate future is both certain and to be desired."

20. For the very questionable interpretation that "to be with Christ" here refers to an intermediate state between the death of Paul and the end–time, see Stefan Schreiber, "Paulus im 'Zwischenzustand': Phil 1.23 und die Ambivalenz des Sterbens als Provokation," *NTS* 49 (2003): 336–59. See also E. B. Treiyer, "S'en aller et être avec Christ: Philippiens 1:23," *AUSS* 34 (1996): 47–64; O'Brien, *Philippians*, 132–37.

21. O'Brien, *Philippians*, 125: "The whole phrase, τὸ ζῆν ἐν σαρκί, does not signify an antithesis to the absolute τὸ ζῆν in the preceding verse. Rather, it is a more precise definition of it so that in both places Paul is speaking of life 'here below'. "

22. Hans-Theo Wrege, "καρπός," *EDNT* 2.252: "'Fruit of the work' in Phil 1:22 (cf. Isa 3:10; Jer 17:10; 32:19) refers to the missionary activity of Paul." Ware, *Mission*, 210: " Ἔργον and its cognates are frequently used by Paul with reference to the work of spreading the gospel. Already in the thanksgiving period Paul has referred to the Philippians' partnership with him for the gospel as an ἔργον ἀγαθόν (1:6)."

23. Fee, *Philippians*, 144: "[W]hat is in tension is not a choice between 'life' and 'death' per se—as if he really had such a choice—but between the ultimate 'gaining' *of Christ* and present 'fruitful labor' *for Christ*."

choose I do not know; I am constrained between the two" (1:22c–23a). Since the imprisoned Paul does not really have full control of his destiny here, his "choice" is more rhetorical than actual. But much to their relief and delight, further encouraging them, the audience are assured that they are to receive the benefit of the resolution of Paul's dilemma. Although he has the deep desire for "release," that is, release from this life through death, and to be with Christ, thus further specifying how "to die is gain" (1:21b), for being with Christ is much better for Paul, as he expresses with an assonant and emphatic superlative—"for that is much better by far (πολλῷ [γὰρ] μᾶλλον κρεῖσσον)" (1:23bc).[24] Nevertheless, to remain alive in the flesh is more "necessary" (ἀναγκαιότερον), that is, divinely necessary or compelled by God's plan, "on account of you," the Philippian audience (1:24).[25]

The audience thus hear a further development, through the chiastic parallels, of the fellowship for the gospel that they share with Paul—from the assertion that Christ being proclaimed will lead to Paul's salvation "through" (διά) the petition of "you" (ὑμῶν) (1:19) in the "a" sub-element to the admission that for Paul to remain alive in the flesh is more necessary "on account of you" (δι' ὑμᾶς) (1:24) in the "a′" sub-element. To sum up, in this A element of the chiasm in 1:19–30, then, the audience, through their experience of the mini-chiasm in 1:19–24, are to be fur-

---

24. O'Brien, *Philippians*, 130: "For the apostle so intimate is the bond between the believer and his Lord that death cannot break it. Instead, death ushers him into an even deeper fellowship with Christ, so that he can say that this union beyond death is 'far, far better' and is a consummation earnestly to be desired."

25. O'Brien, *Philippians*, 131–32: "Here at Phil. 1:24 the comparative 'more necessary' (ἀναγκαιότερον) corresponds to the comparative 'better' (κρεῖσσον) of v. 23. In a sense either alternative, 'living' or 'dying', was necessary just as both were advantageous. But against (δέ is adversative) his personal desires Paul puts the concern for others first (δι' ὑμᾶς). . . . the language arises out of the special relationship that he has with the readers and that he naturally expresses in a letter to them. . . . this necessity or constraint of his apostolate, which was decisive, is similar to the divine compulsion of preaching the gospel (1 Cor. 9:16)." See also Fee, *Philippians*, 150 n. 51. Ware, *Mission*, 212: "As we have seen, the entire section 1:18b–26 functions paraenetically to present Paul as a model for the Philippians. Paul's presentation in 1:21–24 therefore does not directly reflect Paul's own situation, but his situation as interpreted and presented by him so as to apply to the needs of the Philippians. . . . Paul in 1:21–24 presents himself as a model of Christian decision-making, as one who, like Timothy (2:20–22) and Epaphroditus (2:30), subordinates his own interests to those of Christ and the work of the gospel. Moreover, Paul's thinking in 1:21–24 models a reversal of values, in which Christ is all and the alternatives of earhtly life or death are thus radically relativized. The language of choice and decision in 1:21–24 reflects this rhetorical and didactic function of the pericope, not an actual choice which Paul could exercise in his own situation." See also Samuel Vollenweider, "Die Waagschalen von Leben und Tod: Zum antiken Hintergrund von Phil 1,21–26," *ZNW* 85 (1994): 93–115. For a questionable interpretation that Paul is contemplating the possibility of suicide here, see Arthur J. Droge, "*Mori Lucrum*: Paul and Ancient Theories of Suicide," *NovT* 30 (1988): 263–86; James L. Jaquette, "A Not-So-Noble Death: Figured Speech, Friendship and Suicide in Philippians 1:21–26," *Neot* 28 (1994): 177–92; idem, "Life and Death, *Adiaphora*, and Paul's Rhetorical Strategies," *NovT* 38 (1996): 30–54. See also Stefano Bittasi, "La prigionia de Paolo nella lettera ai Filippesi e il problema di una sua morte possibile. I. Una lettura di *Fil* 1, 12–26," *RdT* 45 (2004): 19–34; idem, "La prigionia de Paolo nella lettera ai Filippesi e il problema di una morte possibile. 2. Il nuovo sguardo sul potere imperiale," *RdT* 45 (2004): 189–206.

ther encouraged to contribute to the future joy of Paul (1:18) by continuing their own proclamation of Christ, having been brought to the realization of how their partnership for the gospel is mutually beneficial for Paul and for themselves. Their petition to God is beneficial for Paul's salvation (1:19) and that Paul remain alive in the flesh so that Christ is magnified in his body is necessary for them (1:20–24).

2. *Phil 1:25–27a (B): Joy in the Faith as Citizens of the Gospel*

The audience then begin to hear why it is more necessary on their account that Paul remain alive in the flesh (1:24): "And having confidence of this, I know that I will remain, indeed I will remain beside all of you for your advancement and joy in the faith" (1:25). The audience were reassured by Paul's confidence in what God will do for them—"having confidence of this very thing, that (πεποιθὼς αὐτὸ τοῦτο, ὅτι) he who began in you a good work will perfect it until the day of Christ Jesus" (1:6). And now they are again reassured by Paul's confidence in what God will do for him in allowing him to remain alive, as it is more necessary within the divine plan that "I remain in the flesh on account of you" (1:24)—"and having confidence of this (τοῦτο πεποιθώς), I know that (ὅτι) I will remain, indeed I will remain beside all of you" (1:25ab).[26]

That it is more necessary that Paul "remain" alive in the flesh is emphatically underscored for the audience by the progression of a wordplay on various forms of the Greek verb with the root μένω—from the infinitive of the compound verb "to remain (ἐπιμένειν) in the flesh" (1:24) to the future active first-person singular of the simple form of the verb, the confidently asserted "I will remain" (μενῶ), immediately reinforced by the future active first-person singular of another form of the compound verb, the reassuring assertion that "I will remain beside (παραμενῶ) all of you" (1:25b).[27] That it is more necessary that Paul remain alive in the flesh on account of "you" (ὑμᾶς) (1:24) is more directly, comprehensively, and elaboratively applied to the audience, as Paul boldly promises that "I will remain beside all of you (ὑμῖν) for your (ὑμῶν) advancement and joy in the faith" (1:25bc). And that Paul will remain beside "*all* (πᾶσιν) of you" continues his pointed address of the audience as the total, unified community of all the holy ones at Philippi—"to all (πᾶσιν) those holy ones in Christ Jesus" (1:1; see also 1:4, 7, 8).[28]

The audience have heard that Paul's imprisonment has actually led to a progress in the preaching of the gospel—"the things concerning me have come rather to an advancement (προκοπήν) of the gospel" (1:12). And now they hear how

---

26. O'Brien, *Philippians*, 139: "τοῦτο as the object of πεποιθὼς refers to what has preceded rather than to what follows."

27. Fee, *Philippians*, 152 n. 10: "Gk. μενῶ καὶ παραμενῶ (cf. ἐπιμένῳ v. 24), which could otherwise be synonyms (the second expressing a slight intensification), but here must be nuanced toward 'remaining alive' and 'abiding with you,' especially because of the way the second is qualified."

28. Fee, *Philippians*, 152: "The surprise comes from the qualifier, that 'I will continue with *all* of you.' This otherwise unnecessary mention of 'all' most likely points to the friction that is currently at work among them."

Paul's survival of his imprisonment and remaining alive on account of them (1:24) will lead to *"your"* (ὑμῶν in emphatic position) progress in the faith—"I will remain beside all of you for your advancement (προκοπήν) and joy in the faith" (1:25bc).[29] The implication for the Philippian audience is that their "advancement" in the faith is closely related to their own "advancement" of the preaching of the gospel, as they are partners in fellowship with Paul for the gospel (1:5; cf. 1:7).[30]

That Paul's remaining beside all of the believers at Philippi is necessary not only for their "advancement" in the faith but for their closely co-ordinated "joy" (χαράν) in the faith (1:25c) implies that Paul wants to persuade them to share his "joy" that is oriented toward advancing the gospel, as it recalls how he makes every petition on behalf of his audience with "joy" (χαρᾶς, 1:4) at their fellowship with him for the gospel (1:5). Indeed, the implication is that the presence beside them of Paul, their partner in the gospel, will lead them to share in and appropriate for themselves Paul's declaration that "Christ is proclaimed, and in this I rejoice (χαίρω). And indeed I will be joyful (χαρήσομαι)" (1:18). The Philippian audience can likewise "rejoice" and they "will be joyful," if Christ continues to be proclaimed not only by others, but most especially by themselves.[31]

The audience then hear the purpose of Paul's remaining beside all of them for their advancement and joy in the faith (1:25bc): "so that your boast may abound in Christ Jesus in me through my presence again with you" (1:26). Just as the love of the audience is even more and more to "abound" (περισσεύη) in knowledge and every perception, in order that they may determine the things that matter (1:9–10), so their "boast" (καύχημα), that is, what they can place their confident trust in and thus glory or joyously exult in, is to "abound" (περισσεύη) "in Christ Jesus" (ἐν Χριστῷ Ἰησοῦ), that is, within the sphere or domain of their being in union

---

29. Fee, *Philippians*, 153: "The 'your,' which modifies both 'progress' and 'joy,' stands in the emphatic first position, thus putting the accent first of all on the Philippians themselves. It is for their sakes that he expects to be released, which he now elaborates to mean specifically for their 'progress' and their 'joy.' These two words together summarize his concerns for them in this letter: the first refers to the quality or character of their life in Christ, and especially to their 'advancing,' moving forward, in such; the second denotes the quality of their experience of it."

30. Ware, *Mission*, 214: "The progress of the Philippians (τὴν ὑμῶν προκοπήν, 1:25) is thus related to the progress of the gospel (προκοπὴν τοῦ εὐαγγελίου, 1:12), in that the former is the precondition of the latter. . . . the missionizing partnership of the Philippians with Paul (τῇ κοινωνίᾳ ὑμῶν εἰς τὸ εὐαγγέλιον, 1:5) is dependent upon their own progress and joy in faith (1:25; cf. 1:9–11). Thus Paul's release and personal pastoral care of the Philippians will be necessary (ἀναγκαιότερον, 1:24) if the Philippians are to continue and grow in this partnership and fulfill this active missionizing task. Thus both the force of Paul's example (1:21–24), and his understanding of God's purposes in his upcoming release from prison (1:25–26), function to exhort the Philippians to boldly spread the message of the gospel." Michael Barram, *Mission and Moral Reflection in Paul* (Studies in Biblical Literature 75; New York: Lang, 2006), 125: "From Paul's perspective, the relationship approximates an ideal apostle-community bond—one characterized by reciprocal, ongoing nurture from the start." See also W. Paul Bowers, "Fulfilling the Gospel: The Scope of the Pauline Mission," *JETS* 30 (1987): 197.

31. Fee, *Philippians*, 154: "His [Paul's] concern here is with the joy that is theirs in the gospel itself, although they will undoubtedly also experience joy in seeing Paul again."

with Christ Jesus, as they indeed are holy ones "in Christ Jesus" (ἐν Χριστῷ Ἰησοῦ, 1:1). The more specific and special cause or ground for their boast to abound "in" Christ Jesus is "in me" (ἐν ἐμοί), that is, in Paul himself, who is also within the sphere of Christ Jesus. Indeed, as the audience have just heard, "for to me (ἐμοί) to live is Christ" (1:21a).

That the boast of the audience may abound "in me," in Paul himself (note the use of the emphatic first-person singular pronoun, ἐμοί), within the sphere of both the audience and Paul being in union with Christ Jesus, is further delineated as "through my (ἐμῆς, emphatic first-person singular possessive adjective) presence again with you" (1:26b). With its pointed stress on the presence of Paul himself, as well as its striking alliteration of "p" and "s" sounds—διὰ τῆς ἐμῆς παρουσίας πάλιν πρὸς ὑμᾶς, this prepositional phrase promising Paul's presence again with "you" (ὑμᾶς) emphatically reinforces why it is more necessary for Paul to survive his imprisonment and remain alive in the flesh on account of "you" (ὑμᾶς), the Philippian audience (1:24).[32]

For the first time in the letter the audience are addressed by Paul with a direct command through a verb in the imperative mood: "Only, live as citizens worthy of the gospel of the Christ" (1:27a).[33] In accord with the fellowship for the "gospel" (εὐαγγέλιον, 1:5) that they share with Paul, and in a complementary correspondence to the way that Paul's role within the Roman political system as a prisoner in bonds serves to advance the gospel, so the audience, residing as free citizens in the Roman colony of Philippi, are to "live as citizens" (πολιτεύεσθε) worthy of the

---

32. O'Brien, *Philippians*, 141: "Here καύχημα means the matter or ground of glorying, rather than the act of glorying, for which καύχησις would normally have been used. ὑμῶν is subjective, referring to the Philippians' ground of glorying.... ἐν Χριστῷ Ἰησοῦ, which goes with περισσεύῃ rather than with καύχημα, indicates the element or sphere in which the abounding is to take place and consequently characterizes it.... the Philippians would have ample cause to exult and that reason would be found in Paul himself—but it would all be in the sphere of Christ (ἐν ἐμοί is a special cause or ground within the sphere designated by ἐν Χριστῷ Ἰησοῦ).... The particular ground of true rejoicing Paul has in mind is spelled out in the final words of the sentence: διὰ τῆς ἐμῆς παρουσίας πάλιν πρὸς ὑμᾶς ('because of my coming to you again'). This concluding phrase is connected with ἐν ἐμοί as a special instance. If God is pleased to grant it, then the ground of the Philippians' rejoicing would be the apostle, not imprisoned in some distant cell, but with them again." Fee, *Philippians*, 154–55: "The Greek word καύχημα is especially difficult to render into English. Although it can lean toward 'joy,' there is no reason to think it here means other than what it ordinarily means to Paul, to 'boast' or 'glory' in someone.... 'Boast,' therefore, does not mean to 'brag about' or to 'be conceited'; rather, it has to do first with putting one's full 'trust or confidence in' something or someone and thus, second, in 'glorying' in that something or someone.... In cases such as this one, where the boast is 'in someone,' the 'boast' is still 'in Christ.' What he has done in and for Paul serves both as the ground for their 'glorying in Christ' and the sphere in which such boasting overflows. Thus this part of the clause accents the relationship he and they have with Christ."

33. O'Brien, *Philippians*, 145: "[T]he adverb [μόνον, 'only'] ... brings out the emphatic nature of the imperative statement that follows."

"gospel" (εὐαγγελίου) of the Christ.[34] Paul's imprisonment, which has been in the defense and confirmation of the "gospel" (εὐαγγελίου, 1:7, 16), has rather come to an advancement of the "gospel" (εὐαγγελίου, 1:12), since, despite and/or because of Paul's imprisonment, Christ is proclaimed (1:18). For the audience to "live as citizens worthy of the gospel of the Christ" thus implies that they are to conduct their lives as citizens, in both the Roman colony and the believing community, in a way that promotes the gospel and likewise results in Christ being proclaimed.[35]

In sum, then, in this B element (1:25–27a) of the chiasm the audience, assured by a Paul confident in God that he will survive his imprisonment, remain alive in the flesh, and come to them again, in the meantime are to live as citizens worthy of the gospel of the Christ, with the implication that, by so living, the gospel will be advanced and Christ will continue to be proclaimed in Philippi.

3. Phil 1:27b (C): Whether Coming and Seeing You

The audience then begin to hear the reason they are to live as citizens worthy of the gospel of the Christ (1:27a): "so that, whether coming and seeing you" (1:27b). The audience have just heard of Paul's hope that Christ will be magnified in his body whatever may be the alternative regarding the outcome of his impris-

---

34. On the Jewish background of "live as citizens" here, see Ernest C. Miller, "πολιτεύεσθε in Phil 1:27: Some Philological and Thematic Observations," *JSNT* 15 (1982): 86–96. Ware, *Mission*, 218: "The verb πολιτεύεσθε in its regular usage had specific political and civic connotations, and Paul will directly contrast the Philippians' earthly and heavenly πολίτευμα in 3:20. . . . Jewish writers commonly used this term to refer to citizenship in the Jewish nation . . . Paul thus employs this traditional Jewish language to describe the Philippian community as an alternative polis in contrast to that earthly Roman city in which the Philippian believers reside."

35. Ware, *Mission*, 216: "The mention of the gospel (τοῦ εὐαγγελίου) recalls not only 1:5, but the repeated references to the gospel throughout the first portion of the letter. In addition, the words τοῦ Χριστοῦ echo the references to the preaching of Christ in 1:15–18a. Moreover, the phrase τὸ εὐαγγέλιον τοῦ Χριστοῦ which Paul employs here is in Paul never used of the instruction of the Christian community, but always refers to the missionizing proclamation. The opening imperative of the letter thus accents Paul's interest in a missional purpose of the life and conduct of the community at Philippi as a means of attracting outsiders to the message of Christ." O'Brien, *Philippians*, 148: "[T]hey will walk worthily of the gospel by holding fast to it, preaching and confessing it in spite of opposition and temptation." Fee, *Philippians*, 161–62: "Paul is here making a play on their 'dual citizenship'—of the empire by virtue of their being Philippians; of heaven by virtue of their faith in Christ and incorporation into the believing community. . . . by joining it with the adverb 'worthily,' Paul now uses the verb metaphorically, not meaning 'live as citizens of Rome'—although that is not irrelevant—but rather 'live in the Roman colony of Philippi as worthy citizens of your heavenly homeland.' . . . Thus this is the fitting verb for the setting. It would be full of meaning in light of their privileged status as Roman citizens, now addressing them as to their 'civic' responsibilities in the new 'polis,' the believing community." Bockmuehl, *Philippians*, 98: "The rhetorical force of Paul's language is to play on the perceived desirability of citizenship in Roman society at Philippi, and to contrast against this the *Christian* vision of enfranchisement and belonging." See also Timothy C. Geoffrion, *The Rhetorical Purpose and the Political and Military Character of Philippians: A Call To Stand Firm* (Lewiston, NY: Mellen, 1993), 42–48; Edgar Krentz, "Military Language and Metaphors in Philippians," in *Origins and Methods: Towards a New Understanding of Judaism and Christianity: Essays in Honour of John C. Hurd* (ed. Bradley H. McLean; JSNTSup 86; Sheffield: Sheffield Academic Press, 1993), 105–27.

onment—"whether (εἴτε) through life or (εἴτε) through death" (1:20). "Whether (εἴτε) coming and seeing you (ὑμᾶς)" thus reiterates and reinforces Paul's expectation that the alternative will indeed be life rather than death and he will come again to "you" (ὑμᾶς, 1:26), because of his conviction that it is more necessary that he remain alive in the flesh on account of "you" (ὑμᾶς, 1:24). But "whether coming and seeing you" also introduces another alternative for the audience to consider.

4. Phil 1:27c (C´): Or Being Absent, I Hear the Things concerning You

The audience are then presented with the other half of the alternative to Paul's coming and seeing them: "or being absent, I hear the things concerning you" (1:27c). With these words the audience experience the central pivot of the chiasm in 1:19–30, from "whether coming (εἴτε ἐλθών)" (1:27b) in the C element to its parallel alternative, "or being absent (εἴτε ἀπών)" (1:27c), in the C´ element. Reminding the audience of the previous alternative, "or (εἴτε) through death" (1:20), "or (εἴτε) being absent" implies Paul's absence from Philippi because of the possibility of his death. But such a possibility does not appear to be imminent, as the audience hear the words, "I hear the things concerning you." The audience are to realize, then, that the possibility of Paul's "being absent", for whatever reason, will not prevent his hearing reports about them.[36]

Indeed, if Paul returns to Philippi, he expects to see "you" (1:27b), and if he is absent, he expects to hear reports of "the things concerning you (τὰ περὶ ὑμῶν)" (1:27c), thus recalling and reciprocating the knowledge Paul gave the audience of "the things regarding me" (τὰ κατ᾿ ἐμέ, 1:12),[37] which, in turn, recalls that the audience are to determine "the things (τά) that matter", especially with regard to Paul's imprisonment (1:10).

5. Phil 1:27d (B´): Struggling Together for the Faith of the Gospel

The audience are then presented with a specification of the things concerning them that Paul wants to see if he comes to them (1:27b) and to hear if he remains absent (1:27c): "that you are standing firm in one Spirit, with one mind struggling together for the faith of the gospel" (1:27d). At this point the audience hear a progression, via the chiastic parallels, from Paul's concern for their advancement and joy "in the faith" (τῆς πίστεως, 1:25), as they live as citizens worthy of "the gospel"

---

36. Holloway, *Consolation*, 116 n. 72: "Just as Paul is indifferent to the antipathy of his rivals (εἴτε προφάσει εἴτε ἀληθείᾳ; 1:18a) and to the ultimate outcome of his trial (εἴτε διὰ ζωῆς εἴτε διὰ θανάτου; 1:20), so the Philippians must accept as a matter of indifference his presence or absence (εἴτε ἐλθών . . . εἴτε ἀπών . . .)." O'Brien, *Philippians*, 149: "In the words εἴτε ἐλθών . . . εἴτε ἀπών ('whether I come . . . or be absent') the issue is not whether Paul will be liberated or remain in prison; rather, assuming his release he desires to continue his apostolic journeys and to come again to the Philippians." Bockmuehl, *Philippians*, 99: "Paul may well expect to hear about the Philippian situation when Timothy returns from his imminent mission (2.19ff.)."

37. Bittasi, *Gli esempi*, 48: "Dopo la narrazione della vicenda di Paolo (1,12: τὰ κατ᾿ ἐμέ) l'attenzione si sposta sui destinatari della lettera (1,27: τὰ περὶ ὑμῶν)."

(τοῦ εὐαγγελίου, 1:27a) in the B element (1:25–27a) to their struggling together for "the faith of the gospel" (τῇ πίστει τοῦ εὐαγγελίου) in the B´ element (1:27d) of this chiastic unit.

The audience have heard the implication that it is through their petitioning of God on behalf of Paul that Paul will receive the supply of the "Spirit" (πνεύματος) of Jesus Christ, that is, that Paul will be fully supplied with the Spirit that comes from Jesus Christ, so that Christ being proclaimed even while Paul is imprisoned will lead to Paul's salvation (1:19). And now the audience are to make sure that they themselves are standing in this same "Spirit"—"in one Spirit (πνεύματι)," the Spirit that comes from Jesus Christ and unites them not only with Paul but with one another (1:27d).[38]

Paul has expressed his confident expectation of remaining beside all of the members of the audience at Philippi for their advancement and joy in "the faith" (τῆς πίστεως, 1:25). The audience were then made to realize that their advancement and joy in the faith includes their living as citizens worthy of "the gospel" (τοῦ εὐαγγελίου) of the Christ (1:27a). And now they are made aware that their standing united in the one Holy Spirit includes their struggling together with one mind for "the faith of the gospel" (τῇ πίστει τοῦ εὐαγγελίου, 1:27d).[39] By their conduct as believers in Philippi they are thus to promote the faith whose origin and object is the gospel of Christ, mindful that it is for the defense of "the gospel" (τοῦ εὐαγγελίου, 1:7, 16) that Paul, with whom they share a fellowship for "the gospel" (τὸ εὐαγγέλιον, 1:5), is in prison. Just as Paul's conduct in prison has led to an advancement of "the gospel" (τοῦ εὐαγγελίου, 1:12), so by their standing united in one Spirit and, against all opposition, struggling together with one mind for "the faith of the gospel" (1:27d), the audience may advance in their own joy in "the faith" (1:25).[40]

---

38. Fee, *God's Empowering Presence*, 745–46: "What is missing in Paul is any hint that 'spirit' might be an anthropological *metaphor* for a *community disposition*. Although the French have a word for it (*esprit de corps* = 'spirit of the body'), the Greeks apparently did not; and it is highly questionable whether Paul is here creating such a usage. . . . and most significantly, Paul has used this identical language (ἐν ἑνὶ πνεύματι, 'in one Spirit') in a recent letter (Eph 2:18; cf. 4:4) as well as in 1 Cor 12:13 to describe the Holy Spirit, *precisely in passages where the emphasis is on believers' common experience of the one Spirit as the basis for unity*. No one would imagine in these cases that 'in one Spirit' refers to the *esprit de corps* of the community. Paul's obvious concern is that their being one in Christ is the direct result of the Spirit's presence in their individual and community life" (Fee's emphases). See also Fee, *Philippians*, 163–66, esp. 165: "Thus, just as he has (indirectly) asked for their prayers that he might be supplied afresh with the Spirit of Christ as he faces his ordeal (v. 19), so now in the midst of their ordeal he urges them to stand firm in, and thus by, that same Spirit, the one and only Spirit whom they have in common." Garland, "Philippians," 209: "This directive would complement Paul's request that he be supplied by the Spirit to face his ordeal (1:19)."

39. Note the mini-chiasm, which underlines that their unity as a community flows from their being within the realm of the one Holy Spirit: (a) you are standing (στήκετε) (b) in one Spirit (ἐν ἑνὶ πνεύματι), (b´) with one mind (μιᾷ ψυχῇ) (a´) struggling together (συναθλοῦντες). See also Fee, *Philippians*, 164 n. 36; Silva, *Philippians*, 82.

40. James George Samra, *Being Conformed to Christ in Community: A Study of Maturity, Maturation and the Local Church in the Undisputed Pauline Epistles* (LNTS 320; London: Clark, 2006), 154–55:

6. Phil 1:28–30 (A´): A Demonstration of Your Salvation, Having the Same Struggle

The audience's standing in one Spirit, struggling together for the faith of the gospel (1:27d) is then further elaborated: "and not being intimidated in anything by the opponents, which is for them a demonstration of destruction, but of your salvation, and this is from God" (1:28). At this point the audience hear a progression, via the chiastic parallels, from a focus on Paul's "salvation" to a focus on the "salvation" of the audience—from "I know that this for me will lead to salvation (σωτηρίαν) . . . that in nothing (ἐν οὐδενί) I will be put to shame" (1:19–20) in the A element (1:19–24) to "not being intimidated in anything (ἐν μηδενί)," which is a demonstration of "your salvation (σωτηρίας)" (1:28) in the A´ element (1:28–30) of this chiastic unit.

Paul's confident hope that "in nothing" (ἐν οὐδενί) he will be put to shame (by God, divine passive) (1:20) lends weight and force to his directive for the audience not to be intimidated "in anything" (ἐν μηδενί) by their opponents at Philippi (1:28).[41] Just as Christ being proclaimed in the gospel while Paul is imprisoned (1:18) will lead to his "salvation" (σωτηρίαν) (1:19), so the audience are assured that their not being intimidated by opponents,[42] as they struggle together for the

---

"To 'stand firm' (στήκω) implies opposition. . . . Συναθλέω means 'to strive together with'. Paul is saying that through mutual support and encouragement—being unified in one Spirit and contending as one person—the church at Philippi can strive together so that they might endure this opposition. . . . Therefore whether Paul is absent or present (1.27), the believers in Philippi will become more like Christ (i.e. act worthy of the gospel of Christ) because the believers are enabling one another to endure suffering." O'Brien, *Philippians*, 152: "The Philippians are to stand united in their struggle for the cause of the faith—its spread and growth, the same goal that was set before all of Paul's work." Fee, *Philippians*, 167: "Thus it turns out that their own 'progress and joy in the faith' (mutual love and unity) is directly related to their contending side by side 'for the faith of the gospel' in the face of current opposition in Philippi." Fowl, *Philippians*, 64: "'[S]truggling together for the faith of the gospel' indicates that faith refers both to the reason for the Philippians' common struggle and to the end toward which that struggle is directed." On the military language and metaphors in 1:27–30, see Krentz, "Military Language and Metaphors in Philippians".

41. Ware, *Mission*, 217–18: "The opponents at Philippi are not identified, but their ability to bring adversity upon the young community strongly suggests that they included, or were in a position to influence, the pagan populace of the city. . . . the threat of persecution from the wider civic community at Philippi, and its importance for Paul's hortatory aims in the letter, is increasingly recognized in current research." In this regard, see Craig Steven de Vos, *Church and Community Conflicts: The Relationships of the Thessalonian, Corinthian, and Philippian Churches with Their Wider Civic Communities* (SBLDS 168; Atlanta: Scholars Press, 1999), 263–86; Mikael Tellbe, *Paul Between Synagogue and State: Christians, Jews, and Civic Authorities in 1 Thessalonians, Romans, and Philippians* (ConBNT 34; Stockholm: Almqvist & Wiksell, 2001), 210–78; Peter Oakes, "God's Sovereignty Over Roman Authorities: A Theme in Philippians," in *Rome in the Bible and the Early Church* (ed. Peter Oakes; Carlisle: Paternoster, 2002), 126–41; idem, "Re-Mapping the Universe: Paul and the Emperor in 1 Thessalonians and Philippians," *JSNT* 27 (2005): 301–22.

42. Ware, *Mission*, 219–20: "The command to be unafraid clearly has not a psychological but a social force—the Philippians are to exhibit their courage in the face of the opponents' threats. How are the Philippians to do so? This is clear from the studied focus on courage and fearlessness in the paradigms which Paul has already provided in 1:12–26. In Philippians 1:14 Paul describes the daring

faith of the gospel (1:27d), will be for these opponents a demonstration, on the one hand, of destruction but, on the other hand, of "your salvation (σωτηρίας)."[43] And all of this is from God (1:28).[44] That the audience have already been greeted with a wish for them of the grace and peace that comes "from God" (ἀπὸ θεοῦ) our Father (1:2) fortifies this assurance of their salvation with a divine foundation—it comes "from God" (ἀπὸ θεοῦ, 1:28).[45]

The audience are then presented with further explanation of the manner of their salvation that comes from God (1:28): "for to you has been granted that which is on behalf of Christ, not only in him to believe but also on behalf of him to suffer, having the same struggle, such as you saw in me and now hear in me" (1:29-30). At this point the audience hear a progression, via the chiastic parallels, from the use of the present active participle "having" in reference to Paul to the use of the same present active participle in reference to the audience, from Paul "having (ἔχων) the desire for release and to be with Christ" (1:23) in the A element (1:19-24) to the audience "having (ἔχοντες) the same struggle" (1:30) as Paul in the A´ element (1:28-30) of this chiastic unit.[46]

---

fearlessness of the Roman Christians *to speak the word of God.* In Philippians 1:19-20 Paul accented his unashamed *bold speech* in behalf of the gospel, and through allusion to LXX Job 13:16 emphasized his bold testimony to the gospel in defiance of Roman power. Thus clearly in Philippians 1:28, Paul's practical application to the Philippians of the paradigms set forth in 1:12-26, the Philippians, following the example of Paul and of the Christians at Rome, are to display their own fearlessness through their bold confession and proclamation of the gospel in the Roman colony at Philippi. Paul envisions the mission of the Philippians through conduct and suffering (1:27) as complemented by an active mission of verbal proclamation (1:28)" (Ware's emphases).

43. Garland, "Philippians," 210: "The unity of the church and their refusal to cower in the face of persecution become the proof of their own salvation and the perdition in store for their enemies. . . . Destruction is the necessary opposite of salvation, if salvation is to have any meaning, and refers to the result of judgment on the day of Christ." Ware, *Mission,* 220: "Paul's reference to the Philippians' salvation recalls the delineation of his own paradigm in 1:19-20, in which Paul's bold speech in behalf of the gospel results in his salvation. Paul's wording also recalls the persecuted righteous figure of Wisdom 2:12-5:13 . . . whose persecution and death (Wis 2:12-20) result in the *destruction* of his persecutors (ἀπωλείας, 5:7) but his *salvation* (σωτηρίας, 5:2). Paul's exhortation in 1:27-28, as his own example in 1:19-20, thus involves an implicit warning to the Philippians: the way to salvation involves suffering and affliction on behalf of the gospel message." O'Brien, *Philippians,* 155: "The point is not that the adversaries themselves see this . . . but that it seals their doom as the enemies of the gospel and confirms the eternal salvation of the faithful who endure to the end. . . . the undauntedness of the believers in the context of persecution is a sign of perdition and salvation whether the persecutors recognize it or not. The apostle is stating the facts of the case—not the possible psychological effects on the opponents of the Philippian Christians." For an interpretation that to the opponents it is a sign of the destruction of the Phlilippians, see Fowl, *Philippians,* 67-68.

44. O'Brien, *Philippians,* 157: "The antecedent τοῦτο is neuter and refers back to the whole episode of opposition in its double effect, leading the opponents to destruction and the believers to eternal salvation."

45. That these are the only two occurrences in the letter of the prepositional phrase "from God" (ἀπὸ θεοῦ) enhances this connection.

46. The only time the audience have heard the verb "have" (ἔχειν) previously in the letter was in 1:7, but as an infinitive rather than as a present participle.

Recalling the prayer-wish of "grace to you" (χάρις ὑμῖν) from God (1:2) and that "all of you (ὑμᾶς)" are Paul's fellow sharers of "the grace (χάριτος)" (1:7), "for *to you* (ὑμῖν, in emphatic position) has been granted (ἐχαρίσθη)" as a grace by God (divine passive) "that which is on behalf of Christ" (1:29a) not only reinforces that "your (ὑμῶν) salvation," the salvation of the audience, is a grace or gift from God (1:28), but introduces what God has granted to the audience as a gift to do on behalf of Christ.[47] God has granted the audience, who are to "live as citizens worthy of the gospel of the Christ (Χριστοῦ)" (1:27), what is on behalf of Christ (Χριστοῦ), namely, "not only in him to believe but also on behalf of him to suffer" (1:29b).

The audience are to realize that their advancement and joy in the "faith" (πίστεως, 1:25), that is, the faith with which God has granted them as a grace "to believe" (πιστεύειν) in Christ (1:29), includes not only their struggling together with one another and with Paul for the "faith" (πίστει) of the gospel (1:27), but also includes the grace God has granted them "to suffer" (πάσχειν) on behalf of Christ (1:29).[48] The pointed alliteration, assonance, and repetition that reverberates in the ears of the audience as they hear the progression that commences with "that which is on behalf (τὸ ὑπέρ) of Christ," continues with "in him to believe" (τὸ εἰς αὐτὸν πιστεύειν), and reaches a climactic, emphatic conclusion with "on behalf of him to suffer" (τὸ ὑπὲρ αὐτοῦ πάσχειν).[49] This artful sequence reinforces the close interrelationship between the audience's "believing" (πιστεύειν) in Christ and their "suffering" (πάσχειν) on behalf of Christ.

That the audience are "having" (ἔχοντες) the same struggle as Paul (1:30a) recalls Paul's own suffering on behalf of Christ in his imprisonment, which includes his "having" (ἔχων) the desire for release and to be with Christ (1:23). And that the audience are having the same "struggle" (ἀγῶνα) as Paul reinforces their solidarity with Paul in "struggling together" (συναθλοῦντες), not only with Paul but with one another, for the faith of the gospel (1:27). That the audience are having the same struggle that "you saw" (εἴδετε) in Paul when he was with them in Philippi (cf. Acts 16:19–40) and that now "you hear" (ἀκούετε) in Paul during his imprisonment (1:30b) establishes the basis for the reciprocality of Paul "seeing" (ἰδών) the audience if he comes again to Philippi or "hearing" (ἀκούω) the things concerning them if he remains absent from them (1:27). And that the audience have the same struggle that they saw "in me" (ἐν ἐμοί) and now hear "in me" (ἐν

---

47. O'Brien, *Philippians*, 159: "[T]the passive voice is again used to signify that the gracious activity was God's. . . . while the emphatically placed ὑμῖν corresponds with the previous ὑμῶν."

48. Ware, *Mission*, 221: "Not only the faith of Paul's converts, but also their sharing in Paul's ἀγών of suffering for the extension of the gospel is, Paul emphasizes, the result of the grace of God given to them."

49. O'Brien, *Philippians*, 159–60: "[T]he πάσχειν, which has been prepared for by τὸ ὑπὲρ Χριστοῦ, is finally introduced and especially emphasized: . . . but also for him—*to suffer*. . . . The present tense of πάσχειν suggests that their suffering for Christ was continuous, even up to the time of writing" (O'Brien's emphasis).

ἐμοί), Paul (1:30),[50] reinforces how their boast may abound in Christ Jesus "in me" (ἐν ἐμοί) through Paul's coming again to them in Philippi (1:26).[51]

In sum, in this A´ element (1:28–30) the audience are not to be intimidated "in anything" by their opponents at Philippi, just as Paul will be shamed "in nothing" because of his imprisonment (1:20). This will be a demonstration of their "salvation" from God, just as Paul hopes that Christ being preached while he is imprisoned will lead to his "salvation" (1:18–19). God granted the audience the grace not only to believe in Christ but to suffer on behalf of Christ, as they are "having" the same struggle at Philippi that they saw Paul was involved in there and that they now hear that Paul is experiencing in his imprisonment at Rome, which includes Paul's "having" the desire for release and to be with Christ (1:23)—the ultimate goal for Paul as well as for the audience.

B. SUMMARY ON PHILIPPIANS 1:19–30

1. The audience are to be further encouraged to contribute to the future joy of Paul (1:18) by continuing their own proclamation of Christ, having been brought to the realization of how their partnership for the gospel is mutually beneficial for Paul and for themselves. Their petition to God is beneficial for Paul's salvation (1:19) and that Paul remain alive in the flesh so that Christ is magnified in his body is necessary for them (1:20–24).

2. The audience, assured by a Paul confident in God that he will survive his imprisonment, remain alive in the flesh, and come to them again, in the meantime are to live as citizens worthy of the gospel of the Christ, with the implication that, by so living, the gospel will be advanced and Christ will continue to be proclaimed in Philippi (1:25–27a).

3. If Paul returns to Philippi, he expects to see "you" (1:27b), and if he is absent, he expects to hear reports of "the things concerning you" (1:27c), thus recalling and reciprocating the knowledge Paul gave the audience of "the things regarding me" (1:12), which, in turn, recalls that the audience are to determine "the things that matter," especially with regard to Paul's imprisonment (1:10).

---

50. Fee, *Philippians*, 173 n. 68: "Paul's Greek is a bit more emphatic: οἷον εἴδετε ἐν ἐμοί = 'of a kind that you saw *in me*.' This does not mean simply 'which you saw I experienced,' but 'which you saw taking place in my life and experience among you.'"

51. O'Brien, *Philippians*, 162: "Although they face special trials, the apostle asserts, in an emphatic way, that they 'share the *same* conflict' (τόν αὐτὸν ἀγῶνα ἔχοντες). Their 'fellowship in the gospel' (1:5), that is, their active participation in the spread of the gospel from the time of their conversion until the present, meant that they were involved in the same conflict as Paul. The latter's entire apostolic mission is understood as *one* ἀγών (not several ἀγῶνες) for the gospel. This is because Paul regards his experience during that first visit to Philippi and his present imprisonment with its trials as aspects of one and the same conflict. These two sets of circumstances, separated in time and by distance, are part of the one apostolic ἀγών for the gospel." Fee, *Philippians*, 172: "The accent falls on 'the same,' which minimally points to their common suffering on Christ's behalf brought on by those who oppose the gospel. Very likely . . . 'the same' reflects the common source as well, the Roman Empire."

4. Just as Paul's conduct in prison has led to an advancement of "the gospel" (1:12), so by their standing united in one Spirit and, against all opposition, struggling together with one mind for "the faith of the gospel" (1:27d), the audience may advance in their own joy in "the faith" (1:25).

5. The audience are not to be intimidated "in anything" by their opponents at Philippi, just as Paul will be shamed "in nothing" because of his imprisonment (1:20). This will be a demonstration of their "salvation" from God, just as Paul hopes that Christ being preached while he is imprisoned will lead to his "salvation" (1:18–19). God granted the audience the grace not only to believe in Christ but to suffer on behalf of Christ, as they are "having" the same struggle at Philippi that they saw Paul was involved in there and that they now hear that Paul is experiencing in his imprisonment at Rome, which includes Paul's "having" the desire for release and to be with Christ (1:23)—the ultimate goal for Paul as well as for the audience (1:28–30).

7

PHILIPPIANS 2:1–16: JOY IN HUMILITY FOR THE DAY OF CHRIST WHO HUMBLED HIMSELF TO THE POINT OF DEATH (E)

Be Conformed to Christ Who Was Obedient Even to Death on a Cross

A: [2:1] If then there is any encouragement in Christ, if there is any consolation of *love*, if there is any fellowship of Spirit, if there is any affection and compassion, [2] fill up my joy and think the same thing, having the same *love*, united in mind, thinking the one thing, [3] nothing according to self–seeking nor according to *vainglory*, but in humility considering one another more important than *yourselves*, [4] each of you looking out not for the things of *yourselves*, but everyone also for the things of others. [5] This go on thinking in you, which is also in Christ Jesus,

    B: [6] who, *existing* in the form *of God*, not something to be exploited did he *consider* being equal to God, [7] but emptied himself, taking the form of a slave, becoming in the *likeness* of human beings, and in outward appearance found to be as a human being,

        C: [8a] he humbled himself, becoming obedient to the point of *death*,

        C′: [8b] even of *death* on a cross.

    B′: [9] therefore indeed God *exalted* him and *granted* him the name that is above every name, [10] so that at the *name* of Jesus every knee should bend, of those in heaven and of those on earth and of those under the earth, [11] and every tongue confess that Jesus Christ is Lord to the glory *of God* the Father.[1]

---

1. For a selection of some of the more recent works from the extensive scholarly treatment of Phil 2:5–11, see R. A. Wortham, "Christology as Community Identity in the Philippians Hymn: The Philippians Hymn as Social Drama (Philippians 2:5–11)," *PRSt* 23 (1996): 269–87; Claudio Basevi, "Estudio literario y teológico del himno cristológico de la epístola a los Filipenses (Phil 2,6–11)," *ScrTh* 30 (1998): 439–72; James D. G. Dunn, "Christ, Adam, and Preexistence," in *Where Christology Began: Essays on Philippians 2* (ed. Ralph P. Martin and Brian J. Dodd; Louisville: Westminster John Knox, 1998), 74–83; Lincoln D. Hurst, "Christ, Adam, and Preexistence Revisited," in *Where Christology Began: Essays on Philippians 2* (ed. Ralph P. Martin and Brian J. Dodd; Louisville: Westminster John Knox, 1998), 84–95; Stephen E. Fowl, "Christology and Ethics in Philippians 2:5–11," in *Where Christology Began: Essays on Philippians 2* (ed. Ralph P. Martin and Brian J. Dodd; Louisville: Westminster John Knox, 1998), 140–53; Samuel Vollenweider, "Der 'Raub' der Gottgleichheit: Ein Religionsgeschich-

A′: [12]So that, my *beloved*, just as you have always obeyed, not as in my presence only, but now much more in my absence, with reverence and awe continue to work out *your own* salvation. [13]For God is the one working in you both to desire and to work for the sake of his good pleasure. [14]Do everything without grumbling or questioning, [15]so that you may become blameless and innocent, children of God without blemish in the midst of a crooked and perverse generation, among whom you shine as lights in the world, [16]holding forth the word of life, so that my boast for the day of Christ—that I did not run in vain or labor in vain.[2]

A. AUDIENCE RESPONSE TO PHILIPPIANS 2:1–16

1. Phil 2:1–5 (A): Have the Same Love, Looking Out Not for Your Own Things

Having heard that they were granted the grace not only to believe in Christ but to suffer on behalf of Christ, as they have the same struggle that they saw and now hear taking place in Paul (1:29–30), the audience are presented with a stirring, passionate appeal from Paul: "If then there is any encouragement in Christ, if there is any consolation of love, if there is any fellowship of Spirit, if there is any affection and compassion, fill up my joy and think the same thing, having the same love, like minded, thinking the one thing" (2:1–2).

When the audience hear the word "Christ" (Χριστῷ) in the reference to "encouragement in Christ" (2:1a), they hear the transitional word that links this chiastic unit (2:1–16) with the previous one (1:19–30), whose conclusion contains the phrase "on behalf of Christ (Χριστοῦ)" (1:29). The audience have been led to deduce that indeed there is encouragement for both Paul and themselves "in Christ" (ἐν Χριστῷ), that is, in their being united with Christ within the realm or domain established by the Christ event. The audience recall that the "bonds" of Paul's imprisonment have become "in Christ" (ἐν Χριστῷ) manifest in the whole praetorium and to all the rest (1:13), resulting in an advancement of the gospel (1:12). And the audience, addressed as the holy ones "in Christ Jesus" (ἐν Χριστῷ Ἰησοῦ) who are in Philippi (1:1), also recall that their "boast" may abound "in Christ Jesus" (ἐν Χριστῷ Ἰησοῦ) when Paul comes to them again (1:26) for their

---

tlicher Vorschlag zu Phil 2.6(–11)," *NTS* 45 (1999): 413–33; N. Capizzi, "*Fil* 2,6–11: una sintesi della cristologia?," *RdT* 40 (1999): 353–68; idem, "Soteriologia in Fil 2:6–11?" *Greg* 81 (2000): 221–48; Adela Yarbro Collins, "Psalms, Philippians 2:6–11, and the Origins of Christology," *BibInt* 11 (2003): 361–72; Rainer Schwindt, "Zur Tradition und Theologie des Philipperhymnus," *Studien Zum Neuen Testament und Seiner Umwelt* 31 (2006): 1–60; Joseph A. Marchal, *Hierarchy, Unity, and Imitation: A Feminist Rhetorical Analysis of Power Dynamics in Paul's Letter to the Philippians* (SBLAbib 24; Atlanta: Society of Biblical Literature, 2006), 133–35; idem, "Expecting a Hymn, Encountering an Argument: Introducing the Rhetoric of Philippians and Pauline Interpretation," *Int* 61 (2007): 245–55; Park, *Submission*, 10–37; Michael Peppard, "'Poetry', 'Hymns' and 'Traditional Material' in New Testament Epistles or How to Do Things with Indentations," *JSNT* 30 (2008): 319–42.

2. For the establishment of Phil 2:1–16 as a chiasm, see ch. 2.

advancement and joy in the faith (1:25). These are reasons for the encouragement of both Paul and the audience "in Christ" (2:1a).

The conditional clause, "if there is any (εἴ τις) encouragement (παράκλησις)" in Christ (2:1a), is followed by an alliterative echo—"if there is any (εἴ τι) consolation (παραμύθιον) of love" (2:1b). In addition to their alliteration, there is a close conceptual relationship between the near synonyms, "encouragement" (παράκλησις) and "consolation" (παραμύθιον). The audience have heard that there is indeed a "consolation of love (ἀγάπης)" for Paul, since some have preached the Christ "out of love (ἀγάπης, 1:16)," knowing that Paul was imprisoned for the defense of the gospel (1:15–16). And Paul has affirmed the "love" (ἀγάπη) of the audience, while praying that such love may even more and more abound (1:9). The audience know, then, that there is a most definite "consolation of love" for both Paul and themselves.

The chain of identically introduced conditional clauses continues with "if there is any (εἴ τις) fellowship of Spirit" (2:1c). The alliteration likewise continues with the progression of words introduced by "p," from παράκλησις (encouragement) to παραμύθιον (consolation) to πνεύματος (Spirit). That there is a "fellowship" (κοινωνία) of Spirit uniting Paul and the audience recalls Paul's joy "at your fellowship (κοινωνία) for the gospel from the first day until now" (1:5). This fellowship for the gospel is also a fellowship of the "Spirit" (πνεύματος) shared by Paul and the audience. This follows from Paul's implied dependence upon the audience's petition to God that Paul be supplied with the "Spirit" (πνεύματος) of Jesus Christ (1:19). And it is in the Spirit of Jesus Christ—"the one Spirit (πνεύματι)"—that the audience are to be standing firm at Philippi, struggling together with one another and with Paul for the faith of the gospel (1:27).[3]

For the fourth time the audience hear the introduction to a conditional clause, "if there is any" (εἴ τις), this time followed by the terms "affection and compassion" (2:1d). The first syllable of the first term, "affection" (σπλάγχνα), of this closely related pair continues the chain of "p" sounds linking together this passionate quadruplet of conditional clauses (2:1). That there is certainly "affection and compassion" between Paul and his audience follows from the audience's having heard how Paul not only has them in his heart (1:7), but longs for all of them with the explicit "affection" (σπλάγχνοις) of Christ Jesus (1:8). Because of the close "fellowship" for the gospel of Christ Jesus that unites the audience to Paul (1:5, 7), there is

---

3. Fee, *God's Empowering Presence*, 750: "'[F]ellowship of the Spirit' . . . refers to the sharing 'in the Spirit' that believers have first with God through the Spirit and then with one another because they live and breathe by the same Spirit. They not only live and breathe by means of the Spirit whom God has given them, but they are also thereby united to Christ and to one another in Christ. The Spirit is the empowering agent of all that God is currently doing among them . . . The experienced reality that has brought them together into Christ and has given them this mutual love in Christ is their common participation in the life of the Spirit."

a strong implication, indeed a passionate plea, for the audience's reciprocal "affection and compassion" for Paul, their imprisoned partner.[4]

Paul draws upon this implied "affection and compassion" of the audience, urging them to actualize it, in his appeal for them to "fulfill my joy" (2:2a). The close relation between this appeal and the four previous conditional clauses (2:1) is enhanced by the chain of alliterative "p" sounds linking these conditional clauses (παράκλησις –παραμύθιον –πνεύματος), climaxed by the alliterative progression from the "pl" sound in the first syllable of "affection" (σπλάγχνα) to that in the appeal for the audience to "fulfill" (πληρώσατέ) Paul's joy.[5] The audience, who have been "filled up" (πεπληρωμένοι) by God (divine passive) with the fruit of righteousness that is through Jesus Christ for the glory and praise of God (1:11), are now themselves to "fulfill" *my* (μου in emphatic position) joy.[6] In other words, out of reciprocation for the "affection" (σπλάγχνοις, 1:8) that Paul, their partner in fellowship for the gospel, has for them, the audience are to demonstrate their "affection and compassion" for Paul in his present situation of imprisonment by fulfilling or making complete his joy.[7]

Paul has already made known to the audience that he makes every petition to God on behalf of all of them with "joy" (χαρᾶς, 1:4) at the fellowship they share for the gospel (1:5). Furthermore, Paul has emphatically expressed his joy that, no matter what the motivation, Christ is being proclaimed even while Paul is in the bonds of imprisonment—"in this I rejoice (χαίρω). And indeed I will be joyful (χαρήσομαι)" (1:18b). Thus, just as Paul's presence with the audience when he returns to Philippi will result in their advancement and "joy" (χαράν) in the faith (1:25), so now the audience are to fulfill the "joy" (χαράν) of Paul, their partner (2:2a). But how are they to do this?

How the audience can fulfill Paul's joy is explained by an epexegetical ἵνα (here translated as "and") clause in the form of the following mini-chiasm: (a) *think* (φρονῆτε) *the* (τό) same thing,[8] (b) having the same love, (a´) united in mind, *thinking* (φρονοῦντες) *the* (τό) one thing.[9]

---

4. Silva, *Philippians*, 88: "[V]erse 1 is not intended to function as a set of four rational, theological arguments but rather as impassioned pleading."

5. O'Brien, *Philippians*, 176: "Because πληρώσατε is the only main verb in the paragraph, it appears to spell out the content of Paul's appeal and provide the climax to which the fourfold basis of v. 1 is moving."

6. On the possessive pronoun "my" (μου) as emphatic here, see Fee, *Philippians*, 184 n. 52.

7. Fee, *Philippians*, 177: "The 'if' clauses turn out not to express supposition, but presupposition, and should therefore be translated something closer to 'since there is . . .'; and the apodosis, instead of expressing the 'then' side of a supposition, takes the form of an imperative based on the presuppositions."

8. On the verb "think" (φρονέω), Fee (*Philippians*, 184–85) explains: "[T]he word does not mean 'to think' in the sense of 'cogitate'; rather it carries the nuance of 'setting one's mind on,' thus having a certain disposition toward something (e.g., life, values, people) or a certain way of looking at things, thus 'mind-set.'"

9. On this threefold structural arrangement, see also Fee, *Philippians*, 183 n. 47.

After the unparalleled central and pivotal "b" sub-element, "having the same love" (2:2c), the audience hear a chiastic parallel progression from the imperative "think" (φρονῆτε), with its object, "the same thing," introduced by the neuter definite article "the" (τό), in the "a" sub-element (2:2b), to the participle "thinking" (φρονοῦντες), with its object, "the one thing," also introduced by the neuter definite article "the" (τό) in the "a′" sub-element (2:2d).

For the audience to "think" (φρονῆτε) the same thing (2:2b) means for them not only to be united among themselves in thinking the same thing, but to be united with Paul, their partner, in thinking the same thing that Paul thinks about them. The audience have heard that it is right for Paul to "think" (φρονεῖν) "this" on behalf of all of them (1:7), namely, that the God who began the good work in them by making them sharers with Paul in the fellowship for the gospel will perfect it until the day of Christ Jesus (1:5–6). The audience are thus to think this same thing, both among themselves and together with Paul, namely, that the goal of their fellowship for the gospel is still to be divinely perfected.

The audience then hear the progression from the imperative to think "the same thing" (τὸ αὐτό, 2:2b) to the participle that begins to elaborate upon and develop the imperative—having "the same" (τὴν αὐτήν) love (2:2c). That the audience are to have the same "love" (ἀγάπην) means for them to have the same love for one another that Paul has for all of them, recalling the consolation of "love" (ἀγάπης) that there is with Paul and among them (2:1b), the "love" (ἀγάπη) that Paul prays may even more and more abound (1:9). But it also means that they are to have "the same love" for Paul as those who, out of "love" (ἀγάπης, 1:16), preach the Christ, knowing that it is for the defense of the gospel that Paul is imprisoned (1:15–16). The audience, then, are to "think (φρονῆτε) the (τό) same thing" (2:2b) by being "united in mind" (σύμψυχοι),[10] "thinking (φρονοῦντες) the (τό) one thing" (2:2d), which includes their "having the same love" (2:2c) for one another and for Paul, as partners in fellowship for the gospel of Christ.[11]

How, more specifically with regard to their behavior as a united community, the audience can fulfill and bring to completion Paul's joy by the way that they think among themselves (2:2) Paul continues to elaborate for them: "nothing according to self-seeking nor according to vainglory, but in humility considering one another more important than yourselves, each of you looking out not for the things of yourselves, but everyone also for the things of others. This think in you, which is also in Christ Jesus" (2:3–5).

In contrast to those who, on account of envy of and rivalry with the imprisoned Paul (1:15), proclaim the Christ out of "self-seeking" (ἐριθείας, 1:17), the audience are to think of doing nothing according to "self-seeking" (ἐριθείαν, 2:3a).

---

10. Fee, *Philippians*, 185 n. 60: "Gk. σύμψυχοι, formed from σύν (together with) and ψυχή (soul), picking up and by means of the compound reinforcing the μιᾷ ψυχῇ of v. 27. The word here means something close to 'harmonious' or 'together as one person.'"

11. O'Brien, *Philippians*, 177: "So the means by which Paul's joy is to be made full is by the readers being like-minded, having the same love, being united in spirit and intent on one purpose."

That they are to think of doing "nothing according to self-seeking" (μηδὲν κατ' ἐριθείαν) is immediately underlined and elaborated by a nearly synonymous alliterative and assonant follow-up—"nor according to vainglory (literally, 'empty glory')" (μηδὲ κατὰ κενοδοξίαν, 2:3b).[12] Rather, in "humility" or "lowliness of mind" (ταπεινοφροσύνη), recalling and developing, with the aid of an alliterative and assonant link of "phro" (φρο) sounds, the directive for them to "think" (φρονῆτε) the same thing, which includes "thinking" (φρονοῦντες) the one thing and having the same love (2:2), the audience are to consider one another as more important than themselves (2:3c).[13]

Continuing the series of negative expressions beginning with "nothing (μηδέν) according to self-seeking" (2:3a) and "nor (μηδέ) according to vainglory" (2:3b), "not (μή) for the things of yourselves (ἑαυτῶν)" (2:4a) begins to further explain what it means for the audience to consider one another more important than "yourselves" (ἑαυτῶν, 2:3c).[14] With a noteworthy occurrence of the singular of the indefinite adjective "each one" (ἕκαστος), sandwiched between the plural expressions—"your own (ἑαυτῶν, plural reflexive pronoun) things" and "looking out for" (σκοποῦντες, plural participle), Paul more directly addresses each and every individual member of his Philippian audience. *Each one* of them is "not to be looking out for the things of yourselves" (2:4a).[15]

The contrastive "but (ἀλλά) in humility considering one another more important than yourselves" (2:3c) is developed by a parallel contrastive—"but (ἀλλά) everyone also for the things of others" (2:4b). Through these contrasts the audience hear a progression in the focus of their thinking from a consideration of themselves to a consideration of others, that is, from considering one another more important than "yourselves" (ἑαυτῶν, 2:3c) and not looking out for "the things of yourselves" (τὰ ἑαυτῶν, 2:4a) to looking out also for "the things of others" (τὰ ἑαυτῶν, 2:4b).[16] And this new focus in their way of thinking is reinforced by a pointed progression from "each one" (ἕκαστος, singular indefinite adjective) of them, as an individual member of the community, not looking out for "the things of yourselves" (2:4a) to "everyone" (ἕκαστοι, plural indefinite adjective) of them, that is, "each and all" of

12. O'Brien, *Philippians*, 180: "κενοδοξία probably means more than 'vanity' and signifies 'vain, empty glory.'"

13. On the alliteration and assonance here, see O'Brien, *Philippians*, 181; Fee, *Philippians*, 187 n. 73: "Gk. ταπεινοφροσύνη, a compound word from 'lowly' and 'mind' (from the verb φρονεῖν in v. 2)."

14. Fee, *Philippians*, 189: "[I]t is not so much that others in the community are to be thought of as 'better than I am,' but as those whose needs and concerns 'surpass' my own."

15. O'Brien, *Philippians*, 185: "[T]he presence of ἕκαστος ('each one') indicates that every believer at Philippi was to take the injunction to heart."

16. O'Brien, *Philippians*, 185: "Paul does not prohibit any interest in one's own affairs. It is the selfish preoccupation with them that he condemns."

them, as a group of individuals united together within the community, looking out also for "the things of others" (2:4b).[17]

With an emphatic "this" (τοῦτο), referring not only to "the same thing" (τὸ αὐτό) they are to "think" (φρονῆτε) (2:2b), further elaborated as "the one thing" (τὸ ἓν) they are to be "thinking" (φρονοῦντες) (2:2d), Paul continues his directives to his audience regarding the new focus to their way of thinking: "*This* go on thinking (φρονεῖτε) in you" (2:5a).[18] But "this," "same," "one thing" that they are to go on thinking among themselves, that is, "in you" (ἐν ὑμῖν), is that "which" (ὁ) is also "in Christ Jesus" (ἐν Χριστῷ Ἰησοῦ) (2:5b). That the audience are to go on thinking "in" themselves that which is also "in" Christ Jesus means that they are to have the same attitude of humble concern for others (2:3-4) that was (and still is) in the person of Christ Jesus. But, at the same time, it also means that they are to have an attitude of humble concern for others that is appropriate for themselves as those who are presently within the realm or domain of being in union with Christ Jesus—those who are the holy ones "in Christ Jesus" (ἐν Χριστῷ Ἰησοῦ) at Philippi (1:1), and those whose "boast" in Paul may abound "in Christ Jesus" (ἐν Χριστῷ Ἰησοῦ) when Paul comes again to them (1:26).[19]

The encouragement that is available for Paul and his audience as those who are "in Christ" (ἐν Χριστῷ) introduced the motivation of love (2:1) from which the audience are to fulfill Paul's joy by their way of thinking with a humble consideration of others (2:2-4). The audience, as those who are "in Christ Jesus" (1:1, 26), are now poised to hear what this way of thinking, which was and is also "in Christ Jesus" (ἐν Χριστῷ Ἰησοῦ), more specifically entails for them (2:5).

In sum, then, in the A element (2:1-5) of this chiastic unit (2:1-16), the audience are directed, out of a motivation of their compassionate love, to fulfill Paul's joy by adopting among themselves an attitude of humble consideration for others

---

17. On the structure of 2:1-4, see David Alan Black, "Paul and Christian Unity: A Formal Analysis of Philippians 2:1-4," *JETS* 28 (1985): 299-308. O'Brien, *Philippians*, 185: "The ἕκαστοι is unusual; normally in the NT the singular is used in this distributive appositional sense. . . . it is best to take it here as one of emphasis, perhaps even as denoting an earnest repetition, giving the meaning 'each and all.'" See also Fee, *Philippians*, 190 n. 86.

18. Fee, *Philippians*, 199-200: "He begins with an emphatic 'this,' which is best understood as pointing backward, in this case to vv. 2-4. . . . Thus the basic imperative sums up the whole of vv. 2-4: 'This mind-set (i.e., that which I have just described) have among yourselves.'"

19. Bockmuehl, *Philippians*, 123-24: "Grammatically, therefore, the simplest reading is to supply the *present* tense of 'to be': 'have this attitude amongst yourselves, which *is* also in Christ Jesus.' . . . this reading has the advantage that the indicated attitudes of the mind of Christ are seen to be not just a past fact of history but a *present reality*. . . . In some sense, therefore, the 'mind-set' of unselfish compassion which Paul encourages in the Philippians 'is present' in Christ Jesus both historically and eternally." Thurston, *Philippians*, 80: "The Philippians are either to imitate Christ or to be what they already are in him (or both!)." Michael J. Gorman, *Apostle of the Crucified Lord: A Theological Introduction to Paul and His Letters* (Grand Rapids: Eerdmans, 2004), 433: "Paul wants to draw a parallel between the attitude and behavior he expects of the Philippians who live in Christ and the attitude and behavior he finds in Christ himself." See also Richard A. Burridge, *Imitating Jesus: An Inclusive Approach to New Testament Ethics* (Grand Rapids: Eerdmans, 2007), 146.

as more important than themselves (2:1–4), an attitude that was also in the person of Christ Jesus (2:5), and that is most appropriate for them as those who are holy ones within the domain of being "in Christ Jesus" (1:1, 26).

2. Phil 2:6–7 (B): In the Form of God Becoming in the Likeness of Human Beings

The audience then hear more specifically described the way of thinking that was in the person of Christ Jesus and that they are to adopt as those who are united together in and with Christ Jesus (2:5): "who, existing in the form of God, not something to be exploited did he consider being equal to God, but emptied himself, taking the form of a slave, becoming in the likeness of human beings, and in outward appearance found to be as a human being" (2:6–7).

The audience were directed to adopt the mind-set of "considering (ἡγούμενοι) one another more important than yourselves (ἑαυτῶν), each of you looking out not for the things of yourselves (ἑαυτῶν), but everyone also for the things of others" (2:3–4). Christ Jesus is the motivation and model for this mind-set. In his pre–incarnational situation Christ was existing in the "form" (μορφῇ) of God, that is, in the state or mode of existence in which he was identified with or character-ized as God (2:6a).[20] But not "something to be exploited or grasped" (ἁρπαγμόν) for the benefit or advantage of himself did he "consider" (ἡγήσατο) his being equal to God (2:6b), as part of his being in the form of God.[21] The audience are to adopt

---

20. According to Fee (*Philippians*, 204), "form" (μορφή) means "that which truly characterizes a given reality." O'Brien, *Philippians*, 210–11: "The phrase ἐν μορφῇ θεοῦ is best interpreted against the background of the glory of God, that shining light in which, according to the OT and intertestamental literature, God was pictured. The expression does not refer simply to external appearances but pictures the preexistent Christ as clothed in the garments of divine majesty and splendour. He was in the form of God, sharing God's glory. ἐν μορφῇ θεοῦ thus corresponds with Jn. 17:5 ('the glory I had with you before the world began') and reminds one of Heb. 1:3 ('the radiance of God's glory and the exact repre-sentation of his being')." See also Markus N. A. Bockmuehl, "'The Form of God' (Phil. 2:6): Variations on a Theme of Jewish Mysticism," *JTS* 48 (1997): 1–23; Denny Burk, "On the Articular Infinitive in Philippians 2:6: A Grammatical Note with Christological Implications," *TynBul* 55 (2004): 253–74; Dennis W. Jowers, "The Meaning of μορφή in Philippians 2:6–7," *JETS* 49 (2006): 739–66.

21. Fee, *Philippians*, 207 n. 62: "[B]y putting 'not ἁρπαγμόν' in the emphatic first position, Paul indicates that the infinitive [τὸ εἶναι ἴσα θεῷ, 'being equal to God'] that follows *refers back* [Fee's em-phasis] to the initial participial phrase [ἐν μορφῇ θεοῦ ὑπάρχων, 'existing in the form of God'], in a kind of A-B-A structure. Thus, 'in his being in the form of God (A), not ἁρπαγμόν did Christ consider (B) his being equal with God (A')'" and p. 207: "This, then, is what it means for Christ to be 'in the "form" of God'; it means 'to be equal with God,' not in the sense that the two phrases are identical, but that both point to the same reality." O'Brien, *Philippians*, 216: "The expression οὐχ ἁρπαγμὸν ἡγήσατο empha-sizes that Jesus refused to use for his own gain the glory that he had from the beginning." Bockmuehl, *Philippians*, 130: "Christ did not consider his existing divine status as a possession to be exploited for selfish interests." See also Roy W. Hoover, "The HARPAGMOS Enigma: A Philological Solution," *HTR* 64 (1971): 95–119; Nicholas Thomas Wright, "ἁρπαγμός and the Meaning of Philippians 2:5–11," *JTS* 37 (1986): 321–52.

a similar mind-set by "considering" one another more important than themselves, thinking nothing according to self-seeking (2:3).[22]

While remaining equal to and in the form of God, Christ emptied "himself" (ἑαυτόν), taking the "form" (μορφήν) of a slave, that is, the state or mode of existence by which he was identified with and characterized as a slave (2:7a).[23] That Christ "emptied" (ἐκένωσεν) himself stands in direct contrast to the "vainglory" or "empty glory" (κενοδοξίαν) that is not to be part of the audience's way of thinking (2:3).[24] He took on the form of a slave by becoming in the likeness of human beings, and by being found in outward appearance as a human being (2:7b)—he not only became similar to all human beings, but was himself an actual, individual human being.[25] The audience are thus to have this same non-exploiting, selfless mind-set, by considering one another more important than "themselves," each looking out not only for the things of "themselves" but also of others (2:3b–4).

The senders of the letter, Paul and Timothy, introduced themselves to the audience as metaphorical "slaves" (δοῦλοι) of Christ Jesus (1:1a), suggesting their selfless, humble submission to Christ as their "owner" or "master." But now the audience hear that Christ himself took on the form, metaphorically assuming the identity or status, of a "slave" (δούλου, 2:7a). The implication that the audience are to imitate Paul and Timothy in likewise becoming "slaves" of Christ Jesus is now reinforced by the directive that they are to adopt the non-exploiting, selfless way of thinking exhibited by Christ Jesus, their "master," who, while in the form of and equal to God, took on the form of a "slave," when he became a human being in similarity to and identified with all other human beings (2:7b).[26]

---

22. Fee, *Philippians*, 202: "Thus, he reminds the Philippians that everything Christ did in bringing them salvation was the exact opposite of the 'selfish ambition' censured in v. 3."

23. Fee, *Philippians*, 210: "Christ did not empty himself *of* anything; he simply 'emptied *himself*,' poured himself out. This is a metaphor, pure and simple. The *modifier* is expressed in the modal participle that follows; he 'poured himself out *by* having taken on the "form" of a slave' (Fee's emphases)." O'Brien, *Philippians*, 223–24: "[I]t seems best, on balance, to understand the expression μορφὴν δούλου λαβών against the background of slavery in contemporary society. Slavery pointed to the extreme deprivation of one's rights, even those relating to one's own life and person. When Jesus emptied himself by embracing the divine vocation and becoming incarnate he became a slave, without any rights whatever. He did not exchange the nature or form of God for that of a slave; instead, he displayed the nature or form of God in the nature or form of a slave, thereby showing clearly not only what his character was like, but also what it meant to be God." See also Glancy, *Slavery*, 100–101.

24. Fee, *Philippians*, 211: "Rather than doing anything on the basis of 'empty glory,' Christ on the contrary 'emptied himself' . . . 'made himself nothing.'"

25. Fee, *Philippians*, 213 n. 94: "Gk. ἀνθρώπων; the plural is purposeful, implying his identity with the whole human race, which is then particularized in the next phrase ('as a human being [himself]')" and p. 213: "Thus he came in the 'likeness' of human beings, because on the one hand he has fully identified with us, and because on the other hand in becoming human he was not 'human' only. He was God living out a truly human life, all of which is safeguarded by this expression."

26. That the word "slave" (δοῦλος) occurs only in 1:1 and 2:7 within the letter enhances this connection. Bockmuehl, *Philippians*, 135: "The distinction may be a fine one; but it seems on balance

In sum, in this B element (2:6–7) the way of thinking demonstrated by Christ Jesus, who "considered" his being equal to God while in the form of God not something to be selfishly exploited for his own benefit, but emptied "himself" by taking on the form of a slave when he became a human being is the motivation and model for the audience's way of thinking (2:5) in selflessly "considering" one another more important than "themselves," with each one looking out not for the things of "themselves" but everyone also for the things of others (2:3–4). Following the lead of Paul and Timothy (1:1), the audience are to be "slaves" in imitation of the selfless mind-set of the "slave" Christ Jesus.

3. Phil 2:8a (C): He Humbled Himself, Becoming Obedient to the Point of Death

The selfless, slave-like mind-set exhibited by Christ Jesus in becoming a human being while being equal to God (2:6–7), a way of thinking the audience are to adopt for themselves (2:5), receives further development and intensification: "He humbled himself, becoming obedient to the point of death" (2:8a).[27] At this point the audience experience the following mini-chiasm in 2:7–8a: (a) himself (ἑαυτόν) he emptied, taking the form of a slave, (b) becoming in the likeness of human beings (ἀνθρώπων), (b′) and in outward appearance found to be as a human being (ἄνθρωπος), (a′) he humbled himself (ἑαυτόν), becoming obedient to the point of death.

At the center of this mini-chiasm the audience hear the pivot in parallels from Christ becoming in the likeness of "human beings" in general in the "b" sub-element (2:7b), thus focusing on his incarnation, to his being found in outward appearance as an individual "human being" in the "b′" sub-element (2:7c), thus underlining his humanity. With the statement that Christ humbled "himself," becoming obedient to the point of death, in the "a′" sub-element (2:8a), expressing the humility of his death as a human being, the audience hear the development of the statement that Christ emptied "himself," taking the form of a slave, in the "a" sub-element (2:7a), expressing the humility of his becoming a human being even

---

more likely that Christ is here said to have *been* a metaphorical slave, rather than to have been *like* a literal one. In any case it is true that the word δοῦλος, as in 1.1, carries vividly evocative overtones in a Graeco-Roman setting" (Bockmuehl's emphases). Park, *Submission*, 120–21: "Selflessness demonstrated by the refusal to exploit rights in 2.6 is reiterated and emphatic in the term δοῦλος. . . . a slave by definition is one who has no rights. Paul underscores this vivid contrast of rights and privileges versus absence of rights and privileges by the double use of μορφή in μορφὴ θεοῦ and μορφὴ δούλου. Christ's submission begins with the determination not to exploit his rights, status and privileges which is indicative of a mind-set focused not on self-glory or self-advantage: it is selfless."

27. O'Brien, *Philippians*, 229–30: "μέχρι θανάτου means 'to the extremity of death'. These words draw attention to the utmost limit of the Son's obedience. μέχρι is here used as a preposition of degree or measure, not merely of a temporal goal, that is, as long as he lived. By indicating the extreme depth of the humiliation μέχρι θανάτου at the same time points to its end. . . . only a divine being can accept death as obedience; for ordinary human beings it is a necessity, to which they are appointed by their humanity (Heb. 9:27)."

while in the form of and equal to God.[28] In addition, the audience hear an emphasis on Christ's death as a human being through the repetition of the participle "becoming"—"becoming" (γενόμενος) in the likeness of human beings (2:7b) and "becoming" (γενόμενος) obedient to the point of death (2:8a).

Christ not only humbled himself when he emptied "himself" (ἑαυτόν) by taking on the form of a slave and "becoming" in the likeness of human beings as an actual, individual human being (2:7), but he further humbled "himself" (ἑαυτόν) by "becoming" obedient to the point of death.[29] That he "humbled" (ἐταπείνωσεν) himself to this extent—not only becoming a human being but dying the death of a human being—is the motivation and model for the audience similarly in "humility" (ταπεινοφροσύνῃ) to consider one another more important than "yourselves" (ἑαυτῶν), with each one of them looking not to the things of "yourselves" (ἑαυτῶν), but each and everyone of them also for the things of others (2:3–4).

In sum, in the C element (2:8a) of this chiastic unit (2:1–16) the audience are to have the same humble way of thinking in considering one another more important than themselves and looking out not just for themselves but for others (2:3–4) that Christ demonstrated when he humbled himself by becoming obedient to the human condition even to the point of death as a human being.

4. Phil 2:8b (C´): Even of Death on a Cross

The humility of Christ is further intensified as the audience hear that he humbled himself by becoming obedient not only to the point of death (2:8a), but "even of death on a cross" (2:8b). At this juncture the audience experience the pivot of the chiasm from Christ becoming obedient to the point of "death" (θανάτου) in the C element (2:8a) to its chiastic parallel, even of "death" (θανάτου) on a cross in the C´ element (2:8b).

The humble way of thinking demonstrated by Christ Jesus has thus reached a third and climactic level. First, while being in the form of God and equal to God (2:6), he emptied himself by taking on the form of a slave in entering into the human condition by himself becoming a human being (2:7). Second, he further

---

28. O'Brien, *Philippians*, 227–28: "Although some interpreters see little difference in meaning between 'he emptied himself' (v. 7) and 'he humbled himself' (v. 8), since Christ's whole life from the cradle to the grave was marked by genuine humility, the former relates to his incarnation, the latter to his humanity: he emptied himself in becoming a human being and then, having become human, he humbled himself further. ἐταπείνωσεν is not synonymous with ἐκένωσεν but carries the thought further." Fee, *Philippians*, 215: "'In the form of God' he emptied himself; now 'in the appearance of a human being' he humbled himself."

29. Fee, *Philippians*, 216–17: "'Obedience unto death,' therefore, points to the degree to which obedience took him, the readiness of him who, as one of us, *chose* the path that led to death . . . Which is quite in keeping with him who, as God, impoverished himself by taking on the role of a slave" (Fee's emphasis). Bockmuehl, *Philippians*, 138–39: "Just as we were not told explicitly whose slave Christ was, so there is no indication of the one *to whom* he was obedient. . . . An implicit reference to God's will seems most plausible, since Paul understands Christ's death on the cross as being in response to God's will (Gal. 1.4)" (Bockmuehl's emphasis).

humbled himself by dying the death of a human being, thus fully embracing the human condition (2:8a). And third, he not only underwent death as a human being but the most degrading, shameful, and humiliating manner of death a human being of his time could experience, namely, public execution by being crucified as a criminal—death on a cross (2:8b).[30] Thus, the threefold humility exhibited by Christ in not only becoming human and dying as a human, but dying an utterly humiliating death for any human, death on a cross (2:6–8), serves as the motivation and model for the audience to emulate in the humble way of thinking that is to unite them with one another and with Paul, as they all selflessly look out for the welfare of others (2:2–5).[31]

5. Phil 2:9–11 (B´): Jesus Exalted and Granted a Superior Name to the Glory of God

The audience are then made aware of God's response to the threefold obedient humility demonstrated by Christ Jesus (2:6–8): "therefore indeed God exalted him and granted him the name that is above every name, so that at the name of Jesus every knee should bend, of those in heaven and of those on earth and of those under the earth, and every tongue confess (cf. LXX Isa 45:23) that Jesus Christ is Lord to the glory of God the Father" (2:9–11). At this point the audience

---

30. Williams, *Enemies of the Cross*, 132–33: "The final phrase, 'death on a cross,' . . . loses its rhetorical effect if it is not realized that it is more than a mere 'addition.' Its rhetorical effect lies in the repetition of the word θάνατος ('death') . . . These words (θανάτου δὲ σταυροῦ) are the important rhetorical climax to which the preceding verses have been pointing. . . . In this context the cross is the climax to the narrative about Jesus Christ's privilege and loss (or voluntary abdication) of status." Bockmuehl, *Philippians*, 139–40: "It has the effect of an arresting musical syncopation, marking the end of the downward narrative but leaving one on the edge of one's seat for what comes next. These words stand out both syntactically and thematically, drawing attention to the centrality of the cross as both the climax of Christ's exemplary humility and the final purpose of the incarnation itself." Fee, *Philippians*, 217: "In its own clause its effect lies in the repetition of 'death' back to back: 'unto death, death, that is, of a cross.' At the same time it combines with 'in the form of God' (v. 6) to frame the narrative to this point with the sharpest imaginable contrast: God and the cross." O'Brien, *Philippians*, 230–31: "[I]t was 'death on a cross', the most loathsomely degrading death of all, that he endured. . . . Here the rock bottom of Jesus' humiliation was reached. . . . crucifixion as a penalty in the Graeco–Roman world . . . was very widespread as a political and military punishment, inflicted by the Romans especially on the lower classes, including slaves, violent criminals, and unruly elements in provinces such as Judea. In order to be an efficient deterrent crucifixion was carried out publicly, usually in some prominent place. . . . According to Jewish law anyone who was crucified died under the curse of God (Dt. 21:23; cf. Gal. 3:13)." See also Martin Hengel, *Crucifixion: In the Ancient World and the Folly of the Message of the Cross* (Philadelphia: Fortress, 1977), esp. 86–90; Otfried Hofius, *Der Christushymnus Philipper 2,6–11: Untersuchungen zu Gestalt und Aussage eines urchristlichen Psalms* (2d ed.; WUNT 17; Tübingen: Mohr Siebeck, 1991), 3–17; John Granger Cook, "Envisioning Crucifixion: Light from Several Inscriptions and the Palatine Graffito," *NovT* 50 (2008): 262–85.

31. On Phil 2:5–8, see A. J. McClain, "The Doctrine of the Kenosis in Philippians 2:5–8," *MSJ* 9 (1998): 85–96; D. J. MacLeod, "Imitating the Incarnation of Christ: An Exposition of Philippians 2:5–8," *BSac* 158 (2001): 308–30; Jan Lambrecht, "Paul's Reasoning in Philippians 2,6–8," *ETL* 83 (2007): 413–18.

hear the chiastic development, via a series of predominantly alliterative parallels, from what Christ Jesus, "existing (ὑπάρχων) in the form of God (θεοῦ)," "considered (ἡγήσατο)," in "becoming in the likeness (ὁμοιώματι) of human beings" in the B element (2:6–7) to how "God exalted (ὑπερύψωσεν) him" and "granted (ἐχαρίσατο) him" a superior name, so that "at the name (ὀνόματι) of Jesus,"[32] as the climax of "the name (ὄνομα) that is above every name (ὄνομα)," there should be a cosmic confession of this superior name, Lord, "to the glory of God (θεοῦ)" in the B′ element (2:9–11).

In correspondence to the fact that Jesus "considered" (ἡγήσατο) his being equal to God, while "existing" (ὑπάρχων) in the form of God, not something to be exploited (2:6), God "exalted" (ὑπερύψωσεν) and "granted" (ἐχαρίσατο) him the name that is above every other name in the universe (2:9).[33] This reminds the audience that it has been likewise "granted" (ἐχαρίσθη) to them by God to suffer on behalf of Christ (1:29), thus further uniting them with and conforming them to Christ as beneficiaries of the grace of God.[34] In correspondence to the fact that Jesus became in the "likeness" (ὁμοιώματι) of human beings and was found to be in appearance as a human being (2:7), it is at the "name" (ὀνόματι)—the name that is above every other name, the name or title of "Lord," given to this human being Jesus by God that everyone in the cosmos is to confess him as the universal Lord (2:10–11).[35]

And in correspondence to the threefold intensification of the humility of Jesus in (1) becoming a human being (2:7), (2) becoming obedient to death (2:8a), and (3) undergoing death on a cross (2:8b), there results a most appropriate threefold cosmic homage and confession to his exaltation. The lordship of Jesus will be

---

32. O'Brien, *Philippians*, 240: "[I]t is not 'the name of Jesus', but 'the name which belongs to Jesus' that is meant.... It is not without significance that the concrete name Ἰησοῦ is used for the first time in the hymn. In such a context it serves to emphasize the reality of his humanity: it is the real human being of whom the first part of the hymn has spoken (vv. 7–8) who has been exalted. The one who humbled himself, Jesus, has been enthroned as Lord of the universe, and the day will come when all will acknowledge this." See also Fee, *Philippians*, 223 n. 31.

33. O'Brien, *Philippians*, 237–38: "Here in v. 9 ὄνομα is not used simply of an individual designation as a proper name. The phrase ὑπὲρ πᾶν ὄνομα ('above every [other] name') shows that something additional is in view. Older commentators who sought to interpret τὸ ὄνομα ('the name') simply of a personal designation given to the glorified Christ missed this important point regarding all the qualities and powers that give meaning and substance to the title." Bockmuehl, *Philippians*, 142: "In the ancient world, and in Judaism in particular, a name was of interest for what it signified, and not simply as a label." Fee, *Philippians*, 221 n. 20: "In this case *the* name, meaning 'the well-known' name, probably reflects an OT phenomenon where 'the name' was a periphrasis for Yahweh" (Fee's emphasis).

34. Williams, *Enemies of the Cross*, 134: "Verse 9 expresses the name that is 'graced' or 'freely given' (ἐχαρίσατο) to Jesus by God just as the Philippians have been graced or freely given (ἐχαρίσθη), 1.29) to suffer on Christ's behalf."

35. O'Brien, *Philippians*, 233: "But now, by way of vindication and approval of Jesus' total self-humbling, the Father has magnificently exalted his Son to the highest station and graciously bestowed on him the name above all other names, that is, his own name, Lord (= Yahweh), along with all that gives substance and meaning to the name. In his exalted state Jesus now exercises universal lordship."

honored by every knee and confessed by every tongue (2:10–11) of (1) "those in heaven"—the location of his being in the form of and equal to God (2:6), (2) "those on earth"—the location of his becoming a human being (2:7), and (3) "those under the earth"—the realm of the dead (2:8). The honor and confession rendered thus includes that by angelic beings in heaven, human beings on earth, and the dead under the earth.[36]

At the opening of the letter, Paul and Timothy, as slaves of "Christ Jesus," addressed the audience as all the holy ones in "Christ Jesus" at Philippi (1:1) with the following greeting: "grace to you and peace from God (θεοῦ) our Father (πατρός) and the Lord (κυρίου) Jesus Christ" (1:2). The audience were later reminded that, together with their "brother" believers, they are in the realm or domain of being "in the Lord (κυρίῳ)" (1:14). In addition, the audience have heard Paul's prayer that they "may be sincere and blameless for the day of Christ, having been filled up with the fruit of righteousness that is through Jesus Christ for the glory (δόξαν) and praise of God (θεοῦ)" (1:10–11). The audience can be sincere and blameless for the day of Christ and for the glory and praise of God, and thus play their role, as among "those on earth" (2:10), in the cosmic confession that "Jesus Christ" is "Lord" (κύριος) for the "glory" (δόξαν) of "God the Father" (θεοῦ πατρός) (2:11) by conforming themselves to the same selfless and humble way of thinking that was in "Christ Jesus" (2:5).[37]

---

36. Bockmuehl, *Philippians*, 146: "More specifically, the reference is to angelic beings, to human beings and to the dead: 'under the earth' is more likely to refer to the realm of the dead than that of demonic powers."

37. O'Brien, *Philippians*, 252: "It has been suggested that, because of the later connotations of the term, it is better to speak of Paul's ethics as having to do with 'conformity' to Christ's likeness rather than an 'imitation' of his example." Fee, *Philippians*, 229: "The Philippians—and we ourselves—are not called upon simply to 'imitate God' by what we do, but to have this very mind, the mind of Christ, developed in us, so that we too bear God's image in our attitudes and relationships within the Christian community—and beyond." Fowl, *Philippians*, 105: "Paul wants them to see that what this passage asserts about Christ has deep and profound implications for the ways in which they order their life together. The habits, dispositions, and actions Christ displays in 2:6–11 are precisely the habits, dispositions, and actions Paul wants the Philippians to display toward each other." Bockmuehl, *Philippians*, 147: "[T]his assertion introduces into the daily reality of Christian life at Philippi a profoundly double–edged political point: one who confesses *Jesus* as Lord enters at once into the same freedom to serve that he himself exercised, to promote the welfare of others rather than one's own. At the same time, one who says 'Jesus Christ is *Lord*' cannot also agree that 'Caesar (or any other human potentate) is Lord': a Christian is forbidden to render to other powers, or to require from them, the allegiance that belongs to Christ alone" (Bockmuehl's emphasis). For a treatment of 2:6–11 that focuses especially on the significance of 2:9–11 for an indication of early worship of Jesus, see Larry W. Hurtado, *How on Earth Did Jesus Become a God? Historical Questions About Earliest Devotion to Jesus* (Grand Rapids: Eerdmans, 2005), 83–107; idem, *Lord Jesus Christ: Devotion to Jesus in Earliest Christianity* (Grand Rapids: Eerdmans, 2003), 118–23.

6. Phil 2:12–16 (A´): As Beloved Work Out Your Own Salvation

The audience then hear a further development of their conformity to Christ by adopting his way of thinking: "So that, my beloved, just as you have always obeyed, not as in my presence only, but now much more in my absence, with reverence and awe continue to work out your own salvation. For God is the one working in you both to desire and to work for the sake of his good pleasure. Do everything without grumbling or questioning, so that you may become blameless and innocent, children of God without blemish in the midst of a crooked and perverse generation (cf. LXX Deut 32:5), among whom you shine as lights in the world (cf. LXX Dan 12:3), holding forth the word of life, so that my boast for the day of Christ—that I did not run in vain or labor in vain" (2:12–16).[38]

At this point the audience experience a progression of chiastic parallels from the A (2:1–5) to the A´ element (2:12–16), from the consolation of "love" (ἀγάπης, 2:1), the same "love" (ἀγάπην, 2:1), that they share with Paul to their being addressed as those "beloved" (ἀγαπητοί, 2:12) by Paul, from considering one another more important than "yourselves" (ἑαυτῶν, 2:3), not looking out only for the things of "yourselves" (ἑαυτῶν, 2:4), to working out "your own" (ἑαυτῶν, 2:12) salvation, and from the audience not thinking according to "vainglory" (κενοδοξίαν, 2:3) to Paul's not running in "vain" (κενόν, 2:16) or laboring in "vain" (κενόν, 2:16).

That Paul addresses his audience as "my beloved" (2:12), reminding them of his love for them, reinforces his appeal for them, since there is such a consolation from "love" (2:1), to fill up his joy by sharing the same "love" with him (2:2). Paul's affirmation of his beloved audience's obedience, "just as you have always obeyed (ὑπηκούσατε, 2:12), reminds them how they have already begun to adopt the mind-set of Christ Jesus (2:5), who "humbled himself, becoming obedient (ὑπήκοος) to the point of death" (2:8).[39]

Although they can expect Paul's "presence" (παρουσίας) with them again (1:26), the audience are to continue their humble obedience not only in his "presence" (παρουσία) but now all the more in his absence (2:12, cf. 1:27). Although they are to consider one another more important than "yourselves" (2:3), looking out not only for the things of "yourselves" (2:4), they are with reverence and awe to continue to work out "your own" salvation (2:12).[40] Just as the proclaiming

---

38. Peter Oakes, "Quelle devrait être l'influence des échos intertextuels sur la traduction? Le cas de l'épître aux Philippiens (2,15–16)," in *Intertextualités: La bible en échos* (ed. Daniel Marguerat and A. Curtis; Paris: Labor et Fides, 2000), 266–85. See also Bormann, "Triple Intertextuality," 92.

39. Bockmuehl, *Philippians*, 150: "[I]n the present context it is best seen as obedience to God and to the gospel."

40. O'Brien, *Philippians*, 284: "As we have seen, of special importance is the fact that in both the LXX and Paul φόβος καὶ τρόμος [reverence and awe] is the appropriate response to God's mighty acts. The point comes out clearly and explicitly in Phil. 2:12–13: the readers are to fulfill the injunction to work out their own salvation with the utmost seriousness, precisely because God is mightily at work in their midst." Ware, *Mission*, 246: "Implicit in τὴν ἑαυτῶν σωτηρίαν ('*your own* salvation') is a comparison or contrast between the Philippians and another person or persons. It is possible that the

of Christ despite opposition (1:12–18) will lead to Paul's "salvation" (σωτηρίαν, 1:19), and the audience's not being intimidated by opponents by living in accord with the gospel and proclaiming Christ will be a demonstration of their "salvation" (σωτηρίας, 1:28), so now they are to continue to work out their own "salvation" (σωτηρίαν, 2:12).[41]

But for "you to continue to work out (κατεργάζεσθε) your own salvation" (2:12) depends upon the working of God himself. For God is the one "working" (ἐνεργῶν) within the audience both to desire and to "work" (ἐνεργεῖν) for the sake of his good pleasure (2:13).[42] Recalling how some, on account of "good pleasure" (εὐδοκίαν), that is, God's good pleasure,[43] preach the Christ while Paul is in prison (1:15), that God is the one working within the audience for the sake of his "good pleasure" (εὐδοκίας) underlines the implication that the audience may continue to work out their own salvation by continuing to live worthy of the gospel (1:27–28) as they, like the Christians where Paul is imprisoned and like Paul himself, proclaim the Christ (1:12–18).[44]

For the audience to have the same humble and obedient mind-set as Christ Jesus (2:5) has present and future ramifications. Just as they have "always" (πάντοτε)

---

emphatic pronoun ἑαυτῶν functions to juxtapose the activity of the Philippians with the example of Paul, whose paradigmatic role for the Philippians is evoked, as we have seen, by the language of presence and absence in 2:12a. Just as Paul's bold speech in behalf of the gospel will result in his salvation (1:19–20), so the Philippians, through their own bold proclamation of the gospel, are to work their own (ἑαυτῶν) salvation (2:12)."

41. Ware, *Mission*, 244: "In both 1:19–20 and 1:27–28 the bold confession and proclamation of the gospel in the face of persecution brings salvation (σωτηρία). Paul's use of σωτηρία in 2:12 recalls this carefully developed thematic pattern, and indicates that the activity whereby the Philippians are to work their own salvation is their fearless confession of the gospel despite persecution and suffering."

42. Ware, *Mission*, 248–49: "The source of the Philippians' activity is the activity of God. The verb ἐνεργέω stresses the efficacious nature of this divine activity. . . . The phrase ἐν ὑμῖν does not mean here 'among you' or 'in your midst,' but 'in you.' The phrase refers to God's activity within the hearts and minds of the Philippian Christians, for Paul envisages this divine operation as affecting not only the actions of the Philippians but also their wills (καὶ τὸ θέλειν καὶ τὸ ἐνεργεῖν). The twofold καὶ in this phrase is emphatic, and accents the comprehensiveness of this inward divine operation, embracing the Philippians' willing as well as their doing. Verse 2:13 in a sense qualifies and reinterprets verse 2:12: the activity of the *Philippians* in working out their own salvation is the result of *God's* activity in them" (Ware's emphases). See also Chris VanLandingham, *Judgment & Justification in Early Judaism and the Apostle Paul* (Peabody, Mass.: Hendrickson, 2006), 186–87; J. Ross Wagner, "Working Out Salvation: Holiness and Community in Philippians," in *Holiness and Ecclesiology in the New Testament* (ed. Kent E. Brower and Andy Johnson; Grand Rapids: Eerdmans, 2007), 257–74.

43. Ware, *Mission*, 189–91; Bockmuehl, *Philippians*, 79; see also Robert Mahoney, "εὐδοκία," *EDNT*, 2.75–76.

44. That these two occurrences (1:15; 2:13) are the only occurrences of "good pleasure" (εὐδοκία) in the letter enhances this recall and connection on the part of the audience. Ware, *Mission*, 250: "Strikingly, in the only other occurrence of the word in Philippians, it is directly connected with the proclamation of the gospel (δι᾽ εὐδοκίαν τὸν Χριστὸν κηρύσσουσιν, 1:15). Likewise in 2:13, Paul uses the term to refer to the divine good pleasure which is actively at work in the spread of the gospel. In this way Paul again traces the mission activity of the Philippians to God's activity."

obeyed (2:12), so, in working out their own salvation, they are to do "everything" (πάντα) without disobedient grumbling or questioning (2:14),[45] so that they might become blameless and innocent, children of the God working in them as they work out their own salvation, without blemish in the midst of the present "crooked and perverse generation" in which they are living, but among whom they "shine as stars in the world" (2:15).[46] They are to hold forth the "word" (λόγον) of life, the "word" (λόγον) of the gospel about Christ (cf. 1:12–15),[47] so that, as a complement to Paul's wish that their "boast" (καύχημα) may abound in Christ Jesus in him through his presence again with them (1:26), Paul may likewise have a "boast" (καύχημα) for the day of Christ, namely, that he did not run in vain or labor in vain with regard to them (2:16).[48]

The audience have heard Paul's prayers that the God who began in them a good "work" (ἔργον) will perfect it until the "day of Christ" (ἡμέρας Χριστοῦ) Jesus (1:6) and that they may be sincere and faultless "for the day of Christ" (εἰς ἡμέραν Χριστοῦ) (1:10). And now they hear how they can play their role in fulfilling those prayers as "you work out" (κατεργάζεσθε) "your own salvation" (2:12) with the help of the God who "works" (ἐνεργῶν) in them both to desire and to

---

45. O'Brien, *Philippians*, 290, 292: "Paul's language in v. 14 echoes that of ΟΤ descriptions of the generation of Israelites who passed through the wilderness under Moses' leadership. . . . They had repeatedly complained about their hardships and wished that they had never left Egypt (Nu. 11:1–6; 14:1–4; 20:2; 21:4, 5). . . . Here the term probably draws attention to the Philippians' divisive actions, such as 'quarrels' or 'disputes,' presumably within the congregation (perhaps even with their leaders), and possibly with outsiders. They are to avoid such behaviour, for the lesson to be learned from the Israelites in the wilderness is that such quarrelling is against God."

46. O'Brien, *Philippians*, 292, 294: "Unlike the wilderness generation of Moses' day who had ceased to be God's children 'because of their blemish,' the apostle wants his readers to be God's perfect children as they live and witness in the midst of the entire unbelieving world—a world that stands under divine judgment, though it is not without hope, as the following words show. These Christians have replaced Israel as God's people and shine in the world like stars lighting up the sky, a privilege that had belonged to Israel of old. . . . in Phil. 2:15 the standing reproach of Israel is now applied by the apostle to the whole unbelieving world, in whose midst these Philippian believers live and witness."

47. After an extensive investigation of the meaning of ἐπέχοντες in 2:16, Ware (*Mission*, 269–70) concludes: "The sense *hold forth* is consequently the only possible meaning for the verb ἐπέχω in Philippians 2:16a. The clause is accordingly to be translated 'holding forth the word of life.' This sense of the verb is also demanded by the missional context of the immediately preceding clause, which, as we have seen, describes the Philippians as 'lights of the world' (2:15b). The 'word of life' which Paul's Philippian converts are to hold forth is identical with 'the word of God' which Paul describes the Roman Christians as daring to speak fearlessly (1:14), and is a designation for the gospel message. The clause λόγον ζωῆς ἐπέχοντες is thus an exhortation to spread the gospel." See also Thurston, *Philippians*, 96; Garland, "Philippians," 226. This interpretation is *contra* Vern Sheridan Poythress, "'Hold Fast' Versus 'Hold Out' in Philippians 2:16," *WTJ* 64 (2002): 45–53. Fee, *Philippians*, 248: "Their role in Philippi, by the very nature of things, puts them in strong contrast (hence, in opposition) to the paganism of Philippi, while at the same time they offer 'life,' the life that Christ has provided through his death and resurrection, to those who will take the time to hear."

48. O'Brien, *Philippians*, 298–99: "καύχημα ['boast'], as in 1:26, focuses attention on the ground of glorying rather than on the act of exulting. There Paul hopes that his arrival in Philippi will be the basis for their glorying; here it is the Philippians themselves who are the ground for Paul's exultation."

"work" (ἐνεργεῖν) for the sake of God's good pleasure (2:13), so that Paul may have a boast "for the day of Christ" (εἰς ἡμέραν Χριστοῦ)—that he has not run or labored in vain (2:16).[49] By doing nothing according to "vainglory" (κενοδοξίαν) (2:3), as they work out their own salvation, the audience can assure that Paul did not run in "vain" (κενόν) or labor in "vain" (κενόν) in bringing them the word of life, the gospel about Christ, so that they too, in turn, can spread the gospel and proclaim the Christ (2:16).[50]

In sum, in this A′ element (2:12–16) just as Christ was humbly obedient to death on a cross (2:8), so Paul's beloved audience have always been obedient (2:12). Although they are humbly to consider one another more important than themselves, as they selflessly look out not only for their own things but those of others (2:3–4), they are to work out their own salvation, which includes their living worthy of the gospel and proclaiming the Christ, with the help of the God who is working in them for his good pleasure (2:12–13). By doing nothing according to "vainglory" (2:3), they can assure that Paul did not run in "vain" or labor in "vain" in bringing them the word of life, the gospel about Christ (2:14–16).

B. SUMMARY ON PHILIPPIANS 2:1–16

1. The audience are directed, out of a motivation of their compassionate love, to fulfill Paul's joy by adopting among themselves an attitude of humble consideration for others as more important than themselves (2:1–4), an attitude that was also in the person of Christ Jesus (2:5), and that is most appropriate for them as those who are holy ones within the domain of being "in Christ Jesus" (1:1, 26).

2. The way of thinking demonstrated by Christ Jesus, who "considered" his being equal to God while in the form of God not something to be selfishly exploited for his own benefit, but emptied "himself" by taking on the form of a slave when he became a human being is the motivation and model for the audience's

---

49. Ware, *Mission*, 243–44, 249: "In 1:5–6 Paul specifically describes the Philippians' partnership for the gospel, as an ἔργον ἀγαθόν (1:6). This would strongly suggest that κατεργάζεσθε in 2:12 is to be read in light of the ἔργον ἀγαθόν of 1:6, and the systematic use of cognates of ἔργον throughout the letter with reference to mission activity, and thus refers to the extension of the gospel in some way through the Philippian community. . . . The similarity of Philippians 2:12–13 to 1:5–6 is especially striking, in the notable way in which the activity of the Philippians and the activity of God in them are juxtaposed in each passage. This would indicate that in 2:12–13, as in 1:5–6, the activity for which God is at work in the Philippians is their partnership for the extension of the gospel."

50. O'Brien, *Philippians*, 300: "[T]he repetition of εἰς κένον with the negative (an echo of Is. 49:4, the second Servant Song), draws attention to Paul's great desire that his apostolic efforts on behalf of the Philippians will have been entirely fruitful and that he will not stand before the Judge on that final day with empty hands." Ware, *Mission*, 271: "Paul's boasting in the day of Christ is dependent upon his converts 'holding forth the word of life' (2:16a). Paul thus stakes the success or failure of his apostolic mission on the missionizing activity of his converts. . . . Unless the Philippian Christians hold forth the word of life, Paul's apostolic mission to them will have failed. The crucial place of the mission of the church in Paul's missionary thinking could not be more forcefully expressed."

way of thinking (2:5) in selflessly "considering" one another more important than "themselves," with each one looking out not for the things of "themselves" but everyone also for the things of others (2:3–4). Following the lead of Paul and Timothy (1:1), the audience are to be "slaves" in imitation of the selfless mind-set of the "slave" Christ Jesus (2:6–7).

3. The threefold humility exhibited by Christ in not only becoming human and dying as a human, but dying an utterly humiliating death for any human, death on a cross (2:6–8), serves as the motivation and model for the audience to emulate in the humble way of thinking that is to unite them with one another and with Paul, as they all selflessly look out for the welfare of others (2:2–5).

4. The audience can be sincere and blameless for the day of Christ and for the glory and praise of God (1:10–11), and thus play their role, as among "those on earth" (2:10), in the cosmic confession that "Jesus Christ" is "Lord" for the "glory" of "God the Father" (2:11) by conforming themselves to the same selfless and humble way of thinking that was in "Christ Jesus" (2:5).

5. Just as Christ was humbly obedient to death on a cross (2:8), so Paul's beloved audience have always been obedient (2:12). Although they are humbly to consider one another more important than themselves, as they selflessly look out not only for their own things but those of others (2:3–4), they are to work out their own salvation, which includes their living worthy of the gospel and proclaiming the Christ, with the help of the God who is working in them for his good pleasure (2:12–13). By doing nothing according to "vainglory" (2:3), they can assure that Paul did not run in "vain" or labor in "vain" in bringing them the word of life, the gospel about Christ (2:14–16).

8

PHILIPPIANS 2:17–30: REJOICE WITH THOSE WHO NEARED DEATH
FOR THE WORK OF CHRIST (E´)

Rejoice with Paul over Timothy and Epaphroditus

A: [17] But if indeed I am being poured out like a drink offering upon the sacrifice and *service* of your faith, I am *rejoicing*, indeed I am *rejoicing with* all of you. [18] And in the same way you are to be *rejoicing*, indeed you are to be *rejoicing with* me.

    B: [19a] I *hope in the Lord* Jesus *soon* to *send* Timothy to you,

        C: [19b] so that I also may be heartened, *coming to know* the things concerning you. [20] For I have no one like minded, who genuinely will be anxious for the things concerning you.

            D: [21a] For they all seek *the things* of themselves,

            D´: [21b] not *the things* of Jesus Christ.

        C´: [22] For you *know* his worth, that as a child to a father he served with me for the gospel.

    B´: [23] This one then I *hope* to *send* as soon as I perceive the things concerning me. [24] But I have confidence *in the Lord* that I myself will also come *soon*. [25] I have considered it necessary Epaphroditus, my brother and co-worker and fellow soldier, and your apostle and servant in my need, to *send* to you,

A´: [26] since he was longing for all of you and was distressed, because you heard that he was sick. [27] For indeed he was sick, close to death, but God had mercy on him, not on him only but also on me, so that I might not have sorrow upon sorrow. [28] More eagerly then I send him, so that seeing him you may *rejoice* again and I may be less sorrowful. [29] Welcome him then in the Lord with all *joy* and have such people in esteem, [30] for on account of the work of Christ he came near to the point of death, risking his life, so that he might fill up your lack of *service* toward me.[1]

---

1. For the establishment of Phil 2:17–30 as a chiasm, see ch. 2.

A. CHIASTIC DEVELOPMENT FROM PHILIPPIANS 2:1–16 (E) TO 2:17–30 (E´)

With Phil 2:17–30, the E´ unit within the macrochiastic structure embracing the entire letter, the audience hear resonances, by way of the chiastic parallelism, of 2:1–16, the corresponding E unit in the overall chiasm.[2] "For I have (ἔχω) no one like minded" (2:20) in the E´ unit reverberates with the audience's "having (ἔχοντες) the same love" (2:2) in the E unit.[3] That "they all seek the things of themselves (ἑαυτῶν)" (2:21) in the E´ unit recalls "to work out your own (ἑαυτῶν) salvation" (2:12) and "considering one another more important than yourselves (ἑαυτῶν), each of you looking out not for your own (ἑαυτῶν) things" (2:3–4) in the E unit.[4] "Not the things of Jesus Christ (Χριστοῦ)" (2:21) in the E´ unit recalls "the day of Christ (Χριστοῦ)" (2:16) in the E unit.[5]

"As a child (τέκνον) to a father (πατρί)" (2:22) in the E´ unit reverberates with "to the glory of God the Father (πατρός)" (2:11) and with "children (τέκνα) of God" (2:15) in the E unit.[6] "I have considered (ἡγησάμην) it necessary" (2:25) in the E´ unit recalls "did not consider (ἡγήσατο) being equal to God something to be grasped" (2:6) and "in humility considering (ἡγούμενοι) one another more important than yourselves" (2:3) in the E unit. And, finally, "he came near to the point of death (μέχρι θανάτου)" (2:30) in the E´ unit recalls and parallels "becoming obedient to the point of death (μέχρι θανάτου)" (2:8) in the E unit.[7]

B. AUDIENCE RESPONSE TO PHILIPPIANS 2:17–30

1. Phil 2:17–18 (A): I Am Rejoicing with You and You Are To Be Rejoicing with Me

Having heard how their continuing to "work out" their own salvation through God "working" in them both to desire and to "work" for the sake of God's good pleasure (2:12–13) is interrelated to Paul's boast for the day of Christ that he did not "run" or "labor" in vain for the gospel (2:16), the audience now hear how Paul's joy in his labor is interrelated to their own: "But if indeed I am being poured out like a drink offering upon the sacrifice and service of your faith,[8] I am rejoicing,

---

2. This section is limited to demonstrating the macrochiastic parallels. The exegetical significance of these parallels is presented in the next section.

3. The verb "to have" also occurs in 2:27 and 2:29 of the E´ unit.

4. That these are the only occurrences in the letter of the plural form of the reflexive pronoun enhances the distinctiveness of these parallels.

5. The genitive singular of "Christ" occurs also in 2:30 of the E´ unit, as well as several other times throughout the letter.

6. That these are the only occurrences of the word for "child" in the letter enhances the distinctiveness of this parallel.

7. That these are the only occurrences in the letter of this phrase enhances the distinctiveness of this parallel.

8. Fee, *Philippians*, 253: "The καί that goes with the "if" is almost certainly intensive, heightening the actuality. Thus Paul intends: 'if indeed, as is the case, I am currently being poured out.'"

indeed I am rejoicing with all of you. And in the same way you are to be rejoicing, indeed you are to be rejoicing with me" (2:17–18).[9]

Paul vividly describes the ordeal of his current imprisonment for the sake of defending and promoting the gospel as his "being poured out like a drink offering upon the sacrifice and service" of the audience's "faith" (πίστεως) (2:17a).[10] This cultic metaphor expresses Paul's suffering through imprisonment for the gospel as his "being poured out" (σπένδομαι) like a wine drink offering to the Lord upon the "sacrifice and service" or, as a hendiadys, "sacrificial service" (τῇ θυσίᾳ καὶ λειτουργίᾳ) of the audience's own suffering on behalf of Christ.[11] This recalls and reinforces Paul's desire to hear how the audience, as a unified community, are likewise struggling together for the "faith" (πίστει) of the gospel (1:27). This and Paul's previous assurance that he will remain with them for their advancement and joy in the "faith" (πίστεως) (1:25) aim to motivate them not only to continue to demonstrate progress in the growth of their own faith but to work for the spread of the faith of the gospel of Christ to others.[12]

Despite the suffering on behalf of their advancing of the faith in the gospel of Christ on the part of both Paul and his audience (2:17a), Paul paradoxically proclaims, "I am rejoicing (χαίρω), indeed I am rejoicing with (συγχαίρω) all of you. And in the same way you are to be rejoicing (χαίρετε), indeed you are to

---

9. Ware, *Mission*, 271–72: "In 2:17 Paul depicts his apostolic ministry, which he described in 2:16 under the images of running and labor, as a sacrificial offering. This image accents, even more than the preceding images in 2:16, the severe afflictions and struggles experienced by Paul in his imprisonment for the gospel."

10. O'Brien, *Philippians*, 310: "[I]t is best to consider πίστεως as the sacrificial service itself. The genitive is thus epexegetical, and the context demands that it be understood comprehensively . . . it embraces everything that made up their Christian life as a self-offering to God."

11. Ware, *Mission*, 272: "In both the Jewish cultus and pagan rites the libation was normally only an accompanying element to the sacrifice, and here too in Philippians 2:17 the weight of the verse falls not upon Paul's offering, but the sacrifice and service of the Philippians over which Paul's offering is poured. . . . Paul thus portrays the Philippians as a community of priests." Garland, "Philippians," 227: "Paul links his 'being poured out' and the Philippians' sacrificial service, and he depicts them as priests at an altar, offering up the sacrificial gift of their faith. The image recalls their partnership in the defense and confirmation of the gospel (1:7) and suggests that both he and they are making sacrificial offerings (2:25, 30; 4:18)." See also Gerald L. Borchert, *Worship in the New Testament: Divine Mystery and Human Response* (St. Louis: Chalice, 2008), 144; Martin Vahrenhorst, *Kultische Sprache in den Paulusbriefen* (WUNT 230; Tübingen: Mohr Siebeck, 2008), 234–38.

12. Smith, *Timothy's Task*, 120–21: "In Paul's mind he has been put in prison according to God's will to defend the Gospel (Phil. 1.16). The result has been that the Gospel has advanced (1.12) . . . The Philippians on the other hand are suffering like Paul for 'holding out the word of life' (2.16). This is their ministry of faith (2.17). Paul by preaching in a difficult context (i.e. prison) is suffering but not complaining; rather rejoicing. Similarly Paul wants the Philippians to rejoice too (2.18) and not complain (2.14) or argue as they preach the Gospel. So Paul's wine–libation is his personally–costly (sic) preaching from prison which adds a pleasant aroma to the Philippians' sacrifice of ministering in a comparable difficult context. Together they share the same struggle as one person contending for the Gospel (1.27)."

be rejoicing with (συγχαίρετέ) me" (2:17b–18).[13] In their mutual suffering for the advancement of the gospel of Christ Paul thus emphatically and comprehensively invites "you" (ὑμεῖς, 2:18), that is, "all of you" (πᾶσιν ὑμῖν, 2:17b) with whom he is rejoicing in his audience, to join him in the paradoxical rejoicing they can share with him both now and in the future, as he exuberantly proclaimed it previously when indicating the ironical benefit of his imprisonment for the advancement of the gospel of Christ: "What then? Only that in all manner, whether in pretense or in truth, Christ is proclaimed, and in this I rejoice (χαίρω). And indeed I will be joyful (χαρήσομαι)" (1:18).

When the audience hear that they are to be rejoicing with "me" (μοι, 2:18), they hear the transitional word that links this chiastic unit (2:17–30) with the previous one (2:1–16), which concluded with Paul's appeal regarding "my" (ἐμοί) boast for the day of Christ (2:16). The audience are thus to contribute to Paul's "boasting" for the day of Christ by presently "rejoicing" together with him.

This pointed assertion that not only is Paul "rejoicing with" all in his audience but that all of them are likewise to be "rejoicing with" him (2:17b–18) continues the theme of the joy that unites Paul and his audience in their mutual endeavor of advancing the gospel of Christ despite the suffering it may entail. The audience are to fill up Paul's "joy" (χαράν) by thinking the same thing, having the same love, being like minded, thinking the one thing (2:2). Paul has assured his audience that he, despite his present imprisonment, will remain beside all of them for their advancement and "joy" (χαράν) in the faith (1:25). And Paul has assured them that he makes every petition to God on behalf of them with "joy" (χαρᾶς) at their fellowship with him for the gospel (1:4–5).

In sum, in this A element (2:17–18) of the chiasm all in the audience are strongly urged not only to be rejoicing among themselves but to be rejoicing together with Paul, who is likewise not only rejoicing but rejoicing together with them, despite their mutual suffering through the sacrificial service they are both expending for the advancement of the gospel of Christ.[14]

---

13. Fee, *Philippians*, 256: "To this point every mention of 'joy,' except in 1:25, has had to do with Paul himself. With this imperative a subtle, but noteworthy, shift toward them takes place. What began in 1:25 as concern for their 'progress and *joy* regarding the faith' is now put into the form of an imperative, an imperative that will recur at further points in the rest of the letter; significantly, its first occurrence (1) is totally intertwined with Paul's joy, and (2) is found in the context of rejoicing in the midst of suffering and opposition. . . . Thus, the double repetition, even though it appears unnecessarily redundant, makes perfectly good sense both in the context of the whole letter and at this point in the 'argument.' What Paul is emphasizing in each case is that, first, he and they rejoice on their own accounts for the privilege of serving the gospel, even in the midst of great adversity, and second that they do so mutually, as they have done so much else mutually."

14. Ware, *Mission*, 273–74: "In describing his own self-oblation and the priestly service of the Philippians as a joint offering, Paul again accents the Philippians' partnership with him for the work of the gospel, in which God is effectively at work through the gospel which Paul brought to Philippi to extend the gospel through the Philippians (cf. 1:6–7; 1:29–30; 2:12–13; 2:16). This joint priestly activity is the basis of Paul's joy, and of his mutual joy with the Philippians. So, too, in the thanksgiving period

2. Phil 2:19a (B): I Hope in the Lord Jesus Soon To Send Timothy to You

The audience then begin to hear of Paul's future plans with regard to them: "I hope in the Lord Jesus soon to send Timothy to you" (2:19a). Just as it was within the realm of their being "in the Lord" (ἐν κυρίῳ) that most of the brothers gained confidence by Paul's bonds of imprisonment to more abundantly dare fearlessly to speak the word (1:14), so it is within the realm of his being "in the Lord (ἐν κυρίῳ)" Jesus, the Jesus whom God exalted as heavenly "Lord" (κύριος) after his humiliating death on a cross (2:11), that gives Paul the rather confident hope of sending Timothy, the co-author of the letter and, along with Paul, a "slave" of Christ Jesus (1:1), to his Philippian audience.[15] That Paul hopes soon to send Timothy to "you" (ὑμῖν) provides the audience, just addressed as "all of you (ὑμῖν)" with whom Paul is rejoicing (2:17b), with another reason to rejoice along with Paul—"you (ὑμεῖς) are to be rejoicing, indeed you are to be rejoicing with me" (2:18).

3. Phil 2:19b–20 (C): Coming To Know the Things Concerning You

The audience then hear the reason for Paul's hope soon to send Timothy to them: "so that I also may be heartened, coming to know the things concerning you. For I have no one like minded, who genuinely will be anxious for the things concerning you" (2:19b–20). Having expressed his desire for the audience "to know" (γινώσκειν) "the things regarding me" (τὰ κατ' ἐμέ), namely, that his imprisonment has led to an advancement of the gospel (1:12), now, Paul, with an emphatic "I also" or "I for my part" (κἀγώ), expects to be heartened, reciprocally "coming to know" (γνούς) "the things concerning you" (τὰ περὶ ὑμῶν) (2:19b). Paul reinforces his expectation "to be heartened" (εὐψυχῶ) by "coming

---

(1:3–11), the basis of Paul's joy was the Philippians' partnership for the gospel. Similarly in 1:12–18 the ground of Paul's joy was the wider proclamation of the gospel resulting from his imprisonment. Paul thus throughout Philippians 1:3–2:18 ties his joy to the extension of his mission through the churches." Fee, *Philippians*, 255: "So he rejoices in prayer and thanksgiving as he recalls their faith(fulness) in the gospel (1:4); he rejoices over the advance of the gospel in Rome resulting from his imprisonment, even by those who do so out of 'selfish ambition' (1:18a); he will yet rejoice as he and his gospel are vindicated at his forthcoming trial (1:18b); he wants that joy to be brought to its full measure by their 'obedience' to the present appeal (2:2); and now he insists on rejoicing in the midst of their mutual suffering for Christ. 'I rejoice,' all on my own, as it were, he says first; then he adds 'and I rejoice with all of you as well.'" For an alleged inconsistency of Paul regarding whether his imprisonment will result in execution or not, see B. P. Robinson, "Paul's Character in the Face of Death (Phil. 2:17–18; 2 Tim. 4:6– 8)," *ScrB* 28 (1998): 77–87.

15. O'Brien, *Philippians*, 317: "There may also be the suggestion that the Lord Jesus is the sphere in which his hope moves, or that his plans are formed in a consciousness of his living relationship with his Lord; he is the realm in which Paul and his colleagues think and act." Fee, *Philippians*, 264 n. 18: "The expression 'in the Lord Jesus' is just unusual enough to suggest that Paul is deliberately recalling vv. 9–11, where Jesus has been given the name above every name, the name of the Lord God himself" and p. 264: "Thus, even though 'hope' may be watered down at times (as in our idiom, 'I hope so,' when we have very little confidence about something), this qualifier ["in the Lord Jesus"], plus the change in v. 24 to 'I am persuaded in the Lord' when referring to his own coming, suggests that 'hope' moves much closer to certainty."

to know" (γνούς), after sending Timothy, with a double alliterative wordplay on Timothy being not only "like minded" (ἰσόψυχον) to Paul (2:20a) but "genuinely" (γνησίως) concerned about the Philippians (2:20b).[16] Timothy thus has a sincere solicitude for the Philippians as one "who genuinely will be anxious for the things concerning you (τὰ περὶ ὑμῶν)" (2:20b).[17] The implication is that after Paul sends Timothy to the Philippians, Timothy will eventually rejoin Paul with good news regarding the audience's situation at Philippi.

4. Phil 2:21a (D): For They All Seek the Things of Themselves

The audience continue to hear why Timothy is so valuable both to Paul and to them: "For they all seek the things of themselves" (2:21a). In contrast to all of the other associates available for Paul to send at this time, who selfishly seek "the things of themselves" (τὰ ἑαυτῶν), Timothy selflessly will care for "the things concerning you" (τὰ περὶ ὑμῶν) (2:20), about which Paul expects eventually to be informed by Timothy (2:19b).[18] Timothy behaves and thus serves as a model for the way Paul would like his Philippian audience to behave—"each of you looking out not for the things of yourselves (τὰ ἑαυτῶν), but everyone also for the things of others (τὰ ἑτέρων)" (2:4).

5. Phil 2:21b (D′): Not the Things of Jesus Christ

In seeking the things of themselves, all of the others except Timothy seek "not the things of Jesus Christ" (2:21b). At this point the audience hear the central pivot of this chiastic unit from "the things of themselves" (τὰ ἑαυτῶν) in the D element (2:21a) to "the things of Jesus Christ" (τὰ Ἰησοῦ Χριστοῦ.) in the D′ element (2:21b). That all the others seek "the things of themselves" rather than "the things of Jesus Christ" alerts the audience to the fact that these others to whom Paul refers have not adopted the humble way of thinking which is also in *Christ Jesus,* and which Paul recommends for the audience (2:5). After Jesus selflessly humbled himself to the point of dying on the cross (2:6–8), God exalted him so that every tongue may confess that *Jesus Christ* is Lord to the glory of God the Father (2:9–11).[19]

---

16. This double alliterative wordplay—εὐψυχῶ-ἰσόψυχον and γνούς-γνησίως—thus underscores how Timothy is the one who will both inform and hearten Paul about the situation of the Philippians.

17. Bockmuehl, *Philippians,* 165: "[I]n a positive sense, he [Timothy] is 'anxious' for their welfare."

18. O'Brien, *Philippians,* 321: "οἱ πάντες corresponds to the οὐδένα of the preceding verse, which is the object of the verb ἔχω ('have') and refers not to all whom Paul knows, or to all Christians generally, but to those who might have been available to be sent." Fowl, *Philippians,* 134: "While the precise referent of 'all' is difficult to determine, the more significant move in v. 21 is Paul's connection of concern with the needs of others rather than one's own interests with 'seeking the things of Jesus Christ.' In this way Paul further draws together his own disposition toward his circumstances, the common life he desires for the Philippians, Timothy's disposition toward the Philippians, and the story of Christ narrated in 2:6–11."

19. Park, *Submission,* 128: "Timothy's selflessness coheres with Christ's selflessness in 2.6–8."

In seeking "the things of themselves" rather than "the things of *Jesus Christ*" (2:21), as the audience are to realize, means that these others are not really seeking to advance the gospel about Jesus Christ, the enterprise in which Paul and his audience are closely united as partners (1:5–7, 12–18). Indeed, in alluding to the gospel of Jesus Christ, "the things of Jesus Christ" (τὰ Ἰησοῦ Χριστοῦ) are a central element in "the things concerning you" (τὰ περὶ ὑμῶν) about which Paul expects to be informed by Timothy (2:19b), who himself will be anxious about "the things concerning you" (τὰ περὶ ὑμῶν) (2:20). This is confirmed as the audience recalls Paul's request that they "live as citizens worthy of the gospel of the *Christ*, so that, whether coming and seeing you, or being absent, I hear the things concerning you (τὰ περὶ ὑμῶν), that you are standing firm in one Spirit, with one mind struggling together for the faith of the gospel" (1:27).[20]

In sum, the audience expect Paul soon to send to them his like minded associate, Timothy, who, in contrast to all of Paul's other associates who selfishly seek "the things of themselves," seeks "the things of Jesus Christ" (2:21). These "things of Jesus Christ" include the gospel about Jesus Christ who, rather than seeking "the things of himself," selflessly humbled himself to death on the cross and was exalted by God (2:1–11). The "things of Jesus Christ" thus embrace "the things concerning you" (1:27; 2:19, 20), the things concerning the audience about which Paul expects to be informed by Timothy, the things involved in the audience's struggling together with one another and with Paul for the faith of the gospel of Jesus Christ (1:27; 2:19–21).

6. Phil 2:22 (C´): You Know His Worth in How
He Served with Me for the Gospel

The audience are then impressed with Paul's further commendation of Timothy: "For you know his worth, that as a child to a father he served with me for the gospel" (2:22). At this point the audience hear the progression, via the chiastic parallels, from Paul's "coming to know" (γνούς) from Timothy (2:19a) the things concerning the audience (2:19b) in the C element (2:19b–20) to the audience's "knowing" (γινώσκετε) the worth of Timothy in the C´ element (2:22).

The acknowledgment that the audience know of Timothy's worth, how as a child to a father together with Paul he "served" or "worked as a slave" (ἐδούλευσεν) (2:22) reminds them that Timothy not only exemplifies the humble, selfless, and submissive behavior of Christ, who emptied himself by taking the form of a "slave (δούλου)" (2:7), but that both Timothy and Paul, as co-authors of the letter, were introduced to the Philippians as "slaves" (δοῦλοι) of Christ Jesus (1:1).[21] That Timo-

---

20. Thurston, *Philippians*, 101: "Throughout this letter what is important is 'the things of Jesus Christ.' That would include his example (set forth in 2:6–11) of how to live as individuals and as a community as well as the mission of the Gospel."

21. Fee, *Philippians*, 269 n. 40: "Gk. ἐδούλευσεν (lit. 'performed the duties of a slave'), which in this case almost certainly intentionally echoes the noun in 1:1 (referring to himself and Timothy) and 2:7 (Christ)."

thy served together with Paul "for the gospel" (εἰς τὸ εὐαγγέλιον) (2:22; cf. 1:7, 12, 16, 27) reminds the audience that just as they are in fellowship with Paul "for the gospel" (εἰς τὸ εὐαγγέλιον) (1:5), so is Timothy.[22] This confirms for the audience, who "know" the worth of Timothy in serving for the gospel, that Paul's "coming to know" from Timothy "the things concerning you" (2:19–20) has to do primarily with his learning about their own service for the gospel that embraces "the things of Jesus Christ" (2:21).

In sum, in this C′ element (2:22) Timothy's proven worth, as one who like a child to a father served as a "slave" together with Paul for the gospel, is known to the audience. Timothy is thus commended to the audience not only as a model for them to imitate in their own fellowship with Paul for advancing the gospel, but also as the one who will make known to Paul the status of the Philippian audience's own humble, selfless, and submissive service for the gospel that is about "the things of Jesus Christ" (2:19–21).

7. Phil 2:23–25 (B′): I Hope to Send Not Only Timothy but Epaphroditus to You

The audience then learn that after Paul sends Timothy, he himself plans to come, but before that, he must send Epaphroditus to them: "This one then I hope to send as soon as I perceive the things concerning me. But I have confidence in the Lord that I myself will also come soon. I have considered it necessary Epaphroditus, my brother and co-worker and fellow soldier, and your apostle and servant in my need, to send to you" (2:23–25). At this point the audience hear the progression, via the chiastic parallels, from "I hope in the Lord (ἐλπίζω δὲ ἐν κυρίῳ) Jesus" to "send" (πέμψαι) Timothy to you "soon" (ταχέως) in the B element (2:19a) to "I hope to send" (ἐλπίζω πέμψαι) this one (Timothy) (2:23), to "I have confidence in the Lord (δὲ ἐν κυρίῳ)" that "I also will come soon (ταχέως)" (2:24), and to "I have considered it necessary" Epaphroditus "to send (πέμψαι) to you" (2:25) in the B′ element (2:23–25).

The audience hear this B′ element (2:23–25) as a mini–chiasm: (a) This one then I hope *to send* (πέμψαι) as soon as I perceive the things concerning me. But I have confidence in the Lord that I myself will also come soon (vv. 23–24). (b) I have considered it necessary Epaphroditus, *my* (μου) brother and co-worker and fellow soldier (v. 25a), (b′) and your apostle and servant in *my* (μου) need (v. 25b), (a′) *to send* (πέμψαι) to you (v. 25c).

At the center of this mini-chiasm the audience hear a pivot of parallels from "my (μου) brother and co-worker and fellow soldier" in the "b" sub-element (2:25a) to "your apostle and servant in my (μου) need" in the "b′" sub-element (2:25b).

---

22. O'Brien, *Philippians*, 325: "The servant role of Jesus has been set forth as an example for the Philippians; Timothy has followed that model, and as one genuinely concerned for their welfare he has made himself a slave, along with Paul, in the furtherance of the gospel." Park, *Submission*, 128: "Given the emphasis on Timothy's selfless character in 2.20–21, Timothy's service to Paul is to be interpreted as a voluntary submission which implies selflessness, humility and obedience. Timothy's submission exemplified in selflessness is consistent with Christ's and Paul's submission."

The audience then hear a progression from "this one (Timothy) then I hope to send (πέμψαι)" in the "a" sub-element (2:23) to "to send (πέμψαι) (Epaphroditus) to you" in the "a'" sub-element (2:25c).

Recalling his previous expression of confident hope—"I hope in the Lord (ἐλπίζω δὲ ἐν κυρίῳ) Jesus to send (πέμψαι) Timothy to you soon (ταχέως)" (2:19a), Paul not only reiterates and thus reinforces this confident hope, but adds to it: "This one then I hope (ἐλπίζω) to send (πέμψαι) as soon as I perceive the things concerning me. But I have confidence in the Lord (δὲ ἐν κυρίῳ) that I myself will also come soon (ταχέως)" (2:23–24). That Paul hopes to send Timothy as soon as he perceives "the things concerning me" (τὰ περὶ ἐμέ) (2:23) recalls how "the things regarding me" (τὰ κατ᾽ ἐμέ) during the bonds of his current imprisonment "have come rather to an advancement of the gospel" (1:12). "The things concerning me" correlate with "the things concerning you" (τὰ περὶ ὑμῶν, 2:19b–20), which center on "the things of Jesus Christ" (τὰ Ἰησοῦ Χριστοῦ, 2:21b), and thus on advancing the gospel, rather than on "the things of yourselves" (τὰ ἑαυτῶν, 2:21a; cf. 2:4). In referring to "the things concerning me" here, Paul underlines for the audience the fellowship he shares with them (and Timothy) in advancing the gospel and thus "the things" of Jesus Christ in their respective situations—Paul in prison, his audience in Philippi.[23]

The audience can expect a visit not only from Timothy but from Paul himself. While Paul's being "in the Lord" (ἐν κυρίῳ) gives him the confident hope of sending Timothy (2:19a), his being "in the Lord" (ἐν κυρίῳ) has confidently persuaded him of his own eventual visit as well (2:24). That "I have confidence (πέποιθα) in the Lord that I myself will also come soon" reinforces and develops Paul's previously expressed confident persuasion regarding his audience—"And having confidence (πεποιθὼς) of this, I know that I will remain, indeed I will remain beside all of you for your advancement and joy in the faith" (1:25). It recalls how "most of the brothers, in the Lord having confidence (ἐν κυρίῳ πεποιθότας) by my bonds, more abundantly dare fearlessly to speak the word" (1:14). And it recalls Paul's "having confidence (πεποιθὼς) of this very thing, that he who began in you a good work will perfect it until the day of Christ Jesus" (1:6). As all of these previous "persuasions" allude, in one way or another, to advancing the gospel, Paul's present "persuasion in the Lord" assures the audience of his future visit for the presumed purpose of furthering their mutual joy in the fellowship they share for the gospel.

While it is "more necessary" (ἀναγκαιότερον) on account of his Philippian audience for Paul to remain in the flesh (1:24) rather than be put to death and

---

23. Fee, *Philippians*, 270: "Thus Timothy's reason for coming is twofold; in the first instance for Paul's sake, to see how the letter has affected them; and second their sakes, to be encouraged and brought up to speed about the outcome of his imprisonment." On Timothy as Paul's replacement here, see Paul Andrew Holloway, "*Alius Paulus*: Paul's Promise to Send Timothy at Philippians 2.19–24," *NTS* 54 (2008): 542–56.

be with Christ (1:20–23), Paul now considers it "necessary" (ἀναγκαῖον) to send
Epaphroditus (2:25). That Epaphroditus is described as my "brother" (ἀδελφόν)
indicates that he is a fellow Christian and likens him not only to most of the "brothers" (ἀδελφῶν) who dare to speak the word of the gospel while Paul is imprisoned
(1:14), but also to the audience themselves, whom Paul has addressed as "brothers" (ἀδελφοί) (1:12). That he is described as my "co-worker" (συνεργόν) suggests
that he is a partner with Paul in the fruitful "work" (ἔργου) of advancing the gospel
(1:22), the same good "work" (ἔργον) God has begun in the audience (1:6). And
that he is described as my "fellow soldier" completes the rhetorical triplet of the
characterization closely relating him to Paul (2:25a), as it points to his association
with Paul in the "battle" of advancing the gospel.[24]

Whereas the audience have heard how closely Epaphroditus is related to Paul,
now, by way of the pivot of parallels at the center of the mini-chiasm (2:23–25),
from the "b" (2:25a) to the "b′" (2:25b) sub-element, they are reminded of how
closely Epaphroditus is related to themselves. While he is the brother, co-worker,
and fellow soldier of "me" (μου), Paul, he is also "your" (ὑμῶν), the audience's,
apostle and servant in "my" (μου) need.[25] That he is "your apostle (ἀπόστολον)"
indicates that he was sent by the audience to represent them, and that he is "your
servant (λειτουργόν)in my need" indicates that he was sent by the audience to
serve Paul's needs during his imprisonment. The audience thus experience a chiastic pivot not only from "my" brother, co-worker, and fellow soldier to "your"
apostle and servant but also from "my" brother, co-worker, and fellow soldier to
"my" need. Through this emphatic chiastic pivot the audience are to realize that
the Epaphroditus they sent to Paul as their apostle and servant in his need he is
now sending back to them to be welcomed also as the brother, co-worker, and fellow soldier of Paul.

That Paul considers it necessary "to send" (πέμψαι) Epaphroditus back to the
audience in the "a′" sub-element (2:25c) develops, via the chiastic parallels, his
confident hope "to send" (πέμψαι) Timothy to them as soon as he perceives the
things concerning him in the "a" sub-element (2:23). Whereas the audience can
expect Paul to send Timothy and then to come himself eventually, they can expect
Paul to send Epaphroditus back to them even sooner.

In sum, in this B′ element (2:23–25), the audience can expect a visit first from
Epaphroditus, whom Paul considers it necessary to send back to the Philippians,
who had sent him as their apostle and servant in Paul's need, but who is also the

---

24. Fee, *Philippians*, 275–76: "Military imagery is not common in Paul; very likely it was evoked
by the surroundings (the Praetorian Guard, 1:13), or by the fact that Roman Philippi originated as a
military colony."

25. Note the emphatic contrast at the pivotal center of the mini-chiasm from μου ("my") to
ὑμῶν δέ ("and your"). O'Brien, *Philippians*, 331–32: "If the first three predicates draw attention to
Epaphroditus's relationship with Paul, the next two, by contrast, focus upon his special responsibilities
on behalf of the Philippians: the ὑμῶν, which is in an emphatic position and qualifies both nouns of the
hendiadys, ἀπόστολος and λειτουργός, stands in sharp contrast to (δέ) the preceding μου."

brother, co-worker, and fellow soldier of Paul. Then they can expect a visit from Timothy, whom Paul confidently hopes to send as soon as he perceives the things concerning himself with regard to the advancement of the gospel during his imprisonment. And finally, they can expect a visit from Paul himself, with whom they are to rejoice (2:18) in the fellowship of joy they share with him for the gospel (1:4, 25; 2:2).

8. Phil 2:26–30 (A´): You May Rejoice Again with All Joy

The audience then hear more specifically why it is necessary for Paul to send Epaphroditus to them (2:25): "since he was longing for all of you and was distressed, because you heard that he was sick. For indeed he was sick, close to death, but God had mercy on him, not on him only but also on me, so that I might not have sorrow upon sorrow. More eagerly then I send him, so that seeing him you may rejoice again and I may be less sorrowful.[26] Welcome him then in the Lord with all joy and have such people in esteem, for on account of the work of Christ he came near to the point of death, risking his life, so that he might fill up your lack of service toward me" (2:26–30).

At this point the audience hear, via the chiastic parallels, a progression in the letter's theme of joy from "I am rejoicing (χαίρω), indeed I am rejoicing with (συγχαίρω) all of you. And in the same way you are to be rejoicing (χαίρετε), indeed you are to be rejoicing with (συγχαίρετέ) me" (2:17b–18) in the A element to "you may rejoice (χαρῆτε) again" and "welcome him then in the Lord with all joy (χαρᾶς)" (2:28–29) in the A´ element. In addition, the audience hear a progression, which also serves as a literary inclusion for this unit, from the "service (λειτουργίᾳ) of your faith" (2:17a) in the A element to "your lack of service (λειτουργίας) toward me" (2:30) in the A´ element.

This A´ element (2:26–30) as a whole presents the audience with a mini-chiastic structure of its own: (a) since he was longing for all of you (ὑμᾶς) and was distressed, because you heard that he was sick (v. 26). (b) For indeed he was sick, close to *death* (θανάτῳ), but God had mercy on him, not on him only but also on me (v. 27a), (c) so that I might not *have* (σχῶ) sorrow upon sorrow (v. 27b). (d) More eagerly then I send him, so that seeing him you may *rejoice* (χαρῆτε) again (v. 28a) (e) and I may be less sorrowful (v. 28b). (d´) Welcome him then in the Lord with all *joy* (χαρᾶς) (v. 29a) (c´) and *have* (ἔχετε) such people in esteem (v. 29b), (b´) for on account of the work of Christ he came near to the point of *death* (θανάτου), risking his life (v. 30a), (a´) so that he might fill up *your* (ὑμῶν) lack of service toward me (v. 30b).

After the audience hear the unparalleled center of the mini-chiasm in the

---

26. Fee, *Philippians*, 280: "But did Paul here intend 'see him again and rejoice' or 'see him and again rejoice,' since the placement of the 'again' is perfectly ambiguous? Pauline *usage* clearly favors the latter, since this adverb almost always precedes the verb it modifies. Paul, therefore, probably intended that in seeing him they would 'rejoice again,' which is quite in keeping with the repetition of this imperative in the letter."

"e" sub-element—"and I may be less sorrowful" (2:28b), they hear progressions, via the chiastic parallels: from "you may rejoice (χαρῆτε) again" in the "d" sub-element (2:28a) to "with all joy (χαρᾶς)" in the "d′" sub-element (2:29a); from "I might not have (σχῶ) sorrow upon sorrow" in the "c" sub-element (2:27b) to "have (ἔχετε) such people in esteem" in the "c′" sub-element (2:29b); from "close to death (θανάτῳ)" in the "b" sub-element (2:27a) to "the point of death (θανάτου)" in the "b′" sub-element (2:30a); and from "all of you (ὑμᾶς)" in the "a" sub-element (2:26) to "your (ὑμῶν) lack of service" in the "a′" sub-element (2:30b).

That Epaphroditus "was longing for all of you (ἐπιποθῶνήν πάντας ὑμᾶς) and was distressed, because you heard that he was sick" (2:26) further associates him with Paul in the close relationship of both of them to the Philippian audience, as it resonates with Paul's previous disclosure of "how I long for all of you (ἐπιποθῶ πάντας ὑμᾶς) with the affection of Christ Jesus" (1:8). That Epaphroditus was indeed sick, suffering to the point of coming close to "death" (θανάτῳ) (2:27a), associates him not only with the suffering of Christ, who humbled himself by actually dying, becoming obedient to the point of "death" (θανάτου), even of "death" (θανάτου) on a cross (2:8), but also with the suffering of Paul, who in his imprisonment is ready for Christ to be magnified in his body whether through life or through "death" (θανάτου) (1:20).

The audience are to appreciate that God, who exalted Jesus to heavenly lordship after his humiliating death on a cross (2:8–11), had mercy on Epaphroditus, who in his sickness came close to death (2:27a). In sparing Epaphroditus from death, God demonstrated his mercy not only toward Epaphroditus but also toward Paul. This means that Paul need not have "sorrow upon sorrow" (2:27a), that is, presumably, sorrow at the loss of Epaphroditus as Paul's "brother, co-worker, and fellow soldier" (2:25a) on top of sorrow at the loss of Epaphroditus as the audience's "apostle and servant in my need" (2:25b). This talk of not having "sorrow" (λύπη), the opposite of "joy" (χαρά), amounts to a double negative that functions as a rhetorical understatement to express joy, aimed at developing the mutual rejoicing the audience are to share with Paul (2:17–18), as it now embraces God's sparing of Epaphroditus from death.

Paul is more eagerly sending Epaphroditus to the audience, so that, upon their seeing him who, as they heard, was sick (2:26), "you may rejoice" (χαρῆτε), and Paul himself may be "less sorrowful" (2:28), and thus "more joyful".[27] That the Philippian audience may "rejoice" upon seeing Epaphroditus alive and well adds to Paul's "being poured out like a drink offering upon the sacrifice and service of your faith" another reason for the mutual and reciprocal rejoicing of Paul with his

---

27. Note the clever wordplay between the comparative adverb "more eagerly" (σπουδαιοτέρως), which introduces this sentence, and the comparative adjective "less sorrowful" (ἀλυπότερος), which concludes it. Thus, Paul's sending of Epaphroditus "more eagerly" contributes to his joy, as it results in his being "less sorrowful." Fee, *Philippians*, 281: "Thus, their renewed joy, which was undoubtedly a cause for joy for Paul as well, is here expressed in terms of its opposite, and in response to 'sorrow upon sorrow' in v. 27."

audience—"I am rejoicing (χαίρω), indeed I am rejoicing with (συγχαίρω) all of you. And in the same way you are to be rejoicing (χαίρετε), indeed you are to be rejoicing with (συγχαίρετέ) me" (2:17–18). This mutual and reciprocal rejoicing is reinforced by the fact that upon the audience's seeing of Epaphroditus not only may they rejoice, but Paul may be "less sorrowful" (ἀλυπότερος). That Paul, who now need not have "sorrow upon sorrow" (λύπην ἐπὶ λύπην) (2:27b) at the possible loss of Epaphroditus to both Paul and the Philippians, may be "less sorrowful" ambivalently expresses his bitter sweet joy. While the sending away of Epaphroditus may still be sorrowful for Paul, the return of Epaphroditus to Philippi after coming close to death will be joyful for both the Philippians and Paul.

The audience are enjoined to welcome Epaphroditus "in the Lord with all joy" (2:29a). That they are to welcome him with all joy within the realm of their being "in the Lord" (ἐν κυρίῳ) underlines the mutual joy they share with Paul within this realm, as it recalls that it is also "in the Lord" (ἐν κυρίῳ) that Paul not only hopes to send Timothy but to come himself to Philippi (2:19, 24). Not only may "you"—the audience—"rejoice" (χαρῆτε) upon seeing Epaphroditus (2:28a), but "you" are to welcome him in the Lord with all "joy" (χαρᾶς), a joy whose source is the fact that God, in sparing Epaphroditus from death, has been merciful to both Epaphroditus and Paul (2:27).[28] By welcoming Epaphroditus with "all joy," the audience may not only fill up the "joy" (χαράν) of Paul (2:2), reciprocating the "joy" (χαρᾶς) with which Paul prays for all of them (1:4), but also advance in the "joy" (χαράν) Paul wants to further for them when he himself comes to Philippi (1:25; 2:24).

Whereas Paul may not "have" (σχῶ) "sorrow upon sorrow," that is, he may have joy, because God had mercy in sparing Epaphroditus from death (2:27), the audience's welcoming of Epaphroditus with all joy includes their "having" (ἔχετε) such people in esteem (2:29). The reason for this is that it was on account of the "work" (ἔργον) of Christ, recalling the fruitful "work" (ἔργου) of Paul (1:22) and the good "work" (ἔργον) of the audience (1:6) in their fellowship of advancing the gospel of Christ, that Epaphroditus came near to the point of death, risking his life (2:30a).[29] That Epaphroditus not only came close to "death" (θανάτῳ) in his sickness (2:27a), but also came near "to the point of death" (μέχρι θανάτου, 2:30) in risking his life for the work of Christ, further underscores how his suffering conforms to that of Christ, who humbled himself in becoming obedient "to the point of death" (μέχρι θανάτου, 2:8), and thus how Epaphroditus serves as a model for the audience, who are to have him in esteem.[30]

Epaphroditus neared to the point of death, risking his life, that he might fill

28. Fee, *Philippians*, 279: "Paul probably does not mean simply that in God's good mercy Epaphroditus simply got better, but that God had a direct hand in it."

29. O'Brien, *Philippians*, 342: "ἔργον Χριστοῦ here at 2:30 describes in general terms the 'work' of the gospel (cf. 1:5) to which the Philippians, Epaphroditus, and Paul were committed."

30. O'Brien, *Philippians*, 343: "The echo is deliberate, particularly if Paul is presenting Epaphroditus as a model of unselfish service to the Philippians." Bockmuehl, *Philippians*, 174: "His willingness to expend himself in the service of others, to risk his life and come close to death (μέχρι θανάτου)

up "your" (ὑμῶν) lack of service toward Paul (2:30b), adding another reason for his longing for all of "you" (ὑμᾶς), since they heard of his sickness (2:26). As their apostle sent to be the "servant" (λειτουργόν) of Paul in his need (2:25) during his imprisonment, Epaphroditus was able to substitute for and represent the audience in filling up the lack of their "service" (λειτουργίας) toward Paul due to their absence.[31] The filling up the audience's lack of "service" toward Paul by Epaphroditus, whom they are to welcome with all joy, as they rejoice in seeing him (2:28–29), thus reinforces Paul's appeal for the audience to rejoice along with him because of his being poured out like a drink offering upon the sacrifice and "service" (λειτουργίᾳ) of their faith (2:17–18).[32]

In sum, in this A´ element (2:26–30) the audience are to esteem Epaphroditus, who risked his life and came near to the point of death on account of the work of Christ (2:30), providing an example for the audience to follow in their imitation of the selfless humility of Jesus, who humbled himself, becoming obedient to the point of death (2:8). In rejoicing upon seeing Epaphroditus and welcoming him with all joy (2:29) as the "servant" they sent as their representative to fill up their own lack of "service" to Paul in his need during his imprisonment (2:30), the audience may rejoice along with Paul as he is being poured out like a drink offering upon the sacrifice and "service" of their faith (2:17–18).

C. SUMMARY ON PHILIPPIANS 2:17–30

1. All in the audience are strongly urged not only to be rejoicing among themselves but to be rejoicing together with Paul, who is likewise not only rejoicing but rejoicing together with them, despite their mutual suffering through the sacrificial service they are both expending for the advancement of the gospel of Christ (2:17–18).

2. The audience expect Paul soon to send to them his like minded associate, Timothy, who, in contrast to all of Paul's other associates who selfishly seek "the things of themselves," seeks "the things of Jesus Christ" (2:21). These "things of Jesus Christ" include the gospel about Jesus Christ who, rather than seeking "the things of himself," selflessly humbled himself to death on the cross and was exalted

---

for the 'work of Christ' echoes something of the 'mind' of Christ himself, who was 'obedient to death (μέχρι θανάτου)' (2.8)."

31. Thurston, *Philippians*, 105: "[W]hat is in focus is not the Philippians' shortcomings, but Epaphroditus' service. The point is that he is to be esteemed for risking his life in Christ's work and for his service to Paul. He, like Timothy, is an example of one who has lived the kind of life Paul commends to the Philippians in 2:1–4."

32. For a discussion of 2:25–30 against the background of the ancient notion of friendship, see Rainer Metzner, "In aller Freundschaft: Ein frühchristlicher Fall freundschaftlicher Gemeinschaft (Phil 2.25–30)," *NTS* 48 (2002): 111–31. For a text-centered treatment of the rhetorical function of 2:19–30, according to which Paul is assuring the Philippians that his future plans are for the advancement of the gospel, see Andreas H. Snyman, "Philippians 2:19–30 from a Rhetorical Perspective," *Acta Patristica et Byzantina* 16 (2005): 289–307.

by God (2:1–11). The "things of Jesus Christ" thus embrace "the things concerning you" (1:27; 2:19, 20), the things concerning the audience about which Paul expects to be informed by Timothy, the things involved in the audience's struggling together with one another and with Paul for the faith of the gospel of Jesus Christ (1:27; 2:19–21).

3. Timothy's proven worth, as one who like a child to a father served as a "slave" together with Paul for the gospel, is known to the audience (2:22). Timothy is thus commended to the audience not only as a model for them to imitate in their own fellowship with Paul for advancing the gospel, but also as the one who will make known to Paul the status of the Philippian audience's own humble, selfless, and submissive service for the gospel that is about "the things of Jesus Christ" (2:19–21).

4. The audience can expect a visit first from Epaphroditus, whom Paul considers it necessary to send back to the Philippians, who had sent him as their apostle and servant in Paul's need, but who is also the brother, co-worker, and fellow soldier of Paul. Then they can expect a visit from Timothy, whom Paul confidently hopes to send as soon as he perceives the things concerning himself with regard to the advancement of the gospel during his imprisonment. And finally, they can expect a visit from Paul himself (2:23–25), with whom they are to rejoice (2:18) in the fellowship of joy they share with him for the gospel (1:4, 25; 2:2).

5. The audience are to esteem Epaphroditus, who risked his life and came near to the point of death on account of the work of Christ (2:26–30), providing an example for the audience to follow in their imitation of the selfless humility of Jesus, who humbled himself, becoming obedient to the point of death (2:8). In rejoicing upon seeing Epaphroditus and welcoming him with all joy (2:29) as the "servant" they sent as their representative to fill up their own lack of "service" to Paul in his need during his imprisonment (2:30), the audience may rejoice along with Paul as he is being poured out like a drink offering upon the sacrifice and "service" of their faith (2:17–18).

9

PHILIPPIANS 3:1–21: GAIN IN FAITH IN THE DEATH OF CHRIST AND THE BODY OF HIS GLORY (D´)

Become My Fellow Imitators as We Await the Lord Jesus Christ

A: [3:1a]Furthermore, my brothers, rejoice in the *Lord*.

  B: [1b]To write the same things to *you*, to me is not burdensome, but to *you* is assuring.

   C: [2]Beware of the dogs, beware of the evil workers, beware of the mutilation. [3]For we are the circumcision, the ones who by the Spirit of God are worshiping and boasting *in Christ Jesus*, and not having put confidence in the flesh, [4]although *I myself have* confidence even in the flesh. If someone else supposes to be confident in the flesh, *I* even more, [5]with circumcision on the eighth day, from the race of Israel, tribe of Benjamin, a Hebrew from Hebrews, according to the *Law* a Pharisee, [6]according to zeal *persecuting* the church, according to *righteousness* that is in the *Law* I became blameless.

    D: [7]But whatever things were for me *gains*, these things I have considered on account of the Christ a loss. [8a]But indeed I even *consider all things* to be a loss

     E: [8b]on account of the surpassing greatness of the knowledge of Christ Jesus my Lord,

    D´: [8c]on account of whom I have suffered the *loss* of *all things*, indeed I *consider* them rubbish, that Christ I may *gain*

   C´: [9]and I may be found in him, not *having* my own *righteousness* that is from the *Law* but that is through faith in Christ, the—from God—*righteousness* based on the faith, [10]to know him and the power of the rising of him and the fellowship of the sufferings of him, being conformed to the death of him, [11]if somehow I may arrive to the resurrection from the dead. [12]Not that I have already taken it or already been perfected, but I am *pursuing* it, if indeed I may apprehend it, for which indeed I have been apprehended by Christ Jesus. [13]Brothers, I do not consider that *I* myself have apprehended. But just one thing—forgetting the things behind but stretching out for the things

114

ahead, [14]according to the goal, I am *pursuing* to the prize of the upward calling of God in Christ Jesus.

B´: [15]As many as then (would be) perfect, this let us think. And if something otherwise you are thinking, this also God will reveal to *you*.
[16]Nevertheless, to what we have attained, to the same hold fast. [17]Become
my fellow imitators, brothers, and look at those who are thus walking,
just as you have us as a model. [18]For many are walking, about whom
many times I told *you*, and now even weeping I tell you, that they are the
enemies of the cross of Christ. [19]Their end is destruction, their God is
their stomach and their glory is in their shame, those who are thinking
the things of the earth.

A´: [20]For our citizenship is existing in heaven, from which indeed a savior
we are awaiting, the *Lord* Jesus Christ, [21]who will transform the body of our
humbleness (to be) conformed to the body of his glory according to the working that empowers him even to subject to himself all things.[1]

A. Chiastic Development from Philippians 1:19–30 (D) to 3:1–21 (D´)

With Phil 3:1–21, the D´ unit within the macrochiastic structure embracing
the entire letter, the audience hear resonances, by way of the chiastic parallelism,
of 1:19–30, the corresponding D unit in the overall chiasm.[2] The closely connected,
threefold occurrence of the phrase "in the flesh"—"do not put confidence in the
flesh (ἐν σαρκί), although I myself have confidence even in the flesh (ἐν σαρκί). If
someone else supposes to be confident in the flesh (ἐν σαρκί)" (3:3–4) in the D´
unit resonates with the twofold occurrence of the same phrase—"But to remain in
the flesh (ἐν τῇ σαρκί) is more necessary on account of you" (1:24) and "If it is to
live in the flesh (ἐν σαρκί)" (1:22)—in the D unit.[3]

The words expressing "gain"—"for me gains (κέρδη)" (3:7) and "Christ I may
gain (κερδήσω)" (3:8) in the D´ unit recall "to die is gain (κέρδος)" (1:21) in the
D unit.[4] "The righteousness from God based on the faith (τῇ πίστει)" (3:9) in the
D´ unit recalls "struggling together for the faith (τῇ πίστει)" (1:27) in the D unit.[5]
"Their end is destruction (ἀπώλεια)" (3:19) in the D´ unit recalls "a demonstra-

---

1. For the establishment of Phil 3:1–21 as a chiasm, see ch. 2.

2. This section is limited to demonstrating the macrochiastic parallels. The exegetical significance of these parallels is presented in the next section.

3. That these are the only occurrences in the letter of the phrase "in the flesh" enhances the
distinctiveness of these parallels.

4. That these are the only occurrences in the letter of these particular forms of the Greek noun
and verb to express "gain" enhances the distinctiveness of these parallels.

5. These are the only occurrences in the letter of the phrase "the faith" in the dative case,
enhancing the distintinctiveness of this parallelism; the phrase occurs in the genitive case in 1:25;
2:17; 3:9a.

tion of destruction (ἀπωλείας,)" (1:28) in the D unit.[6] And the double occurrence of the word "body"—"who will transform the body (σῶμα) of our humility (to be) conformed to the body (σώματι) of his glory" (3:21)—in the D´ unit reverberates with its occurrence in the D unit—"Christ will be magnified in my body (σώματί)" (1:20).[7]

B. Audience Response to Philippians 3:1–21

1. Phil 3:1a (A): My Brothers, Rejoice in the Lord

Paul then continues to encourage and reassure his audience regarding their joy: "Furthermore, my brothers, rejoice in the Lord" (3:1a). Paul's address of the audience as "my brothers" (ἀδελφοί μου) recalls that Paul likewise referred to Epaphroditus as "my brother (ἀδελφὸν . . . μου)" (2:25). It thus reminds the Philippians that they share with Epaphroditus a close, "brotherly," relationship to Paul. It also associates them with "most of the brothers (ἀδελφῶν)," who were persuaded to speak the word of the gospel while Paul is imprisoned (1:14), thus subtly reminding them that as "brothers" they too have this responsibility. Indeed, Paul's address to the audience here as "my brothers" makes even more personal and intimate his previous address to them simply as "brothers (ἀδελφοί)" in that same context of speaking about their mutual, "brotherly" fellowship for advancing the gospel of Christ (1:12).

When the audience hear Paul's directive for them, as his brothers, to "rejoice" (χαίρετε) in the Lord (3:1a), they hear the transitional word that links this chiastic unit (3:1–21) with the previous one (2:17–30), which concludes with the directive for them to welcome Epaphroditus in the Lord with all "joy" (χαρᾶς) (2:29), as they may "rejoice" (χαρῆτε) again in seeing him (2:28). Paul's urging of them to rejoice within the realm of being "in the Lord" (ἐν κυρίῳ) thus reinforces the appeal he has just issued for them to welcome Epaphroditus within the same realm of being "in the Lord" (ἐν κυρίῳ).[8] It also reinforces Paul's previous directive to the audience, when he stated, "I am rejoicing (χαίρω), indeed I am rejoicing with

---

6. That these are the only two occurrences in the letter of this particular Greek word for "destruction" enhances the distinctiveness of this parallelism.

7. That these are the only occurrences in the letter of the word for "body" enhances the distinctiveness of these parallels.

8. O'Brien, *Philippians*, 349–50: "For the first time in Philippians the admonition χαίρετε is immediately followed by ἐν κυρίῳ. This addition does not draw attention to some new or special element in the joy here inculcated upon the readers, as though the earlier references in the epistle could designate another joy that was not ἐν κυρίῳ. . . . If, however, ἐν κυρίῳ is taken in an incorporative sense, 'because of your union with the Lord,' then it indicates the ground of their rejoicing and the sphere in which it thrives; that is, you are able to rejoice because of your union with him and you do so as those who are in Christ Jesus the Lord." Fee, *Philippians*, 291–92: "As with the Psalmists whose language Paul is using, the Lord who saves is both the basis and focus of joy, which in this imperative does not refer to a feeling but an activity. It means to verbalize with praise and singing. . . . the phrase 'in the Lord' refers to the grounds (or sphere) of their present existence, and thus points to

(συγχαίρω) all of you. And in the same way you are to be rejoicing (χαίρετε), indeed you are to be rejoicing with (συγχαίρετέ) me" (2:17–18). It thus reminds the audience that they are to continue to rejoice with Paul in the ongoing proclamation of Christ—"Christ is proclaimed, and in this I rejoice (χαίρω). And indeed I will be joyful (χαρήσομαι)" (1:18).

2. Phil 3:1b (B): To Write the Same Things to You Is to You Assuring

Paul underlines for his audience how these repeated appeals that they continue to rejoice and have joy are reassuring for them: "To write the same things to you, to me is not burdensome, but to you is assuring" (3:1b).[9] This reminder, with its double thrust toward the audience—"to you" (ὑμῖν), not only reiterates and reinforces Paul's previous exhortations for them to join him in rejoicing,[10] but also prepares and alerts the audience to hear things they may have heard from Paul (or Timothy, cf. 2:19–23) before but that they have yet to hear in this letter, things aimed at further reassuring them.[11]

3. Phil 3:2–6 (C): We Boast in Christ Jesus

The beginning of Paul's recounting of some of the "same things" that are to be assuring to the audience (3:1b) is heard as a chiastic pattern in 3:2–6:

(a) [3:2] Beware of the dogs, beware of the evil workers, beware of the mutilation (κατατομήν).
    (b) [3a] For we are the circumcision (περιτομή),
        (c) [3b] the ones who by the Spirit of God are worshiping and boasting in Christ Jesus, and not having put confidence in the flesh (ἐν σαρκὶ πεποιθότες),[12]
        (c′) [4] although I myself have confidence even in the flesh (πεποίθησιν καὶ ἐν σαρκί). If someone else supposes to be confident in the flesh (πεποιθέναι ἐν σαρκί), I even more,
    (b′) [5a] with circumcision (περιτομῇ) on the eighth day, from the race of Israel, tribe of Benjamin, a Hebrew from Hebrews,

---

their basic relationship with Christ which should eliminate all attraction to mere religion or religious identity symbols that have no future in them at all."

9. Fee, *Philippians*, 292: "Perhaps anxious lest they take adumbrage over this repetition, he also with a masterful stroke shifts the possibility that such repetition could be 'burdensome' from them to himself." See also Jeffrey T. Reed, "Philippians 3:1 and the Epistolary Hesitation Formulas: The Literary Integrity of Philippians, Again," *JBL* 115 (1996): 63–90.

10. Bockmuehl, *Philippians*, 178: "Paul wants the Philippians to rejoice in 2.28–9 and does not mind saying it once more in this verse."

11. Thurston, *Philippians*, 112: "Placing the phrase 'the same things' first is emphatic and would refer primarily to Paul's imperatives to this point and also allude to the warnings that are to follow." Garland, "Philippians," 234: "But Paul is not simply concerned that they may have heard this before. By calling attention to this repetition, he underscores the importance of what follows."

12. Giuseppe Baldanza, "Il culto per mezzo dello Spirito (Fil 3,3)," *RivB* 54 (2006): 45–64.

(a´) [5b] according to (κατά) the Law a Pharisee, [6] according to (κατά) zeal persecuting the church, according to (κατά) righteousness that is in the Law I became blameless.[13]

At the center of this chiastic pattern the audience hear a pivot in parallels from not "putting confidence in the flesh (ἐν σαρκὶ πεποιθότες)" in the "c" sub-element (3:3b) to having "confidence even in the flesh (πεποίθησιν καὶ ἐν σαρκί)" and being "confident in the flesh (πεποιθέναι ἐν σαρκί)" in the "c´" sub-element (3:4).[14] When the audience then hear the phrase "with circumcision (περιτομῇ)" in the "b´" sub-element (3:5a), they hear the parallel to "we are the circumcision (περιτομή)" in the "b" sub-element (3:3a). Finally, when the audience hear the triple occurrence of the preposition "according to"—"according to (κατά) the Law a Pharisee, according to (κατά) zeal persecuting the church, according to (κατά) righteousness that is in the Law" in the "a´" sub-element (3:5b–6), they hear the alliterative parallel to "beware of the mutilation," in which the preposition κατά serves as the prefix in the word "mutilation" (κατα -τομήν) in the "a" sub-element (3:2).

The audience are jolted by a potent, triple warning from Paul, in which they hear the imperative "beware" (βλέπετε) thrice in a rapid salvo, each time with a derogatory object in an alliterative sequence that strengthens the emphasis.[15] They are to beware of the "dogs" (κύνας), a pejorative metaphorical characterization as unclean animals,[16] they are to beware of the "evil workers" (κακοὺς ἐργάτας),[17] and they are to beware of the "mutilation" (κατατομήν), a blatantly sarcastic wordplay on the Jewish practice of "circumcision" (3:2). With this climactic third biting insult in the triplet of stern warnings, the audience realize that all three warnings are directed against those who may call for the Philippians to be circumcised and thus become Jewish.

In striking contrast to this vilification of the Jewish practice of circumcision as nothing more than a "mutilation," Paul asserts that "we"—he, his audience, and all

---

13. A. J. Thompson, "Blameless Before God? Philippians 3:6 in Context," *Them* 28 (2002): 5–12.

14. Note the pivotal chiastic transition from (a) "in the flesh" (ἐν σαρκί) (b) "putting confidence" (πεποιθότες) to (b´) "confidence" (πεποίθησιν) (a´) "even in the flesh" (καὶ ἐν σαρκί) in 3:3b–4.

15. Fee, *Philippians*, 293 n. 37: "The rhetoric is threefold: the repetition itself; the use of epithets that 'turn the tables' on his opponents; and the assonance with which it is expressed."

16. O'Brien, *Philippians*, 355: "'Dogs' and Gentiles in some contexts were almost synonymous . . . As a religious term it was applied by Jews to Gentiles or lapsed Jews who were ritually unclean and thus outside the covenant. Here at Phil. 3:2 the dogs' association with impurity and their being outside the people of God are the points of the comparison. But in an amazing reversal Paul asserts that it is the Judaizers who are to be regarded as Gentiles; they are 'the dogs' who stand outside the covenant blessings." Fee, *Philippians*, 295: "[B]y trying to make Gentiles 'clean' through circumcision, the Judaizers are unclean 'dogs.'"

17. Fee, *Philippians*, 296: "Such people, Paul proffers, in trying to make Gentiles submit to Torah do not work 'righteousness' at all, but evil." Bockmuehl, *Philippians*, 188: "[T]here may be a deliberate pun on the opponents' claim to be doing the so-called 'works of the Law'."

believers—are the "circumcision" (περιτομή) (3:3a).[18] The implication is that "we," who metaphorically are *the circumcision*, do not need this Jewish form of circumcision that amounts to mutilation.[19] As the circumcision, we are "the ones who by the Spirit of God are worshiping and boasting in Christ Jesus, and not having put confidence in the flesh" (3:3b). In other words, in contrast to those who put confidence "in the flesh" (ἐν σαρκί) by being physically circumcised in order to relate to and worship God, we are relating to and worshiping God not by the "flesh," but by the "Spirit" (πνεύματι) of God himself, and we are "boasting," thus relying upon or putting confidence "in Christ Jesus" (ἐν Χριστῷ Ἰησοῦ) rather than "in the flesh."

That in our relationship to and worship of God we believers, who "are the circumcision," depend not on the actual practice of physical circumcision, which involves putting confidence "in the flesh," but on the "Spirit" (πνεύματι) of God (3:3), reminds the audience of the fellowship of "Spirit" (πνεύματος) they share with one another and with Paul (2:1). It recalls that they are to be "standing firm in one Spirit (πνεύματι), with one mind struggling together for the faith of the gospel" (1:27), and that in his ministry of proclaiming the gospel of Christ, Paul relies upon the "supply of the Spirit (πνεύματος) of Jesus Christ" (1:19).

And we believers, who "are the circumcision," are "boasting" (καυχώμενοι), that is, relying upon our faith for a proper relationship to God at the final judgment (3:3), when Christ comes again, the "day of Christ" (1:5, 10: 2:16).[20] Furthermore, we believers are boasting "in Christ Jesus" (ἐν Χριστῷ Ἰησοῦ) himself, that is, we are boasting within the realm of our being in union with Christ Jesus as the object of our faith. This stands in sharp contrast to the putting of confidence "in the flesh" (ἐν σαρκί), which is epitomized by the Jewish practice of actual physical circumcision (3:3).[21] This "boasting in Christ Jesus" is grounded not "in the flesh" of physical

---

18. Note the wordplay between κατα-τομήν ("multilation") in 3:2 and περι-τομή ("circumcision") in 3:3. Both words have the same root—τομή (cutting, incision), but the first has the preposition κατά as its prefix, yielding a meaning of cutting down or cutting away or cutting off, hence a "mutilation." The second, in contrast, has the preposition περί as its prefix, yielding a meaning of cutting around, hence a "circumcision." O'Brien, *Philippians*, 357: "Clearly, those whom the apostle has in view when he uses this scathing description κατατομή must have insisted on circumcision as a special sign of belonging to the people of God; otherwise the wordplay does not really make sense. The boast of these opponents is overturned by using a word that links literal circumcision with those pagan cuttings of the body which were forbidden by the law of Israel. Circumcision of the flesh has become pagan lacerations. Circumcision, their greatest source of pride, is interpreted by the apostle as a sure sign that they have no part in God's people at all."

19. O'Brien, *Philippians*, 358 n. 71: "The attributive use of the definite article after the verb 'to be' signifies that 'we, and we only, are *the circumcision*'." Bockmuehl, *Philippians*, 191: "He is not saying that uncircumcised Christians are the 'true' (allegorical) circumcision and Jews are not . . . faith in Christ places Gentile believers on the same footing before God as Jewish believers, co-opting them into the Abrahamic covenant which circumcision symbolizes."

20. Trilling, "ἡμέρα," 121.

21. O'Brien, *Philippians*, 364: "It is quite likely that σάρξ does make a passing allusion to circumcision; however, it is clear from the following verses that 'confidence in *the flesh*' is something broader than this. Commentators have taken the phrase ἐν σαρκί in two ways: either (1) as a compre-

circumcision but in the gospel of Christ. If the Philippian audience play their role in advancing the gospel of Christ (2:12–15), then Paul has his "boast" (καύχημα) for the day of Christ (2:16). And if the audience "live as citizens worthy of the gospel of the Christ" (1:27), then their "boast" (καύχημα) may abound "in Christ Jesus" (ἐν Χριστῷ Ἰησοῦ) in Paul through his presence again with them (1:26).

That we believers have not "put confidence in the flesh (ἐν σαρκὶ πεποιθότες)" (3:3b) reminds the audience that our confidence is rather "in the Lord." As Paul previously informed his Philippian audience, "I have confidence in the Lord (πέποιθα δὲ ἐν κυρίῳ) that I myself will also come soon" (2:24). And during Paul's imprisonment most of the brothers, "in the Lord having confidence" (ἐν κυρίῳ πεποιθότας)" by Paul's bonds, more abundantly dare fearlessly to speak the word (1:14; cf. 1:6, 25).

The audience then hear the pivotal transition from the "c" (3:3b) to the "c′" (3:4) sub-element in the chiastic pattern in 3:2–6 as a smaller chiastic pattern in itself:

> (a) although I myself (ἐγώ) have
>> (b) confidence even in the flesh (πεποίθησιν καὶ ἐν σαρκί).
>> (c) If someone else supposes
>> (b′) to be confident in the flesh (πεποιθέναι ἐν σαρκί),
> (a′) I (ἐγώ) even more."

After the unparalleled center of this chiastic pattern, "if someone else supposes" (c), the audience hear a pivot from "confidence even in the flesh (πεποίθησιν καὶ ἐν σαρκί)" (b) to "to be confident in the flesh (πεποιθέναι ἐν σαρκί)" (b′). And when the audience hear "I (ἐγώ) even more" (a′), they hear an emphatic, parallel progression from "although I myself (ἐγώ) have" (a).

In contrast to believers, who boast in Christ Jesus, not "having put confidence in the flesh" (3:3), Paul emphatically singles himself out—"although I myself"—as a believer who not only boasts in Christ Jesus, but also has "confidence even in the flesh" (3:4a). Indeed, Paul boldly maintains that he has more confidence in the flesh than anyone else who claims it—"if someone else supposes to be confident in the flesh, I even more" (3:4b).[22] In addition to the metaphorical or spiritual "circumcision" that we believers are (3:3a), Paul's confidence within the realm of being

---

hensive expression to denote all that in which human beings place their trust, or (2), in the light of the immediately following words, as a more specific reference to the Jewish privileges and achievements Paul rejects as the ground of his confidence before God, for example, circumcision, Jewish descent, and blamelessness in fulfilment of the law. It is possible to combine the two by understanding the phrase in a comprehensive sense here at v. 3, and by regarding the further exposition in vv. 4–7 as a specific example of the former with reference to Paul and Jewish privileges and achievements."

22. O'Brien, *Philippians*, 367–68: "Not only can Paul match the grounds that the Jew or Judaizer had for boasting in himself; he can even outstrip them. These words of v. 4b are not redundant, for although the expression 'confidence in the flesh' is repeated a second time, it serves to draw at-

"in flesh" (3:4), as distinct from the realm of being "in Christ Jesus" (3:3), is based on his actual, physical, fleshly circumcision as a Jew—"with circumcision on the eighth day, from the race of Israel,[23] tribe of Benjamin,[24] a Hebrew from Hebrews" (3:5a).[25]

Paul's brash recalling of his Jewishness as a Pharisee "according to the Law (κατὰ νόμον)" (3:5a) stands in striking contrast, enhanced by an alliterative and ironic wordplay, to his warning for the audience to beware of the "mutilation (κατατομήν)" (3:2c) as a derogatory reference to the Jewish circumcision that is according to the Law.[26] The wordplay is extended as Paul reports that it was "according (κατά) to zeal" that he was persecuting the church,[27] and "according (κατά) to righteousness" that is in the Law that he became blameless (3:6).[28] The "righteousness" (δικαιοσύνην) that is in the Law reminds the audience, by way of contrast, that they are to be "filled up with the fruit of righteousness (δικαιοσύνης) that is through Jesus Christ for the glory and praise of God" (1:11). And that Paul became "blameless" (ἄμεμπτος) according to the righteousness that is in the Law recalls that the audience are to be "blameless" (ἄμεμπτοι) in the world by putting forth the gospel of Christ (2:15–16).

In sum, in this C element (3:2–6), the audience are warned to beware of those calling for them to undergo Jewish circumcision, which amounts to "mutilation" (3:2), since we believers metaphorically "are the circumcision," the ones who worship God and boast "in Christ Jesus," rather than putting confidence "in the flesh," as do those who undergo physical circumcision (3:3–4). Nevertheless, Paul insists

tention in a most emphatic way to the central problem with which Paul has to deal, namely arrogant boasting in one's own achievements as a basis for a saving relationship with God."

23. Fee, *Philippians*, 307: "What the Judaizers hope to achieve by Gentile circumcision is to bring them into the privileges of *belonging* to God's ancient people, 'Isael's race.' Paul had been given this privilege by birth (Fee's emphasis)."

24. O'Brien, *Philippians*, 371: "The tribe of Benjamin stood high in Jewish estimation—it had within its borders the city of Jerusalem and with it the temple (Jdg. 1:21)—and so it was regarded as a special privilege to belong to it."

25. Fee, *Philippians*, 307: "This is the 'swing' term, summing up the preceding three, and setting the stage for the final three. He was in every way a 'Hebrew, born of pure Hebrew stock.'"

26. O'Brien, *Philippians*, 374: "Paul had set himself apart as a κατὰ νόμον Φαρισαῖος and given himself to the service of the law, in order to walk in the way of holiness and perfect righteousness." Bockmuehl, *Philippians*, 197: "The name 'Pharisees' probably means 'the separated ones,' and basically refers to a group that assigned particular significance to the Jewish purity laws with their stress on the distinction of clean and unclean, being concerned to maintain in daily life the standard of purity and holiness required for the Temple. For this reason Pharisees needed to distance themselves from 'unclean' persons like non-observant Jews or Gentiles."

27. Fee, *Philippians*, 308: "In their own way, his Judaizing opponents are also persecuting the church; but Paul surpasses them even here."

28. Fee, *Philippians*, 310: "Paul's present point, of course, is not his sinlessness, but his being without fault in the kind of righteouness that Judaizers would bring one to, by insisting on Torah observance."

that as a model Jew he has more confidence even in the flesh than anyone else (3:5–6).

4. Phil 3:7–8a (D): I Consider All Things Gained to Be a Loss

The audience then begin to hear Paul's reassessment of his former blameless-ness according to the righteousness that is in the Law (3:5–6): "But whatever things were for me gains, these things I have considered on account of the Christ a loss. But indeed I even consider all things to be a loss" (3:7–8a). Previously the audience heard Paul use the word "gain," in a somewhat surprising and provocative way, with regard to his relationship with Christ: "For to me to live is Christ and to die is gain (κέρδος). . . having the desire for release and to be with Christ" (1:21–23). But now, in a further use of financial accounting terminology, the audience hear that whatever things were for Paul "gains" (κέρδη) in regard to his Jewishness (3:5–6),[29] in which Paul could claim to be "even more" confident in the flesh than anyone else (3:4), these very things he has now considered on account of the Christ to be one great and harmful "loss" (3:7).[30] Indeed, the attention of the audience contin-ues to be aroused through the rhetorical emphasis with which Paul maintains that now he considers not only his Jewish heritage but "all things" to be a "loss" (3:8a).

The audience have heard several significant objects of the verb "consider." In humility the audience are to be "considering" (ἡγούμενοι) one another more im-portant than themselves (2:3), in similarity to the humility of Christ, who did not "consider" (ἡγήσατο) being equal to God something to be exploited (2:6). And Paul has "considered" (ἡγησάμην) it necessary to send Epaphroditus back to the Philippians (2:25). But now Paul not only "has come to consider" (ἥγημαι, perfect tense) the things that were "gains" to him as a Jew to be a "loss" on account of the Christ (3:7),[31] but he now "considers" (ἡγοῦμαι) all things to be a "loss" (3:8a).

In sum, in this D element (3:7–8a) within the chiasm, the audience are to real-ize that whatever "gains" in his relationship with God Paul had as a model Jew he has now considered to be a "loss" on account of the Christ. And the audience are to be further impressed and surprised that indeed Paul now considers all things to be a "loss."

---

29. O'Brien, *Philippians*, 384: "As he describes how he once regarded his privileges and achievements of vv. 5 and 6, Paul employs the accounting term κέρδη in the plural: one by one he had carefully counted up the separate items of merit, conscious that when the heavenly audit occurred on the final day, his returns would be seen to be fully in order. . . . these κέρδη were not simply 'advantages' on a human plane; they were for Paul the Pharisee, zealous for God, gains at the divine level." On the marketplace metaphors in 3:7–8, see Ascough, *Paul's Macedonian Associations*, 118–20.

30. O'Brien, *Philippians*, 385: "Here at Phil. 3:7 the singular ζημία (in contrast to the plural κέρδη) indicates that Paul has come to regard his separate and carefully counted gains as one great loss."

31. O'Brien, *Philippians*, 384: "The perfect tense ἥγημαι brings out the present significance of Paul's past change of attitude." Fee, *Philippians*, 316 n. 14: "Gk. ἥγημαι, here purposefully expressed in the perfect tense (what he came to consider loss when he met Christ still holds true)."

5. Phil 3:8b (E): The Surpassing Greatness of the Knowledge of Christ Jesus My Lord

The audience then hear why Paul considers all the things he had gained formerly now to be a loss, namely: "on account of the surpassing greatness of the knowledge of Christ Jesus my Lord" (3:8b). Paul exhorted his audience to consider one another as being "more important" or of "greater significance" (ὑπερέχοντας) than themselves (2:3). And now Paul proclaims that his knowledge of Christ Jesus is of a "greatness surpassing" (ὑπερέχον) not only the things he gained from his thorough Jewishness but all other things as well. By pointing to his "knowledge" of, that is, his close personal relationship to,[32] "Christ Jesus" as "my Lord," Paul echoes, joins, and makes his own the confession of "every tongue" in the cosmos that "Jesus Christ is Lord" (2:10–11), as a result of God exalting him after his death on a cross in humility (2:8–9).[33] The implication is that the audience, whom Paul initially greeted with a prayer-wish of grace and peace from God our Father and the "Lord Jesus Christ" (1:2), will deepen their appreciation for the knowledge they share with Paul of "Christ Jesus" as their "Lord."

In sum, in this E element (3:8b) within the chiasm, the audience are to appreciate that everything Paul gained in his relationship with God from his authentic Jewish heritage has now been greatly surpassed on account of Paul's knowledge of Christ Jesus as his Lord.

6. Phil 3:8c (D´): I Have Suffered the Loss of All Things That Christ I May Gain

The audience continue to hear why all the things that were "gains" for Paul because of his Jewish heritage he now considers to be a total "loss" (3:7–8a) on account of his knowledge of Christ Jesus (3:8b): "on account of whom I have suffered the loss of all things, indeed I consider them rubbish, that Christ I may gain" (3:8c). After the unparalleled, central, and pivotal E element (3:8b) of this chiastic unit, the audience hear a progression, via the chiastic parallelism, from "these things I have considered (ἥγημαι) on account of the Christ a loss (ζημίαν). . . . I

---

32. O'Brien, *Philippians*, 388: "Paul's understanding of γνῶσις here is controlled by OT ideas of knowledge, on the one hand of God's knowledge, that is, his election of his people, and on the other hand of his people's knowledge of him as a loving and obedient response to his grace. . . . To know God was regarded as of paramount importance and meant to be in a close personal relationship with him." Fee, *Philippians*, 318: "As v. 10 will clarify, 'knowing Christ' does not mean to have head knowledge about him, but to 'know him' personally and relationally." See also Koperski, *Knowledge of Christ*, 20–65.

33. O'Brien, *Philippians*, 389: "In using the singular pronoun μου rather than the regular plural 'our,' the apostle is in no way suggesting that his relationship with Christ Jesus is an exclusive one. Rather, the wonder of this knowledge of Christ Jesus as his Lord is so great and the relationship is so intensely personal that he focuses upon it in his testimony." Fowl, *Philippians*, 153: "Paul's identification of Christ Jesus as 'my Lord' may well play on the granting of the name to the exalted Christ in 2:11. Indeed, Paul is narrating himself into the story of salvation that begins, climaxes, and will end with Christ, particularly as related in 2:6–11."

even consider (ἡγοῦμαι) all things (πάντα) to be a loss (ζημίαν)" (3:7b–8a) in the D element to "I have suffered the loss (ἐζημιώθην) of all things (πάντα),[34] indeed I consider (ἡγοῦμαι) them rubbish" (3:8c) in the D´ element. This particular chiastic parallelism reaches its climax as the audience hear the progression from "whatever things were for me gains (κέρδη)" (3:7a) in the D element to "that Christ I may gain (κερδήσω)" (3:8c) in the D´ element.

It is "on account" (δι') of whom, that is, "Christ Jesus my Lord" (3:8b), that "I," Paul, "have suffered the loss" of "all things," to the point that Paul "considers" them mere rubbish or filth (3:8c).[35] This echoes and emphasizes for the audience that Paul "considers" "all things" to be a "loss," which accentuates that he has "considered" the things he gained as a model Jew to be a "loss," "on account" (διά) of the Christ (3:7b). Whatever things were "gains" for Paul in his relationship to God because of his Jewishness and superiority in matters of the "flesh" (3:7a) he has now left behind, so that Christ "I may gain" (3:8c).[36]

In sum, with this D´ element (3:8c), the audience have been persuaded to acknowledge along with Paul that whatever things may be "gains" for them by having themselves circumcised and becoming Jewish must be considered rather as a "loss." Indeed, they must consider all things to be not only a "loss" but mere rubbish in comparison with "gaining" Christ.

7. Phil 3:9–14 (C´): I Am Pursuing the Upward Calling of God in Christ Jesus

Next the audience hear the elaboration of why Paul suffered the loss of all things, and considered them of no value, in order that he may gain Christ (3:8c): "and I may be found in him, not having my own righteousness that is from the Law but that is through faith in Christ, the—from God—righteousness based on the faith, to know him and the power of the rising of him and the fellowship of the sufferings of him, being conformed to the death of him, if somehow I may arrive to the resurrection from the dead. Not that I have already taken it or already been perfected, but I am pursuing it, if indeed I may apprehend it, for which indeed I have been apprehended by Christ Jesus. Brothers, I do not reckon that I myself have apprehended. But just one thing—forgetting the things behind but stretching out for the things ahead, according to the goal, I am pursuing to the prize of the upward calling of God in Christ Jesus" (3:9–14).

---

34. O'Brien, *Philippians*, 389: "ἐζημιώθην draws attention, not to the loss that was inflicted on him, but to his willingness to have everything confiscated or to his voluntary renunciation of everything."

35. Fee, *Philippians*, 319: "The word translated 'rubbish' [σκύβαλα] is well attested as a vulgarity, referring to excrement; on the other hand, it is also well attested to denote 'refuse,' especially of the kind that was thrown out for the dogs to forage through. Although it could possibly mean 'dung' here, more likely Paul is taking a parting shot at the 'dogs' in v. 2."

36. O'Brien, *Philippians*, 291: "'Gaining Christ' is best understood in terms of a relationship with Christ as Lord, and thus is akin to the personal knowledge of Christ already referred to . . . He desires to know Christ more, for he wants this personal relationship with his Lord to deepen. . . . a goal that will be fully realized only at the end."

With this C′ element (3:9–14) the audience hear a progression of a number of parallels from the C element (3:2–6). They hear a progression from Paul's "having" (ἔχων) confidence even in the flesh (3:4), a confidence that includes his being according to the "Law" (νόμον) a Pharisee (3:5), and according to the "righteousness" (δικαιοσύνην) that is in the "Law" (νόμῳ) blameless (3:6) in the C element to his not "having" (ἔχων) his own "righteousness" (δικαιοσύνην) that is from the "Law" (νόμου) but the "righteousness" (δικαιοσύνην) that is from God (3:9) in the C′ element. They hear a development from an emphatic focus upon Paul himself—"although I myself (ἐγώ) have confidence in the flesh" and "I (ἐγώ) even more" (3:4)—in the C element to "I do not reckon that I (ἐγώ) myself have apprehended" (3:13) in the C′ element.

They hear a development from Paul's "persecuting" (διώκων) the church (3:6) in the C element to his "pursuing" (διώκω) the resurrection from the dead (3:11–12), and his "pursuing" (διώκω) to the prize of the upward calling of God (3:14) in the C′ element. And they hear a progression from our boasting "in Christ Jesus" (ἐν Χριστῷ Ἰησοῦ, 3:3) in the C element to Paul's pursuit of the upward calling of God "in Christ Jesus" (ἐν Χριστῷ Ἰησοῦ, 3:14) in the C′ element.

Continuing to delineate what it means for him to gain Christ (3:8c), the statement, "and I may be found (εὑρεθῶ) in him" (3:9a), expresses Paul's desire for a divinely granted ("found" as divine passive) close communion with Christ, who in outward appearance was "found" (εὑρεθείς), by the agency of God or within God's plan ("found" again as divine passive), to be as a human being (2:7), before he humbled himself to the point of death on a cross and was exalted by God to a position of universal lordship (2:8–11).[37] By the gracious agency of the God who granted "him" (αὐτῷ), Christ, the name that is above every name (2:9), Paul wants to be found in "him" (αὐτῷ), the Christ whom Paul now knows as "my lord" (3:8b; cf. 2:11).[38] In sharp contrast to Paul's having become blameless according to righteousness that is "in the Law" (ἐν νόμῳ, 3:6), he now wishes to be found "in him" (ἐν αὐτῷ).

Paul's elaboration of his desire to be found in Christ (3:9a) is heard by the audience as a smaller chiastic pattern in the remainder of this verse:

(a) not having my own righteousness (δικαιοσύνην) (3:9b)
   (b) that is from (τὴν ἐκ) the Law (3:9c)
      (c) but that is through faith in Christ (3:9d),
   (b′) the—from (τὴν ἐκ) God—(3:9e)
(a′) righteousness (δικαιοσύνην) based on the faith (3:9f).

---

37. That these are the only two occurrences in the letter of the verb "find" (εὑρίσκω) enhances this connection for the audience. O'Brien, *Philippians*, 393: "'[T]o be found in Christ' really means 'to be in him' (cf. Phil. 2:7)."

38. That these are the first two occurrences in the letter of the third-person personal pronoun in the dative masculine singular to refer to Christ enhances this recall for the audience; the same form occurs only twice later in 3:16, 21.

After hearing "but that is through faith in Christ," the unparalleled pivot at the center of the chiasm in the "c" sub-element (3:9d), the audience hear a development from "that is from (τὴν ἐκ) the Law" in the "b" sub-element (3:9c) to "the—from (τὴν ἐκ) God" in the "b′" sub-element (3:9e). Finally, the audience hear a progression from "not having my own righteousness (δικαιοσύνην)" in the "a" sub-element (3:9b) to "righteousness (δικαιοσύνην) based on the faith" in the "a′" sub-element (3:9f).

Paul's desire that "I may be found *in him* (αὐτῷ)" (3:9a), that is, in close union with Christ, entails his "not having *my own* (ἐμήν) righteousness" (3:9b). With a pointed emphasis upon his own exceptional status, Paul previously declared, "although I myself have (ἐγὼ ἔχων) confidence even in the flesh" (3:4). In keen contrast, he now describes himself as "not having my own (ἔχων ἐμήν) righteousness." Whereas he had become blameless according to "righteousness" (δικαιοσύνην) that is in the "Law" (νόμῳ) (3:6), Paul now does not have his own "righteousness" (δικαιοσύνην) that is from the "Law" (νόμου, 3:9c). Rather, Paul now has the righteousness, the right relationship with God, that is through faith in "Christ" (Χριστοῦ, 3:9d), recalling and developing for the audience that it is on account of the surpassing greatness of his knowledge of "Christ" (Χριστοῦ) Jesus (3:8b) that Paul gladly suffered the loss of all things that "Christ" (Χριστόν) he may gain (3:8c).[39]

That Paul now has a righteousness that is through "faith" (πίστεως) in Christ (3:9d) reminds the audience of the faith in Christ that he shares with them. Indeed, Paul is "being poured out like a drink offering upon the sacrifice and service of your faith (πίστεως)" (2:17a), which is a cause not only for the rejoicing of Paul but of the audience's rejoicing with him (2:17b–18). Furthermore, Paul is confident that, despite his current imprisonment, he will remain alive and beside all in the audience for their advancement and joy in the "faith" (πίστεως, 1:25), that is, their faith in Christ (cf. 1:26).[40]

In a penetrating contrast to Paul not having his own righteousness that is "from the Law" (ἐκ νόμου, 3:9c) but rather is through faith in Christ (3:9d), the righteousness he now has is emphatically "from God" (ἐκ θεοῦ, 3:9e), with the emphasis enhanced by the insertion of the phrase "from God" between "the" and "righteousness" (3:9f). That this righteousness is emphatically "*from God* (θεοῦ)" and through the faith in Christ that the audience share with Paul reinforces how "we"—Paul and the audience—"are the circumcision, the ones who by the Spirit of *God* (θεοῦ) are worshiping and boasting in Christ Jesus, and not having put confidence in the flesh" (3:3). In a further contrast, the righteousness that Paul now has is not only from God rather than from the Law, but based on the faith

---

39. Veronica Koperski, "The Meaning of δικαιοσύνη in Philippians 3:9," *LS* 20 (1995): 147–69.

40. On the objective genitive meaning here of "faith in Christ," see Veronica Koperski, "The Meaning of *Pistis Christou* in Philippians 3:9," *LS* 18 (1993): 198–216; Fee, *Philippians*, 325 n. 44; Silva, *Philippians*, 161.

(3:9f) rather than on the Law. That this righteousness is based on "the faith" (τῇ πίστει), the faith in Christ that the audience share with one another and with Paul, reminds the audience of Paul's directive that they are to be struggling together with one another and with Paul for "the faith" (τῇ πίστει) of the gospel, the gospel of the Christ (1:27).

As Paul continues by expressing his desire "to know (γνῶναι) him (αὐτόν)" (3:10a), the audience begin to hear an elaboration not only of the "knowledge" (γνώσεως) of Christ Jesus whose great value surpasses anything Paul had previously gained as a model Jew (3:8b), but also of what it means for Paul to be found in "him" (αὐτῷ , 3:9a), the Christ whom Paul wants to gain (3:8c). As the concerted focus on "him" in reference to Christ continues, the audience hear delineated, by means of a rhetorical triplet of climactic emphases upon "him," what it means for Paul to know, that is, to understand and experience, "him" (3:10a):[41] and the power of the rising of *him* (αὐτοῦ, 3:10b) and the fellowship of the sufferings of *him* (αὐτοῦ, 3:10c), being conformed to the death of *him* (αὐτοῦ, 3:10d).

Paul's being "conformed" (συμμορφιζόμενος) to the "death" (θανάτῳ) of *him*, Christ (3:10d), expresses his desire to have the same "form" of humility that Christ manifested by his death. It reminds the audience of how Christ, although being in the "form" (μορφῇ) of God (2:6), humbly emptied himself, taking the "form" (μορφήν)of a slave (2:7), and further humbled himself by becoming obedient to the point of "death" (θανάτου), even of "death" (θανάτου) on a cross (2:8).[42] Paul's desire to be conformed to the humiliating death of Christ as part of the way that "Christ I may gain (κερδήσω)" (3:8c) reinforces his hope that "Christ will be magnified in my body, whether through life or through death (θανάτου, 1:20). For to me to live is Christ and to die is gain (κέρδος, 1:21)."

Paul's being conformed to the humiliating death of *him*, Christ (3:10d), further explains how he is to know *him* (3:10a), by knowing the fellowship of the sufferings of *him* (3:10c), that is, the sufferings implicitly entailed in his humiliating death on a cross (2:8). Paul's desire to know the "fellowship" (κοινωνίαν) of the "sufferings" (παθημάτων) of *him* further draws his audience into this fellowship as well. It reminds them that they share with Paul not only a "fellowship" (κοινωνία) of Spirit (2:1) but also a "fellowship" (κοινωνία) for the gospel (1:5). But this fellowship with Paul also means their sharing with Paul in his sufferings for Christ, as it reminds them that God has granted them not only to believe in Christ, "but also on behalf of him to suffer (πάσχειν, 1:29), having the same struggle, such as you saw in me and now hear in me" (1:30).

---

41. O'Brien, *Philippians*, 402: "Perhaps a paraphrase such as 'understanding and experience' brings out the nuances of Paul's statement."

42. Fee, *Philippians*, 333: "[T]he combination 'being conformed' and 'death' recall the Christ narrative in 2:6–11, offering the strongest kind of linguistic ties between Paul's story and the story of Christ." Bockmuehl, *Philippians*, 216: "[T]he apostle may be deliberately raising the issue of the 'form' of Christ's death to indicate that his own former motivation of pride has given way to one of Christ-like humility."

Paul's being conformed to the humiliating death of *him*, Christ (3:10d), also explains how he is to know *him* (3:10a), by knowing the power of the rising of *him* (3:10b), that is, the power of God implicitly active in God not only raising Jesus to life from his humiliating sufferings and death, but also exalting him to a position of universal lordship (2:9–11). For Paul to know and thus experience the divine power at work in the rising of Jesus from death to exaltation further unfolds for the audience what it means for Paul to gain Christ (3:8c). The audience are thus to realize that Paul wants to know and experience the divine power which raised and exalted Jesus from his humility, the Jesus whom Paul knows as "my Lord (κυρίου)" (3:8b), and whom every tongue may confess as "Lord" (κύριος) to the glory of God the Father (2:11).

The ultimate goal of Paul's hope that "I may gain" (κερδήσω) Christ (3:8c) and that "I may be found" (εὑρεθῶ) in him (3:9a) is that somehow "I may arrive" (καταντήσω) to the resurrection from the dead (3:11).[43] For Paul to know the power of the "rising" (ἀναστάσεως) of *him*, Christ, and the fellowship of the sufferings of *him*, by being conformed to the humiliating death of *him* (3:10), whose humble mind-set Paul and his audience are to share (2:1–8), establishes the basis for his hope. Somehow, by this same divine power active in the rising of Christ from his humility, he hopes to arrive to the final "resurrection" (ἐξανάστασιν) from the dead, the goal of his full and final knowledge of Christ (3:8–10).[44]

As Paul clarifies, "not that I have already taken (ἔλαβον) it or already been perfected" (3:12a), further reminding the audience of the humble mind-set of Christ in "taking" (λαβών) the form of a slave (2:7) and humbling himself (2:8)

---

43. The words εἴ πως, "somehow" or "if possible," should be understood as expressing real doubt and uncertainty on Paul's part about maintaining his faith in light of his impending death and thus attaining to a special resurrection of martyrs, according to R. E. Otto, " 'If Possible I May Attain the Resurrection from the Dead' (Philippians 3:11)," *CBQ* 57 (1995): 324–40. But, as O'Brien (*Philippians*, 412–13) points out, "Paul is not expressing doubt about his participation in this bodily resurrection . . . while the goal of the resurrection is certain, the way or route by which the apostle will reach it is unclear. On this view the element of uncertainty lies with πώς (= 'somehow, in some way'); he might reach the resurrection through martyrdom (or by some other kind of death), or he might be alive at the coming of Christ." Fee, *Philippians*, 336: "[W]hat is uncertain for him is whether his certain future is to be realized by resurrection or by transformation (as implied in vv. 20–21). This matter is in God's hands, to which Paul gladly submits by his use of this language."

44. O'Brien, *Philippians*, 414–15: "ἐξανάστασις ('resurrection') occurs nowhere else in the Greek Bible . . . The addition of the preposition ἐξ- before the usual form of the noun ἀνάστασις (which appears in v. 10) *reinforces* the significance of the preposition ἐκ in ἐκ νεκρῶν, that is, 'out from among dead ones'. . . . Since this raising 'out from among' the dead at the end was the work of God, the apostle could look forward to his goal with confidence and assurance" (O'Brien's emphasis); see also Fee, *Philippians*, 335 n. 68. Fowl, *Philippians*, 158: "Paul is speaking of the true and proper end of his knowledge of Christ, that is, resurrection." For a text-centered analysis of 3:1–11, see Andreas H. Snyman, "A Rhetorical Analysis of Philippians 3:1–11," *Neot* 40 (2006): 259–83. See also Mikael Tellbe, "The Sociological Factors Behind Philippians 3.1–11 and the Conflict at Philippi," *JSNT* 55 (1994): 97–121; Fabian E. Udoh, "Paul's Views on the Law: Questions About Origin (Gal. 1:6–2:21; Phil. 3:2–11)," *NovT* 42 (2000): 214–37.

before God raised and exalted him (2:9–11).[45] In other words, in his own humility Paul has not yet "taken" the resurrection Christ attained after "taking" the form of a slave and humbling himself to the point of death on a cross. But that Paul has not already "taken" it himself is complemented by the fact that "I have not already been perfected (τετελείωμαι)," so that the audience are to realize that it is not merely a matter of Paul actively taking it as a personal achievement, but of passively receiving it through the gracious action of God (divine passive).[46]

The audience then hear a contrasting parallel progression from Paul "according to zeal persecuting or pursuing (διώκων) the church" (3:6a) in his former situation as a model Jew (3:4–6) to Paul, as now a believer in Christ, "pursuing" (διώκω, 3:12b) the resurrection from the dead (3:11). That he is pursuing it "if indeed I may apprehend (καταλάβω) it" (3:12b) reinforces, intensifies, and develops for the audience, through an assonant wordplay with a cognate verb, his disclosure that "I have not already taken (ἔλαβον) it" (3:12a). Paul then quickly complements the notion that he may actively "apprehend" it himself with the notion that it is something for which "I have been apprehended (κατελήμφθην)" by Christ Jesus (3:12c), underlining for the audience that it is ultimately a gift graciously given to him.

That Paul has been apprehended for the resurrection from the dead (3:11) by "Christ Jesus" (Χριστοῦ Ἰησοῦ, 3:12c) develops and reinforces his declaration that he no longer has his own righteousness that is from the Law but that is from faith in "Christ" (Χριστοῦ, 3:9). And that Paul has been apprehended by Christ Jesus further explains for the audience how Paul's knowledge, his personal and profound experience, of "Christ Jesus" (Χριστοῦ Ἰησοῦ) as his Lord greatly surpasses all that he had gained formerly as a model Jew (3:8).[47]

With another direct address of his audience as "brothers" (ἀδελφοί, cf. 1:12; 3:1), his fellow believers, Paul draws their special attention to his announcement

---

45. That these are the only two occurrences in the letter of the verb "take" (λαμβάνω) enhances this connection.

46. O'Brien, *Philippians*, 423: "Here a possible literal rendering of the phrase (with the passive τετελείωμαι) is: 'or have already been perfected'. The expression is parallel with the preceding ἤδη ἔλαβον and is a further explanation in more literal terms of what was described figuratively of obtaining the goal. The ἤ ('or') connects two similar processes, not distinct or alternative ones." Fee, *Philippians*, 344–45: "[S]ince this verb seems intended to further clarify the first one, it carries the sense of having 'been brought to completion,' by having arrived at the final goal with regard to his knowing Christ."

47. Fee, *Philippians*, 346: "While Paul is indeed pursuing the eschatological goal with all his might, that is only because Christ was there first, pursuing him as it were, and 'apprehending' him so as to make Paul one of his own. Paul's point, as always, is that Christ's work is the prior one, and that all his own effort is simply in response to, and for the sake of, that prior 'apprehension' of him by 'Christ Jesus my Lord.'"

that "I do not reckon that I myself have apprehended" (3:13a).[48] This emphasis that "*I myself*" (ἐγὼ ἐμαυτόν) have not yet apprehended the resurrection from the dead (3:11) and thus the final gaining of the knowledge of Christ (3:8–10), as a believer in Christ (3:9), creates a sharply dramatic contrast for the audience with the emphatic focus upon Paul's personal achievement as a model Jew in matters of the "flesh."[49] It recalls his previous pronouncement that "*I myself* (ἐγώ) have confidence even in the flesh. If someone else supposes to be confident in the flesh, *I even more* (ἐγὼ μᾶλλον)" (3:4). Furthermore, that "*I myself*" have not yet "apprehended" (κατειληφέναι) as a personal achievement further underscores for the audience how it is ultimately a divinely given gift for which Paul has been "apprehended" (κατελήμφθην) by Christ Jesus (3:12c).

In contrast to the many things he personally achieved as a model Jew (3:4–6), Paul further draws the attention of his audience to "but just one thing (ἕν)," namely, "forgetting the things behind but stretching out for the things ahead" (3:13b).[50] The "things" (τά) Paul is leaving behind are included in "all the things (τά)" Paul has now suffered as a loss that he may gain Christ (3:8c). No longer focussed on these "things" from his past as a model Jew, Paul wants his fellow brothers in his Philippian audience to know that he is now, with imagery connoting an athletic race or contest, "stretching out" for the "things" (τοῖς) that lie ahead for him in the future as a believer in Christ. Furthermore, that Paul is so totally focussed on this "one thing" (ἕν) reminds his audience how they are to be thinking the "one thing" (ἕν) as they unite themselves by adopting the humble mind-set of Christ Jesus (2:2).

In a direct contrast to formerly "according to zeal persecuting (κατὰ ζῆλος διώκων) the church" (3:6a), Paul, continuing the imagery of an athletic contest, is now "according to the goal pursuing (κατὰ σκοπὸν διώκω) to the prize of the upward calling of God in Christ Jesus" (3:14). In addition, the audience are to realize that, since Paul "has been apprehended" for the resurrection from the dead (3:11) by Christ Jesus (3:12c), he is "pursuing" (διώκω) it to "apprehend" (3:12b) what he has not yet "apprehended" (3:13a), not so much as a personal achievement, but he is, according to the goal, "pursuing" (διώκω) to the "prize" that will be graciously given to him by God at the end of the contest (3:14).

---

48. O'Brien, *Philippians*, 425–26: "ἀδελφοί ('brothers'), often employed as an affectionate term of address, is no perfunctory opening to the sentence. Here it is probably intended to arrest the attention of the readers, so as to stress that what follows is important."

49. O'Brien, *Philippians*, 426: "Because of its position at the beginning of the clause ἐγώ gains special emphasis, while the presence of ἐμαυτόν, which is syntactically unnecessary, provides further weight to this strong judgment." Fee, *Philippians*, 346 n. 34: "[T]he ἐμαυτὸν ('myself') is best understood as the subject of the infinitive. Bringing it forward in the sentence is what creates the emphasis."

50. Fee (*Philippians*, 347 n. 41) notes how this pair of participles, "forgetting" (ἐπιλανθανόμενος) and "stretching out" (ἐπεκτεινόμενος), is especially poetic. This "probably accounts for both the choice of the first verb and the fact that 'what lies before' is plural. The two participles express 'manner.' The second brings special vividness to the imagery, picturing the runner who is extending himself or herself by leaning toward the goal."

That Paul is pursuing "to" (εἰς) the prize of the "upward" (ἄνω) calling of God
in Christ Jesus (3:14) tells his audience that Paul's hope of arriving "to" (εἰς) the
"resurrection" (ἐξανάστασιν), the "upward" movement, from the dead (3:11) is
based on his faith in Christ Jesus that this "prize" of resurrection and thus the
final gaining of the knowledge of Christ will be given to him through the calling of God.[51] And that Paul is, according to the goal, pursuing to the prize of the
"upward" calling of God in Christ Jesus explains for his audience the ultimate
goal of his hope to know, that is, to personally experience, the power of the "rising" (ἀναστάσεως), the "upward" movement, of *him*, Christ Jesus (3:10a). This
"upward" calling of God reminds the audience of how God is calling believers in
Christ Jesus to participate in God's exaltation, God's "upward" calling, that Christ
Jesus experienced after he humbled himself to the point of death on a cross (2:6–
11). The audience are to respond to and participate in this "upward" calling of God
by adopting a Christ-like humble mind-set (2:1–5).[52]

That Paul is pursuing to the prize of the upward calling of "God" (θεοῦ) "in
Christ Jesus" (ἐν Χριστῷ Ἰησοῦ) (3:14) is aimed at persuading the audience that,
as believers in Christ, they, like Paul, now have the righteousness that is not from
the Law but from "God" (θεοῦ), the righteousness based on the faith, faith in
"Christ" (Χριστοῦ) (3:9). It is aimed at further persuading the audience not to have
themselves circumcised and become Jewish (3:2), because we believers are "the
circumcision," those who are worshiping by the Spirit of "God" (θεοῦ) himself,
and boasting "in Christ Jesus" (ἐν Χριστῷ Ἰησοῦ) (3:3). Like Paul, the audience,
as believers boasting within the realm of being "in Christ Jesus," are to pursue, according to the goal of arriving to the resurrection from the dead (3:11) and thus to
knowing Christ finally and fully (3:8–10), to the prize of the upward calling of God
to be graciously given to them through their faith in Christ Jesus.[53]

In sum, in this C′ element (3:9–14), the audience have been persuaded that
Paul now has a righteousness that is not from the Law, according to which he
was circumcised as a Jew, but that is from God and through faith in Christ (3:9).
Therefore, the audience are not to have themselves circumcised and become Jew-

---

51. Fee, *Philippians*, 348 n. 45: "The εἰς is best understood as telic, indicating the purpose or
goal of his 'pursuit,' rather than simply directional."

52. David J. Williams, *Paul's Metaphors: Their Context and Character* (Peabody, Mass.: Hendrickson, 1999), 278 n. 35: "Here the prize is defined by the genitive, 'of the upward call" (τῆς ἄνω
κλήσεως). Because they are 'in Christ,' those who have endured to the end—who have run with
patience the race set before them—are 'called up' at last by God to receive the final issue of their
salvation." On "calling" (κλῆσις) here, Fee (*Philippians*, 349 n. 49) states that "this noun, which accents the event of calling rather than status or condition, is a nearly technical term for God's call of
the believer to himself."

53. Fee, *Philippians*, 350: "[I]n this case God's call has been effected for him and them 'in
Christ Jesus.' As throughout the letter, this preposition is probably locative, not instrumental,
pointing to the sphere in which God's calling took place; it happened 'in Christ Jesus,' meaning in
his death and resurrection, and it has been effected for Paul as one who trusts in and therefore lives
'in Christ Jesus.' Thus Christ is both the means and the end of God's call."

ish (3:2). Rather, as those worshiping by the Spirit of God himself and boasting in Christ Jesus (3:3), they, like Paul, are to have the hope of arriving to the resurrection from the dead by the divine power active in the rising of Christ (3:10–11). Through their faith in Christ Jesus they are to pursue to the prize of this upward calling of God (3:12–14).

8. Phil 3:15–19 (B´): This Also God Will Reveal to You and Many Times I Told You

The audience are further drawn into Paul's way of thinking and behaving: "As many as then (would be) perfect, this let us think. And if something otherwise you are thinking, this also God will reveal to you. Nevertheless, to what we have attained, to the same hold fast. Become my fellow imitators, brothers, and look at those who are thus walking, just as you have us as a model. For many are walking, about whom many times I told you, and now even weeping I tell you, that they are the enemies of the cross of Christ. Their end is destruction, their God is their stomach and their glory is in their shame, those who are thinking the things of the earth" (3:15–19).

By way of the chiastic parallels with this B´ element (3:15–19), the audience hear a progression from the B element (3:1b) in direct references to them as "you." That Paul's writing the same things "to you" (ὑμῖν), is not burdensome for him, but "to you" (ὑμῖν) is assuring (3:1b) progresses to what God will reveal "to you" (ὑμῖν, 3:15) and to what Paul many times has told "to you" (ὑμῖν, 3:18).

The audience experience this B´ element as a chiastic pattern in itself:

(a) [3:15a] As many as then (would be) perfect, this let us think (φρονῶμεν). And if something otherwise you are thinking (φρονεῖτε),

   (b) [15b] this also God (θεός) will reveal to you.

      (c) [16] Nevertheless, to what we have attained, to the same hold fast. [17a] Become my fellow imitators, brothers, and look at those who are thus walking (περιπατοῦντας),

         (d) [17b] just as you have us as a model.

      (c´) [18] For many are walking (περιπατοῦσιν), about whom many times I told you, and now even weeping I tell you, that they are the enemies of the cross of Christ.

   (b´) [19a] Their end is destruction, their God (θεός) is their stomach and their glory is in their shame,

(a´) [19b] those who are thinking (φρονοῦντες) the things of the earth.

After hearing "just as you have us as a model" in the "d" sub-element (3:17b), the unparalleled and pivotal center of this chiastic pattern, the audience hear a progression from "look at those who are thus walking (περιπατοῦντας)" in the "c" sub-element (3:16–17a) to "many are walking (περιπατοῦσιν)" in the "c´" sub-element (3:18). They then hear a development from "this also God (θεός) will reveal to you" in the "b" sub-element (3:15b) to "their God (θεός) is their stomach" in the "b'" sub-element (3:19a). And finally, the audience hear a progression from "this let us think (φρονῶμεν)" and "if something otherwise you are thinking (φρονεῖτε)" in the "a" sub-element (3:15a) to "those who are thinking (φρονοῦντες) the things of the earth" in the "a'" sub-element (3:19b).

Having heard that Paul has not yet been "perfected" (τετελείωμαι, 3:12), but that he desires to be "perfected" by God (divine passive), that is, to arrive to the resurrection from the dead (3:11), and thus to the full and final knowledge and gaining of Christ (3:8–10), the audience are invited to join Paul in his pursuit of such a future "perfection," as he presents them with an attractive offer, "as many as then (would be) perfect (τέλειοι), this let us think" (3:15a).[54] "This" (τοῦτο), that is, being "perfect," arriving at the "perfection" of fully and finally knowing and gaining Christ, is what Paul exhorts his audience to be "thinking" about along with him, that is, having the same attitude or mind-set as Paul, a way of thinking attuned and focussed on this kind of God-given "perfection" as their life's goal.

Paul's exhortation, "this let us think (τοῦτο φρονῶμεν) and if something otherwise you are thinking (φρονεῖτε)," resonates for his audience with his previous directive to them, "this go on thinking (τοῦτο φρονεῖτε) in you, which is also in Christ Jesus" (2:5), before he exhorted them to have the same humble mind-set as Christ, before God exalted him upward to being Lord over all (2:6–11). This is similar to the "upward calling of God" (3:14), for which Paul and his audience are to be "thinking" about being "perfect" (τέλειοι) (3:15a). This humble mind-set of Christ is the "one thing" the audience, united in mind, are to be "thinking" (φρονοῦντες), the "same thing" they are to "think" (φρονῆτε) in order to fill up Paul's joy (2:2). Paul is thus exhorting them to the same sort of mind-set according to which it is right for him to "think" (φρονεῖν, 1:7) that the God who began in them a good work "will perfect" (ἐπιτελέσει) it until the day of Christ Jesus (1:6).[55]

But if the audience adopt a different mind-set and are thinking something otherwise (3:15a), this God (θεός), the God (θεοῦ) who is calling them upward in Christ Jesus (3:14), will reveal to them. Indeed, that God will reveal this "to you" (ὑμῖν) reinforces for the audience that Paul's writing the same things "to you (ὑμῖν), to me is not burdensome, but to you (ὑμῖν) is assuring" (3:1b).

Rather than allowing themselves to become Jews by being physically circumcised, and thus "mutilated" (3:2), the audience are, along with Paul, to hold fast

---

54. The opening Greek clause states literally, "as many as then perfect" (ὅσοι οὖν τέλειοι), and thus has no explicit verbal form, but the most natural implicit verbal notion to be supplied, based on Paul's not yet having been perfected, is "would be"—"as many as then would be (like Paul) perfect, this let us (Paul and his audience) think."

55. O'Brien, *Philippians*, 437: "As has already been shown, φρονέω is a significant term in this letter, and it has to do with a person's whole disposition or direction of life. In this context it involves continually pursuing the same Christ-centered ambition Paul has."

to what "we have attained" (ἐφθάσαμεν) (3:16).[56] This reminds them that "we are" (ἐσμεν) the "circumcision," the ones who by the Spirit of God are worshiping and boasting in Christ Jesus, and not having put confidence in the flesh (3:3).

Addressed yet again as "brothers" (cf. 1:12; 3:1, 13), fellow believers with Paul, the audience are to become "fellow imitators" (συμμιμηταί) of "me" (μου) (3:17a), of the Paul who knows Christ Jesus as "my" (μου) Lord (3:8). They are to join Paul in imitating the Christ who became Lord not only of Paul but of the universe (2:6–11), by adopting the same humble mind-set (2:5) which resulted in God exalting Jesus to this lordship over all. They are thus to imitate Paul as he imitates the way that Jesus, by his humble way of thinking, responded to "the upward calling of God" (3:14).[57] They are to be fellow imitators of Paul, who according to the "goal" (σκοπόν) is pursuing to the prize of this upward calling of God in Christ Jesus (3:14). They are to do this by "looking at" (σκοπεῖτε), thus keeping as their "goal," those who are thus "walking," that is behaving and living as fellow imitators of Paul (3:17a).[58]

As a model of those who are thus "walking" as fellow imitators of Paul, the audience have "us" (3:17b). This model includes, first of all, Paul himself, whose knowledge of the Christ he hopes to fully and finally gain and entails being conformed to the humility of his death (3:10; cf. 2:8), to the point that he can say, "For to me to live is Christ and to die is gain" (1:21). But it also includes Epaphroditus, who, on account of the work of Christ came near to the point of death, recalling Christ's actual death on a cross (cf. 2:8), "risking his life, so that he might fill up your lack of service toward me" (2:30). That "you have" (ἔχετε) us as a model (3:17b) resonates with Paul's previous directive for the audience to "have" (ἔχετε) such people as Epaphroditus in esteem (2:29). And the model also includes Timothy, as Paul has no one as like minded as him, who, unlike others, seeks the things of Jesus Christ, and has selflessly served with Paul for the gospel (2:20–22).[59]

The audience are to look at those who are thus "walking" (περιπατοῦντας), just as they have "us," which includes Paul, Timothy, and Epaphroditus, as a model

---

56. Rainer Metzner, "Paulus und der Wettkampf: Die Rolle des Sports in Leben und Verkündigung des Apostels (1 Kor 9.24–7; Phil 3.12–16)," *NTS* 46 (2000): 565–83.

57. Fee, *Philippians*, 364: "In every case 'imitation' of Paul means 'as I imitate Christ' (expressly so in 1 Cor 11:1; cf. 1 Thess 1:6)."

58. Thurston, *Philippians*, 132: "The verb σκοπεῖτε has the same root as "goal" (σκοπός) in v. 14." Silva, *Philippians*, 179: "The imperative σκοπεῖτε may also reflect a contrast with the βλέπετε of verse 2; considering the Judaizers, or watching out for them, must not prevent the Philippians from keeping their eyes on the positive examples that God has provided for them."

59. See O'Brien (*Philippians*, 450), who "regards ἡμᾶς as referring to both Paul, the dominant member of the team, and his associates such as Timothy and Epaphroditus." Fee, *Philippians*, 362 n. 3: "[B]oth Timothy (who looks out for the interests of Christ Jesus) and Epaphroditus (who risked his life for the sake of the gospel) are set before them as among those who 'imitate' Christ in this way." For a recent discussion of 3:17 in relation to the issue of the integrity of the letter, see Angela Standhartinger, " 'Join in Imitating Me' (Philippians 3.17): Towards an Interpretation of Philippians 3," *NTS* 54 (2008): 417–35.

(3:17), because many are "walking" (περιπατοῦσιν), that is, behaving and living, as enemies of the cross of Christ (3:18).[60] That they are enemies of the "cross" (σταυροῦ) of Christ—whatever else this may involve—tells the audience that they have not adopted the humble mind-set of Christ, who humbled himself to the point of death, even of death on a "cross" (σταυροῦ, 2:8).[61] Paul's lamentful statement that about these people "many times I told you (ὑμῖν), and now even weeping I tell you, that they are the enemies of the cross of Christ" (3:18), further reinforces his previous declaration that "to write the same things to you (ὑμῖν), to me is not burdensome, but to you (ὑμῖν) is assuring" (3:1b).

In a contrasting wordplay to as many in the audience as would be "perfect" (τέλειοι, 3:15), and thus be "perfected" (τετελείωμαι, 3:12) as Paul hopes to be, by fully and finally knowing and gaining Christ (3:8–10), the "end" (τέλος) of the enemies of the cross of Christ is final destruction (3:19a). They will thus not be truly "perfected" nor arrive at the "end" of the resurrection from the dead (3:11). That the end of these enemies of the cross of Christ is "destruction" (ἀπώλεια, 3:19a) reinforces Paul's previous exhortation for his audience not to be "intimidated in anything by the opponents, which is for them a demonstration of destruction (ἀπωλείας, 1:28), but of your salvation, and this is from God, for to you has been granted that which is on behalf of Christ, not only in him to believe but also on behalf of him to suffer, having the same struggle, such as you saw in me and now hear in me" (1:28–30).[62]

The true God (θεός), the God (θεοῦ) who is calling them upward in Christ Jesus (3:14) and the God (θεοῦ) by whose Spirit they are worshiping (3:3), will reveal to the audience whether they are thinking something different than becoming perfect by adopting the humble mind-set of Christ (3:15b). But the false "God" (θεός) of these enemies of the cross of Christ is their stomach or belly (3:19a), which, based on the previous context (3:2–6), would seem to refer to matters of the "flesh," including their concern for circumcision and perhaps the food laws of Judaism.[63]

---

60. O'Brien, *Philippians*, 451: "περιπατοῦσιν ('walk, live') is deliberately used by way of antithesis to the godly example of those who walk (περιπατοῦντας), v. 17) in conformity with the Pauline model." Fee, *Philippians*, 365 n. 13: "Gk. περιπατοῦντας: only here and in v. 18 in this letter, but the primary verb in Paul for paraenesis. The usage derives from his Jewish heritage, where God's people are to 'walk in the ways of the Lord'."

61. That these are the only two occurrences in the letter of the word "cross" enhances the significance of this connection. Fee, *Philippians*, 370: "Paul's concern is for the Philippians to 'walk' in a way that conforms to the death of Christ, even death on the cross. Those who are to be 'marked' as walking *contrary to the pattern Paul set* for them are first of all described as 'enemies of the cross of Christ'" (Fee's emphasis).

62. On "destruction" (ἀπώλεια) here Fee (*Philippians*, 371 n. 35) notes : "This is the language of eternal loss; it is generally reserved by Paul to describe the eternal destiny of those outside of Christ."

63. "Stomach" (κοιλία) here should be interpreted as a euphemism for the circumcised member, according to J. Moiser, "The Meaning of *Koilia* in Philippians 3:19," *ExpTim* 108 (1997): 365–66.

Their "glory" (δόξα) is in their "shame" (3:19a)—a further vilification of the "mutilation" of Jewish circumcision (3:2), rather than in the acknowledgment of the universal lordship of Jesus Christ "to the glory (δόξαν) of God the Father" (2:11).[64] Their concern for righteousness from the Jewish Law (3:9) opposes them to the audience who are to be "filled up with the fruit of righteousness that is through Jesus Christ for the glory (δόξαν) and praise of God" (1:11). And that their glory is in their "shame" (αἰσχύνη) ironically indicates to the audience that the basis for their present "glory," the "shame" of Jewish circumcision, will ultimately lead to their being "shamed" by God in the final judgment. This stands in pointed contrast to the hope of Paul that "in nothing I will be put to shame (αἰσχυνθήσομαι) but in all boldness as always and now Christ will be magnified in my body, whether through life or through death" (1:20).[65]

These enemies of the cross of Christ are those who are "thinking" (φρονοῦντες) the things of the earth (3:19b). This pits them against the audience, who are not to be "thinking" (φρονεῖτε) something otherwise than following Paul's exhortation that "we think" (φρονῶμεν) about becoming "perfect" (3:15a) by answering the calling of God upward (3:14) in adopting the humble mind-set of Christ. He was exalted from his humility upward to the status of universal lordship (2:6–11).

The audience are to realize that these enemies of the cross of Christ, by thinking the things "of the earth" (ἐπίγεια), are models not to be imitated, since they are failing to number themselves among "those on earth" (ἐπιγείων) whose "knee should bend at the name of Jesus" (2:10), as they look beyond the things of the earth upward (3:14) to the things of heaven in confessing Jesus Christ as Lord to the glory of God the Father (2:11).[66] In thinking "the things" (τά) of the earth, these enemies are thus providing the audience with examples of those who seek "the

---

O'Brien, *Philippians*, 456: "[I]t has been suggested that κοιλία is being employed here similarly to Paul's use of σάρξ in an ethical sense to describe the old earthbound humanity from which the believer has been rescued into the new humanity in Christ. . . . accordingly, those who are enemies of Christ's cross have failed to accept the death of the old life, the κοιλία, and have disqualified themselves from the new." For other ways of interpreting κοιλία in Paul, see Karl Olav Sandnes, *Belly and the Body in the Pauline Epistles* (STNSMS 120; New York: Cambridge University Press, 2002); Brian S. Rosner, *Greed as Idolatry: The Origin and Meaning of a Pauline Metaphor* (Grand Rapids: Eerdmans, 2007), 94–98.

64. O'Brien, *Philippians*, 457: "Accordingly, the apostle is heaping bitter scorn on the rite of circumcision (cf. 3:2) when it becomes the thing in which one boasts and the ground of their salvation."

65. O'Brien, *Philippians*, 457: "The apostle could then be saying that they glory in these things, namely their circumcision and spiritual experience, but it will turn out to be their disgrace (αἰσχύνη) at the final judgment."

66. That these are the only two occurrences in the letter of the term "earthly" or "of the earth" facilitates this connection. Thurston, *Philippians*, 133: "The enemies' habitual attitude is directed toward what is of the earth, not the 'upward call' commended in v. 14."

things" (τά) of themselves rather than "the things" (τά) of Jesus Christ (2:21). It is his humble way of thinking the audience are to imitate along with Paul (3:17).[67]

In this B´ element (3:15–19), then, the audience are invited to become fellow imitators of Christ along with Paul by following such models as Paul, Timothy, and Epaphroditus in imitating Christ's humble way of thinking manifested in his death on a cross, which led to his exaltation upward to a heavenly status of universal lordship (3:15–17). They are not to imitate the enemies of the cross of Christ, whose final "end" is destruction, as they are thinking the things of the earth, rather than the heavenly "perfection" of the upward calling of God that the audience are to pursue along with Paul in Christ Jesus (3:18–19).

9. Phil 3:20–21 (A´): We Are Awaiting the Lord Jesus Christ

The audience then hear of the inspiring and hopeful final outcome of their adoption, as imitators of and with Paul, of the humble mind-set of Christ: "For our citizenship is existing in heaven, from which indeed a savior we are awaiting, the Lord Jesus Christ, who will transform the body of our humbleness (to be) conformed to the body of his glory according to the working that empowers him even to subject to himself all things" (3:20–21). At this point the audience experience a climactic progression, via the chiastic parallels, from the exhortation to rejoice in the "Lord" (κυρίῳ) in the A element (3:1a) to the hope-filled announcement that a savior we are awaiting, the "Lord" (κύριον) Jesus Christ (3:20), in the A´ element (3:20–21).

In sharp contrast to the enemies of the cross of Christ (3:18), who are thinking "the things of the earth" (τὰ ἐπίγεια, 3:19), "our" (ἡμῶν)—Paul's and the Philippians'—citizenship is already existing "in the heavens" (ἐν οὐρανοῖς) (3:20a).[68] This "citizenship" (πολίτευμα) is an appropriately attractive and meaningful status for the Philippians, who reside in a distinguished Roman colony (cf. Acts 16:12).[69]

---

67. O'Brien, *Philippians*, 458: "What determines the whole pattern of living of the opponents referred to in Phil. 3:19 is ultimately the earthly sphere of sin. They are concerned with values that pass away—they have neither divine origin nor eternal worth." Bockmuehl, *Philippians*, 232: "After all is said and done, however, we will do well to recall that in the present context Paul's interest in these enemies of the cross is general and rhetorical rather than specific and sustained. They are evidently of no acute importance to Paul, and their sole appearance in this letter serves merely to give sharper definition to the Christ-centered orientation which Paul wants to commend to his readers."

68. O'Brien, *Philippians*, 459: "[T]he position of ἡμῶν shows that those described are emphatically contrasted with the opponents of the preceding verse." Fee, *Philippians*, 378 n. 14: "Gk. ἡμῶν γάρ, where the 'our' stands in the emphatic first position, intending the strongest kind of contrast to 'them.'" And note the similarity between 3:21a and 3:3a.

69. O'Brien, *Philippians*, 461: "So, writing to Christians in a city proud of its relation to Rome, Paul tells the Philippians that they belong to a heavenly commonwealth, that is, their state and constitutive government is in heaven, and as its citizens they are to reflect its life." Fee, *Philippians*, 379: "Citizens of the Roman 'commonwealth' they may well be, and proudly so, but the greater reality is that they are subjects of the heavenly 'Lord' and 'Savior,' Jesus Christ, and therefore their true 'commonwealth' exists in heaven."

It resonates with and reinforces Paul's previous imperative for the audience "to live as citizens (πολιτεύεσθε) worthy of the gospel of the Christ" (1:27). That it is already "existing" (ὑπάρχει) for them "in the heavens" reminds the audience that Christ Jesus was "existing" (ὑπάρχων) in the form of God, and thus in a heavenly status (2:6),[70] before God exalted him from the humility of his death on a cross (2:8) to a universal lordship (2:11) confessed by all, including "those in heaven" (ἐπουρανίων) (2:10).[71]

It is from this heavenly position of universal lordship, then, that "a savior we are awaiting, the Lord Jesus Christ" (3:20b). Paul thus invites his audience to confidently await, along with him, a "savior" (σωτῆρα), who will bring both Paul and the Philippians to their final "salvation" (σωτηρία, cf. 1:19, 28; 2:12).[72] That "we are awaiting" Jesus Christ as the heavenly "Lord" (κύριον) over all draws the audience further into sharing with Paul the surpassing knowledge of Christ Jesus as "my Lord (κυρίου)" (3:8b). And it reinforces, with a further exhilarating motivation, Paul's previous imperative for the audience to rejoice in the "Lord" (κυρίῳ) (3:1a).[73] Furthermore, the word order of the full, emphatic title "Lord Jesus Christ" here recalls for the audience the climactic and universal confession that "Lord is Jesus Christ" (2:11).

The hope of Paul that "Christ will be magnified in my body (σώματί), whether through life or through death" (1:20) now expands to embrace both Paul and his audience. The Jesus Christ whom "we are awaiting" with hope is the Lord (3:20b) who will transform the "body" (σῶμα) of our humbleness to be conformed to the "body" (σώματι) of his glory (3:21a). The hope that he will transform the body of our "humbleness" (ταπεινώσεως) reinforces Paul's previous exhortation for the audience, in "humility" (ταπεινοφροσύνη), to consider one another more important than themselves (2:3), as they imitate the humble mind-set of Christ Jesus who "humbled" (ἐταπείνωσεν) himself to the point of a humiliating death on a cross (2:8).[74]

---

70. That these are the only two occurrences in the letter of the verb "exist" (ὑπάρχω) enhances this connection.

71. O'Brien, *Philippians*, 461: "This heavenly commonwealth is a present reality—note the important present tense ὑπάρχει ('is, exists, is present')—and believers are, while living in this present world, already citizens of it."

72. O'Brien, *Philippians*, 462 n. 120: "[A]lthough σωτήρ is not a title its appropriateness is apparent in the context of a letter to Philippi, where the Emperor was regarded as 'saviour'." Fee, *Philippians*, 380 n. 23: "Gk. σωτῆρα, which stands in the emphatic first position (the object before the verb) and without the definite article. But it is doubtful that Paul intended merely 'a Savior,' as some contend. Rather the anarthrous usage is emphatic, as with the anarthrous κύριον Ἰησοῦν Χριστόν that follows. This is probably a variation on 'Colwell's rule,' that a definite predicate noun that precedes the verb is usually anarthrous." Garland, "Philippians," 250: "The term 'savior' is rare in Paul and is probably used because it was a title given to Caesar as 'savior of the world.'"

73. Fee, *Philippians*, 381: "Here is the ultimate reason for their rejoicing *in the Lord*" (Fee's emphasis).

74. The translation, "he will transform our body characterized by humility," for 3:21a is proposed by Peter Doble, "'Vile Bodies' or Transformed Persons? Philippians 3.21 in Context," *JSNT* 86 (2002): 3–27.

Paul's being "conformed" (συμμορφιζόμενος) to the death (3:10) of the Lord
Jesus Christ, as a model of humility for the audience, is now complemented by
the hope of being "conformed" (σύμμορφον) to the body of his glory (3:21a).[75]
In keen contrast to the enemies of the cross of Christ whose "glory" (δόξα) is in
their shame (3:19), the hope for Paul and his audience is that our body will be conformed to the "glory" (δόξης) of the Lord Jesus Christ, whose universal lordship is
ultimately for the "glory" (δόξαν) of God (2:11; 1:11).

The transformation of the body of our humbleness to be conformed to the
body of his glory (3:21a) will take place "according to the working that empowers him even to subject to himself all things" (3:21b). This divine "working"
(ἐνέργειαν) reminds the audience how "God is the one working (ἐνεργῶν) in you
both to desire and to work (ἐνεργεῖν) for the sake of his good pleasure (2:13). This
working that "empowers" (δύνασθαι) him is the same divine "power" (δύναμιν)
that effected his rising (3:10) from the humility of his death on a cross to his exaltation as universal Lord (2:6–11). That this working empowers him even to subject
to himself "all things" (πάντα) emphatically and climactically reinforces for the
audience the confession of his universal lordship as the one whom God exalted
and "granted him the name that is above _every_ (πᾶν) name, so that at the name of
Jesus _every_ (πᾶν) knee should bend, of those in heaven and of those on earth and
of those under the earth, and _every_ (πᾶσα) tongue confess that Jesus Christ is Lord
to the glory of God the Father" (2:9–11).[76]

In sum, in this A´ element (3:20–21) the audience are assured that they have
a citizenship already existing in the heavens in contrast to the enemies of the cross
of Christ (3:18), who are thinking the things of the earth (3:19). Paul's imperative
for the audience to rejoice in the Lord (3:1a) is bolstered by the hope that we are
awaiting the Lord Jesus Christ as a savior from heaven, who will transform the
body of our humbleness, as we imitate the humble mind-set of Christ, to be conformed to the body of his exalted glory according to the force of the divine power

---

75. O'Brien, *Philippians*, 465: "Here by means of the adjective σύμμορφος Paul indicates that
the bodies the people of Christ will possess in the age to come will be of the same heavenly order as
his own resurrected and glorified body. His resurrection is the guarantee of their resurrection, and
his resurrected body is the prototype and paradigm of theirs."

76. O'Brien, *Philippians*, 467: "The Philippians have been exhorted to be conformed to Christ's
likeness in humility. At 2:6–11 nothing was said about their exaltation. Now in these concluding
verses of chap. 3 Paul spells out what will happen to Christians at the appearance of the Lord Jesus
Christ. They will be exalted when he transforms them into his own likeness." Bockmuehl, *Philippians*, 236: "It serves as a confirmation of Paul's high christology that the equivalent act of subjec-
tion was in 2.9–11 ascribed to God." See also David A. DeSilva, "No Confidence in the Flesh: The
Meaning and Function of Philippians 3:2–21," *TJ* 15 (1994): 27–54; Darrell J. Doughty, "Citizens of
Heaven: Philippians 3.2–21," *NTS* 41 (1995): 102–22; G. L. Nebeker, "Christ as Somatic Transformer
(Phil 3:20–21): Christology in an Eschatological Perspective," *TJ* 21 (2000): 165–87; Andreas H.
Snyman, "A Rhetorical Analysis of Philippians 3:12– 21," *Acta Patristica et Byzantina* 17 (2006):
327–48.

that raised him from the humility of his death and empowered him to subject to himself all things.

C. SUMMARY ON PHILIPPIANS 3:1–21

1. The audience are to continue to rejoice with Paul in the ongoing proclamation of Christ (3:1a).

2. The audience are alerted to hear things they may have heard from Paul before but that they have yet to hear in this letter, things aimed at further reassuring them (3:1b).

3. The audience are warned to beware of those calling for them to undergo Jewish circumcision, which amounts to "mutilation," since we believers metaphorically "are the circumcision," the ones who worship God and boast "in Christ Jesus," rather than putting confidence "in the flesh," as do those who undergo physical circumcision. Nevertheless, Paul insists that as a model Jew he has more confidence even in the flesh than anyone else (3:2–6).

4. The audience are to realize that whatever "gains" in his relationship with God Paul had as a model Jew he has now considered to be a "loss" on account of the Christ. And the audience are to be further impressed and surprised that indeed Paul now considers all things to be a "loss" (3:7–8a).

5. The audience are to appreciate that everything Paul gained in his relationship with God from his authentic Jewish heritage has now been greatly surpassed on account of Paul's knowledge of Christ Jesus as his Lord (3:8b).

6. The audience have been persuaded to acknowledge along with Paul that whatever things may be "gains" for them by having themselves circumcised and becoming Jewish must be considered rather as a "loss." Indeed, they must consider all things to be not only a "loss" but mere rubbish in comparison with "gaining" Christ (3:8c).

7. The audience have been persuaded that Paul now has a righteousness that is not from the Law, according to which he was circumcised as a Jew, but that is from God and through faith in Christ. Therefore, the audience are not to have themselves circumcised and become Jewish. Rather, as those worshiping by the Spirit of God himself and boasting in Christ Jesus, they, like Paul, are to have the hope of arriving to the resurrection from the dead by the divine power active in the rising of Christ. Through their faith in Christ Jesus they are to pursue to the prize of this upward calling of God (3:9–14).

8. The audience are invited to become fellow imitators of Christ along with Paul by following such models as Paul, Timothy, and Epaphroditus in imitating Christ's humble way of thinking manifested in his death on a cross, which led to his exaltation upward to a heavenly status of universal lordship. They are not to imitate the enemies of the cross of Christ, whose final "end" is destruction, as they are thinking the things of the earth, rather than the heavenly "perfection" of the

upward calling of God that the audience are to pursue along with Paul in Christ Jesus (3:15–19).

9. The audience are assured that they have a citizenship already existing in the heavens in contrast to the enemies of the cross of Christ (3:18), who are thinking the things of the earth (3:19). Paul's imperative for the audience to rejoice in the Lord (3:1a) is bolstered by the hope that we are awaiting the Lord Jesus Christ as a savior from heaven, who will transform the body of our humbleness, as we imitate the humble mind-set of Christ, to be conformed to the body of his exalted glory according to the force of the divine power that raised him from the humility of his death and empowered him to subject to himself all things (3:20–21).

10

PHILIPPIANS 4:1–5: REJOICE IN THE LORD, REJOICE (C′)

Rejoice in the Lord Who Is Near

A: ^{4:1} So that, my brothers beloved and longed for, my *joy* and crown, thus stand firm *in the Lord*, beloved. ² Euodia I exhort and Syntyche I exhort to think the same thing *in the* Lord.

 B: ^{3a}Yes, I ask also you, genuine *yokemate,*

  C: ^{3b} *bring them together,*

  C′: ^{3c}those who in the gospel *have struggled together* with me,

 B′: ^{3d}with also Clement and the rest of my *co-workers,* whose names are in the book of life.

A′: ⁴*Rejoice in the Lord* always. Again I will say, *rejoice.* ⁵ Let your forbearance be known to all human beings. The *Lord* is near.¹

A. CHIASTIC DEVELOPMENT FROM PHILIPPIANS 1:12–18 (C) TO 4:1–5 (C′)

With Phil 4:1–5, the C′ unit within the macrochiastic structure embracing the entire letter, the audience hear resonances, by way of the chiastic parallelism, of 1:12–18, the corresponding C unit in the overall chiasm.² The mention of Clement and the "rest" (λοιπῶν) of my co-workers (4:3) in the C′ unit recalls how the bonds of Paul have become in Christ manifest in the whole praetorium and to *all* the "rest" (λοιποῖς) in the C unit, as references to those associated with Paul.³ The twofold occurrence of the verb for "rejoice" in Paul's imperatives for the audience to "rejoice" (χαίρετε) in the Lord always and again he will say "rejoice" (χαίρετε) (4:4) in the C′ unit recalls and complements the twofold occurrence of the same verb to express Paul's joy, "Christ is proclaimed, and in this I rejoice (χαίρω). And indeed I will be joyful (χαρήσομαι)" (1:18), in the C unit.

---

1. For the establishment of 4:1–5 as a chiasm, see ch. 2.

2. This section is limited to demonstrating the macrochiastic parallels. The exegetical signifi-cance of these parallels is presented in the next section.

3. That these are the only two occurrences in the letter of the plural adjectival form for "rest" enhances the significance of this connection. The formulaic τὸ λοιπόν, "furthermore" or "finally," oc-curs in 3:1 and 4:8.

B. Audience Response To Philippians 4:1–5

1. Phil 4:1–2 (A): As My Joy Stand Firm and Think the Same in the Lord

Paul puts forth further consequences of what he has been saying to the audience he holds to be especially dear to him: "So that, my brothers beloved and longed for, my joy and crown, thus stand firm in the Lord, beloved. Euodia I exhort and Syntyche I exhort to think the same thing in the Lord" (4:1–2). Paul's direct address of his audience here not only resonates with but elaborately develops previous direct addresses of his audience, especially those employing the first-person singular possessive pronoun to underline Paul's close personal relationship to his audience to whom he is issuing a particular directive.

Thus, first of all, Paul's address to his audience as "my brothers (ἀδελφοί μου) beloved and longed for, my (μου) joy and crown" (4:1a), with the general directive for them to stand firm in the Lord (4:1b) reinforces his more specific previous directive for them to become "my (μου) fellow imitators, brothers (ἀδελφοί)," that is, for them to imitate along with Paul the humble mind-set of the Lord Jesus Christ (3:17). Paul's address and directive for his audience, as "my brothers (ἀδελφοί μου) beloved and longed for, my joy (χαρά) and crown," to "thus stand firm in the Lord (ἐν κυρίῳ)" also resonates with and reinforces his previous address and directive, "Furthermore, my brothers (ἀδελφοί μου), rejoice (χαίρετε) in the Lord (ἐν κυρίῳ)" (3:1a).[4] When the audience hear Paul's directive for them to stand firm in the "Lord" (κυρίῳ), they hear the transitional word that links this chiastic unit (4:1–5) with the previous one (3:1–21), which concludes on the note that we are awaiting the "Lord" (κύριον) Jesus Christ (3:20).[5]

After proclaiming the universal lordship of Jesus Christ that followed upon the humble obedience demonstrated by his death on a cross (2:8–11), Paul drew out its consequences for his audience, addressed as his "beloved": "So that (ὥστε), my beloved (ἀγαπητοί), just as you have always obeyed, not as in my presence only, but now much more in my absence, with reverence and awe continue to work out your own salvation" (2:12). Similarly, now, after referring to the Lord Jesus Christ as the savior we are awaiting, who will transform the body of our humbleness to be conformed to the body of his glory in accord with his universal lordship (3:20–21), Paul draws out the consequences of this for his audience, twice

---

4. In 1:12 and 3:13 the audience are addressed simply as "brothers" (ἀδελφοί), but without a first-person singular possessive pronoun in reference to Paul, when Paul informs them of details about himself without issuing a directive for the audience.

5. Fee, *Philippians*, 388–89: "During their present distress they are to 'stand fast *in the Lord*,' firmly planted in relationship with the same Lord whose coming they eagerly await and who will then subject all to himself (3:20–21). And they are to '*thus* stand firm, referring probably to the whole of 3:1–21, but especially to their 'imitation' of Paul by their upright 'walk' even as they bend every effort to attain the eschatological prize. With these words, then, Paul renews the appeal to steadfastness with which the exhortations in this letter began (1:27), but does so by way of the more recent exhortation (3:15–21)" (Fee's emphases).

and thus emphatically addressed as his "beloved": "So that (ὥστε), my brothers beloved (ἀγαπητοί) and longed for, my joy and crown, thus stand firm in the Lord, beloved (ἀγαπητοί)" (4:1).

The audience are "longed for (ἐπιπόθητοι)" (4:1) especially by Epaphroditus: "since he was longing for (ἐπιποθῶν) all of you and was distressed, because you heard that he was sick" (2:26). And that the audience are "longed for" also recalls and reinforces how "I long for" (ἐπιποθῶ) all of you with the affection of Christ Jesus (1:8), thus underlining that the audience are "beloved" not only by Paul but by God and the Lord Jesus Christ.[6]

The directive for the audience to thus "stand firm (στήκετε) in the Lord" (4:1) reinforces Paul's previous exhortation regarding their unity, how he expects to hear that "you are standing firm (στήκετε) in one Spirit, with one mind struggling together for the faith of the gospel" (1:27). The audience are to stand firm in the Lord as Paul's "joy (χαρά) and crown" by themselves "rejoicing" (χαίρετε) in the Lord (3:1). That they are here addressed as Paul's "joy" further develops the theme of the mutual joy shared by Paul and his Philippian audience within the realm of their being "in the Lord." The audience are to welcome Epaphroditus in the Lord with all "joy" (χαρᾶς) (2:29). They are to fill up Paul's "joy" (χαράν) by having the same humble mind-set appropriate for those who are in the Lord Jesus Christ (2:2). Paul is confident that he will remain beside them for their advancement and "joy" (χαράν) in the faith (1:25), so that their boast may abound within the realm of their being in Christ Jesus (1:26). And in his every petition on behalf of his audience Paul is making the petition with "joy" (χαρᾶς) (1:4) at the fellowship they share for the gospel (1:5).[7]

Paul's general directive for the audience as a whole to stand firm "in the Lord" (ἐν κυρίῳ, 4:1) receives specification as he exhorts two women in his audience, Euodia and Syntyche, to think the same thing within the realm of their being "in the Lord" (ἐν κυρίῳ, 4:2).[8] That he addresses each with the verb "I exhort" (παρακαλῶ) indicates not only his respect for each as an individual member of the community, but how each has an equal responsibility to fulfill Paul's exhortation

---

6. O'Brien, *Philippians*, 475 n. 4: "Often in Paul ἀγαπητός ('beloved') characterizes Christians as chosen of God and members of his covenant."

7. O'Brien, *Philippians*, 475-76: "It has already been shown that the theme of joy is very important in this letter. Here Paul, with a deep sense of gratitude, states that the Philippians are his joy. χαρά, by metonymy, describes that which causes joy or is the object of joy. . . . Paul rejoices over them as he writes the letter; they *are* his present delight even if this is in prospect of the day of Christ. These converts are already a source of joy to him. . . . As χαρά, so also στέφανος ['crown'; cf. 1 Thess 2:19] here describes what the Philippians are presently to Paul: they are already the cause of his honour, the source of his pride and joy . . . they are his crown even now."

8. Fee, *Philippians*, 390: "We do not know who Euodia and Syntyche were. Their names, which (roughly) mean 'Success' and 'Lucky,' tell us very little except that the latter, named after the goddess of fortune, indicates pagan origins, and that both were given names indicative of parental desire for their making good in the world. What we do know is that in v. 3 Paul refers to them as his co-workers, having 'contended at his side in the gospel.'"

for the benefit of the unity of the community. Singling them out for individual exhortations while they are listening to the letter along with the rest of the audience places a certain communal pressure upon each of them to conform to Paul's exhortation.[9]

That Euodia and Syntyche are "to think the same thing" (τὸ αὐτὸ φρονεῖν) in the Lord individualizes Paul's previous directive for the entire audience to "fill up my joy and think the same thing (τὸ αὐτὸ φρονῆτε), having the same love, united in mind, thinking the one thing (τὸ ἓν φρονοῦντες)" (2:2). Like the audience as a whole, Euodia and Syntyche, whatever may be their differences, are to resolve them as individuals who are to "go on thinking" (φρονεῖτε) that which is also in Christ Jesus (2:5). In other words, they are to adopt the same humble mind-set demonstrated by the Jesus who humbled himself to the point of death on a cross (2:6–8), which for them means thinking "nothing according to self–seeking nor according to vainglory, but in humility considering one another more important than yourselves, each of you looking out not for the things of yourselves, but everyone also for the things of others" (2:3–4). By adopting the same selfless, humble mind-set as the Lord Jesus Christ, Euodia and Syntyche can play their roles in meeting Paul's directive for the entire audience, as Paul's "joy and crown," to stand firm in the Lord (4:1–2).

2. Phil 4:3a (B): Yes, I Ask Also You, True Comrade

Paul then singles out another individual member of the audience: "Yes, I ask also you, genuine yokemate" (4:3a). With an introduction initialized by an emphatically affirmative "yes,"[10] Paul alerts the audience to a special request of an anonymous individual whom he addresses as "genuine yokemate (σύζυγε)," or, "genuine yokefellow," evidently an associate of Paul well known within the Philippian community.[11] That he is characterized as a "genuine (cf. 2:20) yokemate"

---

9. O'Brien, *Philippians*, 477–78: "παρακαλῶ is repeated and this heightens the effect, as Paul refuses to take sides but makes the same appeal to both. It is as if . . . he is exhorting each separately face to face." Fee, *Philippians*, 392: "He appeals to both women—indeed the identical repetition of their names followed by the verb has rhetorical effect—to bury their differences by adopting the 'same mind-set,' which in this case, as in the immediately preceding imperative, is qualified '*in the Lord*.' Here is the evidence that we are not dealing with a personal matter, but with 'doing the gospel' in Philippi. Having 'the same mind-set *in the Lord*' has been specifically spelled out in the preceding paradigmatic narratives, where Christ (2:6–11) has humbled himself by taking the 'form of a slave' and thus becoming obedient unto death on a cross, and Paul (3:4–14) has expressed his longing to know Christ, especially through participation in his sufferings so as to be conformed into the same cruciform lifestyle. The way such a 'mind-set' takes feet is by humbly 'looking out for the interests of others' within the believing community (2:3–4)" (Fee's emphases). See also Nils Alstrup Dahl, "Euodia and Syntyche and Paul's Letter to the Philippians," in *The Social World of the First Christians: Essays in Honor of Wayne A. Meeks* (ed. L. Michael White and O. Larry Yarbrough; Minneapolis: Fortress, 1995), 1–15.

10. O'Brien, *Philippians*, 479: "The particle ναί ('yes, indeed, certainly'), which can denote affirmation, agreement, or emphasis, here strengthens Paul's appeal."

11. O'Brien, *Philippians*, 480–81: "Who is the person singled out by the expession γνήσιε σύζυγε ('true yokefellow')? Clearly it was unecessary to name the person (unless Σύζυγε is itself a proper

singles him out within a community who shares a fellowship for the gospel with Paul (1:5), as his "fellow sharers" (συγκοινωνούς) of the grace (1:7).[12]

3. Phil 4:3b (C): Bring Them Together

The audience then learn of the special request Paul is making of the "genuine yokemate": "bring them together" (4:3b). Singled out as one associated with Paul and known by the audience, the "genuine yokemate" is given the responsibility of bringing together Euodia and Syntyche, so that they may resolve whatever differences are dividing them by thinking the same thing in adopting the humble mind-set of Jesus within the realm of their being in the Lord (4:2–3a). In fulfilling Paul's request to bring together Euodia and Syntyche, the "genuine yokemate" has the opportunity of himself demonstrating the humble and selfless mind-set of Jesus that Paul is enjoining for the entire audience. Indeed, as the audience cannot fail to miss the alliterative wordplay, it would be most appropriate for the "genuine yokemate," the one who is "yoked together" (σύζυγε) with Paul, to "bring together" (συλλαμβάνου) these two divided women members of the Philippian community.

4. Phil 4:3c (C'): Those Who in the Gospel Have Struggled Together with Me

The audience hear Euodia and Syntyche, the two divided women members of the community whom the "genuine yokemate" is to bring together (4:2–3b), further described as "those who in the gospel have struggled together with me" (4:3c). At this point, the audience experience the chiastic pivot involving a similarity of verbal forms, from the request for the "genuine yokemate" to "bring them together" (συλλαμβάνου) in the C element (4:3b) to the description of those who "have struggled together" (συνήθλησάν) in the C' element (4:3c).

The resolution of the differences separating Euodia and Syntyche is important both for the sake of the unity of the community and of the fellowship they share with one another and with Paul for advancing the gospel. That it was in the work of advancing the "gospel" (εὐαγγελίῳ) that these two women "struggled together"

---

name), since everyone at Philippi, including the one so addressed, would know who was intended. . . . It is no longer possible to determine with certainty just whom Paul has in mind; 'faithful partner' suggests a coworker in the apostolic mission who was no doubt well known to the Philippians. He was probably some prominent and influential member of the congregation, perhaps a person of tact as well as influence." On σύζυγε as possibly a proper name, Fee (Philippians, 393 n. 44) notes: "Not only is such a 'name' unknown, but it is difficult to imagine the circumstances in which a parent would give a child such an unusual moniker; finally, the qualifier 'genuine' almost totally disqualifies it as a proper noun."

12. For a questionable and highly speculative allegorical interpretation of the individuals addressed in 4:2–3, see P. Carls, "Identifying Syzygos, Euodia, and Syntyche, Philippians 4:2f," Journal of Higher Criticism 8 (2001): 161–82. For a very interesting but ultimately speculative interpretation of the "genuine yokemate" in 4:3 as Paul's co-worker and the author of the "we-sections" in Acts, namely Luke, see Eduard Verhoef, "Σύζυγος In Phil 4:3 and the Author of the 'We-Sections' in Acts," Journal of Higher Criticism 5 (1998): 209–19.

(συνήθλησάν) with Paul further commends the worthiness of the resolution of their differences as a priority not only for the "genuine yokemate," who is to bring them together, but for the audience as a whole, whom Paul expects similarly to be "with one mind struggling together (συναθλοῦντες) for the faith of the gospel (εὐαγγελίου)" (1:27).

5. Phil 4:3d (B΄): With the Rest of My Co-Workers

The audience are further informed about the character and significance of Euodia and Syntyche as those who struggled together not only with Paul but "with also Clement and the rest of my co-workers, whose names are in the book of life" (4:3d). At this point, the audience hear a progression, by way of alliterative and conceptual chiastic parallels, from genuine "yokemate" (σύζυγε) in the B element (4:3a) to my "co-workers" (συνεργῶν) in the B΄ element (4:3d).

Euodia and Syntyche have "struggled together" (συνήθλησάν) in the gospel (4:3c) not only with Paul but with Clement, a named and apparently prominent member of the audience, as well as with the rest (cf. 1:13) of Paul's "co-work-ers" (συνεργῶν).[13] This associates them with Epaphroditus, another "co-worker" (συνεργόν) of Paul well known to the audience (2:25) and places them within the fellowship for the gospel shared by Paul and his Philippian audience. It further commends the resolution of their differences by their being "brought together (συλλαμβάνου)" (4:3b) with the help of the "genuine yokemate (σύζυγε)" (4:3a) and the communal oversight of the audience as a whole (4:3d), who are likewise "struggling together" (συναθλοῦντες) for the faith of the gospel (1:27).[14]

The names of Euodia and Syntyche, as among the rest of Paul's co-workers, are in the book of "life" (ζωῆς, 4:3d, cf. LXX Ps 68:29), the new, eschatological "life" available in the gospel as the word of "life" (ζωῆς) the audience are to hold forth (2:16) in the fellowship for the gospel they share with Paul (1:5), as his fellow sharers of the grace (1:7). Thus, the prominent status of Euodia and Syntyche as Paul's co-workers in the gospel, whose names are in the book of life, climactically confirms for the audience how important is the resolution of their differences by being brought together to think the same thing in adopting the humble mind-set of Jesus that the audience as a whole are also to adopt.[15]

---

13. O'Brien, Philippians, 482: "'Clement' is otherwise unknown to us. His name is Latin, and he may well have been a Philippian Christian who was well known within the church, since Paul does not need to identify him."

14. O'Brien, Philippians, 482: "The notion of fellowship or participation is brought out in the repetition of the prefix συν- in the terms σύζυγος, συναθλέω, and συνεργοί. They were highly valued co-workers who had energetically participated in Paul's apostolic mission, perhaps even when the congregation at Philippi was founded. The apostle's concern that they be helped to reconcile their differences was, therefore, all the more urgent."

15. Thurston, Philippians, 141: "In Hellenistic cities registers were kept of the names of citizens of the city. Thus the phrase ['book of life'] may connect with 1:27 and 3:19 with their 'citizenship' metaphors. . . . To be listed in the Book of Life is to be a citizen of God's commonwealth (3:20)."

6. Phil 4:4–5 (A'): Rejoice Always in the Lord Who Is Near

The entire audience then receive an exuberant exhortation from Paul: "Rejoice in the Lord always. Again I will say, rejoice. Let your forbearance be known to all human beings. The Lord is near" (4:4–5). At this point, the audience hear a progression, via the chiastic parallels, in expressions for joy—from "my joy (χαρά) and crown" (4:1) in the A element to "rejoice (χαίρετε) in the Lord always. Again I will say, rejoice (χαίρετε)" (4:4) in the A´ element. They also hear a progression in references to the Lord—from "stand firm in the Lord (κυρίῳ)" (4:1) and "think the same thing in the Lord (κυρίῳ)" (4:2) in the A element to "rejoice in the Lord (κυρίῳ)" (4:4) and "the Lord (κύριος) is near" (4:5) in the A´ element.

The audience hear Paul's double exhortation to rejoice as an alliterative and assonant mini–chiasm in itself, thus enhancing its rhetorical artistry and potency: (a) rejoice (χαίρετε) (b) in the Lord always (πάντοτε). (b´) Again (πάλιν) I will say, (a´) rejoice (χαίρετε) (4:4).[16] Paul's double exhortation for the audience, as his "joy (χαρά) and crown" (4:1), to "rejoice in the Lord (χαίρετε ἐν κυρίῳ) always. Again I will say, rejoice (χαίρετε)" (4:4), emphatically reinforces his previous exhortation for them to "rejoice in the Lord" (χαίρετε ἐν κυρίῳ) (3:1), and thus, by so rejoicing as Paul's "joy," to stand firm "in the Lord" (ἐν κυρίῳ) (4:1).[17] The audience, who have "always" (πάντοτε) obeyed (2:12), are thus to rejoice within the realm of their being in the Lord not only repeatedly but "always" (πάντοτε).[18]

Paul's double exhortation for the audience to "rejoice" (χαίρετε) in the Lord always (4:4) advances the theme of the mutual joy the audience are to share with him. As "my joy (χαρά) and crown" (4:1), the audience are to contribute to Paul's rejoicing in the Lord by following the directives he is giving them in the letter, including in the matter of resolving the differences between Euodia and Syntyche (4:2–3). That the audience themselves are to rejoice in the Lord always reinforces Paul's previous exhortation regarding their mutual rejoicing. Just as Paul is rejoicing even in the midst of his sufferings for the gospel—"I am rejoicing (χαίρω), indeed I am rejoicing with (συγχαίρω) all of you" (2:17), so the audience in the same way are to be rejoicing despite their difficulties—"you are to be rejoicing

---

16. See also Fee, *Philippians*, 404 n. 19.

17. Note how the emphatic double exhortation for the audience to "rejoice" (4:4) corresponds to the emphatic double address of the audience as Paul's "beloved" (4:1).

18. O'Brien, *Philippians*, 485: "In a sense, this adverb might be said to look to the future (as well as the present) and to possible future trials: 'keep on rejoicing in the Lord at all times, regardless of what may come upon you.'" Silva, *Philippians*, 194: "Clearly Paul does not have in view the kind of superficial happiness that manifests itself only when things go well. No, it is a rejoicing that can be had πάντοτε, because it depends not on changing circumstances but on the one who does not change: 'Rejoice *in the Lord*.' And, in a manner reminiscent of 1:18, Paul repeats the command with reference to the future: 'again I will say, rejoice!'" (Silva's emphasis). Garland, "Philippians," 252: "Since joy is commanded, it is not a feeling like happiness. It is a mental attitude, a life stance. Whereas happiness depends on what happens, joy does not. Joy derives from a conviction that despite present circumstances, God is in control and will save those who belong to Christ. Joy derives from the Philippians' union with Christ, the promise of the resurrection, and their partnership with one another."

(χαίρετε), indeed you are to be "rejoicing with (συγχαίρετέ) me" (2:18; cf. 1:18; 2:28).

Paul's exhortation for the audience to "let your forbearance be known to all human beings" (4:5a), as they rejoice always within the realm of their being "in the Lord" (4:4), resonates with his previous exhortations for them to adopt a selfless, humble mind-set in imitation of the Lord Jesus Christ. Indeed, their "forbearance" (ἐπιεικές) seems to aptly summarize and capture the essence of the attitude they are to exhibit, when Paul told them to "fill up my joy and think the same thing, having the same love, united in mind, thinking the one thing, nothing according to self–seeking nor according to vainglory, but in humility considering one another more important than yourselves, each of you looking out not for the things of yourselves, but everyone also for the things of others. This go on thinking in you, which is also in Christ Jesus" (2:2–5).[19] As the humble mind-set of Jesus in obediently forbearing the suffering of death on a cross (2:6–8) resulted in the universal acknowledgment of his lordship by "every" (πᾶσα) tongue (2:11), so, similarly, the audience are to let their humble "forbearance" toward one another (including Euodia and Syntyche) and toward their sufferings for the sake of the gospel be known to "all" (πᾶσιν) human beings.[20]

His exhortation for the audience to rejoice in the "Lord" (κυρίῳ) always (4:4) Paul bolsters with his confident assertion that the "Lord" (κύριος) is near (4:5b). This resonates with and reinforces Paul's previous proclamation that "a savior we are awaiting, the Lord (κύριον) Jesus Christ, who will transform the body of our humbleness (to be) conformed to the body of his glory according to the working that empowers him even to subject to himself all things" (3:20–21). That the Lord is "near" (ἐγγύς), temporally as well as spatially (cf. LXX Ps 144:18), provides a confident yet urgent hopefulness as further motivation for the audience not only to let their humble forbearance be known to all human beings (4:5a), but to "rejoice" in the Lord always, indeed to truly "rejoice" (4:4).[21] By so rejoicing "in the

---

19. On the meaning of ἐπιεικές, BDAG (371) states: "not insisting on every right of letter of law or custom, yielding, gentle, kind, courteous, tolerant." Heinz Giesen, "ἐπιεικής," EDNT 2.26: "According to Phil 4:5 the Christians should make known to all their *forbearance* (τὸ ἐπιεικές), which lives from the joy in the Lord, who is near." Fee, *Philippians*, 406–7: "It is used by hellenistic writers and in the LXX primarily to refer to God (or the gods) or to the 'noble,' who are characterized by their 'gentle forbearance' with others. That is most likely its sense here, only now as the disposition of *all* of God's people" (Fee's emphasis). Silva, *Philippians*, 194: "The thrust of this command is then essentially the same as that of 2:3–4. And just as in chapter 2 Paul followed up his exhortation with an appeal to the humility of Christ, before whom we all bow at the parousia (2:5–11), so here in 4:5 Paul reinforces his command with the simple but powerful comment ὁ κύριος ἐγγύς (the Lord is near). It may well be that the apostle wants to remind us of the one who personifies the grace of ἐπιείκεια, and that his approaching return should awaken us to follow his example."

20. O'Brien, *Philippians*, 488: "The universality of the expression πᾶσιν ἀνθρώποις ('to everybody') indicates that it is not only among the circle of believers that this ἐπιείκεια is to be known."

21. O'Brien, *Philippians*, 489: "The apostle may have intended to include both ideas of time and space with his use of ἐγγύς: the Lord who may return at any time came near in his incarnation (2:6–8),

Lord" always, and thinking the same thing, adopting with Euodia and Syntyche a humble mind-set "in the Lord" (4:2), the audience will stand firm "in the Lord" as Paul's "joy" and crown (4:1).

C. SUMMARY ON PHILIPPIANS 4:1–5

1. By adopting the same selfless, humble mind-set as the Lord Jesus Christ (2:2–8), Euodia and Syntyche can play their roles in meeting Paul's directive for the entire audience, as Paul's "joy and crown," to stand firm in the Lord (4:1–2).

2. It would be most appropriate for the "true comrade" in the audience, the one who is "yoked together" with Paul (4:3a), to "bring together" (4:3b) Euodia and Syntyche, two divided women members of the Philippian community (4:2).

3. That it was in the work of advancing the "gospel" that Euodia and Syntyche "struggled together" with Paul (4:3c) further commends the worthiness of the resolution of their differences as a priority not only for the "genuine yokemate" (4:3a), who is to bring them together (4:3b), but for the audience as a whole, whom Paul expects similarly to be "with one mind struggling together for the faith of the gospel" (1:27).

4. The prominent status of Euodia and Syntyche as Paul's co-workers (4:3d) in the gospel (4:3c), whose names are in the book of life (4:3d), climactically confirms for the audience how important is the resolution of their differences by being brought together (4:3b) to think the same thing (4:2) in adopting the humble mind-set of Jesus that the audience as a whole are also to adopt.

5. That the Lord is near (4:5b) provides a confident yet urgent hopefulness as further motivation for the audience not only to let their humble forbearance be known to all human beings (4:5a), but to "rejoice" in the Lord always, indeed, to truly "rejoice" (4:4). By so rejoicing "in the Lord" always, and thinking the same thing, adopting with Euodia and Syntyche a humble mind-set "in the Lord" (4:2), the audience will stand firm "in the Lord" as Paul's "joy" and crown (4:1).

---

and is continually near to his people." Fee, *Philippians*, 408: "Since their present suffering is at the hands of those who proclaim Caesar as Lord, they are reminded that the true 'Lord' is 'near.' Their eschatological vindication is close at hand. At the same time, by using the language of the Psalter, Paul is encouraging them to prayer in the midst of their present distress, because the 'Lord is near' in a very real way to those who call on him now." Bockmuehl, *Philippians*, 246: "Whether one eventually opts for a primarily spatial or a primarily temporal interpretation, for the New Testament writers each one in any case implies the other: the Lord's nearness to believers is a nearness of the one who is coming to save; and vice versa, his imminent parousia assures believers that he is close at hand."

11

Philippians 4:6–20: Glory to God Who Will Fulfill You as I Am Filled and Abound (B′)

My God Will Fulfill Your Every Need in Christ Jesus

A: [6] Be anxious about nothing, but in everything, by prayer and petition, with thanksgiving, let your requests be made known before *God*. [7] And the peace of *God* that surpasses all understanding will guard your hearts and your minds *in Christ Jesus*. [8] Furthermore, brothers, whatever is true, whatever is honorable, whatever is right, whatever is pure, whatever is pleasing, whatever is commendable, if there is any excellence, and if there is any praise, these things consider. [9] And the things you have learned and received and heard and saw in me, these things practice. And the *God* of peace will be with you.

B: [10] I am joyful in the Lord greatly that now at last you have begun again to think on behalf of me, for which indeed you were thinking, but had no opportunity. [11] Not that I say this on account of want, for I have learned in whatever things I am involved to be content. [12] I know indeed to be humble, I know indeed to *abound*. In every situation and in all things I have learned the secret, both to be satisfied and to hunger, both to *abound* and to be in want. [13] I am strong for *everything* in the one who empowers me!

C: [14] Nevertheless, you did well, sharing with me in my affliction. [15] And you indeed know, Philippians, that in the beginning of the gospel, when I went out from Macedonia, not a single church shared with me *in an account* of *giving* and receiving except you alone,

D: [16] for even in Thessalonica not only once but twice you sent to me in my need.

C′: [17] Not that I am seeking the *gift*, but I am seeking the fruit that increases *in your account*.

B′: [18a] For I have received in full *everything* and I am *abounding*. I have been filled up, having received from Epaphroditus the things from you, an aroma of fragrance, an acceptable sacrifice,

A′: [18b] well pleasing to *God*. [19] My *God* will fill up your every need according to his wealth in glory *in Christ Jesus.* [20] To our *God* and Father, glory to the ages of the ages, Amen.[1]

A. CHIASTIC DEVELOPMENT FROM PHILIPPIANS 1:3–11 (B) TO 4:6–20 (B′)

With Phil 4:6–20, the B′ unit within the macrochiastic structure organizing the entire letter, the audience hear resonances, by way of the chiastic parallelism, of 1:3–11, the corresponding B unit in the overall chiasm.[2] The mention of the "prayer and petition (δεήσει), with thanksgiving (εὐχαριστίας)," of the audience (4:6) in the B′ unit recalls Paul's petitions for the audience, when he stated, "I thank (εὐχαριστῶ) my God at every remembrance of you, always in my every petition (δεήσει) on behalf of all of you, making the petition (δέησιν) with joy" (1:3–4), in the B unit. Paul's promise that the peace of God will guard your "hearts" (καρδίας) (4:7) in the B′ unit recalls the reference to Paul's own heart—"I have you in my heart (καρδίᾳ)" (1:7)—in the B unit.[3] "Whatever is right (δίκαια)" (4:8) in the B′ unit recalls that "it is right (δίκαιον) for me" (1:7) in the B unit.[4] "If there is any praise (ἔπαινος)" (4:8) in the B′ unit recalls "for the glory and praise (ἔπαινον) of God" (1:11) in the B unit.[5] That "you have begun again to think on behalf of me (ὑπὲρ ἐμοῦ φρονεῖν)" (4:10) in the B′ unit reciprocally recalls "for me to think this on behalf of all of you (φρονεῖν ὑπὲρ πάντων ὑμῶν)" (1:7) in the B unit.

The threefold occurrence of the verb "abound"—"I know indeed to abound (περισσεύειν)" (4:12), "both to abound (περισσεύειν) and to be in need" (4:12), and "I am abounding" (περισσεύω) (4:18)—in the B′ unit recalls "that your love even more and more may abound (περισσεύῃ)" (1:9) in the B unit. That "I am seeking the fruit (καρπόν)" (4:17) in the B′ unit recalls "the fruit (καρπόν) of righteousness" (1:11) in the B unit.[6] The twofold occurrence of the verb "fill up"— "I have been filled up" (πεπλήρωμαι) (4:18) and "my God will fill up (πληρώσει)" (4:19)—in the B′ unit recalls "having been filled up" (πεπληρωμένοι) (1:11) in the B unit. And finally, the twofold occurrence of "glory"—"according to his wealth in glory (δόξῃ)" (4:19) and "glory (δόξα) to the ages of the ages" (4:20)—

---

1. For the establishment of 4:6–20 as a chiasm, see ch. 2.

2. This section is limited to demonstrating the macrochiastic parallels. The exegetical significance of these parallels is presented in the next section.

3. That these are the only two occurrences of the word "heart" (καρδία) in the letter enhances the significance of this parallelism for the macrochiastic structure.

4. That these are the only two occurrences in the letter of the word "right" (δίκαιος) enhances the significance of this parallelism for the macrochiastic structure.

5. That these are the only two occurrences in the letter of the word "praise" (ἔπαινος) enhances the significance of this parallelism for the macrochiastic structure.

6. That these are the only two occurrences of the word "fruit" (καρπός) in the accusative singular enhances the significance of this parallelism for the macrochiastic structure ("fruit" occurs in the nominative singular in 1:22).

in the B´ unit recalls "for the glory (δόξαν) and praise of God" (1:11) in the B unit.

B. AUDIENCE RESPONSE TO PHILIPPIANS 4:6–20

1. Phil 4:6–9 (A): The Peace of God That Is in Christ Jesus

Paul continues to exhort his Philippian audience: "Be anxious about nothing, but in everything, by prayer and petition, with thanksgiving, let your requests be made known before God. And the peace of God that surpasses all understanding will guard your hearts and your minds in Christ Jesus. Furthermore, brothers, whatever is true, whatever is honorable, whatever is right, whatever is pure, whatever is pleasing, whatever is commendable, if there is any excellence, and if there is any praise, these things consider. And the things you have learned and received and heard and saw in me, these things practice. And the God of peace will be with you" (4:6–9).

The audience hear this series of directives from Paul in the form of the following chiastic pattern:

(a) [4:6] Be anxious about nothing, but in everything, by prayer and petition, with thanksgiving, let your (ὑμῶν) requests be made known before God (θεόν). [7] And the peace (εἰρήνη) of God (θεοῦ) that surpasses all understanding will guard your (ὑμῶν) hearts and your (ὑμῶν) minds in Christ Jesus.

(b) [8] Furthermore, brothers, whatever is true, whatever is honorable, whatever is right, whatever is pure, whatever is pleasing, whatever is commendable, if there is any excellence, and if there is any praise, these things (ταῦτα) consider.

(b´) [9a] And the things you have learned and received and heard and saw in me, these things (ταῦτα) practice.

(a´) [9b] And the God (θεός) of peace (εἰρήνης) will be with you (ὑμῶν).

At the center of this chiastic pattern the audience hear a pivot in parallels from Paul's command to consider "these things" (ταῦτα) (4:8) in the "b" sub-element to his complementary command to practice "these things" (ταῦτα) (4:9a) in the "b´" sub-element. When the audience hear Paul's promise that the "God (θεός) of peace (εἰρήνης) will be with you (ὑμῶν)" (4:9b) in the "a´" sub-element, they hear a progression in parallels to Paul's exhortation for them to "let your (ὑμῶν) requests be made known before God (θεόν)" (4:6b) and his promise that "the peace (εἰρήνη) of God (θεοῦ) that surpasses all understanding will guard your (ὑμῶν) hearts and your (ὑμῶν) minds in Christ Jesus" (4:7) in the "a" sub-element.

Paul previously assured the audience that Timothy, whom he hopes to send to them soon (2:19), "genuinely will be anxious (μεριμνήσει) for the things concerning you" (2:20). Now, he reassures them to "be anxious (μεριμνᾶτε) about nothing"

(4:6a).[7] Rather, "in everything, by prayer and petition (δεήσει), with thanksgiving (εὐχαριστίας)," they are to let their requests be known before God (4:6), with the corresponding promise that the peace of God will guard their hearts and their minds in Christ Jesus (4:7). This directive regarding their thankful petitions in things concerning themselves develops Paul's previous confident hope regarding their petition for him, when he asserted, "for I know that this for me will lead to salvation through the petition (δεήσεως) of you and supply of the Spirit of Jesus Christ" (1:19). And it also further complements Paul's own thankful petitions for his Philippian audience, when he proclaimed, "I thank (εὐχαριστῶ) my God at every remembrance of you, always in my every petition (δεήσει) on behalf of all of you, making the petition (δέησιν) with joy" (1:3–4).

When the audience hear Paul's directive to "let your requests be known (γνωριζέσθω) to God" (4:6b), they hear the transitional word that links this chiastic unit (4:6–20) with the previous one (4:1–5), which concluded with Paul's directive for them to "let your forbearance be known (γνωσθήτω) to all human beings" (4:5). The transition thus moves the focus of the audience from the forbearance they are to make known to all human beings in their communal fellowship to the requests they are to make known to God in their communal worship.

Paul's promise that "the peace (εἰρήνη) of God (θεοῦ) that surpasses all understanding will guard your hearts and your minds in Christ Jesus (ἐν Χριστῷ Ἰησοῦ)" (4:7) reinforces, even as it elaborates upon, Paul's introductory prayer-wish, "grace to you and peace (εἰρήνη) from God (θεοῦ) our Father and the Lord Jesus Christ" (1:2), which follows his address of the audience as "all those holy ones in Christ Jesus (ἐν Χριστῷ Ἰησοῦ)" (1:1b). That this peace of God that "surpasses" (ὑπερέχουσα) all understanding will guard your hearts and your minds in Christ Jesus resonates with, and thus hints at a close relationship to, "the surpassing greatness (ὑπερέχον) of the knowledge of Christ Jesus my Lord" (3:8b).[8]

---

7. Thurston, *Philippians*, 145: "Paul's command is made in the context of any number of things they might well be anxious about: persecution, opponents, divisiveness, and enemies. Certainly Paul has spoken of the Philippians' anxiety about him (1:12–26; 2:17–3:1)."

8. O'Brien, *Philippians*, 497–98: "Paul is telling his readers that God's peace or salvation that stands guard over them is more wonderful than they can imagine.... Paul pictures God's peace as a garrison keeping guard over the Philippians' hearts and minds, protecting them from all assaults. Since the city of Philippi was guarded by a Roman garrison at the time, the metaphor would have been easily understood and appreciated by the readers." Fee, *Philippians*, 410–11: "[I]t is the 'peace of God' that 'transcends all understanding.' This could mean 'beyond all human comprehension,' which in one sense is certainly true. More likely Paul intends that God's peace 'totally transcends the merely human, unbelieving mind,' which is full of anxiety because it cannot think higher than itself. Because the God to whom we pray and offer thanksgiving, whose ways are higher than ours, is also totally trustworthy, our prayer is accompanied by his peace. And that, not because he answers according to our wishes, but because his peace totally transcends our merely human way of perceiving the world." For an interpretation that the "peace of God" here surpasses the "peace" known as the *pax Romana* in the social environment of Paul's Philippian audience, see Wiard Popkes, "Philipper 4.4–7: Aussage und situativer Hintergrund," *NTS* 50 (2004): 246–56. See also W. Mostert, "Meditation über Philipper 4,4–7," *BTZ* 16 (1999): 120–31.

The Paul who has assured his audience that "I have you in my heart (καρδίᾳ)" (1:7), further reassures them now with his promise that "the peace of God that surpasses all understanding will guard your hearts (καρδίας) and your minds in Christ Jesus."[9] This promise regarding the peace of God (4:7) is thus the result of the audience making known their requests before God (4:6).[10]

Previously Paul extended his directive for the audience to welcome Epaphroditus with joy (2:29–30) by adding a further directive regarding their joy: "Furthermore, my brothers (τὸ λοιπόν, ἀδελφοί μου), rejoice in the Lord" (3:1a). Now, similarly, Paul extends his directive for the audience to let their requests be made known before God, so that the peace of God that surpasses all understanding will guard their hearts and their minds in Christ Jesus (4:7), by adding a further directive regarding the kind of mental activity that accords with the promise about the peace of God: "Furthermore, brothers (τὸ λοιπόν, ἀδελφοί),[11] whatever is true,[12] whatever is honorable,[13] whatever is right,[14] whatever is pure,[15]

---

9. According to O'Brien (*Philippians*, 496), "the peace of God" here refers to "that peace which God himself possesses or has . . . at the same time, ἡ εἰρήνη τοῦ θεοῦ refers to the peace that he bestows or gives and is thus equivalent to the eschatological salvation that has been effected in Christ Jesus and that the Philippians have received for themselves." Thurston, *Philippians*, 146: "Note the distinction between 'heart,' in biblical anthropology the core of the person, the center of willing, feeling, and thinking, and thus of personality, and 'mind,' Paul's term for the rational, thinking self."

10. O'Brien, *Philippians*, 495–96: "[A]s a consequence of the Philippians letting their requests be made known to God with thanksgiving, his peace will guard them. V. 7 is not a concluding wish . . . it is a specific and certain promise about God's peace that is attached to the encouraging admonition of v. 6. Most significantly, this promise about God's peace guarding the Philippians is given irrespective of whether their concrete requests are granted or not. This word of assurance is independent of their petitions being answered by God in the affirmative. God's peace will be powerfully at work in their lives as a result (καί) of their pouring out their hearts in petition with thanksgiving, not because they have made requests that are perfectly in line with the will of God."

11. According to Bockmuehl (*Philippians*, 249), "furthermore" (τὸ λοιπόν) here "should be seen not as beginning a separate final conclusion but as introducing implications loosely related to the promise of Christ's peace and the preceding exhortations to an attitude of Christ-centered joy, gentleness, prayer and thanksgiving." See also Fowl, *Philippians*, 184 n. 9.

12. Bockmuehl, *Philippians*, 251: "Truth for Paul always has its focus in God and the gospel of Christ."

13. O'Brien, *Philippians*, 504: "The adjective σεμνός and its cognate noun σεμνότης were used in the Greek world to describe what was serious, sublime, dignified, majestic, or august. The adjective was a frequent epithet for divinities and related holy things, for example, the temple, the law, and the sabbath."

14. According to O'Brien (*Philippians*, 504), "whatever is right" has a broad sense, "not simply in relation to humans but in accordance with the divine standard, and thus fulfilling all obligations to God, others, and themselves." Fee, *Philippians*, 417–18: "As with 'truth,' what is 'right' is always defined by God and his character."

15. O'Brien, *Philippians*, 504: "This adjective [ἁγνά], deriving from a verb that meant to stand in awe of someone, was used in religious language from early times as an attribute of deity and everything belonging to it; later it was employed in a transferred moral sense of holy or pure."

whatever is pleasing,[16] whatever is commendable,[17] if there is any excellence, and if there is any praise,[18] these things consider" (4:8).

The Paul who stated what "I do not consider (λογίζομαι)," namely, that he himself has yet apprehended (3:13) the future resurrection of the dead (3:11) for which he has been apprehended by Christ Jesus (3:12), as he pursues the prize of the upward calling of God within the realm of his being "in Christ Jesus" (3:14), now enjoins his audience what they are to "consider" (λογίζεσθε) (4:8), what they are to take into account in their hearts and their minds, namely, the things that accord with the promise that the peace of God that surpasses all understanding will guard their hearts and their minds within the realm of their being "in Christ Jesus" (4:7). The accumulation of appropriate things the audience are to consider has the rhetorical effect of shaping their mental activity as they think about what requests they are to make known in their prayer and petition before God (4:6) and within the realm of their being "in Christ Jesus" (4:7).

Indeed, the phrase "before God and in Christ Jesus" would seem to be implicit after each item in the list of virtues the audience are to consider—"whatever is true (before God and in Christ Jesus), whatever is honorable (before God and in Christ Jesus), whatever is right (before God and in Christ Jesus)" (4:8), and so on. This is confirmed by those items in the list that have been mentioned previously in the letter. "Whatever is true (ἀληθῆ)" recalls the "truth" of God involved in the proclamation of the gospel of Christ in Paul's statement of how he will be joyful whenever Christ is proclaimed, whether in pretense of in truth (ἀληθείᾳ)" (1:18). "Whatever is right (δίκαια)" recalls how it is "right (δίκαιον)" (1:7) before God and in Christ Jesus for Paul to think that the God "who began in you a good work will perfect it until the day of Christ Jesus" (4:6). And "if there is any praise (ἔπαινος)" recalls the "praise" of God through Jesus Christ in Paul's prayer that the audience may "determine the things that matter, so that you may be sincere and faultless for the day of Christ, having been filled up with the fruit of righteousness that is through Jesus Christ for the glory and praise (ἔπαινον) of God" (1:10–11).[19]

The list of virtues before God and in Christ Jesus that the audience are to consider in their way of thinking (4:8) is complemented by a list of things they are to practice in imitation of Paul in their way of acting before God and in Christ Jesus: "the things you have learned and received and heard and saw in me, these things

---

16. O'Brien, *Philippians*, 505: "προσφιλῆ appears only here in the NT and is not found in the contemporary lists of virtues in the ancient world. The basic meaning of the word is 'that which calls forth love, love-inspiring', and here it has the passive sense of 'lovely, pleasing, agreeable, amiable.'"

17. O'Brien, *Philippians*, 499–500: "These six clauses in synonymous parallelism are grammatically unconnected and as a result very emphatic."

18. O'Brien, *Philippians*, 500: "The conditional clauses do not express doubt about the presence of ἀρετή ('moral excellence') or ἔπαινος ('what is worthy of praise'), for the conjunction εἰ signifies 'since' or 'if, as is the case.'"

19. Noteworthy is that the list of virtues the audience are to consider in 4:8 begins ("true") and ends ("praise") with items that thus frame the list with resonances of previous references in the letter.

practice" (4:9a). The reference to the things the audience have "heard and saw in me (ἠκούσατε καὶ εἴδετε ἐν ἐμοί)" recalls that the audience, in their suffering on behalf of Christ (1:29), have the same struggle that "you saw in me and now hear in me (εἴδετε ἐν ἐμοὶ καὶ νῦν ἀκούετε ἐν ἐμοί)" (1:30). Here Paul is thus reinforcing his exhortation for the audience to "live as citizens worthy of the gospel of the Christ, so that, whether coming and seeing (ἰδών) you, or being absent, I hear (ἀκούω) the things concerning you, that you are standing firm in one Spirit, with one mind struggling together for the faith of the gospel" (1:27). The audience at Philippi, then, are to imitate and practice what they have learned, received, heard and saw "in me," that is, embodied in Paul himself, as they struggle together in unity with one another and with him for the faith of the gospel (see also 3:17).[20]

Paul's promise that flows from and follows upon the things the audience are to consider and the things they are to practice (4:8–9a) is that "the God of peace will be with you" (4:9b). Paul's previous promise to the audience, who are to be anxious about nothing, but in everything, by prayer and petition, with thanksgiving, are to let their requests be made known before God (4:6), was that the peace of God that surpasses all understanding will then guard their hearts and their minds in Christ Jesus (4:7). That promise is now climatically intensified in its personal dimensions. Not only will "the peace of God" (ἡ εἰρήνη τοῦ θεοῦ), the profound peace that comes from God, guard "your" (ὑμῶν) hearts and "your" (ὑμῶν) minds—the center and core of their beings, but "the God of peace" (ὁ θεὸς τῆς εἰρήνης), the very person of the God who is the source of that profound peace, will be "with you" (μεθ' ὑμῶν)—present with the very persons themselves of those in the audience at Philippi.[21]

In sum, in this A element (4:6–9), the audience are to be anxious about nothing, but in everything, in their prayer and petition, with thanksgiving, to make their requests known before God, so that the profound peace that comes from

---

20. O'Brien, *Philippians*, 511: "[I]t is possible that ἐν ἐμοί has been placed at the end for rhetorical effect, that is, to indicate in an emphatic way that everything they had learnt, received, heard, and seen had been embodied in Paul himself." Fee, *Philippians*, 420: "Given the overall context of this letter, one may rightly assume that, whatever the specifics, Paul is once again calling them to the kind of cruciform existence he has been commending and urging on them throughout. Only as they are 'conformed to Christ's death,' as Paul himself seeks continually to be, even as they eagerly await the final consummation at his coming, will they truly live what is 'virtuous' and 'praiseworthy' from Paul's distinctively 'in Christ' perspective."

21. O'Brien, *Philippians*, 512: "At v. 7 they were promised that God's peace would keep them safe; here they are assured that the God of peace himself will be with them. The two promises are similar, with only a slight difference of emphasis: in the former, the focus is upon God's salvation guarding them; in the latter, it is upon his presence to bless and to save them. Since the gift of his peace cannot be separated from his presence as the giver, these two assurances are closely related in meaning." For an Epicurean interpretation of 4:8–9, see Paul Andrew Holloway, "*Bona Cogitare*: An Epicurean Consolation in Phil 4:8–9," *HTR* 91 (1998): 89–96. See also R. J. Taylor, "Paul's Way to Peace—Philippians 4:4–9," *ScrC* 27 (1997): 502–12; Andreas H. Snyman, "Philippians 4:1–9 from a Rhetorical Perspective," *Verbum et Ecclesia* 28 (2007): 224–43.

God and that surpasses all understanding will guard their hearts and their minds within the realm of their being in Christ Jesus (4:6–7). They are to consider the things as well as practice—in imitation of Paul—the things that will enable them to experience the promise that the very person of the God who is the source of profound peace will be with their very persons (4:8–9), as they struggle together with one another and with Paul in conformity to Christ for the faith of the gospel (1:27–30).

2. Phil 4:10–13 (B): Paul Knows How to Abound in Everything

Paul then discloses to his audience more of his personal attitude, the disposition with which he deals with his present situation of imprisonment: "I am joyful in the Lord greatly that now at last you have begun again to think on behalf of me, for which indeed you were thinking, but had no opportunity. Not that I say this on account of want, for I have learned in whatever things I am involved to be content. I know indeed to be humble, I know indeed to abound. In every situation and in all things I have learned the secret, both to be satisfied and to hunger, both to abound and to be in want. I am strong for everything in the one who empowers me!" (4:10–13).

The audience hear this disclosure from Paul in the form of the following chiastic pattern:

(a) [4:10] I am joyful in the Lord greatly that now at last you have begun again to think on behalf of me (ἐμοῦ), for which indeed you were thinking, but had no opportunity.

    (b) [11a] Not that I say this on account of want (ὑστέρησιν),

        (c) [11b–12a] for I have learned in whatever things I am involved to be content. I know indeed to be humble, I know indeed to abound (περισσεύειν).

            (d) [12b] In every situation (ἐν παντὶ)

            (d´) [12c] and in all things (ἐν πᾶσιν) I have learned the secret,

        (c´) [12d] both to be satisfied and to hunger, both to abound (περισσεύειν)

    (b´) [12e] and to be in want (ὑστερεῖσθαι).

(a´) [13] I am strong for everything in the one who empowers me (με)!

At the center of this chiastic pattern the audience hear a pivot in parallels from "in every situation" (ἐν παντὶ) (4:12b) in the "d" sub-element to "in all things" (ἐν πᾶσιν) (4:12c) in the "d´" sub-element.[22] When the audience hear the infinitive "to abound" (περισσεύειν) (4:12d) in the "c´" sub-element, they hear a progression in parallels from Paul's statement that "I know indeed to abound (περισσεύειν)"

---

22. Although the word "everything" (πάντα) occurs in 4:13, it is not preceded by the preposition "in" (ἐν), as is the case for the parallels in the "d" (4:12b) and "d´" (4:12c) sub-elements.

(4:12a) in the "c" sub-element. When they hear "to be in want" (ὑστερεῖσθαι) (4:12e) in the "b′" sub-element, they hear a progression in parallels from Paul's statement, "Not that I say this on account of want (ὑστέρησιν)" (4:11a), in the "b" sub-element. Finally, when they hear "the one who empowers me (με)" (4:13) in the "a′" sub-element, they hear a progression in parallels from "on behalf of me (ἐμοῦ)" (4:10) in the "a" sub-element.[23]

Paul's declaration that "I am joyful (ἐχάρην) in the Lord (ἐν κυρίῳ) greatly" (4:10a) continues the dominant theme that has been streaming throughout the letter of the joy he shares with his audience with whom he is in fellowship for the gospel within the realm of their mutually being "in the Lord." This theme began when Paul announced, "I thank my God at every remembrance of you, always in my every petition on behalf of all of you, making the petition with joy (χαρᾶς, 1:4) at your fellowship for the gospel" (1:3–5). That the gospel of Christ is the central focus of Paul's joy became evident for the audience when he then disclosed that "in all manner, whether in pretense or in truth, Christ is proclaimed, and in this I rejoice (χαίρω). And indeed I will be joyful (χαρήσομαι)" (1:18). Paul then began to draw his audience into the mutual joy they are to share, as he indicated the importance of his remaining with them for the increase of their joy: "And having confidence of this, I know that I will remain, indeed I will remain beside all of you for your advancement and joy (χαράν) in the faith" (1:25).

The audience were then made aware of the key role they are to play with regard to the advancement of Paul's joy, when he exhorted them to "fill up my joy (χαράν) and think the same thing, having the same love, united in mind, thinking the one thing" (2:2). The audience then were emphatically exhorted to share the joy of Paul even in their common suffering for the faith: "But if indeed I am being poured out like a drink offering upon the sacrifice and service of your faith, I am rejoicing (χαίρω), indeed I am rejoicing with (συγχαίρω) all of you. And in the same way you are to be rejoicing (χαίρετε), indeed you are to be rejoicing with (συγχαίρετέ) me" (2:17–18). The audience may rejoice in Paul's return to them of Epaphroditus, their mutual partner, who suffered in the work of Christ: "More eagerly then I send him, so that seeing him you may rejoice (χαρῆτε) again and I may be less sorrowful. Welcome him then in the Lord with all joy (χαρᾶς) and have such people in esteem, for on account of the work of Christ he came near to the point of death, risking his life, so that he might fill up your lack of service toward me" (2:28–30).

The audience then were directly and affectionately exhorted to rejoice within the realm of their being "in the Lord": "Furthermore, my brothers, rejoice (χαίρετε) in the Lord (ἐν κυρίῳ)" (3:1a). After being again affectionately addressed by Paul as "my brothers beloved and longed for, my joy (χαρά) and crown, thus stand firm

---

23. These are the only two occurrences in this chiastic pattern of the first-person singular pronoun used as a grammatical object; this pronoun occurs in 4:11 as the grammatical subject of the sentence.

in the Lord (ἐν κυρίῳ), beloved" (4:1), the audience were exuberantly and emphatically exhorted to "rejoice (χαίρετε) in the Lord (ἐν κυρίῳ) always. Again, I will say
rejoice (χαίρετε)" (4:4). And so now, Paul's declaration that "I am joyful (ἐχάρην)
in the Lord (ἐν κυρίῳ) greatly" (4:10a) adds to the theme of the mutual joy he
shares with his Philippian audience in their fellowship for the gospel of Christ.[24] It
reinforces these previous repeated exhortations for the audience to rejoice in the
Lord by exemplifying such rejoicing in the Lord for them, thus further providing
them with a model to imitate (4:9a; 3:17).

The reason Paul is now joyful in the Lord greatly is "that now at last you have
begun again to think (φρονεῖν) on behalf of me, for which indeed you were thinking (ἐφρονεῖτε), but had no opportunity" (4:10).[25] That the audience have renewed
their concern for Paul advances the theme of the mutual joy they share with Paul,
as it further indicates how they contribute to Paul's joy by the way that they think.[26]
Previously, Paul exhorted them to "fill up my joy and think (φρονῆτε) the same
thing, having the same love, united in mind, thinking (φρονοῦντες) the one thing"
(2:2). The same one thing they are to think, the mind-set they are to adopt, is
the selfless, humble mind-set demonstrated by Jesus in his obedient acceptance of
death on a cross (2:6–8), which they are to adopt within the realm of their being
"in Christ Jesus": "This go on thinking (φρονεῖτε) in you, which is also in Christ
Jesus" (2:5).

That the audience have now at last begun again to think "on behalf of me"
(ὑπὲρ ἐμοῦ) (4:10) further contributes to Paul's rejoicing in the Lord greatly as it
reciprocates Paul's own thinking on behalf of them. Paul previously asserted how
it is right for him to "think" (φρονεῖν) this—that God will perfect the good work
for the gospel that he began in them (1:6)—"on behalf of all of you" (ὑπὲρ πάντων
ὑμῶν) (1:7). He asserted this after declaring that he makes every petition "on behalf of all of you" (ὑπὲρ πάντων ὑμῶν) with joy (1:4) at the fellowship they share
with him for the gospel (1:5).[27]

---

24. Fee, *Philippians*, 428: "As he twice exhorted them (3:1; 4:4), his rejoicing was 'in the Lord,'
another subtle indication of the three-way bond (between him, them, and Christ) that holds the letter
together. Paul rejoiced 'in the Lord,' the author of their common salvation, over the tangible evidence
that they together belong to the Lord and thus to one another." See also Fowl, *Philippians*, 192.

25. Thurston, *Philippians*, 152: "The word for 'thinking' in this verse reflects the familiar (nine
times in the letter) and important verb φρονέω, 'to be minded,' 'to have as a habitual attitude' (see, e.g.,
1:7; 2;2; 4:2). . . . The Philippians were thinking of Paul all along; 'without opportunity' means they had
had no chance to show their concern."

26. Fee, *Philippians*, 429: "The verb 'you have renewed' [ἀνεθάλετε] is a botanical metaphor,
meaning to 'blossom again'—like perennials or the Spring shoots of deciduous trees and bushes."

27. O'Brien, *Philippians*, 518: The key word φρονέω appears again, and here it describes the
'thoughtful concern' of the Philippians, who take an active interest in Paul's affairs since they are bound
up with the progress of the gospel." Silva, *Philippians*, 208–9: "Paul, after assuring the Philippians that
he had the right frame of mind toward them (1:7), and then rebuking them for not having the right
frame of mind toward one another (2:2, 5; 3:15; 4:2), here at the end encourages them by recognizing
a very positive trait in their attitude."

Although the audience have been appreciatively acknowledged by Paul for taking the opportunity of the current situation of his imprisonment to think on behalf of him (4:10), they are to realize that Paul was not necessarily seeking their material support in this situation, as he asserts, "Not that I say this on account of want (ὑστέρησιν)" (4:11a). After all, Paul has already informed his audience of how Epaphroditus has filled up their "lack" (ὑστέρημα) of service toward him (2:30). Paul's insistence, intensified by its emphatic use of the first-person singular pronoun, "for I (ἐγώ) have learned (ἔμαθον) in whatever things I am involved to be content" (4:11b),[28] resonates with his previous exhortation to his audience, also intensified by its emphatic use of the first-person singular pronoun, "And the things you have learned (ἐμάθετε) and received and heard and saw in me (ἐμοί), these things practice" (4:9a). The implication is that the audience are to learn what Paul himself has personally learned, and thus further imitate him by likewise being content with their material provisions in whatever things they find themselves involved within their fellowship with Paul for the gospel of Christ Jesus.

The audience then begin to hear an elaboration of what it means for Paul to be content in his current situation of imprisonment: "I know indeed to be humble, I know indeed to abound" (4:12a).[29] That Paul indeed knows what it means "to be humble" (ταπεινοῦσθαι) further likens and conforms him to Jesus, who "humbled (ἐταπείνωσεν) himself, becoming obedient to the point of death, even death on a cross" (2:8). Paul thus adds his own personal example of humility to that of Jesus as a further model for the audience to imitate and be inspired by, as they strive to put into practice Paul's exhortation for them in "humility" (ταπεινοφροσύνη) to consider one another more important than themselves (2:3).

After experiencing an emphatic pivot of parallels involving the word "all" or "every," and thus intensifying the totality of the situations and circumstances "in which" (ἐν οἷς) Paul has found himself (4:11b), from the singular "in every situation" (ἐν παντὶ) (4:12b) to the plural "and in all things (ἐν πᾶσιν)" (4:12c), the audience hear that Paul has learned the secret of how to be content no matter what may be the extremes of his physical and material surroundings.[30] He has learned

---

28. O'Brien, *Philippians*, 520: "The ἐγώ is slightly emphatic and indicates, 'I, for my part, whatever it may be with others', while the aorist ἔμαθον is best rendered by an English perfect 'I have learned.'"

29. O'Brien, *Philippians*, 524: "One might have expected the simpler expression καὶ ταπεινοῦσθαι καὶ περισσεύειν ('*both* to be abased *and* to abound'). But in order to drive home the point that he knows the one secret as well as the other Paul breaks the normal construction by the emphatic repetition of οἶδα" (O'Brien's emphasis).

30. O'Brien, *Philippians*, 525: "He employs the verb μεμύημαι (lit. 'I have been initiated'), a technical term taken from the vocabulary of the mystery religions, to describe the initiatory rites of a devotee who wished to enter their secrets and privileges. Here, however, it describes a learning experience of a different kind: Paul *has come to know* the secret of being content (the perfect tense of μεμύημαι shows that this learning was not instantaneous), while the very emphatic ἐν παντὶ καὶ ἐν πᾶσιν describes the inclusive and varied spheres of Paul's 'initiation'" (O'Brien's emphasis). Bockmuehl, *Philippians*, 261: "Initiation in the metaphorical sense may still be intended, in which case Paul's point is that Christian

the secret "both to be satisfied and to hunger, both to abound and to be in want" (4:12).[31]

That Paul himself knows indeed not only "to abound" (περισσεύειν) (4:12a), but both "to abound" (περισσεύειν) (4:12d) and to be in want (4:12e) in his physical and material circumstances reinforces his previously expressed wishes and prayers regarding the spiritual abundance of his audience. Paul wishes "that your boast may abound (περισσεύῃ) in Christ Jesus in me through my presence again with you" (1:26). And Paul prays "that your love even more and more may abound (περισσεύῃ) in knowledge and every perception" (1:9). That Paul knows the secret both to abound and "to be in want" (ὑστερεῖσθαι) thus further clarifies for his audience why he has not spoken to them on account of any "want" (ὑστέρησιν) (4:11a).[32]

Paul's climactic exclamation that "I am strong for everything in the one who empowers me!" (4:13) complements his previous proclamation that "I am joyful in the Lord greatly" (4:10a).[33] That Paul is strong for "everything" (πάντα) comprehensively sums up for the audience how he is content "in every situation" (ἐν παντί) (4:12b) and "in all things" (ἐν πᾶσιν) (4:12c). That he is strong for everything "in (ἐν) the one who empowers me" develops his being joyful "in (ἐν) the Lord." It advances the theme of Paul's experience of the divine power available for those in conformity with the death and resurrection of the Lord Jesus Christ, a conformity that the audience are to imitate. Paul's being strong in the one who "empowers (ἐνδυναμοῦντί) me" resonates with his deep desire to know Christ and "the power (δύναμιν) of the rising of him and the fellowship of the sufferings of him, being conformed to the death of him" (3:10). And it bolsters the hope that "we are awaiting the Lord Jesus Christ, who will transform the body of our humbleness (ταπεινώσεως, cf. 4:12a) (to be) conformed to the body of his glory

contentment remains unintelligible to those outside and can only be 'learned' from the God of peace (4.7, 9)."

31. O'Brien, *Philippians*, 523: "[T]he verb οἶδα, when followed by an infinitive, usually signifies 'to know how' or 'to be able'. Consequently, the apostle is not simply stating that he has experienced life at both ends of the economic spectrum, though this was true enough. Rather, as an amplification of v. 11b, he is explaining that he knows *how* to live in an appropriate manner under these contrasting circumstances: he knows how to be brought low by poverty or want and to be content" (O'Brien's emphasis).

32. O'Brien, *Philippians*, 524–25: "Paul has the right attitude to both so that even when he has more than enough for his needs he does not succumb to the temptation of finding his satisfaction in such material abundance. And if he knows how to be content in these two extreme conditions, then he is able to cope with the intermediate circumstances as well."

33. Fee, *Philippians*, 434 n. 48: "Gk. ἐν τῷ ἐνδυναμοῦντί, which, given the frequency of the 'in Christ' kind of phrase in Philippians, almost certainly does not primarily express agency here—although such an idea does not lag very far behind. Paul is referring to his being 'in him, that is, in the one who enables'. The problem with translating it 'through him' is that it often leads to a kind of triumphalism." Fowl, *Philippians*, 195: "Although the Lord is not mentioned explicitly in 4:13 as the one who strengthens Paul, at the beginning of this passage Paul began by rejoicing 'in the Lord.'"

according to the working that empowers (δύνασθαι) him even to subject to him-self all things" (3:20–21).

Finally, that Paul is strong for everything in the Lord Jesus Christ as the one who empowers him (4:13) further elucidates for the audience why Paul has not spoken to them of any want (4:11a) while in prison, even though he appreciates that they have begun to think on behalf of him (4:10). The audience are to realize that Paul appreciates their thinking "on behalf of me (ἐμοῦ)," but has not informed them of his present material needs, because "I" (ἐγώ) have learned to be content in all situations and in all circumstances (4:11b), because "I am strong for everything in the one who empowers me (με)!"[34]

In sum, in the B element (4:10–13) the audience are to imitate Paul by being content in whatever physical and material situations and circumstances they find themselves within their fellowship for the gospel of Christ. Like Paul, they are to be in need of nothing materially but "abound" spiritually by being conformed, through a selfless, humble mind-set, to the death and resurrection of the Lord Jesus Christ. They will thereby be able, like Paul, to rejoice greatly in the Lord, in the realm of the one who empowers them to be strong for everything.

3. Phil 4:14–15 (C): You Alone Shared with Me in an Account of Giving and Receiving

Paul then affirms his Philippian audience for their sharing with him within their fellowship for the gospel: "Nevertheless, you did well, sharing with me in my affliction. And you indeed know, Philippians, that in the beginning of the gospel, when I went out from Macedonia, not a single church shared with me in an ac-count of giving and receiving except you alone" (4:14–15).

The audience hear this affirmation from Paul in the form of the following chiastic pattern:

(a) [4:14–15a] Nevertheless, you did well, sharing with (συγκοινωνήσαντές) me (μου) in my affliction. And you (ὑμεῖς) indeed know, Philippians,

    (b) [15b] that (ὅτι) in the beginning of the gospel,

      (b′) [15c] when (ὅτε) I went out from Macedonia,

---

34. O'Brien, *Philippians*, 526–27: "If the verb ἰσχύω (in the active voice) draws attention to Paul's sufficiency or ability to cope, then the highly significant qualifying phrase ἐν τῷ ἐνδυναμοῦντί με makes it perfectly clear that this contentment did not arise from his own inherent or innate resources. . . . and so it was very different from that of the Stoic." Fee, *Philippians*, 435: "He has just urged them to 'prac-tice' what he both taught and modeled (v. 9). In the midst of their own present difficulties, here is what they too should learn of life in Christ, that being 'in him who enables' means to be 'content' whatever their circumstances." Garland, "Philippians," 258: "In this case, 'everything' refers to his ministry as an apostle, not to anything he might set out to do." See also Abraham J. Malherbe, "Paul's Self–Sufficiency (Philippians 4:11)," in *Friendship, Flattery, and Frankness of Speech: Studies on Friendship in the New Testament World* (ed. John T. Fitzgerald; NovTSup 82; Leiden: Brill, 1996), 125–39.

(a´) ¹⁵ᵈ not a single church shared (ἐκοινώνησεν) with me (μοι) in an account of giving and receiving except you (ὑμεῖς) alone.

At the center of this chiastic pattern the audience hear a pivot in parallels involving an alliteration of conjunctions, from "that (ὅτι) in the beginning of the gospel" (4:15b) in the "b" sub-element to "when (ὅτε) I went out from Macedonia" (4:15c) in the "b´" sub-element. When the audience hear that not a single church "shared (ἐκοινώνησεν) with me (μοι)" except "you" (ὑμεῖς) (4:15d) in the "a´" sub-element, they hear a progression in parallels from "sharing with (συγκοινωνήσαντές) me (μου)" (4:14) and "you (ὑμεῖς) indeed know" (4:15a) in the "a" sub-element.

Paul's laudatory acknowledgment of his audience, "nevertheless you did (ἐποιήσατε) well in sharing with me" (4:14) affirms their ability to fulfill Paul's previous directive to them, "do (ποιεῖτε) everything without grumbling or questioning" (2:14).³⁵ Their "sharing with" (συγκοινωνήσαντές) Paul underscores his initial affirmation that both in his bonds and in the defense and confirmation of the gospel they are his "fellow sharers" (συγκοινωνούς) of the grace (1:7). It reinforces their mutual "fellowship" (κοινωνίᾳ) for the gospel (1:5), which includes a "fellowship" (κοινωνία) of Spirit (2:1), and the "fellowship" (κοινωνίαν) of the sufferings of Christ in being conformed to his death (3:10). That they have shared with him in "my affliction (θλίψει)" resonates with the situation of his imprisonment, as it recalls the reference to those who would raise "affliction" (θλῖψιν) for Paul in his bonds (1:17).³⁶

What Paul and his audience respectively "know" is part of their mutual fellowship for the gospel. Paul confidently declared that "I know" (οἶδα) that "this—the preaching of the gospel (1:18)—for me will lead to salvation through the petition of you and supply of the Spirit of Jesus Christ" (1:19). He went on to confidently affirm that "I know (οἶδα) that I will remain, indeed I will remain beside all of you for your advancement and joy in the faith" (1:25). He then asserted that in his situation of imprisonment for the gospel "I know (οἶδα) indeed to be humble, I know (οἶδα) indeed to abound" (4:12). Now, with a direct address and naming of his audience, he begins to emphatically acknowledge what they "know": "And you indeed know (οἴδατε), Philippians" (4:15a).³⁷

---

35. O'Brien, *Philippians*, 528: "Paul's statement is no mere acknowledgement that they had simply done their duty. Rather, it is a generous commendation for their noble and praiseworthy action."

36. Fee, *Philippians*, 439 n. 9: "By bringing the 'my' forward for emphasis, Paul puts θλίψις in the dative as his way of emphasizing the 'togetherness' inherent in the συν. The result is even greater emphasis on their being sharers in the affliction itself, while the 'vernacular possessive' emphasizes that they share it with Paul." Garland, "Philippians," 258: "They share his shame and risk bringing suspicion on themselves through their loyalty to him."

37. O'Brien, *Philippians*, 531: "Here Φιλιππήσιοι is an expression of Paul's affectionate gratitude. But it is not used as a term of earnestness and affection in order to temper his supposed exasperation." Fee, *Philippians*, 439 n. 10: "Gk. οἴδατε δὲ καὶ ὑμεῖς, Φιλιππήσιοι. The δέ marks a transition in the nar-

What the Philippian audience, together with Paul, well know is that in the beginning of their fellowship with Paul for the gospel, that is, when Paul went out from Macedonia, the region wherein Philippi is located, not a single one of the churches he founded there shared with him in a matter of giving and receiving except the Philippians alone (4:15). The phrase "in the beginning of the gospel (εὐαγγελίου)" echoes the many references previously in the letter to the fellowship for the gospel that the Philippians share in.[38] The Philippians Euodia and Syntyche have struggled together with Paul in the "gospel" (εὐαγγελίῳ) (4:3). The Philippian audience know the worth of Timothy, who as a child to a father served with Paul "for the gospel (εὐαγγέλιον)" (2:22). They are to live as citizens worthy of the "gospel (εὐαγγελίου) of the Christ," with one mind struggling together for the faith of the "gospel" (εὐαγγελίου) (1:27). Paul is in prison for "the defense of the gospel (εὐαγγελίου)" (1:16). His being in prison has resulted in "an advancement of the gospel (εὐαγγελίου)" (1:12).

But the most direct and noteworthy resonance of the phrase "in the beginning of the gospel (εὐαγγελίου)" (4:15) is with the thanksgiving that introduces the letter. That the Philippians are the only ones who shared with Paul in the beginning of the gospel especially recalls and elaborates the reason for Paul's joyful thanksgiving to God for their "fellowship for the gospel (εὐαγγέλιον) from the first day until now" (1:5). Indeed, both in Paul's present bonds of imprisonment and in his "defense and confirmation of the gospel (εὐαγγελίου), all of you are my fellow sharers of the grace" (1:7).

That no "church" (ἐκκλησία) has shared with Paul in an account of giving and receiving except the church at Philippi alone (4:15d) emphatically singles out this church for its especially close and cooperative relationship with the Paul who formerly with zeal persecuted "the church (ἐκκλησίαν)" (3:6). And finally, that no church "shared (ἐκοινώνησεν) with me (μοι) in an account of giving and receiving except you (ὑμεῖς) alone" substantiates and adds a further reason for Paul's laudatory acknowledgment of the Philippians as "you (ὑμεῖς) indeed know" (4:15a) and "you did well, sharing with (συγκοινωνήσαντές) me (μου) in my affliction" (4:14).[39]

---

rative; the combination καὶ ὑμεῖς ('even you yourselves') and the vocative, "Philippians,' together create the impression of strong emphasis on what he is about to narrate—a way of saying, 'sit up and take note of what I am about to say.'"

38. O'Brien, *Philippians*, 532: "It is appropriate, then, to regard the time reference as denoting the beginning of the gospel from the standpoint of the Philippians. Again εὐαγγέλιον is used to denote the dynamic progress of that gospel, its onward march, this time in the lives of the Philippians themselves."

39. O'Brien, *Philippians*, 533–34: "Many of the expressions in this clause, particularly the phrase εἰς λόγον δόσεως καὶ λήμψεως, as well as others in the following verses, were key commercial terms. εἰς λόγον was a technical phrase meaning 'to the account of', being used of business transactions in Greek literature and the papyri. The nouns δόσις and λῆμψις, 'giving and receiving', refer to monetary transactions on two sides of a ledger, while the verb κοινωνέω, which had a wide range of applications, so as to describe friends sharing in the good things of life or social intimacies, could refer to a joint

In sum, in this C element (4:14–15) the audience are affectionately praised by Paul as the only church which, at the beginning of the proclamation of the gospel, when Paul went out from Philippi in the region of Macedonia, shared with him in an account of giving and receiving within their fellowship with Paul for the gospel. They have added to the reason for such singular praise by doing well in sharing with him in the present affliction of his imprisonment for the gospel.

4. Phil 4:16 (D): Even in Thessalonica You Sent to Me in My Need

Paul adds yet another reason for his laudatory acknowledgment of his Philippian audience: "for even in Thessalonica not only once but twice you sent to me in my need" (4:16). That "even in Thessalonica," which, like Philippi, is also located in the region of Macedonia, the Philippians sent support to Paul means that they did this even before Paul went out from Macedonia (4:15). That the Philippians not only once but twice sent to "me (μοι) in my need" further underlines their close fellowship with Paul, for whom they did well in "sharing with me in my (μου) affliction" (4:14), and who were the only ones who shared with Paul in an account of giving and receiving, when no other church "shared with me (μοι)" (4:15).[40]

Previously, Paul declared, "I hope in the Lord Jesus soon to send (πέμψαι) Timothy to you" (2:19a), and, "This one then I hope to send (πέμψαι) as soon as I perceive the things concerning me" (2:23). He then announced, "I have considered it necessary Epaphroditus, my brother and co-worker and fellow soldier, and your apostle and servant in my need (χρείας μου), to send (πέμψαι) to you" (2:25), and, "More eagerly then I send (ἔπεμψα) him, so that seeing him you may rejoice again and I may be less sorrowful" (2:28). Now, the Philippian audience are to appreciate that Paul is sending these two co-workers to reciprocate, within the fellowship they share for the gospel, for the fact that they, even back when Paul was still in Thessalonica, "not only once but twice sent (ἐπέμψατε) to me (μοι) in my need (χρείαν)" (4:16).[41]

---

undertaking in business. In this passage it denotes 'financial sharing'. Paul's use of commercial language (cf. v. 17) seems to be both deliberate and sustained." Bockmuehl, *Philippians*, 263–64: "Even Jewish–Hellenistic writers could happily use such common financial terminology either literally (e.g. Sir. 42.7) or metaphorically of a socially reciprocal relationship (e.g. Sir. 41.21). Similar accounting terminology is found in vv. 17 and 18 (and of course previously in 3.7, 8). . . . the undoubted aspects of equality and mutuality in Paul's partnership with the Philippians are underwritten by their common participation in a new identity that is constructed in Christ rather than in social or ethnic status. As the whole letter has been at pains to show, both for Paul (3.2–14) and for the Philippians (1.27; 2.15; 3.20 and *passim*) their citizenship of heaven creates new bonds in Christ and relativizes the norms and expectations of secular society." Garland, "Philippians," 259: "Paul rejoices in their unique bond created by their working partnership—a bond that transcends the conventions of social reciprocity."

40. O'Brien, *Philippians*, 535: "The phrase καὶ ἅπαξ καὶ δίς, (lit.) 'both once and twice', has been taken to mean 'not once but twice' or more specifically 'twice'. It is preferable, however, to regard it as an idiomatic expression for 'more than once.'"

41. Fee, *Philippians*, 446: "If he felt compelled to establish in vv. 11–13 that his joy over their gift was not grounded at this level, which could be viewed as utilitarian, neither did he intend to deny that

In sum, in this D element (4:16), that the Philippian audience even while Paul was still in Thessalonica more than once "sent" to him in his need further singles them out for praise in their mutual fellowship with Paul for the gospel, as it provides a reason for Paul's reciprocal "sending" to them of two key co-workers for the gospel, Timothy and Epaphroditus (2:19–28).

5. Phil 4:17 (C′): Not That I Seek the Gift, but the Fruit That Increases in Your Account

The audience are then made aware of Paul's special concern for them in the matter of their giving and receiving (4:15–16): "Not that I am seeking the gift, but I am seeking the fruit that increases in your account" (4:17). At this point, after hearing the unparalleled central and pivotal D element (4:16) of this chiastic unit (4:6–20), the audience hear a progression of parallels from "in an account of giving (εἰς λόγον δόσεως) and receiving" (4:15) in the C element (4:14–15) to "seeking the gift (δόμα)" and "in your account (εἰς λόγον)" in the C′ element (4:17).

Elaborating upon the commercial terminology of his laudatory acknowledgment of his Philippian audience as the only church to share with him "in an account (εἰς λόγον) of giving (δόσεως) and receiving" (4:15), Paul clarifies that it is not the "gift" (δόμα) in itself that "I am seeking" (ἐπιζητῶ) from them, but rather "I am seeking" (ἐπιζητῶ) the fruit that increases "in your account (εἰς λόγον)" (4:17).[42] "Not that (οὐχ ὅτι) I am seeking the gift" resonates with Paul's previous assertion after acknowledging his audience's concern for him (4:10), "Not that (οὐχ ὅτι) I say this on account of want" (4:11a).[43] The emphatic use of the second-person plural pronoun in Paul's assertion that he is seeking the fruit that increases "in your account," literally, "in the account of you (ὑμῶν)," continues Paul's focus upon the praiseworthy role of his audience in their mutual fellowship for the gospel. It was with similar emphatic uses of the second-person plural pronoun that Paul singled out his audience, when he told them that "you (ὑμεῖς) indeed know" that "no church shared with me in an account of giving and receiving except you (ὑμεῖς) alone" (4:15).

That Paul is seeking the "fruit" (καρπόν) that "increases in the account" of his Philippian audience (4:17) contributes to the mutuality of their fellowship for the gospel, as his commercial terminology becomes more metaphorical.[44] It was in

---

they had in fact ministered to his 'need.'" Garland, "Philippians," 259: "Their support reveals that they were concerned for both the welfare of Paul and the spread of the gospel."

42. O'Brien, *Philippians*, 538: "By repeating the verb ἐπιζητῶ, he emphasizes in an impressive manner what he does set his heart on."

43. Bockmuehl, *Philippians*, 265: "He wants to counteract the idea that he either solicited their gift or is asking for more."

44. O'Brien, *Philippians*, 538–39: "καρπός can mean the 'advantage or profit' gained in a business transaction and thus here probably signifies 'interest'. . . . Accordingly, when the present participle πλεονάζοντα ('continuing to multiply or increase') qualifies the noun καρπόν, it suggests the figure of compound interest. . . . The picture painted by the accounting metaphor is of compound interest that

metaphorical commercial terms that Paul previously declared that as for him, to live is Christ and to die is "gain" (1:21; cf. 3:7–8). He continued, "If it is to live in the flesh, this for me is fruitful work"—literally the "fruit (καρπός) of work" (1:22). And that Paul is seeking the "fruit that increases in your account" resonates with his opening prayer that "your love even more and more may abound in knowledge and every perception in order that you determine the things that matter, so that you may be sincere and faultless for the day of Christ, having been filled up with the fruit (καρπόν) of righteousness that is through Jesus Christ for the glory and praise of God" (1:9–11).[45] In sum, the audience are to realize that within their fellowship with Paul for the gospel their giving of the gift to Paul is even more beneficial for them spiritually as the givers than the material gift itself is for him as the recipient.[46]

6. Phil 4:18a (B´): I Have Received in Full Everything and I Am Abounding

Paul then acknowledges his reception of the gift from Epaphroditus sent to him by his Philippian audience: "For I have received in full everything and I am abounding. I have been filled up, having received from Epaphroditus the things from you, an aroma of fragrance, an acceptable sacrifice" (4:18a). At this point the audience hear a progression, via the chiastic parallels, from "I am strong for everything (πάντα) in the one who empowers me" (4:13) in the B element to "I have received in full everything (πάντα)" (4:18a) in the B´ element. They also hear a progression from "I know indeed to abound (περισσεύειν)" and "both to abound (περισσεύειν) and to be in want" (4:12) in the B element to "I am abounding" (περισσεύω) (4:18a) in the B´ element.

Continuing with his commercial language, Paul announces that he has received in full "everything" (πάντα), referring to all of the material support that he has received from his Philippian audience at the hands of Epaphroditus (4:18a).[47] This resonates with his previous exclamation that he is strong for "everything" (πάντα), referring to all of the various extreme situations he has been divinely enabled to endure in the past and that he is presently enduring in his imprisonment for the gospel "in the one who empowers me" (4:13). The implication is that

---

accumulates all the time until the last day. The apostle has employed this commercial language to show that he has set his heart on an ongoing, permanent gain for the Philippians in the spiritual realm."

45. Bockmuehl, *Philippians*, 265: "Quite plausibly this 'fruit' should be understood in eschatological terms, too, as relating to the future reckoning on the 'day of Jesus Christ' (1.6; 2.16), when in fact the Philippian gift will not only accrue to their own account, but they themselves will be Paul's 'joy and crown' (4.1; cf. 2.16)."

46. Fee, *Philippians*, 448: "Their gift, which serves his 'physical health,' serves more significantly as evidence of their 'spiritual health.'" Garland, "Philippians," 259: "Paul helps them see their relationship with him in the context of their relationship with God. It is not a bilateral but a trilateral relationship. Their sacrificial generosity reveals that God's work is bearing fruit in their lives."

47. O'Brien, *Philippians*, 539: "The apostle continues by introducing a further reason for his not seeking any gift from the Philippians: he has everything he needs and can even write his own receipt for all that he has been given."

the work they have done in sending Paul "everything" that he has received has the same divine origin and impetus from the "one who empowers" Paul. Indeed, Paul previously made his audience aware that "God is the one working in you both to desire and to work for the sake of his good pleasure" (2:13). And in his thanksgiving for the mutual fellowship he shares with his audience for the gospel (1:5), Paul prayed that the God "who began in you a good work will perfect it until the day of Christ Jesus" (1:6).

Paul's declaration that "I am abounding" (περισσεύω), now that he has received in full all of the material support his audience has sent him from Philippi (4:18a), resonates with his previous assertions regarding his ability to "abound": "I know indeed to be humble, I know indeed to abound (περισσεύειν). In every situation and in all things I have learned the secret, both to be satisfied and to hunger, both to abound (περισσεύειν) and to be in want" (4:12). Paul's present "abounding" due to the gift from his audience (4:14–17) underscores their cooperation, within the fellowship they share for the gospel of Christ Jesus, in the divine empowerment that enables Paul to be strong in whatever physical situation and circumstances he finds himself (4:13).

Paul's further declaration that "I have been filled up" (πεπλήρωμαι) as a result of the gift sent to him by his audience through Epaphroditus (4:18a) reinforces the ability of his audience to complete his previous directive for them to "fill up (πληρώσατέ) my joy and think the same thing, having the same love" (2:2). And Paul's declarations that "I am abounding" (περισσεύω) and "I have been filled up" (πεπλήρωμαι) also contribute to the complementarity between Paul and his audience within their fellowship for the gospel, as they resonate reciprocally with Paul's opening prayer for his audience: "And this I pray, that your love even more and more may abound (περισσεύῃ) in knowledge and every perception in order that you determine the things that matter, so that you may be sincere and faultless for the day of Christ, having been filled up (πεπληρωμένοι) with the fruit of righteousness that is through Jesus Christ for the glory and praise of God" (1:9–11).

Paul's acknowledgment of "having received from Epaphroditus the things from you (ὑμῶν)" (4:18a) bolsters the basis for his previous singling out of his Philippian audience with emphatic uses of the second-person plural pronoun. He pointed out that "*you* (ὑμεῖς) indeed know, Philippians, that in the beginning of the gospel, when I went out from Macedonia, not a single church shared with me in an account of giving and receiving except *you* (ὑμεῖς) alone" (4:15). And then he boldly asserted that "I am seeking the fruit that increases in the account of *you* (ὑμῶν)" (4:17).

The metaphorical characterization of the Philippians' gift as "an aroma of fragrance, an acceptable sacrifice (θυσίαν)" (4:18a), with its allusions to a recurrent formulaic phrase describing sacrifices to God in the OT (cf. LXX Gen 8:21; Exod 29:18, 25, 41; Lev 1:9, 13, 17; Ezek 20:41), elaborates upon, as it resonates with, Paul's earlier reference to the sacrificial character of the faith of his audience.[48] He proclaimed that "if indeed I am being poured out like a drink offering upon the sacrifice (θυσίᾳ) and service of your faith, I am rejoicing, indeed I am rejoicing with all of you" (2:17). The gift the Philippians have sent to Paul through Epaphroditus exemplifies the "sacrifice" and service of their faith. This "sacrifice" is acceptable not only to Paul but to the God who prompted it.

In sum, in this B´ element (4:18a) Paul acknowledged that the gift he has received from Epaphroditus sent by his Philippian audience has filled him up and enabled him to abound. Their gift represents a "sacrifice" acceptable not only to Paul but to the God who instigated and facilitated it.

7. Phil 4:18b–20 (A´): My God Will Fill Up Your Every Need in Christ Jesus

Paul then concentrates the focus of his audience directly and emphatically upon God himself—on what God will do for the Philippians who have sent the gift to Paul, as he reinforces how their gift as a sacrifice is acceptable to God, the God to whom eternal glory is due. Their sacrifice in not only acceptable (4:18a) but "well pleasing to God. My God will fill up your every need according to his wealth in glory in Christ Jesus. To our God and Father, glory to the ages of the ages, Amen" (4:18b–20). At this point the audience hear a progression, via the chiastic parallels, of threefold references to God—from "let your requests be made known before God (θεόν)" (4:6), "the peace of God (θεοῦ)" (4:7), and the "God (θεός) of peace" (4:9) in the A element to "well pleasing to God (θεῷ)" (4:18b), "my God (θεός) will fill up" (4:19), and "to our God (θεῷ) and Father" (4:20) in the A´ element. And they hear a progression from "your hearts and your minds in Christ Jesus (ἐν Χριστῷ Ἰησοῦ)" (4:7) in the A element to "his wealth in glory in Christ Jesus (ἐν Χριστῷ Ἰησοῦ)" (4:20) in the A´ element.

In reciprocation for the sacrificial gift of his Philippian audience, which is well pleasing "to God (θεῷ)" (4:18b), the "God" (θεόν) before whom the audience are to make known their requests (4:6), Paul promises that "my God (θεός) will fill up your every need" (4:19a). Paul's promise here thus bolsters and develops his previous promises that "the peace of God (θεοῦ) that surpasses all understanding will guard your hearts and your minds" (4:7) and "the God (θεός) of peace will be with you" (4:9). That God "will fill up" (πληρώσει) your every "need" (χρείαν) reciprocates not only for the filling up of Paul—"I have been filled up (πεπλήρωμαι)"—by their sacrificial gift now while he is in prison (4:18a), but for their having sent "to me in my need (χρείαν)" when Paul was in Thessalonica (4:16). That God will fill up "your" (ὑμῶν) every need reciprocates for "the things from you (ὑμῶν)" that

---

48. O'Brien, *Philippians*, 541: "The original imagery of ὀσμὴν εὐωδίας ['aroma of fragrance'] is that of God taking pleasure in the odour from the sacrifices that his people offer him. The expression is then used figuratively of an offering (or those who offer it) that is pleasing and acceptable to him." Fee, *Philippians*, 451: "Paul has already referred to Epaphroditus's 'ministry' as a 'priestly service' [2:25–30] to Paul on their behalf. Here he spells out what that means with language borrowed directly from the LXX, used to indicate the interplay between the human and the divine in the sacrifices." See also Vahrenhorst, *Kultische Sprache*, 242–45.

Paul has received from Epaphroditus, even as it further specifies "the fruit that increases in your (ὑμῶν) account" (4:17).[49]

Paul's promise that God will fill up the Philippians' *every* need, both material and spiritual, both now and in eternity, according to God's wealth "in glory (δόξῃ) in Christ Jesus (Χριστῷ Ἰησοῦ)" (4:19) resonates with and complements Paul's previous promise regarding the divine "glory" of the resurrected body in the heavenly life. It is the "Lord Jesus Christ (Ἰησοῦν Χριστόν)" (3:20) "who will transform the body of our humbleness (to be) conformed to the body of his glory (δόξης) according to the working that empowers him even to subject to himself all things" (3:21). This sharpens the contrast between the audience and those whose "God is their stomach and their glory (δόξα) is in their shame, those who are thinking the things of the earth" (3:19). The audience, whose way of thinking is to correspond with their "citizenship that is in heaven" (3:20), are assured that God will fill up their every need. That Paul's promise is according to God's wealth in glory for the audience who are within the realm of being in union with Christ Jesus—"in Christ Jesus" (ἐν Χριστῷ Ἰησοῦ)—resonates with and reinforces Paul's previous promise that "the peace of God that surpasses all understanding will guard your hearts and your minds in Christ Jesus (ἐν Χριστῷ Ἰησοῦ)" (4:7).[50]

Paul's climactic closing doxology, "To our God (θεῷ) and Father, glory to the ages of the ages, Amen" (4:20) renders praise to God as reciprocation for his promise that "God (θεός) will fill up your every need" (4:19). And it complements his acknowledgment of his audience's sacrificial gift to him as "well pleasing to God (θεῷ)" (4:18). The employment of the first-person plural pronoun in the address of the doxology, "to our (ἡμῶν) God and Father," further unites the audience with Paul and all other believers, as it flows progressively from the use of the first-person singular and second-person plural pronouns in Paul's promise that "my

---

49. O'Brien, *Philippians*, 547: "[T]he expression πᾶσαν χρείαν ὑμῶν is comprehensive in its range, including the readers' physical needs on the one hand (arising out of 4:10–20) and their spiritual concerns on the other (which have already been mentioned throughout the letter)." Fee, *Philippians*, 452–53: "Although he cannot reciprocate in kind, since their gift had the effect of being a sweet–smelling sacrifice, pleasing to God, Paul assures them that God, whom he deliberately designates as '*my* God,' will assume responsibility for reciprocity. . . . '*My* God,' Paul says, will act for me in your behalf by 'filling to the full *all* your needs'" (Fee's emphases). Bockmuehl, *Philippians*, 266: "God's 'full provision' should be understood to cover material needs, but presumably also their need for the qualities which Paul has been encouraging in this letter: joy and steadfastness in Christ, humility and concord amongst each other."

50. According to O'Brien (*Philippians*, 547–49), the phrase "according to his wealth" (κατὰ τὸ πλοῦτος αὐτοῦ) "draws attention not simply to the source of God's abundant riches (= 'from' or 'out of'), but also particularly indicates that his giving is 'in a manner that befits His wealth—on a scale worthy of His wealth' . . . As one who knows the secret of being content through Christ's overflowing sufficiency Paul assures his dear friends that his God will share with them his limitless resources, both now in their times of trial (cf. 1:28–29) and in the future consummation." Fee, *Philippians*, 454: "This is what the letter has ultimately been all about. It began 'in Christ Jesus'; it now concludes 'in Christ Jesus.'" Bockmuehl, *Philippians*, 266: "Just as the peace of God surpasses all understanding (v. 7), so the riches of God surpass every conceivable human need."

(μου) God will fill up your (ὑμῶν) every (πᾶσαν) need" (4:19), recalling Paul's pronouncement that "I thank my (μου) God at every (πάσῃ) remembrance of you (ὑμῶν)" (1:3).[51] The audience are to appreciate that the God whom Paul serves as "*my* God" is also "*our* God," the God and Father of Paul, the audience, and all other believers, the God to whom glory is due forever.[52]

The transition from Paul's promise for the audience, with its reference to "in glory (δόξῃ) in Christ Jesus" (4:19b), to his doxology, "to our God and Father, glory (δόξα) to the ages of the ages, Amen" (4:20), further leads his audience into the praise of God, based on what God has accomplished for them and all believers in Christ Jesus. At the beginning of the letter the audience heard Paul pray "that your love even more and more may abound in knowledge and every perception in order that you determine the things that matter, so that you may be sincere and faultless for the day of Christ, having been filled up with the fruit of righteousness that is through Jesus Christ for the glory (δόξαν) and praise of God" (1:9–11). Later they heard him proclaim the climactic hymnic conclusion "that at the name of Jesus every knee should bend, of those in heaven and of those on earth and of those under the earth, and every tongue confess that Jesus Christ is Lord to the glory (δόξαν) of God the Father" (2:10–11). And now, the audience are invited to join Paul in his praise that to *our* God, the God who will fill up the audience's "every need according to his wealth in glory in Christ Jesus" (4:19), is "glory to the ages of the ages, Amen" (4:20).[53]

---

51. O'Brien, *Philippians*, 545: "The addition of the personal pronoun μου is emphatic in the light of the immediately preceding τῷ θεῷ and stresses the apostle's consciousness of his close personal relationship with his God. Paul had long since experienced the divine power to meet all his needs; he now assures his dear Christian friends that his God will act on his behalf and fully meet their needs."

52. O'Brien, *Philippians*, 545 n. 213: "ὁ θεός μου means 'the God whom I serve', not 'the God whom I possess'."

53. O'Brien, *Philippians*, 549–50: "At v. 19 Paul used the intensely personal expression ὁ θεός μου to assure the Philippians that his God will act on his behalf to fulfill all their needs. Now he changes to the plural ἡμῶν as he unites himself with his converts in this ascription of praise. . . . To give God glory is not to add something that is not already present; it is rather an active acknowledgment or extolling of what he is or has already done. So, although this and many other doxologies contain no verb, the indicative ἐστιν ('is' or 'belongs') is presupposed, rather than the optative εἴη ('be' or 'may it be')." Fee, *Philippians*, 455: "'My God' is now '*our* God *and Father*'; and the living God, the everlasting one, who belongs to the 'ages of ages,' and who dwells 'in glory,' is now ascribed the 'glory' that is due his name" (Fee's emphases). Bockmuehl, *Philippians*, 267: "Paul's final Amen confirms that this doxology is no mere rhetorical flourish, but gives voice to his own deep conviction. It is the appropriately worshipful response to God's generous and sovereign providence in Christ Jesus." For recent discussions of 4:10–20, see Gerald W. Peterman, "'Thankless Thanks': The Epistolary Social Convention in Philippians 4:10–20," *TynBul* 42 (1991): 261–70; Brian J. Capper, "Paul's Dispute with Philippi: Understanding Paul's Argument in Phil. 1–2 from His Thanksgiving in 4.10–20," *TZ* 49 (1993): 193–214; Gordon D. Fee, "To What End Exegesis? Reflections on Exegesis and Spirituality in Philippians 4:10–20," *BBR* 8 (1998): 75–88; Stephen E. Fowl, "Know Your Context: Giving and Receiving Money in Philippians," *Int* 56 (2002): 45–58; J. Barnet, "Paul's Reception of the Gift from Philippi," *SVTQ* 50 (2006): 225–53. See also Jeffrey A. D. Weima, *Neglected Endings: The Significance of the Pauline Letter Closings* (JSNTSup 101; Sheffield: JSOT, 1994), 191–201.

To sum up, in the A′ element (4:18b–20) the audience's sacrificial gift to Paul is acknowledged as well pleasing to God, the God who will fill up their every material and spiritual need in accord with his wealth demonstrated in the glory of the heavenly, resurrected life of the Lord Jesus Christ, which they hope to share within the realm of their being in union with Christ Jesus. They are invited to join Paul and all other believers in the climactic doxology that "to our God and Father is glory to the ages of the ages, Amen."

C. SUMMARY ON PHILIPPIANS 4:6–20

1. The audience are to be anxious about nothing, but in everything, in their prayer and petition, with thanksgiving, to make their requests known before God, so that the profound peace that comes from God and that surpasses all understanding will guard their hearts and their minds within the realm of their being in Christ Jesus (4:6–7). They are to consider the things as well as practice—in imitation of Paul—the things that will enable them to experience the promise that the very person of the God who is the source of profound peace will be with their very persons (4:8–9), as they struggle together with one another and with Paul in conformity to Christ for the faith of the gospel (1:27–30).

2. The audience are to imitate Paul by being content in whatever physical and material situations and circumstances they find themselves within their fellowship for the gospel of Christ. Like Paul, they are to be in need of nothing materially but "abound" spiritually by being conformed, through a selfless, humble mind-set, to the death and resurrection of the Lord Jesus Christ. They will thereby be able, like Paul, to rejoice greatly in the Lord, in the realm of the one who empowers them to be strong for everything (4:10–13).

3. The audience are affectionately praised by Paul as the only church which, at the beginning of the proclamation of the gospel, when Paul went out from Philippi in the region of Macedonia, shared with him in an account of giving and receiving within their fellowship with Paul for the gospel. They have added to the reason for such singular praise by doing well in sharing with him in the present affliction of his imprisonment for the gospel (4:14–15).

4. That the Philippian audience even while Paul was still in Thessalonica more than once "sent" to him in his need further singles them out for praise in their mutual fellowship with Paul for the gospel, as it provides a reason for Paul's reciprocal "sending" to them of two key co-workers for the gospel, Timothy and Epaphroditus (4:16; cf. 2:19–28).

5. The audience are to realize that within their fellowship with Paul for the gospel their giving of the gift to Paul is even more beneficial for them spiritually as the givers than the material gift itself is for him as the recipient (4:17).

6. Paul acknowledged that the gift he has received from Epaphroditus sent by his Philippian audience has filled him up and enabled him to abound. Their gift

represents a "sacrifice" acceptable not only to Paul but to the God who instigated and facilitated it (4:18a).

7. The audience's sacrificial gift to Paul is acknowledged as well pleasing to God, the God who will fill up their every material and spiritual need in accord with his wealth demonstrated in the glory of the heavenly, resurrected life of the Lord Jesus Christ, which they hope to share within the realm of their being in union with Christ Jesus. They are invited to join Paul and all other believers in the climactic doxology that "to our God and Father is glory to the ages of the ages, Amen" (4:18b–20).

12
PHILIPPIANS 4:21–23: GREETING FROM HOLY ONES AND GRACE FROM THE LORD JESUS CHRIST (A´)

The Brothers and All the Holy Ones Greet You

A: [21a]Greet every holy one in *Christ Jesus.*
   B: [21b]The brothers who are with me *greet you.*
   B´: [22]All the holy ones *greet you*, especially those from the household of Caesar.
A´: [23]The grace of the Lord *Jesus Christ* be with your spirit.[1]

A. CHIASTIC DEVELOPMENT FROM PHILIPPIANS 1:1–2 (A) TO 4:21–23 (A´)

With Phil 4:21–23, the A´ unit within the macrochiastic structure organizing the entire letter, the audience hear resonances, by way of the chiastic parallelism, of 1:1–2, the corresponding A unit in the overall chiasm.[2] The mention of "every holy one" (πάντα ἅγιον) (4:21) and "all the holy ones" (πάντες οἱ ἅγιοι) (4:22) in the A´ unit recalls Paul's opening address to "all those holy ones" (πᾶσιν τοῖς ἁγίοις) (1:1) in the A unit.[3] And Paul's closing greeting, "the grace (χάρις) of the Lord Jesus Christ (κυρίου Ἰησοῦ Χριστοῦ) be with your spirit" (4:23) in the A´ unit, reverberates with his opening greeting, "grace (χάρις) to you and peace from God our Father and the Lord Jesus Christ (κυρίου Ἰησοῦ Χριστοῦ)" (1:2) in the A unit, forming a literary inclusion that frames the entire letter with a worshiping context of prayer-greetings.[4]

B. AUDIENCE RESPONSE TO PHILIPPIANS 4:21–23

1. Phil 4:21a (A): Greet Every Holy One in Christ Jesus

The closing greetings begin as Paul directs his audience: "Greet every holy one in Christ Jesus" (4:21a). The letter opened with Paul and Timothy, characterized as

---

1. For the establishment of 4:21–23 as a chiasm, see ch. 2.
2. This section is limited to demonstrating the macrochiastic parallels. The exegetical significance of these parallels is presented in the next section.
3. That these are the only occurrences in the letter of the term "holy" (ἅγιος) enhances the significance of this parallelism.
4. These are the only two occurrences in the letter of the word "grace" (χάρις) in the nominative singular; it occurs in the genitive singular in 1:7.

"slaves of Christ Jesus," addressing the whole community as "all those holy ones" (πᾶσιν τοῖς ἁγίοις) who are within the realm of being in union with Christ Jesus— "in Christ Jesus" (ἐν Χριστῷ Ἰησοῦ), those who are in Philippi, together with their leaders—the overseers and ministers (1:1). Now, as the letter comes to a close, the audience as a whole are directed to extend the greeting from Paul to "every holy one" (πάντα ἅγιον), each and every individual member of the community of believers within the realm of their being "in Christ Jesus" (ἐν Χριστῷ Ἰησοῦ) (4:21a).[5] This focusing of the whole community on each and every member within it thus resonates with Paul's previous directive for the audience in humility to consider one another more important than themselves (2:3), "each of you looking out not for the things of yourselves, but everyone also for the things of others" (2:4).[6]

When the audience hear the words "in Christ Jesus" (4:21a), they hear the transitional phrase that links this chiastic unit (4:21-23) with the previous one (4:6-20). It was towards the end of that unit that Paul promised that God will fill up every need of the Philippian audience within the realm of their being "in Christ Jesus" (4:19).[7]

In this A element (4:21a), then, the audience as a whole are encouraged to greet each and every "holy one," demonstrating a concern for each and every individual believer at Philippi (cf. 2:3-4), as those who are within the realm of being "in Christ Jesus," the realm in which God will fill up their every need (4:19).

2. Phil 4:21b (B): The Brothers Who Are with Me Greet You

After directing the audience to greet every holy one in Christ Jesus (4:21a), Paul extends to them greetings from those with him: "The brothers who are with me greet you" (4:21b). The "brothers" (ἀδελφοί) who are with Paul include Epaphroditus, whom Paul has described as "my brother (ἀδελφόν) and co-worker and fellow soldier" (2:25), presumably Timothy (1:1; 2:19-23), and perhaps some of the "brothers" (ἀδελφῶν) who have dared fearlessly to speak the word of the gospel while Paul is in the bonds of his imprisonment (1:14). The audience have heard themselves addressed repeatedly and affectionately by Paul as his "brothers" (ἀδελφοί, 1:12; 3:1, 13, 17; 4:1, 8), a most appropriate designation in view of the

---

5. Peter Trummer, "ἀσπάζομαι," EDNT 1.173: "The greeting receives special importance as a constituent part of the Pauline letters, in which Paul not only gives the letter itself a new function, but also gives the greeting formula a new function in the framework of his apostolic activity. In addition to the introductory greetings, the concluding greetings are of interest, inasmuch as their frequency and proportion is surprising in comparison with the Hellenistic culture."

6. O'Brien, Philippians, 553: "Paul may have omitted all personal salutations so as not to give any suggestion of partiality, especially since he had mentioned to them their need to be united (2:1-4; 4:3) and to follow the Lord's example of showing humility to one another (2:5-11)." Fee, Philippians, 457: "The greeting is not to the community lumped together as a whole, but to each member of the community individually. He does not single anyone out, but he does greet each of them in this fashion."

7. Fee, Philippians, 458: "Paul is sending his own greetings to each member of the believing community; they are to pass it on to one another for him, and the greeting is to be 'in Christ Jesus,' who is boh the source and focus of their common life together."

close fraternal fellowship he shares with them for the gospel of Christ Jesus (1:5). Now, the audience, whom Paul considers his "brothers" within their fellowship for the gospel, are assured of the greetings of the "brothers" who are with Paul in his imprisonment, thus reminding them that they share this fraternal fellowship not only with Paul but with these other "brothers" as well.

3. Phil 4:22 (B´): All the Holy Ones Greet You

Paul then continues the communication of greetings to his audience at Philippi: "All the holy ones greet you, especially those from the household of Caesar" (4:22). At this point the audience experience the pivot at the center of this chiastic unit, from "the brothers who are with me greet you (ἀσπάζονται ὑμᾶς)" (4:21b) in the B element to "all the holy ones greet you (ἀσπάζονται ὑμᾶς)" (4:22a) in the B´ element. The audience are assured of the warm greetings not only from the "brothers" closely associated with Paul but from the even broader circle of "all the holy ones," all the believers, where Paul is located. That "all the holy ones" (πάντες οἱ ἅγιοι) with Paul greet the audience, whom Paul addressed as "all those holy ones" (πᾶσιν τοῖς ἁγίοις) in Christ Jesus (1:1), reinforces and further inspires them to fulfill Paul's directive for them in turn to greet "every holy one" (πάντα ἅγιον) in Christ Jesus at Philippi (4:21a). The audience, as "all the holy ones" in Christ Jesus at the prominent Roman colony of Philippi (1:1), are thus to appreciate the greetings that come from, and thus unite them with, "all the holy ones" where Paul is located, especially those involved in the civil service of the Roman empire, those of the "household of Caesar."[8]

4. Phil 4:23 (A´): The Grace of the Lord Jesus Christ Be with Your Spirit

Paul concludes the letter with his own final greeting for the audience: "The grace of the Lord Jesus Christ be with your spirit" (4:23). Here the audience experience a progression, via the chiastic parallels, from Paul's directive for them to greet every holy one "in Christ Jesus (Χριστῷ Ἰησοῦ)" (4:21a) in the A element

---

8. O'Brien, *Philippians*, 554: "Special mention (μάλιστα) is made of one group: οἱ ἐκ τῆς Καίσαρος οἰκίας ('those of the imperial household'). According to the prevailing usage, this expression refers not to the members of the Emperor's family or relations but to the great number of slaves and freedmen from whose ranks the imperial civil service was staffed. These were scattered throughout the provinces of the Empire, although the largest concentration was obviously in Rome . . . Paul sends greetings from these Christian members of the imperial service, whether soldiers, slaves, or freedmen who . . . may have had special links with the citizens of Philippi as a Roman colony." Fee, *Philippians*, 460: "Paul either has found or has made disciples of the 'Lord' Jesus among members of the imperial household, who are thus on the Philippians' side in the struggle against those who proclaim Caesar as Lord!" Fowl, *Philippians*, 203: "Both those Christians in Philippi, who were suffering opposition from Roman citizens of Philippi, and Paul, who suffered at the hands of the empire both in Philippi and now in Rome, could draw encouragement and hope from movements in God's economy of salvation which had brought the gospel into Caesar's household." See also P. R. C. Weaver, *Familia Caesaris: A Social Study of the Emperor's Freedmen and Slaves* (Cambridge: Cambridge University Press, 1972).

to Paul's own final greeting of them with the prayerful wish that the grace of "the Lord Jesus Christ (Ἰησοῦ Χριστοῦ)" be with their spirit in this A´ element.

At the beginning of the letter Paul greeted the audience with the prayerful wish of "grace (χάρις) to you and peace from God our Father and the Lord Jesus Christ" (1:2). The audience were then made aware of how they are already fellow sharers with Paul of "the grace (χάριτος)" (1:7). Now, after the stirring doxology to "our God and Father" (4:20), the focus is more directly on the "grace" (χάρις) as coming from "the Lord Jesus Christ" (4:23). The audience are to appreciate that Paul's wish is for the grace that comes from "the Lord Jesus Christ," as the Lord whom all believers await as their savior (3:20). They are to appreciate that Paul's wish is for the "grace" that comes from "Christ Jesus my Lord," the surpassing greatness of the knowledge of whom has prompted Paul to consider everything else as worthless (3:8). And they are to appreciate that Paul's wish is for the "grace" that comes from the "Jesus Christ" whom God "granted" or "graced" (ἐχαρίσατο) with the name above every name (2:9), so that every tongue is to confess him as "Lord" to the glory of God the Father (2:11).[9]

Paul's wish is that the grace of the Lord Jesus Christ be "with your spirit (πνεύματος)" (4:23), that is, with the human "spirit" that animates and is synonymous with their persons and that embraces their way of thinking, which has been such a central focus in the letter.[10] The grace of the Lord Jesus Christ is to be with the human spirit of the audience, who are part of the fellowship of the divine "Spirit (πνεύματος)" (2:1). It is by this divine "Spirit (πνεύματι) of God" that they worship and boast in Christ Jesus (3:3). They are to be standing firm in this "one Spirit (πνεύματι)" (1:27). Indeed, Paul is confident of salvation through the supply of the "Spirit (πνεύματος) of Jesus Christ" himself (1:19). The "grace" that comes from Jesus Christ thus includes the "Spirit" that comes from Jesus Christ. Hence, Paul's wish that the grace of the Lord Jesus Christ be with the "spirit" of each individual member of the audience is the wish for the grace that will enable each of them to adopt the same selfless and humble mind-set (2:2–5) which resulted in God's exaltation of Jesus Christ as the universal Lord (2:6–11).[11]

---

9. O'Brien, *Philippians*, 555: "The phrase ['the grace of the Lord Jesus Christ'] describes not a character or quality of Jesus but something he shows and does. The Lord Jesus who is the source of grace bestows it freely on the congregation at Philippi. It will sustain the community, for it is by grace alone that they will stand."

10. Jacob Kremer, "πνεῦμα, *EDNT* 3.118–19: "πνεῦμα refers to the human being who is (and does not merely have) also *spirit*" (Kremer's emphasis).

11. Fee, *Philippians*, 461: "[T]he distributive singular, 'with your (pl.) spirit (sing.),' in effect, as with the first of the greetings in v. 21, individualizes the grace–benediction, so that each of them (in the 'spirit' of each) will experience the desired grace that is here prayed for." Thurston, *Philippians*, 161: "[T]he grace comes from Jesus. This was made especially clear in Philippians with its vivid depiction of how God made Jesus 'Lord' (2:9–11)." For a recent discussion of Phil 4:10–23, see Andreas H. Snyman, "Philippians 4:10–23 from a Rhetorical Perspective," *AcT* 27 (2007): 168–85.

C. Summary on Philippians 4:21–23

1. The audience as a whole are encouraged to greet each and every "holy one," demonstrating a concern for each and every individual believer at Philippi (cf. 2:3–4), as those who are within the realm of being "in Christ Jesus" (4:21a), the realm in which God will fill up their every need (4:19).

2. The audience, whom Paul considers his "brothers" within their fellowship for the gospel, are assured of the greetings of the "brothers" who are with Paul in his imprisonment, thus reminding them that they share this fraternal fellowship not only with Paul but with these other "brothers" as well.

3. The audience, as "all the holy ones" in Christ Jesus at the prominent Roman colony of Philippi (1:1), are thus to appreciate the greetings that come from, and thus unite them with, "all the holy ones" where Paul is located, especially those involved in the civil service of the Roman empire, those of the "household of Caesar" (4:22).

4. Paul's wish that the grace of the Lord Jesus Christ be with the "spirit" of each individual member of the audience (4:23) is the wish for the grace that will enable each of them to adopt the same selfless and humble mind-set (2:2–5) which resulted in God's exaltation of Jesus Christ as the universal Lord (2:6–11).

13

SUMMARY AND CONCLUSION

Let Us Rejoice in Being Conformed to Christ

The preceding chapters have provided detailed summary conclusions for each of the ten chiastic units comprising Paul's letter to the Philippians. This final chapter presents an overview of how this letter, through the rhetorical dynamics of its intricate and intriguing chiastic structures, encourages its audience to rejoice along with Paul in their being conformed to the selfless, humble mindset that enabled Jesus to obediently accept the sufferings and death which resulted in his exaltation as the universal Lord.

The opening chiastic A unit (1:1–2) introduces the senders of the letter as Paul and Timothy, characterized as obedient "slaves" under the authority of *Christ Jesus* (1:1a). The audience then experience a pivot of chiastic parallels involving the address to them as the recipients of the letter—from "to all *those* holy ones *in* Christ Jesus" (1:1b) to "*those* who are *in* Philippi with overseers and ministers" (1:1c). The climactic conclusion of the chiasm prepares the audience, as "holy ones" within the realm of being in union with Christ Jesus, to further receive and experience, by listening to the letter, the empowerment that comes from the grace and peace Paul and Timothy wish for them as special gifts from "God our Father and the Lord *Jesus Christ*" (1:2) (ch. 3).

At the center of the chiastic B unit (1:3–11) the audience hear Paul declare, "For my witness is God" (1:8a). The audience then experience a chiastic parallel progression from Paul's assertion that "*all of you* are my fellow sharers of the grace" (1:7) to his disclosure of "how I long for *all of you* with the affection of Christ Jesus" (1:8b). They then hear a progression from "your fellowship for the gospel from the first *day* until now" (1:5) and "that he who began in you a good work will perfect it until the *day of Christ* Jesus" (1:6) to Paul's prayer "that you may be sincere and faultless for the *day of Christ*" (1:10). In the conclusion of the chiasm the audience experience a parallel progression from Paul's pronouncement that "I thank my *God* at every remembrance of you" (1:3) to his reference to the audience as those "having been filled up with the fruit of righteousness that is through Jesus Christ for the glory and praise of *God*" (1:11) (ch. 4).

At the center of the chiastic C unit (1:12–18) the audience hear Paul's reference to those who preach the Christ "out of love, knowing that for the defense of the gospel I am set" (1:16). They then hear a parallel progression of references from those who "on account of good pleasure, preach *the Christ*" (1:15) to those who "out of self-seeking, proclaim *the Christ*" (1:17a). In the conclusion of the chiasm the audience experience a parallel progression from Paul's disclosure "that *my bonds* have become in Christ manifest in the whole praetorium and to *all* the rest, and most of the brothers, in the Lord having confidence by *my bonds*, more abundantly dare fearlessly to speak the word" (1:13–14) to his notice that some proclaim the Christ "not sincerely, supposing to raise affliction in *my bonds*. What then? Only that in *all* manner, whether in pretense or in truth, Christ is proclaimed, and in this I rejoice. And indeed I will be joyful" (1:17b-18) (ch. 5).

At the center of the chiastic D unit (1:19–30) the audience listen to a chiasti-cally parallel pivot from the imprisoned Paul's notifications that "*whether coming and seeing you*" (1:27b) to "*or being absent, I hear the things concerning you*" (1:27c). They then hear a parallel progression from Paul's desires "for your ad-vancement and joy in *the faith*" (1:25) and that they "live as citizens worthy of *the gospel* of the Christ" (1:27a) to his expectation "that you are standing firm in one Spirit, with one mind struggling together for *the faith of the gospel*" (1:27d). In the conclusion of the chiasm the audience experience a parallel progression from Paul's statements about his own situation, that "I know that this for me will lead to *salvation*" (1:19), "that *in nothing* I will be put to shame" (1:20), and "having the desire for release and to be with Christ" (1:23), to his encouragement for the audience not be "intimidated *in anything* by the opponents, which is for them a demonstration of destruction, but of your *salvation*, and this is from God, for to you has been granted that which is on behalf of Christ, not only in him to believe but also on behalf of him to suffer, *having* the same struggle, such as you saw in me and now hear in me" (1:28–30) (ch. 6).

The center of the chiastic E unit (2:1–16) leads the audience in a parallel pivot from the assertion that Christ "humbled himself, becoming obedient to the point of *death*" (2:8a) to its intensification, "even of *death* on a cross" (2:8b). They then hear a parallel progression from the description of Christ as he "who, *existing* in the form *of God*, not something to be exploited did he *consider* being equal to God, but emptied himself, taking the form of a slave, becoming in the *likeness* of human beings" (2:6–7) to the proclamation that "God *exalted* him and *granted* him the name that is above every name, so that at the *name* of Jesus . . . every tongue confess that Jesus Christ is Lord to the glory *of God* the Father" (2:9–11). In the conclusion of the chiasm the audience experience a parallel progression from references to "any consolation of *love*" (2:1), "having the same *love*" (2:2), and "nothing according to self-seeking nor according to *vainglory*, but in humility considering one another more important than *yourselves*, each of you looking out not for the things of *yourselves*" (2:3–4) to the references to "my *beloved*" (2:12), "work out *your own* salvation" (2:12), and "my boast for the day of Christ—that I did not run in *vain* or labor in *vain*" (2:16) (ch. 7).

With Phil 2:17–30, the E′ unit within the macrochiastic structure organizing the entire letter, the audience hear resonances, by way of the chiastic parallelism, with the corresponding E unit (2:1–16), which together with the E′ unit forms the pivotal center within the macrochiasm. "For I *have* no one like minded" (2:20) in the E′ unit reverberates with the audience's "*having* the same love" (2:2) in the E unit. That "they all seek the things of *themselves*" (2:21) in the E′ unit recalls "to work out *your own* salvation" (2:12) and "considering one another more important than *yourselves*, each of you looking out not for *your own* things" (2:3–4) in the E unit. "Not the things of Jesus *Christ*" (2:21) in the E′ unit recalls "the day of *Christ*" (2:16) in the E unit. "As a *child* to a *father*" (2:22) in the E′ unit reverberates with "to the glory of God the *Father*" (2:11) and with "*children* of God" (2:15) in the E unit. "I have *considered* it necessary" (2:25) in the E′ unit recalls "did not *consider* being equal to God something to be grasped" (2:6) and "in humility *considering* one another more important than yourselves" (2:3) in the E unit. And, finally, "he came near *to the point of death*" (2:30) in the E′ unit recalls and parallels "becoming obedient *to the point of death*" (2:8) in the E unit.

The center of the chiastic E′ unit (2:17–30) leads the audience in a parallel pivot from the declaration that "they all seek *the things* of themselves" (2:21a) to its contrast, "not *the things* of Jesus Christ" (2:21b). They then hear a parallel progression from "*coming to know* the things concerning you" (2:19b) to "you *know* his worth" (2:22). They also hear a parallel progression from "I *hope in the Lord* Jesus *soon* to *send* Timothy to you" (2:19a) to "this one then I *hope* to *send* as soon as I perceive the things concerning me. But I have confidence *in the Lord* that I myself will also come *soon*. I have considered it necessary Epaphroditus . . . to *send* to you" (2:24–25). In the conclusion of the chiasm the audience experience a parallel progression from "I am being poured out like a drink offering upon the sacrifice and *service* of your faith, I am *rejoicing*, indeed I am *rejoicing with* all of you. And in the same way you are to be *rejoicing*, indeed you are to be *rejoicing with* me" (2:17–18) to "you may *rejoice* again . . . with all *joy* and have such people in esteem, for on account of the work of Christ he came near to the point of death, risking his life, so that he might fill up your lack of *service* toward me" (2:28–30) (ch. 8).

With Phil 3:1–21, the D′ unit within the macrochiastic structure embracing the entire letter, the audience hear resonances of the corresponding D unit (1:19–30) in the overall chiasm. The closely connected, threefold occurrence of the phrase "in the flesh"—"do not put confidence *in the flesh*, although I myself have confidence even *in the flesh*. If someone else supposes to be confident *in the flesh*" (3:3–4) in the D′ unit resonates with the twofold occurrence of the same phrase— "But to remain *in the flesh* is more necessary on account of you" (1:24) and "If it is to live *in the flesh*" (1:22)—in the D unit. The words expressing "gain"—"for me *gains*" (3:7) and "Christ I may *gain*" (3:8) in the D′ unit recall "to die is *gain*" (1:21) in the D unit. "The righteousness from God based on *the faith*" (3:9) in the D′ unit recalls "struggling together for *the faith*" (1:27) in the D unit. "Their end is *destruction*" (3:19) in the D′ unit recalls "a demonstration of *destruction*" (1:28) in the D unit. And the double occurrence of the word "body"—"who will transform the *body* of our humility (to be) conformed to the *body* of his glory" (3:21)—in the D´ unit reverberates with its occurrence in the D unit—"Christ will be magnified in my *body*" (1:20).

At the center of the chiastic D´ unit (3:1–21) the audience listen to Paul's declaration about "the surpassing greatness of the knowledge of Christ Jesus my Lord" (3:8b). They hear a parallel progression from "whatever things were for me *gains*, these things I have *considered* on account of the Christ a *loss*. But indeed I even *consider all things* to be a *loss*" (3:7–8a) to "I have suffered the *loss* of *all things*, indeed I *consider* them rubbish, that Christ I may *gain*" (3:8c). They hear a progression from Paul's "boasting *in Christ Jesus* . . . although *I myself have* confidence even in the flesh. . . . I even more . . . according to the *Law* a Pharisee, according to zeal *persecuting* the church, according to *righteousness* that is in the *Law* I became blameless" (3:3–6) to "not *having* my own *righteousness* that is from the *Law* but that is through faith in Christ, the—from God—*righteousness* based on the faith . . . but I am *pursuing* it . . . I do not consider that I myself have apprehended. . . . I am *pursuing* to the prize of the upward calling of God *in Christ Jesus*" (3:9–14).

They also hear a progression from Paul's clarification that "to write the same things to *you*, to me is not burdensome, but to *you* is assuring" (3:1b) to "this also God will reveal to *you*" (3:15) and "many times I told *you*" (3:18). In the conclusion of this chiastic D´ unit the audience experience a parallel progression from Paul's directive, "Furthermore, my brothers, rejoice in the *Lord*" (3:1a) to his declaration, "For our citizenship is existing in heaven, from which indeed a savior we are awaiting, the Lord Jesus Christ" (3:20) (ch. 9).

With Phil 4:1–5, the C´ unit within the macrochiastic structure organizing the entire letter, the audience hear resonances, by way of the chiastic parallelism, of 1:12–18, the corresponding C unit in the overall chiasm. The mention of Clement and "the *rest* of my co-workers" (4:3) in the C´ unit recalls how the bonds of Paul have become in Christ manifest in the whole praetorium and "to all the *rest*" in the C unit, as references to those associated with Paul. The twofold occurrence of the verb for "rejoice" in Paul's imperatives for the audience to "*rejoice*" in the Lord always and again he will say "*rejoice*" (4:4) in the C´ unit recalls and complements the twofold occurrence of the same verb to express Paul's joy, "Christ is proclaimed, and in this *I rejoice*. And indeed *I will be joyful*" (1:18), in the C unit.

At the center of the chiastic C´ unit (4:1–5) the audience hear a parallel pivot from Paul's directive regarding Euodia and Syntyche, "*bring them together*" (4:3b), to his description of them as "those who in the gospel *have struggled together* with me" (4:3c). They listen to a parallel progression from Paul's address to the "genuine *yokemate*" (4:3a) to his reference regarding "the rest of my *co-workers*" (4:3d). In the conclusion of this chiasm the audience experience a parallel progression from his address to "my brothers beloved and longed for, my *joy* and crown, thus stand firm *in the Lord*, beloved. Euodia I exhort and Syntyche I exhort to think the same thing *in the Lord*" (4:1–2) to his stirring exhortation, "*Rejoice in the Lord* always.

Again I will say, *rejoice*. Let your forbearance be known to all human beings. The *Lord* is near" (4:4–5) (ch. 10).

With Phil 4:6–20, the B′ unit within the macrochiastic structure organizing the entire letter, the audience hear resonances, by way of the chiastic parallelism, of 1:3–11, the corresponding B unit in the overall chiasm. The mention of the "prayer and *petition*, with *thanksgiving*," of the audience (4:6) in the B′ unit recalls Paul's petitions for the audience, when he stated, "I *thank* my God at every remembrance of you, always in my every *petition* on behalf of all of you, making the *petition* with joy" (1:3–4), in the B unit. Paul's promise that the peace of God will guard your "*hearts*" (4:7) in the B′ unit recalls the reference to Paul's own heart—"I have you in my *heart*" (1:7)—in the B unit. "Whatever is *right*" (4:8) in the B′ unit recalls that "it is *right* for me" (1:7) in the B unit. "If there is any *praise*" (4:8) in the B′ unit recalls "for the glory and *praise* of God" (1:11) in the B unit. That "you have begun again *to think on behalf of me*" (4:10) in the B′ unit reciprocally recalls "for me *to think this on behalf of all of you*" (1:7) in the B unit.

The threefold occurrence of the verb "abound"—"I know indeed to *abound*" (4:12), "both to *abound* and to be in need" (4:12), and "I am *abounding*" (4:18)—in the B′ unit recalls "that your love even more and more may *abound*" (1:9) in the B unit. That "I am seeking the *fruit*" (4:17) in the B′ unit recalls "the *fruit* of righteousness" (1:11) in the B unit. The twofold occurrence of the verb "fill up"—"I have been *filled up*" (4:18) and "my God will fill up" (4:19)—in the B′ unit recalls "having been filled up" (1:11) in the B unit. And finally, the twofold occurrence of "glory"—"according to his wealth in *glory*" (4:19) and "*glory* to the ages of the ages" (4:20)—in the B′ unit recalls "for the *glory* and praise of God" (1:11) in the B unit.

At the center of the chiastic B′ unit (4:6–20) the audience hear Paul remind them that "even in Thessalonica not only once but twice you sent to me in my need" (4:16). They then hear a parallel progression from Paul's statements that "not a single church shared with me *in an account* of *giving* and receiving except you alone" (4:15) to "not that I am seeking the *gift*, but I am seeking the fruit that increases *in your account*" (4:17). They also hear a progression from Paul's declarations that "I know indeed to *abound*" (4:12), "both to *abound* and to be in want" (4:12), and "I am strong for *everything* in the one who empowers me" (4:13) to "I have received in full *everything* and I am *abounding*" (4:18a). In the conclusion of the chiasm the audience experience a parallel progression in threefold references to God from "let your requests be made known before *God*" (4:6), "the peace of *God* that surpasses all understanding will guard your hearts and your minds *in Christ Jesus*" (4:7), and "the *God* of peace will be with you" (4:9), to "well pleasing to *God*" (4:18b), "my *God* will fill up your every need according to his wealth in glory *in Christ Jesus* (4:19), and "to our *God* and Father, glory to the ages of the ages, Amen" (4:20) (ch.11).

With Phil 4:21–23, the A′ unit within the macrochiastic structure organizing the entire letter, the audience hear resonances, by way of the chiastic parallelism, of 1:1–2, the corresponding A unit in the overall chiasm. The mention of "*every holy one*" (4:21) and "*all the holy ones*" (4:22) in the A′ unit recalls Paul's opening address to "*all those holy ones*" (1:1) in the A unit. And Paul's closing greeting, "the *grace* of the Lord Jesus Christ be with your spirit" (4:23) in the A′ unit, reverberates with his opening greeting, "*grace* to you and peace from God our Father and the Lord Jesus Christ" (1:2) in the A unit, forming a literary inclusion that frames the entire letter within a worshiping context.

At the center of the chiastic A′ unit (4:21–23) the audience hear a parallel pivot from "the brothers who are with me *greet you*" (4:21b) to "all the holy ones *greet you*" (4:22). And in the conclusion of the chiasm the audience experience a parallel progression from "greet every holy one in *Christ Jesus*" (4:21a) to "the grace of the Lord *Jesus Christ* be with your spirit" (4:23) (ch. 12).

In sum, the chiastic structure of Philippians begins with Paul's address to all the holy ones in Christ Jesus who are also in Philippi (1:1), on behalf of whom Paul thanks God with joy for the fellowship he shares with them for the gospel (1:3–5), praying that they conform their way of thinking to be in accord with Jesus Christ for the glory and praise of God (1:9–11). At the pivotal center of the chiastic structure of the letter the audience are exhorted to adopt the selfless, humble mindset of Jesus himself, whom God graciously exalted to a position of universal Lord, after he obediently humbled himself to the point of dying on a cross (2:1–16). By conforming their way of thinking, like Paul and his co-workers, to that of Jesus Christ, they may, in the midst of their struggling along with Paul (1:29–30), also rejoice with him in accord with his emphatic exhortation: "I am rejoicing, indeed I am rejoicing with all of you. And in the same way you are to be rejoicing, indeed you are to be rejoicing with me" (2:17–18). The basis of such rejoicing is the hope of sharing in the exaltation of Jesus (3:9–14). And the ultimate source of this profound rejoicing even in the midst of suffering is the grace and peace that come from God our Father and the Lord Jesus Christ (1:1; 2:11; 4:23).

In conclusion, listening to and experiencing the rhetorical dynamics of the intricate and intriguing chiastic patterns of Paul's letter to the Philippians encourages and empowers its audience to a hope-filled, worshipful rejoicing as they conform their sufferings for the gospel to the sufferings and obedient death of Jesus Christ by adopting his selfless, humble way of thinking, from which God exalted him to universal lordship. In short, Philippians functions as a concerted encouragement for its audience, both within and outside of their worshiping assembly, to rejoice in being conformed to Christ.

Bibliography

Alexander, Loveday C. A. "Hellenistic Letter-Forms and the Structure of Philippians." *JSNT* 37 (1989): 87–101.

Allan, John A. "The 'In Christ' Formula in Ephesians." *NTS* 5 (1958–59): 54–62.

Ascough, Richard S. *Paul's Macedonian Associations: The Social Context of Philippians and 1 Thessalonians.* WUNT 161. Tübingen: Mohr Siebeck, 2003.

Aune, David E. *The Westminster Dictionary of New Testament and Early Christian Literature and Rhetoric.* Louisville: Westminster John Knox, 2003.

Bailey, J. L. "Perspectives from Prison: Reading Philippians." *Trinity Seminary Review* 27 (2006): 83–97.

Baldanza, Giuseppe. "Il culto per mezzo dello Spirito (Fil 3,3)." *RivB* 54 (2006): 45–64.

Barnet, J. "Paul's Reception of the Gift from Philippi." *SVTQ* 50 (2006): 225–53.

Barram, Michael. *Mission and Moral Reflection in Paul.* Studies in Biblical Literature 75. New York: Lang, 2006.

Basevi, Claudio. "Estudio literario y teológico del himno cristológico de la epístola a los Filipenses (Phil 2,6–11)." *ScrTh* 30 (1998): 439–72.

Berger, Klaus. "Apostelbrief und apostolische Rede: Zum Formular frühchristlicher Briefe." *ZNW* 65 (1974): 190–231.

Beutler, Johannes. "ἀδελφός." *EDNT* 1.28–30.

———. "μάρτυς." *EDNT* 2.393–95.

Bittasi, Sefano. "La prigionia de Paolo nella lettera ai Filippesi e il problema di una morte possibile. 2. Il nuovo sguardo sul potere imperiale." *RdT* 45 (2004): 189–206.

———. *Gli esempi necessari per discernere: Il significato argomentativo della struttura della lettera di Paolo ai Filippesi.* AnBib 153. Rome: Editrice Pontificio Istituto Biblico, 2003.

———. "'... per scegliere ciò che conta di piú' (*Fil* 1,10): Il criterio cristologico dello scegliere nella lettera di san Paolo ai Filippesi." *RdT* 47 (2006): 831–49.

———. "La prigionia de Paolo nella lettera ai Filippesi e il problema di una sua morte possibile. I. Una lettura di Fil 1, 12–26." *RdT* 45 (2004): 19–34.

Black, David Alan. "The Discourse Structure of Philippians: A Study in Textlinguistics." *NovT* 37 (1995): 16–49.

———. "Paul and Christian Unity: A Formal Analysis of Philippians 2:1–4." *JETS* 28 (1985): 299–308.

Blomberg, Craig L. *From Pentecost to Patmos: An Introduction to Acts Through Revelation.* Nashville: Broadman & Holman, 2006.

Bloomquist, L. Gregory. *The Function of Suffering in Philippians.* JSNTSup 78. Sheffield: JSOT, 1993.

———. "Subverted by Joy: Suffering and Joy in Paul's Letter to the Philippians." *Int* 61 (2007): 270–82.

Bockmuehl, Markus N. A. *The Epistle to the Philippians.* BNTC 11. London: Hendrickson, 1998.

187

———. "'The Form of God' (Phil. 2:6): Variations on a Theme of Jewish Mysticism." *JTS* 48 (1997): 1–23.

Borchert, Gerald L. *Worship in the New Testament: Divine Mystery and Human Response.* St. Louis: Chalice, 2008.

Bormann, Lukas. *Philippi: Stadt und Christengemeinde zur Zeit des Paulus.* NovTSup 78. Leiden: Brill, 1995.

———. "Triple Intertextuality in Philippians." Pp. 90–97 in *The Intertextuality of the Epistles: Explorations of Theory and Practice.* Ed. Thomas L. Brodie, Dennis R. MacDonald, and Stanley E. Porter. NTM 16. Sheffield: Sheffield Phoenix, 2006.

Botha, Pieter J. J. "The Verbal Art of the Pauline Letters: Rhetoric, Performance and Presence." Pp. 409–28 in *Rhetoric and the New Testament: Essays from the 1992 Heidelberg Conference.* Ed. Stanley E. Porter and Thomas H. Olbricht. JSNTSup 90. Sheffield: JSOT, 1993.

Bouttier, Michel. *En Christ: Étude d'exégèse et de théologie pauliniennes.* Paris: Presses Universitaires, 1962.

Bowers, W. Paul. "Fulfilling the Gospel: The Scope of the Pauline Mission." *JETS* 30 (1987): 185–98.

Böttrich, Christfried. "Verkündigung aus 'Neid und Rivalität'? Beobachtungen zu Phil 1, 12–18." *ZNW* 95 (2004): 84–101.

Breck, John. "Biblical Chiasmus: Exploring Structure for Meaning." *BTB* 17 (1987): 70–74.

Brucker, Ralph. *'Christushymnen' oder 'epideiketische Passagen'? Studien zum Stilwechsel im Neuen Testament und seiner Umwelt.* FRLANT 176. Göttingen: Vandenhoeck & Ruprecht, 1997.

Burk, Denny. "On the Articular Infinitive in Philippians 2:6: A Grammatical Note with Christological Implications." *TynBul* 55 (2004): 253–74.

Burridge, Richard A. *Imitating Jesus: An Inclusive Approach to New Testament Ethics.* Grand Rapids: Eerdmans, 2007.

Büchsel, Friedrich. "'In Christus' bei Paulus." *ZNW* 42 (1949): 141–58.

Byrskog, Samuel. "Co-Senders, Co-Authors and Paul's Use of the First Person Plural." *ZNW* 87 (1996): 230–50.

Capizzi, N. "*Fil* 2,6–11: una sintesi della cristologia? ." *RdT* 40 (1999): 353–68.

———. "Soteriologia in Fil 2:6–11?" *Greg* 81 (2000): 221–48.

Capper, Brian J. "Paul's Dispute with Philippi: Understanding Paul's Argument in Phil. 1–2 from His Thanksgiving in 4.10–20." *TZ* 49 (1993): 193–214.

Carls, P. "Identifying Syzygos, Euodia, and Syntyche, Philippians 4:2f." *Journal of Higher Criticism* 8 (2001): 161–82.

Carter, Warren, and John Paul Heil. *Matthew's Parables: Audience-Oriented Perspectives.* CBQMS 30. Washington: Catholic Biblical Association, 1998.

Cassidy, Richard J. *Paul in Chains: Roman Imprisonment and the Letters of St. Paul.* New York: Crossroad, 2001.

———. *Four Times Peter: Portrayals of Peter in the Four Gospels and at Philippi.* Collegeville, Minn.: Liturgical Press, 2007.

Chang, H.-K. "(ἀπο)καραδοκία bei Paulus und Aquila." *ZNW* 93 (2002): 268–78.

Clarke, Andrew D. "Equality or Mutuality? Paul's Use of 'Brother' Language." Pp. 151–64 in *The New Testament in Its First Century Setting: Essays on Context and Background in Honour of B. W. Winter on His 65th Birthday.* Ed. P. J. Williams, Andrew D. Clarke, Peter M. Head, and David Instone-Brewer. Grand Rapids: Eerdmans, 2004.

Collins, Adela Yarbro. "Psalms, Philippians 2:6–11, and the Origins of Christology." *BibInt* 11 (2003): 361–72.

Collins, Raymond F. *The Power of Images in Paul.* Collegeville, Minn.: Liturgical Press, 2008.

Cook, John Granger. "Envisioning Crucifixion: Light from Several Inscriptions and the Palatine Graffito." *NovT* 50 (2008): 262–85.

Croy, N. Clayton. "'To Die Is Gain' (Philippians 1:19–26): Does Paul Contemplate Suicide?" *JBL* 122 (2003): 517–31.

Dahl, Nils Alstrup. "Euodia and Syntyche and Paul's Letter to the Philippians." Pp. 1–15 in *The Social World of the First Christians: Essays in Honor of Wayne A. Meeks*. Ed. L. Michael White and O. Larry Yarbrough. Minneapolis: Fortress, 1995.

Dalton, William J. "The Integrity of Philippians." *Bib* 60 (1979): 97–102.

Davis, Casey Wayne. "Oral Biblical Criticism: Raw Data in Philippians." Pp. 96–124 in *Linguistics and the New Testament: Critical Junctures*. Ed. Stanley E. Porter and D. A. Carson. JSNTSup 168. Sheffield: Sheffield Academic Press, 1999.

———. *Oral Biblical Criticism: The Influence of the Principles of Orality on the Literary Structure of Paul's Epistle to the Philippians*. JSNTSup 172. Sheffield: Sheffield Academic Press, 1999.

de Vos, Craig Steven. *Church and Community Conflicts: The Relationships of the Thessalonian, Corinthian, and Philippian Churches with Their Wider Civic Communities*. SBLDS 168. Atlanta: Scholars Press, 1999.

Debanné, Marc J. *Enthymemes in the Letters of Paul*. LNTS 303. New York: Clark, 2006.

Denton, D. R. "Ἀποκαραδοκία." *ZNW* 73 (1982): 138–40.

DeSilva, David A. "No Confidence in the Flesh: The Meaning and Function of Philippians 3:2–21." *TJ* 15 (1994): 27–54.

———. "X Marks the Spot? A Critique of the Use of Chiasmus in Macro-Structural Analyses of Revelation." *JSNT* 30 (2008): 343–71.

Dewey, Joanna. "Mark as Aural Narrative: Structures as Clues to Understanding." *Sewanee Theological Review* 36 (1992): 45–56.

Doble, Peter. "'Vile Bodies' or Transformed Persons? Philippians 3.21 in Context." *JSNT* 86 (2002): 3–27.

Doughty, Darrell J. "Citizens of Heaven: Philippians 3.2–21." *NTS* 41 (1995): 102–22.

Droge, Arthur J. "*Mori Lucrum*: Paul and Ancient Theories of Suicide." *NovT* 30 (1988): 263–86.

Droge, Arthur J., and James D. Tabor. *A Noble Death: Suicide and Martyrdom Among Jews and Christians in Antiquity*. San Francisco: Harper Collins, 1992.

Dunn, James D. G. *The Theology of Paul the Apostle*. Grand Rapids: Eerdmans, 1998.

— — —. "Christ, Adam, and Preexistence." Pp. 74–83 in *Where Christology Began: Essays on Philippians 2*. Ed. Ralph P. Martin and Brian J. Dodd. Louisville: Westminster John Knox, 1998.

Fatehi, Mehrdad. *The Spirit's Relation to the Risen Lord in Paul: An Examination of Its Christological Implications*. WUNT 128. Tübingen: Mohr Siebeck, 2000.

Fee, Gordon D. *Paul's Letter to the Philippians*. NICNT. Grand Rapids: Eerdmans, 1995.

———. *Pauline Christology: An Exegetical–Theological Study*. Peabody, Mass.: Hendrickson, 2007.

———. *God's Empowering Presence: The Holy Spirit in the Letters of Paul*. Peabody, Mass.: Hendrickson, 1994.

———. "To What End Exegesis? Reflections on Exegesis and Spirituality in Philippians 4:10–20." *BBR* 8 (1998): 75–88.

Finlan, Stephen. *The Apostle Paul and the Pauline Tradition*. Collegeville, Minn.: Liturgical Press, 2008.

Fitzgerald, John T. "Philippians in the Light of Some Ancient Discussions of Friendship." Pp. 141–60 in *Friendship, Flattery, and Frankness of Speech: Studies on Friendship in the New Testament World*. Ed. John T. Fitzgerald. NovTSup 82. Leiden: Brill, 1996.

Fitzmyer, Joseph A. "The Consecutive Meaning of ἐφ ᾧ in Romans 5.12." *NTS* 39 (1993): 321–39.

Fowl, Stephen E. *Philippians*. Grand Rapids: Eerdmans, 2005.

———. "Christology and Ethics in Philippians 2:5–11." Pp. 140–53 in *Where Christology Began: Essays on Philippians 2*. Ed. Ralph P. Martin and Brian J. Dodd. Louisville: Westminster John Knox, 1998.

———. "Know Your Context: Giving and Receiving Money in Philippians." *Int* 56 (2002): 45–58.

Garland, David E. "Philippians." Pp. 177–261 in *The Expositor's Bible Commentary: Revised Edition*, Vol. 12. Ed. Tremper Longman and David E. Garland. Grand Rapids: Zondervan, 2006.

——. "Philippians 1:1–26: The Defense and Confirmation of the Gospel." *RevExp* 77 (1980): 327–36.

——. "The Composition and Unity of Philippians: Some Neglected Literary Factors." *NovT* 27 (1985): 141–73.

Geoffrion, Timothy C. *The Rhetorical Purpose and the Political and Military Character of Philippians: A Call To Stand Firm*. Lewiston, NY: Mellen, 1993.

Giesen, Heinz, "ἐπιεικής." *EDNT* 2.26.

——. "Eschatology in Philippians." Pp. 217–82 in *Paul and His Theology*. Ed. Stanley E. Porter. Pauline Studies 3. Leiden: Brill, 2007.

Gilfillan Upton, Bridget. *Hearing Mark's Endings: Listening to Ancient Popular Texts Through Speech Act Theory*. BIS 79. Leiden: Brill, 2006.

Glancy, Jennifer A. *Slavery in Early Christianity*. Minneapolis: Fortress, 2006.

Gorman, Michael J. *Apostle of the Crucified Lord: A Theological Introduction to Paul and His Letters*. Grand Rapids: Eerdmans, 2004.

Guthrie, George H. "Cohesion Shifts and Stitches in Philippians." Pp. 36–59 in *Discourse Analysis and Other Topics in Biblical Greek*. Ed. Stanley E. Porter and D. A. Carson. JSNTSup 113. Sheffield: Sheffield Academic Press, 1995.

Hainz, Josef. "κοινωνία." *EDNT* 2.303–5.

Harrill, J. Albert. *Slaves in the New Testament: Literary, Social, and Moral Dimensions*. Minneapolis: Fortress, 2006.

Harrison, James R. *Paul's Language of Grace in Its Graeco-Roman Context*. WUNT 172. Tübingen: Mohr Siebeck, 2003.

Harvey, John D. *Listening to the Text: Oral Patterning in Paul's Letters*. Grand Rapids: Baker, 1998.

Hearon, Holly E. "The Implications of Orality for Studies of the Biblical Text." Pp. 3–20 in *Performing the Gospel: Orality, Memory, and Mark: Essays Dedicated to Werner Kelber*. Ed. Richard A. Horsley, Jonathan A. Draper, and John Miles Foley. Minneapolis: Fortress, 2006.

Heil, John Paul. *Ephesians: Empowerment to Walk in Love for the Unity of All in Christ*. Studies in Biblical Literature 13. Atlanta: Society of Biblical Literature, 2007.

——. *The Meal Scenes in Luke-Acts: An Audience-Oriented Approach*. SBLMS 52. Atlanta: Society of Biblical Literature, 1999.

——. *The Rhetorical Role of Scripture in 1 Corinthians*. Studies in Biblical Literature 15. Atlanta: Society of Biblical Literature, 2005.

——. *The Transfiguration of Jesus: Narrative Meaning and Function of Mark 9:2–8, Matt 17:1–8 and Luke 9:28–36*. AnBib 144. Rome: Editrice Pontificio Istituto Biblico, 2000.

——. "The Chiastic Structure and Meaning of Paul's Letter to Philemon." *Bib* 82 (2001): 178–206.

Hengel, Martin. *Crucifixion: In the Ancient World and the Folly of the Message of the Cross*. Philadelphia: Fortress, 1977.

Hofius, Otfried. *Der Christushymnus Philipper 2,6–11: Untersuchungen zu Gestalt und Aussage eines urchristlichen Psalms*. 2d ed. WUNT 17. Tübingen: Mohr Siebeck, 1991.

Holloway, Paul Andrew. *Consolation in Philippians: Philosophical Sources and Rhetorical Strategy*. SNTSMS 112. Cambridge: Cambridge University Press, 2001.

——. "Thanks for the Memories: On the Translation of Phil 1.3." *NTS* 52 (2006): 419–32.

——. "*Bona Cogitare*: An Epicurean Consolation in Phil 4:8–9." *HTR* 91 (1998): 89–96.

———. "*Alius Paulus*: Paul's Promise to Send Timothy at Philippians 2.19–24." *NTS* 54 (2008): 542–56.

Hoover, Roy W. "The HARPAGMOS Enigma: A Philological Solution." *HTR* 64 (1971): 95–119.

Hurst, Lincoln D. "Christ, Adam, and Preexistence Revisited." Pp. 84–95 in *Where Christology Began: Essays on Philippians 2*. Ed. Ralph P. Martin and Brian J. Dodd. Louisville: Westminster John Knox, 1998.

Hübner, Hans. "κεῖμαι." *EDNT* 2.280.

Hurtado, Larry W. *Lord Jesus Christ: Devotion to Jesus in Earliest Christianity*. Grand Rapids: Eerdmans, 2003.

———. *How on Earth Did Jesus Become a God? Historical Questions About Earliest Devotion to Jesus.* Grand Rapids: Eerdmans, 2005.

Jacquett, James L. "A Not-So-Noble Death: Figured Speech, Friendship and Suicide in Philippians 1:21–26." *Neot* 28 (1994): 177–92.

Janzen, J. G. "Creation and New Creation in Phlippians 1:6." *HBT* 18 (1996): 27–54.

Jaquette, James L. "Life and Death, *Adiaphora*, and Paul's Rhetorical Strategies." *NovT* 38 (1996): 30–54.

Jowers, Dennis W. "The Meaning of μορφήin Philippians 2:6–7." *JETS* 49 (2006): 739–66.

Kertelge, Karl. "δικαιοσύνη." *EDNT* 1.324–30.

Koperski, Veronica. *The Knowledge of Christ Jesus My Lord: The High Christology of Philippians 3:7–11.* CBET 16. Kampen: Pharos, 1996.

———. "The Meaning of *Pistis Christou* in Philippians 3:9." *LS* 18 (1993): 198–216.

———. "The Meaning of δικαιοσύνη in Philippians 3:9." *LS* 20 (1995): 147–69.

Kourie, Celia E. T. "In Christ and Related Expressions in Paul." *Theologia Evangelica* 20 (1987): 33–43.

Kremer, Jacob. "πνεῦμα." *EDNT* 3.117–22.

Krentz, Edgar. "Military Language and Metaphors in Philippians." Pp. 105–27 in *Origins and Methods: Towards a New Understanding of Judaism and Christianity: Essays in Honour of John C. Hurd.* Ed. Bradley H. McLean. JSNTSup 86. Sheffield: Sheffield Academic Press, 1993.

Lambrecht, Jan. "Paul's Reasoning in Philippians 2,6–8." *ETL* 83 (2007): 413–18.

Lieu, Judith M. "'Grace to You and Peace': The Apostolic Greeting." *BJRL* 68 (1985): 161–78.

Longenecker, Bruce W. *Rhetoric at the Boundaries: The Art and Theology of the New Testament Chain-Link Transitions.* Waco, Texas: Baylor University Press, 2005.

Luter, A. Boyd. "Grace." *DPL* 372–74.

MacLeod, D. J. "Imitating the Incarnation of Christ: An Exposition of Philippians 2:5–8." *BSac* 158 (2001): 308–30.

Mahoney, Robert. "εὐδοκία." *EDNT* 2.75–76.

Malherbe, Abraham J. "Paul's Self-Sufficiency (Philippians 4:11)." Pp. 125–39 in *Friendship, Flattery, and Frankness of Speech: Studies on Friendship in the New Testament World.* Ed. John T. Fitzgerald. NovTSup 82. Leiden: Brill, 1996.

Marchal, Joseph A. *Hierarchy, Unity, and Imitation: A Feminist Rhetorical Analysis of Power Dynamics in Paul's Letter to the Philippians.* SBLAbib 24. Atlanta: Society of Biblical Literature, 2006.

———. "With Friends Like These . . .: A Feminist Rhetorical Reconsideration of Scholarship and the Letter to the Philippians." *JSNT* 29 (2006): 77–106.

———. "Expecting a Hymn, Encountering an Argument: Introducing the Rhetoric of Philippians and Pauline Interpretation." *Int* 61 (2007): 245–55.

Martin, Dale B. *Slavery as Salvation: The Metaphor of Slavery in Pauline Christianity.* New Haven: Yale University Press, 1990.

McClain, A. J. "The Doctrine of the Kenosis in Philippians 2:5–8." *MSJ* 9 (1998): 85–96.

Metzger, Bruce Manning. *A Textual Commentary on the Greek New Testament: Second Edition.* Stuttgart: Deutsche Bibelgesellschaft, 1994.

Metzner, Rainer. "In aller Freundschaft: Ein frühchristlicher Fall freundschaftlicher Gemeinschaft (Phil 2.25–30)." *NTS* 48 (2002): 111–31.

———. "Paulus und der Wettkampf: Die Rolle des Sports in Leben und Verkündigung des Apostels (1 Kor 9.24–7; Phil 3.12–16)." *NTS* 46 (2000): 565–83.

Miller, Ernest C. "πολιτεύεσθε in Phil 1:27: Some Philological and Thematic Observations." *JSNT* 15 (1982): 86–96.

Moiser, J. "The Meaning of *Koilia* in Philippians 3:19." *ExpTim* 108 (1997): 365–66.

Morrice, William G. "Joy." *DPL*, 511–12.

Mostert, W. "Meditation über Philipper 4,4–7." *BTZ* 16 (1999): 120–31.

Nebeker, G. L. "Christ as Somatic Transformer (Phil 3:20–21): Christology in an Eschatological Perspective." *TJ* 21 (2000): 165–87.

Neugebauer, Fritz. "Das Paulinische 'In Christo'." *NTS* 4 (1957–58): 124–38.

Nobbs, Alanna. "'Beloved Brothers' in the New Testament and Early Christian World." Pp. 143–50 in *The New Testament in Its First Century Setting: Essays on Context and Background in Honour of B. W. Winter on His 65th Birthday.* Ed. P. J. Williams et al. Grand Rapids: Eerdmans, 2004.

Nolland, John. "Grace as Power." *NovT* 28 (1986): 26–31.

O'Brien, Peter Thomas. *The Epistle to the Philippians: A Commentary on the Greek Text.* NIGTC. Grand Rapids: Eerdmans, 1991.

Oakes, Peter. *Philippians: From People to Letter.* SNTSMS 110. Cambridge: Cambridge University Press, 2001.

———. "God's Sovereignty Over Roman Authorities: A Theme in Philippians." Pp. 126–41 in *Rome in the Bible and the Early Church.* Ed. Peter Oakes. Carlisle: Paternoster, 2002.

———. "Quelle devrait être l'influence des échos intertextuels sur la traduction? Le cas de l'épître aux Philippiens (2,15–16)." Pp. 266–85 in *Intertextualitiés: La bible en échos.* Ed. Daniel Marguerat and A. Curtis. Paris: Labor et Fides, 2000.

———. "Re-mapping the Universe: Paul and the Emperor in 1 Thessalonians and Philippians." *JSNT* 27 (2005): 301–22.

Otto, R. E. "'If Possible I May Attain the Resurrection from the Dead' (Philippians 3:11)." *CBQ* 57 (1995): 324–40.

Palmer, D. W. "'To Die Is Gain' (Philippians 1:21)." *NovT* 17 (1975): 203–18.

Park, M. Sydney. *Submission Within the Godhead and the Church in the Epistle to the Philippians: An Exegetical and Theological Examination of the Concept of Submission in Philippians 2 and 3.* LNTS 361. London: Clark, 2007.

Peng, Kuo-Wei. "Do We Need an Alternative Rendering for Philippians 1.3?" *BT* 54 (2003): 415–19.

Peppard, Michael. "'Poetry,' 'Hymns' and 'Traditional Material' in New Testament Epistles or How to Do Things with Indentations." *JSNT* 30 (2008): 319–42.

Peterlin, Davorin. *Paul's Letter to the Philippians in the Light of Disunity in the Church.* NovTSup 79. Leiden: Brill, 1995.

Peterman, Gerald W. *Paul's Gift from Philippi: Conventions of Gift-Exchange and Christian Giving.* SNTSMS 92. Cambridge: Cambridge University Press, 1997.

———. "'Thankless Thanks': The Epistolary Social Convention in Philippians 4:10–20." *TynBul* 42 (1991): 261–70.

Pilhofer, Peter. *Philippi: Die erste christliche Gemeinde Europas.* WUNT 87. Tübingen: Mohr-Siebeck, 1995.

Popkes, Wiard. "Philipper 4.4–7: Aussage und situativer Hintergrund." *NTS* 50 (2004): 246–56.

Porter, Stanley E., and Jeffrey T. Reid. "Philippians as a Macro-Chiasm and Its Exegetical Significance." *NTS* 44 (1998): 213–31.

Poythress, Vern Sheridan. "'Hold Fast' Versus 'Hold Out' in Philippians 2:16." *WTJ* 64 (2002): 45–53.

Reed, Jeffrey T. *A Discourse Analysis of Philippians: Method and Rhetoric in the Debate Over Literary Integrity.* JSNTSup 136. Sheffield: Sheffield Academic Press, 1997.

———. "Philippians 3:1 and the Epistolary Hesitation Formulas: The Literary Integrity of Philippians, Again." *JBL* 115 (1996): 63–90.

Reumann, John. "Church Office in Paul, Especially in Philippians." Pp. 82–91 in *Origins and Method: Towards a New Understanding of Judaism and Christianity: Essays in Honour of John C. Hurd.* Ed. Bradley H. McLean. JSNTSup 86. Sheffield: Sheffield Academic Press, 1993.

———. "Philippians, Especially Chapter 4, as a 'Letter of Friendship': Observations on a Checkered History of Scholarship." Pp. 83–106 in *Friendship, Flattery, and Frankness of Speech: Studies on Friendship in the New Testament World.* Ed. John T. Fitzgerald. NovTSup 82. Leiden: Brill, 1996.

———. "The (Greek) Old Testament in Philippians 1:19 as Parade Example—Allusion, Echo, Proverb?" Pp. 189–200 in *History and Exegesis: New Testament Essays in Honor of Dr. E. Earle Ellis for His 80th Birthday*. Ed. Sang-Won Son. London: Clark, 2006.

Richards, E. Randolph. *Paul and First-Century Letter Writing: Secretaries, Composition and Collection*. Downers Grove, Ill.: InterVarsity, 2004.

Rico, C., and Gregory T. Tatum. "Une métaphore financière de l'Épître aux Philippiens: πεπληρωμένοι καρπῶν δικαιοσύνης (Ph 1,11)." *RB* 114 (2007): 447–53.

Ritt, Hubert. "λόγος." *EDNT* 2.356–59.

Robinson, B. P. "Paul's Character in the Face of Death (Phil. 2:17–18; 2 Tim. 4:6–8)." *ScrB* 28 (1998): 77–87.

Rolland, Philippe. "La structure littéraire et l'unité de l'Épître aux Philippiens." *RevScRel* 64 (1990): 213–16.

Rosner, Brian S. *Greed as Idolatry: The Origin and Meaning of a Pauline Metaphor*. Grand Rapids: Eerdmans, 2007.

Russell, Ronald. "Pauline Letter Structure in Philippians." *JETS* 25 (1982): 295–306.

Samra, James George. *Being Conformed to Christ in Community: A Study of Maturity, Maturation and the Local Church in the Undisputed Pauline Epistles*. LNTS 320. London: Clark, 2006.

Sandnes, Karl Olav. *Belly and the Body in the Pauline Epistles*. STNSMS 120. New York: Cambridge University Press, 2002.

Schelkle, Karl Hermann. "σωτηρία." *EDNT* 3.327–29.

Schenk, Wolfgang. *Die Philipperbriefe des Paulus: Kommentar*. Stuttgart: Kohlhammer, 1984.

Schlosser, J. "La communauté en charge de L'Évangile: A propos de Ph 1,7." *RHPR* 75 (1995): 67–76.

———. "La Figure de Dieu selon l'Épître aux Philippiens." *NTS* 41 (1995): 378–99.

Schoenborn, Ulrich. "δέησις." *EDNT* 1.286–87.

Schreiber, Stefan. "Paulus im 'Zwischenzustand': Phil 1.23 und die Ambivalenz des Sterbens als Provokation." *NTS* 49 (2003): 336–59.

Schubert, Paul. *Form and Function of the Pauline Thanksgiving*. BZNW 20. Berlin: Töpelmann, 1939.

Schunack, Gerd. "δοκιμάζω." *EDNT* 1.341–43.

Schwindt, Rainer. "Zur Tradition und Theologie des Philipperhymnus." *Studien Zum Neuen Testament und Seiner Umwelt* 31 (2006): 1–60.

Seifrid, Mark A. "In Christ." *DPL*, 433–36.

Shiell, William David. *Reading Acts: The Lector and the Early Christian Audience*. BIS 70. Boston: Brill, 2004.

Shiner, Whitney Taylor. *Proclaiming the Gospel: First Century Performance of Mark*. Harrisburg, Pa.: Trinity Press International, 2003.

Silva, Moisés. *Philippians*. BECNT. Grand Rapids: Baker, 2005.

———. "Philippians." Pp. 835–39 in *Commentary on the New Testament Use of the Old Testament*. Ed. Gregory K. Beale and Donald A. Carson. Grand Rapids: Baker, 2007.

Skeat, T. C. "Did Paul Write to 'Bishops and Deacons' at Philippi? A Note on Philippians 1:1." *NovT* 37 (1995): 12–15.

Smith, Craig A. *Timothy's Task, Paul's Prospect: A New Reading of 2 Timothy*. NTM 12. Sheffield: Sheffield Phoenix, 2006.

Snyman, Andreas H. "Philippians 2:19–30 from a Rhetorical Perspective." *Acta Patristica et Byzantina* 16 (2005): 289–307.

———. "Philippians 4:1–9 from a Rhetorical Perspective." *Verbum et Ecclesia* 28 (2007): 224–43.

———. "Philippians 4:10–23 from a Rhetorical Perspective." *AcT* 27 (2007): 168–85.

———. "A Rhetorical Analysis of Philippians 1:1–11." *AcT* 24 (2004): 81–104.

———. "A Rhetorical Analysis of Philippians 3:1–11." *Neot* 40 (2006): 259–83.

———. "A Rhetorical Analysis of Philippians 3:12–21." *Acta Patristica et Byzantina* 17 (2006): 327–48.

Spicq, Ceslas. *Theological Lexicon of the New Testament.* Translated and edited by James D. Ernest. 3 vols. Peabody, Mass.: Hendrickson, 1994.

Standhartinger, Angela. "'Join in Imitating Me' (Philippians 3.17): Towards an Interpretation of Philippians 3." *NTS* 54 (2008): 417–35.

Stirewalt, Luther M. *Paul: The Letter Writer.* Grand Rapids: Eerdmans, 2003.

Stock, Augustine. "Chiastic Awareness and Education in Antiquity." *BTB* 14 (1984): 23–27.

Stowers, Stanley K. "Friends and Enemies in the Politics of Heaven: Reading Theology in Philippians." Pp. 105–21 in *Pauline Theology.* Vol. 1. Ed. Jouette M. Bassler. Minneapolis: Fortress, 1991.

Swift, Robert C. "The Theme and Structure of Philippians." *BSac* 141 (1984): 234–54.

Taylor, R. J. "Paul's Way to Peace—Philippians 4:4–9." *ScrC* 27 (1997): 502–12.

Tellbe, Mikael. "The Sociological Factors Behind Philippians 3.1–11 and the Conflict at Philippi." *JSNT* 55 (1994): 97–121.

———. *Paul between Synagogue and State: Christians, Jews, and Civic Authorities in 1 Thessalonians, Romans, and Philippians.* ConBNT 34. Stockholm: Almqvist & Wiksell, 2001.

Thomas, Kenneth J., and Margaret Orr Thomas. *Structure and Orality in 1 Peter: A Guide for Translators.* UBS Monograph 10. New York: United Bible Societies, 2006.

Thompson, A. J. "Blameless Before God? Philippians 3:6 in Context." *Them* 28 (2002): 5–12.

Thomson, Ian H. *Chiasmus in the Pauline Letters.* JSNTSup 111. Sheffield: Academic Press, 1995.

Thurston, Bonnie B., and Judith M. Ryan. *Philippians and Philemon.* SP 10. Collegeville, Minn.: Liturgical Press, 2005.

Tolmie, D. Francois. *Persuading the Galatians: A Text-Centered Rhetorical Analysis of a Pauline Letter.* WUNT 190. Tübingen: Mohr Siebeck, 2005.

Treiyer, E. B. "S'en aller et être avec Christ: Philippiens 1:23." *AUSS* 34 (1996): 47–64.

Trilling, Wolfgang. "ἡμέρα." *EDNT* 2.119–21.

Trummer, Peter. "ἀσπάζομαι." *EDNT* 1.173.

Udoh, Fabian E. "Paul's Views on the Law: Questions about Origin (Gal. 1:6–2:21; Phil. 3:2–11)." *NovT* 42 (2000): 214–37.

Vahrenhorst, Martin. *Kultische Sprache in den Paulusbriefen.* WUNT 230. Tübingen: Mohr Siebeck, 2008.

VanLandingham, Chris. *Judgment & Justification in Early Judaism and the Apostle Paul.* Peabody, Mass.: Hendrickson, 2006.

Verhoef, Eduard. "Σύζυγος In Phil 4:3 and the Author of the 'We-Sections' in Acts." *Journal of Higher Criticism* 5 (1998): 209–19.

Vollenweider, Samuel. "Die Waagschalen von Leben und Tod: Zum antiken Hintergrund von Phil 1,21–26." *ZNW* 85 (1994): 93–115.

———. "Der 'Raub' der Gottgleichheit: Ein Religionsgeschichtlicher Vorschlag zu Phil 2.6(–11)." *NTS* 45 (1999): 413–33.

Wagner, J. Ross. "Working Out Salvation: Holiness and Community in Philippians." Pp. 257–74 in *Holiness and Ecclesiology in the New Testament.* Ed. Kent E. Brower and Andy Johnson. Grand Rapids: Eerdmans, 2007.

Walter, Nikolaus. "σπλάγχνον." *EDNT* 3.265–66.

Wansink, Craig S. *Chained in Christ: The Experience and Rhetoric of Paul's Imprisonments.* JSNTSup 130. Sheffield: Sheffield Academic Press, 1996.

Ware, James P. *The Mission of the Church in Paul's Letter to the Philippians in the Context of Ancient Judaism.* NovTSup 120. Leiden: Brill, 2005.

Watson, Duane F. "A Rhetorical Analysis of Philippians and Its Implications for the Unity Question." *NovT* 30 (1988): 57–88.

Weaver, P. R. C. *Familia Caesaris: A Social Study of the Emperor's Freedmen and Slaves.* Cambridge: Cambridge University Press, 1972.

Wedderburn, Alexander J. M. "Some Observations on Paul's Use of the Phrases 'in Christ' and 'with Christ.'" *JSNT* 25 (1985): 83–97.

Weima, Jeffrey A. D. *Neglected Endings: The Significance of the Pauline Letter Closings.* JSNTSup 101. Sheffield: JSOT, 1994.

Welch, John W. "Chiasmus in the New Testament." Pp. 211–49 in *Chiasmus in Antiquity: Structures, Analyses, Exegesis.* Ed. John W. Welch. Hildesheim: Gerstenberg, 1981.

———. "Criteria for Identifying and Evaluating the Presence of Chiasmus." Pp. 157–74 in *Chiasmus Bibliography.* Ed. John W. Welch and Daniel B. McKinlay. Provo, Utah: Research, 1999.

White, John L. "Apostolic Mission and Apostolic Message: Congruence in Paul's Epistolary Rhetoric, Structure and Imagery." Pp. 145–61 in *Origins and Method: Towards a New Understanding of Judaism and Christianity: Essays in Honour of John C. Hurd.* Ed. Bradley H. McLean. JSNTSup 86. Sheffield: Sheffield Academic Press, 1993.

White, L. Michael. "Morality between Two Worlds: A Paradigm of Friendship in Philippians." Pp. 201–15 in *Greeks, Romans, and Christians.* Ed. David L. Balch, Everett Ferguson, and Wayne A. Meeks. Minneapolis: Fortress, 1990.

Wick, Peter. *Der Philipperbrief: Der formale Aufbau des Briefs als Schlüssel zum Verständnis seines Inhalts.* BWANT 135. Stuttgart: Kohlhammer, 1994.

Williams, David J. *Paul's Metaphors: Their Context and Character.* Peabody, Mass.: Hendrickson, 1999.

Williams, Demetrius K. *Enemies of the Cross of Christ: The Terminology of the Cross and Conflict in Philippians.* JSNTSup 223. London: Sheffield, 2002.

Wilson, Mark. *The Victor Sayings in the Book of Revelation.* Eugene, OR: Wipf and Stock, 2007.

Witherington, Ben. *Friendship and Finances in Philippi: The Letter of Paul to the Philippians.* Valley Forge, Pa.: Trinity Press International, 1994.

Wortham, R. A. "Christology as Community Identity in the Philippians Hymn: The Philippians Hymn as Social Drama (Philippians 2:5–11)." *PRSt* 23 (1996): 269–87.

Wrege, Hans-Theo. "καρπός." *EDNT* 2.251–52.

Wright, Nicholas Thomas. "ἁρπαγμός and the Meaning of Philippians 2:5–11." *JTS* 37 (1986): 321–52.

Zerwick, Maximilian. *Biblical Greek.* Rome: Biblical Institute, 1963.

Scripture Index

Old Testament

Genesis
8:21   169

Exodus
29:18   169
29:25   169
29:41   169

Leviticus
1:9   169
1:13   169
1:17   169

Deuteronomy
32:5   94

Psalms
Ps 68:29 (lxx)   147
Ps 144:18 (lxx)   149

Job
13:16   62–63

Isaiah
45:23   91

Ezekiel
20:41   169

Daniel
12:3   94

New Testament

Acts of the Apostles
16:1   4, 32
16:11–40   32

16:12   5, 137
16:13–15   5
16:16–23   5
16:19–40   77
16:24–34   5
16:35–40   5
16:37–38   4
17:14–15   4, 32
18:5   4, 32
19:22   4, 32
20:4   4, 32
22:25–29   4
23:23–27:1   4
23:27   4
28:16–31   4

Romans
16:21   4

1 Corinthians
4:17   4
16:10   4

2 Corinthians
1:1   4

Philippians
1:1–2   13, 26, 30, 31, 32–37, 38, 39, 50, 175, 180, 185
1:1   4, 5, 13, 26, 30, 32, 33, 34, 35, 36, 37, 39, 40, 45, 47, 53, 69, 71, 81, 86, 87, 88, 89, 93, 97, 98, 103, 105, 154, 175, 176, 177, 179, 180, 185
1:2   2, 13, 14, 26, 29, 30, 32, 35, 36, 37, 39, 43, 44, 45, 47, 51, 54, 76, 77, 93, 123, 154, 175, 178, 180, 185
1:3–11   14–15, 26, 30, 31, 38–49, 50, 52, 152, 180, 184
1:3–6   43, 48

197

Author Index

Breinigsville, PA USA
09 July 2010
241456BV00001B/1/P